# Millennialism, Persecution, and Violence

Religion and Politics
Michael Barkun, *Series Editor*

# Millennialism, Persecution, and Violence

_Historical Cases_

_Edited by_
Catherine Wessinger

Syracuse University Press

Copyright © 2000 by Syracuse University Press
Syracuse, New York 13244-5160

First Edition 2000
00 01 02 03 04     6 5 4 3 2 1

The paper used in this publication meets the minimum requirements
of American National Standard for Information Sciences—Permanence
of Paper for Printed Library Materials, ANSI Z39.48-1984. ∞™

**Library of Congress Cataloging-in-Publication Data**

Millennialism, persecution, and violence : historical cases / edited
   by Catherine Wessinger.
        p.  cm. — (Religion and politics)
     Includes bibliographical references and index.
      ISBN 0-8156-2809-9 (alk. paper). — ISBN 0-8156-0599-4 (pbk. :
   alk. paper)
      1. Millennialism—History of doctrines.  I. Wessinger, Catherine
   Lowman.  II. Series.
   BL503.2.M55   1999
   291.2'3—dc21                                          99-16575


Manufactured in the United States of America

# Contents

# Acknowledgments _____

The contributors to this volume deserve acknowledgment. The technology of E-mail facilitated distribution of the chapters to all contributors, who then provided their comments to the respective authors. This book is greatly strengthened by the input provided by these excellent scholars to each other on the chapters. As has been the case with my previous edited volumes, I have learned a great deal from every one of the contributors, and I am indebted to them.

I am grateful to Michael Barkun, series editor, and Cynthia Maude-Gembler, acquisitions editor, for approaching me about editing this volume. I was busy with other projects and tried to give this one away, but I am grateful to Mary McCormick Maaga for her wisdom in giving it back to me.

I thank Dale A. Stover for his careful reading and commentary on my introduction and the chapter by Michelene E. Pesantubbee.

For the past thirteen years, Carol Cortazzo, the administrative assistant for the religious studies department at Loyola University, New Orleans, has kept me organized through my various projects including this one. I owe much to Mrs. Cortazzo for her cheerful efficiency and insight.

I was better able to complete this book thanks to a new home computer provided to me by my parents. I am grateful to Bryson and Ellen Lowman for their love and support.

This topic is vitally important. I hope that people in numerous walks of life and professions find this book helpful in explaining the dynamics involving millennial beliefs, persecution, and episodes of tragic violence. I will be happy if we see fewer such episodes.

Catherine Wessinger
Loyola University, New Orleans

# Contributors _____

MICHAEL BARKUN is professor of political science in the Maxwell School at Syracuse University. He is the author or editor of nine books, including *Religion and the Racist Right* (1997), *Millennialism and Violence* (1996), and *Disaster and the Millennium* (1974). He is the recipient of grants and fellowships from the Harry Frank Guggenheim Foundation, the Ford Foundation, and the National Endowment for the Humanities. From 1987 to 1994 he served as editor of *Communal Societies,* the journal of the Communal Studies Association. In 1996 he was a consultant to the FBI during the Montana Freemen standoff. His current projects include a study of conspiracy beliefs in UFO literature and a comparative study of Black and White separatist movements.

ROBERT S. ELLWOOD is professor emeritus of religion from the University of Southern California. He received his Ph.D. in history of religion at the University of Chicago Divinity School in 1967, and taught at USC from 1967 to 1997. In 1998–99 he was Goodwin-Philpott eminent scholar in religion at Auburn University in Alabama. He is the author of more than twenty books, including *Religious and Spiritual Groups in Modern America* (1973/1988), *Alternative Altars* (1979), *The Sixties Spiritual Awakening* (1994), and *The Politics of Myth* (1999).

EUGENE V. GALLAGHER is the Rosemary Park Professor of Religious Studies at Connecticut College, where he teaches courses on new religious movements in comparative and historical perspective. He is the coauthor with James D. Tabor of *Why Waco? Cults and the Battle for Religious Freedom in America* (1995), and the author of *Expectation and Experience: Explaining Religious Conversion* (1990) and *Divine Man or Magician? Celsus and Origen on Jesus* (1982). He has published scholarly articles on early Christianity and other religions of Late Antiquity and on contemporary new religions in the United States.

MASSIMO INTROVIGNE is director of CESNUR, the Center for Studies on New Religions, in Torino, Italy, and professor at the Pontifical Athenaeum Queen of the Apostles in Rome, where he teaches a course on new religious movements. He has been consulted by law enforcement agencies, church bodies, and local and national governments in Europe in connection with various problems concerning new religious movements and millenarian groups. He is the author of more than twenty books in Italian (some of them translated into French and German) on new religious movements and esoteric groups. E-mail: cesnur@tin.it.

JEFFREY KAPLAN holds the Fulbright Bicentennial Chair of American Studies, Renvall Institute of Historical Research, University of Helsinki. He is the author of *Radical Religion in America* (1997), *The Emergence of a Euro-American Radical Right* coauthored with Leonard Weinberg (1998), and the author of *Encyclopedia of White Supremacy* (forthcoming). He has coedited two anthologies: *Nation and Race: The Developing Euro-American Racist Subculture* (1998), and *Cult, Anti-Cult and the Cultic Milieu: A Re-Examination* (forthcoming) and serves as book review editor and member of the editorial board of *Nova Religio: The Journal of Alternative and Emergent Religions*. In addition, he has published a number of articles in journals such as *Terrorism and Political Violence* and the *Christian Century*. He was awarded a Harry Frank Guggenheim Foundation Research Grant in 1995 and the Fulbright Bicentennial Chair at the Renvall Institute of Historical Research of the University of Helsinki in 1998–1999.

SCOTT LOWE is associate professor and chair of the philosophy and religion department at the University of North Dakota, where he teaches courses in world religions and new religious movements. His publications include *Mo tzu's Religious Blueprint for a Chinese Utopia: The Will and the Way* (1992) and *Da: The Strange Case of Franklin Jones* (1996). He started work on his contribution to this volume while participating in a National Endowment for the Humanities Summer Seminar at Northwestern University.

REBECCA MOORE is assistant professor in the department of religious studies at San Diego State University, San Diego, California. She has studied Peoples Temple for twenty years, because friends and relatives died in Jonestown in 1978. Her publications include *A Sympathetic History of Jonestown* (1985); *The Jonestown Letters* (1986); *In Defense of Peoples Temple* (1988); *The Need for a Second Look at Jonestown*, coeditor (1989); and *New Religious Movements, Mass Suicide, and Peoples Temple*, coeditor (1989). She developed a Web site with University of North Dakota student Kevin Hozak called "Alternative Considerations of Peoples Temple and Jonestown" for the twentieth anniversary of the Jonestown deaths, at http://www.und.nodak.edu/dept/philrel/jonestown/. Most recently she has published *Jews and Christians in the Life and Thought of Hugh of St. Victor* (1998).

MICHELENE E. PESANTUBBEE is an assistant professor of religious studies at the University of Colorado, Boulder, where she teaches courses on Native American religious traditions and new religious movements. She earned her Ph.D. in religious studies from the University of California, Santa Barbara. Her area of specialization is Southeastern Native American religious traditions and Native American religious movements. She is the author of "When the Earth Shakes: The Cherokee Prophecies of 1811–12," *American Indian Quarterly* (Summer 1993).

IAN READER is professor of religious studies at Lancaster University. His main research interests focus on the modern Japanese religious situation, and on studies of pilgrimage. His most recent publications include *A Poisonous Cocktail? Aum Shinrikyō's Path to Violence* (1996), *Practically Religious: Worldly Benefits and the Common Religion of Japan* coauthored with George J. Tanabe (1998), and *Religious Violence in Contemporary Japan: The Case of Aum Shinrikyō* (forthcoming). He is writing a book on the Shikoku pilgrimage in Japan.

THOMAS ROBBINS is a sociologist of religion with a Ph.D. from the University of North Carolina. Presently semiretired, he has held teaching or research positions at Queens College (CUNY), Yale University, The New School for Social Research, The Graduate Theological Union, and Central Michigan University. He is the author of *Cults, Converts and Charisma* (1988) and has coedited six collections of original papers including *In Gods We Trust* (1981; rev. ed. 1990), and *Millennium, Messiahs, and Mayhem* (1997). He has published numerous articles and essays on religious movements in social science and religious studies journals.

JEAN E. ROSENFELD earned her Ph.D. in the history of religions at the University of California at Los Angeles. She is an instructor in the Master of Arts in Interdisciplinary Studies program at Marylhurst College, Portland, Oregon, and a staff research associate at the Center for the Study of Religion at the University of California at Los Angeles. She was an adviser to the FBI during the Freemen standoff in 1996. Her publications include articles on Maori millennialism, religion, and violence, and a book entitled *The Island Broken in Two Halves,* on New Zealand prophet movements (1999).

RICHARD C. SALTER is assistant professor of religious studies at Hobart and William Smith Colleges. His dissertation at the University of Chicago Divinity School is a comparative case study of Rastafarian, Pentecostal, and Catholic group formation in Dominica, the West Indies. He is also chair of the seminar on "Rastafari in Global Context" in the American Academy of Religion.

CHRISTINE STEYN is a senior lecturer in the Department of Religious Studies at the University of South Africa where she teaches courses in new and alternative religious movements and research methodology. Besides various articles, she has also authored *Worldviews in Transition: An Investigation of the New Age Movement in South Africa* (1994), and coauthored *The Human Search for Meaning: A Multireligious Introduction to the Religions of Humankind* (1996).

JACQUELINE STONE is associate professor in the Department of Religion at Princeton University, where she teaches courses on Buddhism and Japanese religions. Her area of specialization is medieval Japanese Buddhism, especially the Tendai and Nichiren traditions. She has also worked on appropriations of traditional Buddhist teachings in modern Japan. She is president of the Society for the Study of Japanese Religions, and cochair of the Buddhism section of the American Academy of Religion. She is author of *Original Enlightenment and the Transformation of Medieval Japanese Buddhism* (1999).

GRANT UNDERWOOD is professor of religion at Brigham Young University, Hawaii. His *The Millenarian World of Early Mormonism* (1993) won several awards from scholarly associations, and he has published a number of articles on millennialism and on Mormon history in various journals. He has served a term on the executive council of the Mormon

History Association as well as on the board of editors of the *Journal of Mormon History.* He has been a fellow at the American Jewish Archives and with the National Endowment for the Humanities. His scholarly pursuits are balanced by the humor, heartache, and happiness of rearing a family of seven children.

CATHERINE WESSINGER is professor of the history of religions and women's studies, and chair of the religious studies department at Loyola University, New Orleans. She is a former chair of the New Religious Movements Group at the American Academy of Religion, and a member of the Executive Advisory Committee of *Nova Religio: The Journal of Alternative and Emergent Religions.* She was an adviser to the FBI during the Freemen standoff in 1996. She is the author of *Annie Besant and Progressive Messianism* (1988) and *How the Millennium Comes Violently: From Jonestown to Heaven's Gate* (2000). She is editor of *Women's Leadership in Marginal Religions: Explorations Outside the Mainstream* (1993) and of *Religious Institutions and Women's Leadership: New Roles Inside the Mainstream* (1996). She has articles on Millennialism posted at <http://www.loyno.edu/~wessing>.

# Millennialism, Persecution, and Violence

# Introduction

## The Interacting Dynamics of Millennial Beliefs, Persecution, and Violence

CATHERINE WESSINGER _____

Millennial beliefs are extremely ancient (Cohn 1993), and they will always be among the vital expressions of human religiosity. Whereas numerous millennialists and their respective groups never become involved in violence, there are scenarios in which millennial beliefs combined with the experience of persecution result in violence. By comparative and cross-cultural study, this volume aims to elucidate the interacting dynamics of millennialism and persecution that produce violence.

The Branch Davidian tragedy in 1993 highlighted for me the connection between persecution, millennialism, and violence, and this could be discerned in subsequent events reported in the news. These include the first set of Solar Temple deaths in 1994, Aum Shinrikyō's releasing of sarin gas on the Tokyo subway in 1995, the avoidance of persecution of the Montana Freemen by FBI agents and therefore the peaceful resolution of the standoff in 1996, the Heaven's Gate group suicide in 1997, and the lack of persecution of the Taiwanese group, Chen Tao, in Garland, Texas, in 1998.

Contrary to popular stereotypes, cases of violence involving millennial groups are not all the same. It is important to distinguish between millennial groups that are assaulted because they are perceived by outsiders to be dangerous; fragile millennial groups that initiate violence to preserve their religious goal; and revolutionary

3

millennial groups possessing ideologies or theologies that legitimate violence.[1]

The chapters of this volume will demonstrate variations regarding believers' experiences and perceptions of being persecuted. Some groups are subjected to severe forms of opposition. For other groups, the sense of being persecuted is internally generated. Sometimes the millennial believers are persecuted, and sometimes the millennialists are the persecutors.

## Relevant Terms

With the approach of the new temporal millennium, popular attention is increasingly aware of a pattern of religiosity that scholars of religion term "millennialism" or "millenarianism." Religious imaginations are being stimulated by the approach of the year 2000 to dream of an imminent transition to a new era, a condition of collective salvation.[2] David Koresh had predicted that armageddon[3] would occur in 1995. Koresh's prophecies were validated for the Davidians by the assault of their residence by Bureau of Alcohol, Tobacco, and Firearms (BATF) agents on February 28, 1993, the subsequent fifty-

---

1. The categories of millennial groups involved in violence that I am delineating—assaulted millennial groups, fragile millennial groups, and revolutionary millennial movements—are not as neatly distinguishable from each other as I describe in this introduction. All millennial movements have revolutionary implications, and they all have the potential to become either fragile and therefore initiate violence, or assaulted by law enforcement agents or members of the public. Further complicating the clarity of these typologies, a revolutionary group may become assaulted or fragile, a millennial group may become fragile because the members experience themselves as being assaulted, or a millennial group may become revolutionary because they are assaulted. Although acknowledging the real complexities of these ideal types, I still suggest that it is helpful in understanding why violence occurred in specific cases to determine which category is particularly relevant, that is, whether the group had a revolutionary ideology that motivated the violence, whether the group initiated violence because of its fragility to preserve the religious goal, or whether the group was assaulted.

I am grateful to Eugene V. Gallagher and Thomas Robbins for stressing to me the interplay between these categories (personal communications).

2. The following discussion defining "millennialism" builds on the work of Norman Cohn (1957) and Yonina Talmon (1962, 1966). See my earlier discussion of the definitional issues in Wessinger (1988, 19–27).

3. I am using the word "armageddon" in its popular sense of the final great battle between good and evil. In the New Testament Book of Revelation, Armageddon is the location in the Holy Land where the great battle will occur.

one-day siege conducted by Federal Bureau of Investigation (FBI) agents, and the tank and CS gas assault on April 19, 1993, that culminated in the fire. Members of the Solar Temple believed in the imminent destruction of the world, so they decided to make "transits" using group suicide and murder in three separate episodes in 1994, 1995, and 1997. The Aum Shinrikyō guru, Asahara Shōkō,[4] had predicted that armageddon would occur in 1999 or later. Asahara increasingly brought the date closer in time, directed his scientists to develop weapons of mass destruction, and one such chemical weapon, sarin, was released in the town of Matsumoto in 1994 and on the Tokyo subway in 1995. In 1997 thirty-nine Heaven's Gate believers residing near San Diego believed that planet Earth was soon to be "spaded under," so they opted to "exit" via group suicide to beam up to the mothership and thereby enter into the Kingdom of Heaven. At this writing, the most recent millennial group to attract media attention is Chen Tao, consisting of Taiwanese who moved to Garland, Texas, and whose leader predicted that God would appear at his house on March 31, 1998, and perform miracles. Teacher Chen predicted nuclear holocaust originating in East Asia in 1999. America was the place of safe haven from which the faithful would be picked up in flying saucers by God. God, speaking through Teacher Chen, had issued a strong statement against suicide, including suicide instigated by religious teachers, as always being motivated by devil possession (God—The Supreme Being 1997, 38). Although God did not appear in the manner predicted on March 31, 1998, Teacher Chen did not waver in his predictions of global catastrophe in 1999 and prepared his believers to relocate elsewhere in the United States to await the flying saucers (Wicker 1998a, 1998b).

The chapters of *Millennialism, Persecution, and Violence: Historical Cases* demonstrate that believers may take extreme actions to preserve their religious goal in the face of repeated disconfirmation and when there are stresses internal to the group and "cultural opposition" (Hall 1995) that threaten their religious goal. Millennial believers may also take the nonviolent measures of reinterpreting their doctrines or giving a different weight to apparently disconfirmed predictions. Some may lose faith in the prophecies, leave the group, and move on with their lives. Only time will tell how the Chen Tao

---

4. Japanese names will be given in the Japanese style of family name followed by the given name.

believers will react to continued disconfirmation of Teacher Chen's prophecies.[5]

The word "millennium" refers to "one thousand years," but "millennial" or "millenarian" religious expectations are ancient, and will not disappear after the temporal transition past the year 2000. Based upon his analysis of the data relating to the year 1000 and afterward, Richard Landes has suggested that there may be heightened millennial expectations relating to the period 2000 to 2033 (1996; n.d.).[6] But millennialism will persist indefinitely into the future, because millennial beliefs address the perennial human hope that the limitations of the human condition—conflicted relations, suffering, illness, death—will be overcome once and for all.

Millennialism is an expression of the human hope for the achievement of permanent well-being, in other words, salvation. Michael Barkun (1986) has demonstrated that millennial movements are often responses to the experience of multiple disasters, but even when social disasters are relatively absent, as individuals we are each subjected to the disaster of life—we each grow old, get sick, die, and lose our loved ones in the various tragedies of life; the human condition is the experience of finitude. Religions express the human desire to transcend finitude and gain a permanent state of well-being. In religions, a permanent state of well-being is salvation. Millennial religions promise the overcoming of finitude to collectivities of people.

5. It is important that in America, Chen Tao believers did not experience persecution in 1998. The Garland police were courteous to them, and furthermore the police consulted a religious studies scholar, Dr. Lonnie Kliever of Southern Methodist University, and facilitated his study of the group. Chen Tao attracted a great deal of media attention, but the reporters were generally courteous to the believers (personal communication from Christine Wicker), and Teacher Chen announced that the arrival of so many reporters to help him spread his message proved that God was implementing the plan of salvation (Wicker 1998b). The Chen Tao theology indicated alienation from East Asian culture—85 percent of the population there was described as being devil-possessed—but in 1998 the experience of Chen Tao believers in America was *not* one of persecution. If the absence of persecution continues, the Chen Tao believers may well be able to adjust their theology to continued disconfirmation of prophecies and proceed with the institutionalization of their religion.

6. Richard Landes maintains a Web site for the Center for Millennial Studies at <http://www. mille.org>. Despite the popular belief that Jesus was born in A.D. 1 and died in A.D. 33, the Gregorian calendar is inaccurate in its dating of the birth and death of Jesus Christ. Scholarship indicates that Jesus was probably born between 6 and 4 B.C. If Jesus was thirty-three when crucified, then that event would have occurred earlier than A.D. 33. If Jesus was born in 4 B.C., then 1996 would have been the two-thousand-year anniversary of his birth.

The book of Revelation in the New Testament speaks of the kingdom of God on earth lasting one thousand years. The term "millennium" as now used by religion scholars refers to the perfect age or God's kingdom in which there will be a collective salvation (i.e., collective permanent well-being). Therefore, the scholarly use of the term "millennium" is no longer tied to reference to a period of one thousand years. Religion scholars use the term "millennium" to refer to a condition of collective salvation, either earthly or heavenly,[7] in which the limitations of the human condition are overcome. In this book, to avoid confusion with the temporal millennium that begins with the year 2001, the authors often use the phrase "millennial kingdom" to refer to the expected collective salvation.

"Millennialism" or "millenarianism," therefore, is belief in an imminent transition to the millennial kingdom (the collective salvation). The sense of imminence—that the millennial kingdom will arrive very soon—is important to the millennial religious pattern. The sense of the imminence of the millennial kingdom has the power to draw people together to found new religious movements and to prompt them to radically change their lives and associations. Millennial beliefs are important in the founding of numerous religious traditions, including Christianity, Islam, Baha'i, and Mormonism, to name just a few.[8] The sense of imminence diminishes as the millennial religion's institutionalization, accommodation, and acceptance in society increases. This becomes what Jacqueline Stone (this volume) calls "managed millennialism." Managed millennialism is not likely to stimulate actions that radically oppose widely accepted social norms. But millennial beliefs will be recorded in the tradition's scriptures and continue to be resources that radical individuals can use to initiate additional new religious movements.

"Millennialism" is "religious," even in its atheistic varieties, because religion involves having an "ultimate concern," which has been defined by Robert D. Baird as "a concern which is *more important than anything*

---

7. Most definitions of millennialism stipulate belief in an earthly collective salvation. However, the Solar Temple, Heaven's Gate, and the Branch Davidians remind us that millennialism may well involve belief in an otherworldly or heavenly collective salvation. When the possibility for the earthly collective salvation is disproved, it is not unusual for the group to shift its expectation to a heavenly salvation. Scholars have been attracted to the study of millennial groups expecting the imminent appearance of a collective earthly salvation, because this belief's disconfirmation is so obviously dramatic to nonbelievers.

8. In the history of Judaism, apocalyptic beliefs became prominent during periods of oppression.

*else in the universe for the person [or the group] involved"* (1971, 18). An ultimate concern is the religious goal or religious commitment (Ian Reader in this volume calls it the "mission") as expressed within a belief system. People may change their ultimate concern if it is subjected to disconfirming events, or if they are put under pressure, but some people—perhaps many—cling to their ultimate concern so tightly that they become willing to kill or die for it.

Millennialism, because it involves belief in a collective salvation that may be earthly, and because it involves an allegiance to a principle whose authority is greater than the authority of civil law, is political. Millennialists may actively attempt to build the millennial kingdom on earth, either through peaceful or violent means, and millennialists may also resist imposition of civil authority on them that they regard as secondary to their ultimate authority.

Elsewhere (Wessinger 1997a), I have recommended the terms "catastrophic millennialism" and "progressive millennialism" to indicate two major patterns of belief about how the millennial kingdom is expected to be accomplished. Millennial beliefs can and do change in response to circumstances (Lucas 1997), and groups and individuals may shift back and forth between catastrophic and progressive expectations. When a group is relatively comfortable in society and they achieve some success in building their millennial kingdom, progressive themes may be highlighted. When disaster, opposition, or persecution is encountered, catastrophic themes will receive greater prominence. Catastrophic millennialism and progressive millennialism are not mutually exclusive (Wessinger 1997a, 51), and one may well contain the seeds of the other (see Reader in this volume). The social context, human free will, and predisposition will determine which theme is highlighted.

In "catastrophic millennialism," the belief is that the transition to the millennial kingdom will be accomplished by a great catastrophe (often caused by a superhuman agent)[9] that destroys the currently evil world so that a collective salvation will be accomplished for the saved

---

9. Numerous catastrophic millennial groups express belief that the great cataclysm will be orchestrated by God or some superhuman agent. However, there are catastrophic millennial systems, such as the teachings of Jim Jones or Marshall Herff Applewhite ("Do") of Heaven's Gate, in which the cause of the cataclysm is ambiguous or is attributed to nondivine causes, such as Teacher Chen's recent teaching that nuclear holocaust will be caused, not by God, but by devil-possessed human beings. In all cases of catastrophic millennialism, however, the great cataclysm is closely related to entrance into the millennial kingdom.

(often termed the "Elect" in Christianity). "Apocalypse" refers to biblical literature that reveals the catastrophic events that will occur at the end of the current world (see Underwood this volume, and the Los Angeles Police Department address by Rosenfeld). In popular usage, "apocalypse" has become synonymous with the expected catastrophe, and therefore we can say that "apocalyptic" is synonymous with "catastrophic millennialism."

Catastrophic millennialists have various views about the role humans will play in the expected upheaval. Some catastrophic millennialists believe that they must prepare themselves with faith and ethical living, and watch for the catastrophic change; they are waiting in faith to be included in the millennial kingdom. Some catastrophic millennialists are waiting to be included in the millennial kingdom, but they are armed for self-defense and will fight if attacked by enemies. Some catastrophic millennialists are revolutionaries and believe that the divine or superhuman plan calls for them to participate in overthrowing the evil government (see Freemen chapter by Rosenfeld for delineation of these different action options).

"Progressive millennialism" is belief that humans working in harmony with a divine or superhuman plan can progressively build the millennial kingdom; working under the guidance of a divine or superhuman agent, humans can create the collective salvation. "Progress" is inevitable and under the guidance of a superhuman agent. Many progressive millennialists do not believe catastrophe is required to bring about the millennial kingdom.

Many, perhaps most, millennialists believe in God, but many do not—hence in these definitions of millennialism I have stressed the belief in a "superhuman agent." Increasingly, "extraterrestrials" are cast in the roles formerly played by God, Satan, angels, and devils. These are all normally unseen beings that are believed to have the power to affect human beings for good or ill. There are atheistic forms of millennialism, of which Marxism is a primary example. In this volume, Robert Ellwood discusses Hitler's National Socialism in Germany, Scott Lowe discusses Mao Zedong's Great Leap Forward in the People's Republic of China, and Richard Salter discusses the Khmer Rouge's "super great leap forward" in Cambodia as revolutionary millennial movements. For Hitler and the Nazis, the superhuman agent was the the sacred Aryan race and the collective Aryan "will" that would create the triumphant Third Reich. In Maoism, the superhuman agent was the "consciousness" and determination of the people stimulating their heroic efforts to create the communist state. For the Khmer Rouge, the superhuman agent was the people as a collectivity possessing right Marxist knowledge concerning class struggle and the determination to act rightly according to Khmer Rouge ethics to create the communist state.

Whereas my study (1988) of a peaceful progressive millennial thinker, Annie Besant (1847–1933), had led me to conclude that progressive millennialists were not likely to commit violence, Robert Ellwood in his chapter on German Nazism, Scott Lowe in his treatment of Maoism, and Richard Salter in his chapter on the Khmer Rouge each report that these were progressive millennial movements. Whereas many progressive millennialists can be described as expecting a progressive *noncatastrophic* transition to the collective salvation, Nazis, Maoists, the Khmer Rouge (and others) were believers in progress who used revolutionary violence on a massive scale in their attempt to create the collective earthly salvation for the Elect. Ellwood indicates the violent point of contact between catastrophic millennialism and progressive millennialism by explaining that revolutionary progressive millennialists see revolution as "progress speeded up to an apocalyptic rate," and that for them revolution is a "virtually sacramental rite of accelerating progress."

Catastrophic millennialism and progressive millennialism may be visualized as two polarities on a continuum of ever-shifting millennial thought, which constantly responds and adjusts to physical circumstances. We may imagine that on the two ends of the continuum are the peaceful forms of catastrophic millennialism and progressive millennialism—those catastrophic millennialists who wait for the violent destruction of the world as we know it, and those progressive millennialists who engage in social work to carry out the divine plan to create the millennial kingdom noncatastrophically. Catastrophic millennialism can be observed to be a pessimistic view of human nature and society that sees society and humans as beyond repair; the old must be swept away to initiate the new condition. The peaceful expression of progressive millennialism can be observed to be an optimistic view of society and human nature that is confident that humans working under the guidance of a superhuman agent (or God) can progressively and *noncatastrophically* create the millennial kingdom. Further in on the continuum, having a greater potential for violence, are the catastrophic millennialists who are waiting for divine intervention, but who are armed in case they are attacked by diabolic enemies. Additional case studies are needed to determine whether progressive millennialists may also gather into armed communities prepared for the possibility of attack. Revolutionary progressive millennialism and revolutionary catastrophic millennialism meet each other on this continuum.[10] When progressive millennialism becomes revolutionary, it possesses the same radical dualistic view that is typical of catastrophic millennialism. A dualistic perspective divides people into good vs. evil, us vs. them, and the human vs. the unhuman, demonic, and less than human. Dualism, therefore, can justify violence.

Millennial movements have leaders of different types. "Ideological leaders" (Eichler 1971, 83–85) are leaders of movements in which every person in the movement has access to the respected source of authority. Margrit Eichler (1971) cites the Millerite movement in nineteenth-century America as an ideological movement. Anyone in the movement initiated by William Miller could interpret the Bible, and Miller was not the only person responsible for setting dates for the Second Coming of Jesus Christ. In an ideological movement, the assertions of leaders are either validated or invalidated by their degree of conformity to a source of ideological doctrine, often a scripture or a revered body of literature. The source of authority is available to all in an ideological movement, whether it is a scripture, respected literature, or an unseen source of revelation (Wessinger 1988, 315, 318).

In contrast to ideological authority, "charisma" is a term used by religion scholars to refer to authority derived from an unseen source that is believed to be restricted to the few. "Charisma" designates access to a divine or superhuman source of authority that is not usually shared with many others. That source of authority normally is unseen, so people either believe or disbelieve an individual's claims to revelation. Charisma is socially constructed; if no one in the environment believes an individual's claims to revelation from a superhuman or divine source of authority, a religious movement will not form.

A "prophet" is someone who speaks words of revelation from a normally unseen source (examples are God, angels, ascended masters, and extraterrestrials). A "messiah" also speaks words of revelation from an unseen source; therefore, a messiah is also a prophet, but a messiah goes beyond solely being a prophet. A prophet is not necessarily a messiah, but a messiah is always a prophet. A messiah is an individual believed to be empowered by a superhuman or divine agent to create the millennial

10. A linear continuum is an inadequate metaphor for the relationships between these various forms of millennialism. The reader should recall that millennialists typically shift between catastrophic expectations and progressive noncatastrophic expectations without ever resorting to arms and violence.

kingdom. Both prophets and messiahs have charisma—their followers believe they have access to a divine or superhuman source of authority.

The section of this book entitled "Two Nativist Millennial Movements: Two Nativist Millennial Movements" contains a chapter by Christine Steyn on two South African millennial movements, the Xhosa Cattle-Killing movement and the Israelites at Bulhoek. The Israelites were assaulted by police. The Xhosa were a fragile culture under attack by white colonialists, whose members initiated violence against their means of survival, their cattle, in a desperate effort to escape their oppressors and bring in the millennial kingdom. Because these two different types of movements were treated in a single chapter, I was unable to place Steyn's chapter in either the section "Assaulted Millennial Groups" or the section "Fragile Millennial Groups." Both of the groups treated by Steyn, however, are nativist millennial movements.

A "nativist millennial movement" consists of people who feel under attack by a foreign colonizing government that is destroying their traditional way of life, their culture and religion, and is taking away their land and means of survival. Nativists look with nostalgia to their past and regard it as an idealized golden age to which they long to return.[11] Often the memory of the idealized past is highly embellished. Quite a few nativists have identified themselves with the oppressions and deliverance of the Israelites described in the Old Testament of the Christian Bible, as did the South African Israelites.[12] Nativist millennialists look to the past for their idealized golden age, and they believe that divine intervention will eliminate the oppressors who are destroying their people and traditional way of life.

A number of nativist millennial movements are discussed in this volume: the Native American Ghost Dance movement, the Dreads in

11. Often Wallace's term "revitalization movement" is used for what I am calling "nativist millennial movement." In his classic article, Wallace defines revitalization movement as "a deliberate, organized, conscious effort by members of a society to construct a more satisfying culture" (Wallace 1956, 265). I find this definition to be overly broad to be of great use. As defined by Wallace, "revitalization movement" can be applied to any religious innovation, including those that are not millennial or nativist. The confusion about Wallace's meaning of his term arises from the fact that most of the movements he describes are nativist movements reacting to stress.

12. The members of the Church of Jesus Christ of Latter-day Saints (Mormons) and the Branch Davidians also identified with the Israelites without being nativists. Contemporary Euro-American nativists who are members of the religion called Christian Identity believe that white people are the true Israelites (see Freeman chapter by Rosenfeld).

Dominica, the Taiping revolutionaries in China, Christian Identity in the United States, the Xhosa Cattle-Killing movement and the Bulhoek Israelites in South Africa. Additionally, the Russian Old Believers, the German Nazis, and the American Neo-Nazis can also be considered nativists.

As with other millennialists, nativists display a range of behaviors. The ghost dancers believed that their faithful dancing would bring the return of their ancestors with herds of buffalo, and that through divine intervention the oppressing whites would be eliminated. After a shoot-on-sight law was passed in Dominica, many Dreads retreated to the bush to create their millennial kingdom. Now that Dreads have greater social acceptance, they wait in faith for divine intervention to destroy "Babylon" (a potent and often-used biblical metaphor for the sinful social order) and create the millennial kingdom. The Xhosa in South Africa believed in the imminent return of their ancestors with powerful "new people" to conquer the colonizers, and to show their faith in the imminent millennial kingdom and to purify themselves of all contamination by evil, they killed all their cattle. The Israelites at Bulhoek, South Africa, also awaited divine intervention. In contrast to these nativists awaiting divine intervention, there are revolutionary nativist millennial movements, such as the Russian Old Believers,[13] the Taiping revolutionaries, and the German Nazis, who take violent actions to create the millennial kingdom. However, when the revolutionary movement is not socially dominant, as with the American Neo-Nazis and Identity Christians such as the Freemen, individuals may be cautious about resorting to violence. The Freemen waged "paper warfare" against the federal government through the magical use of their Common Law documents.

Magical thinking and actions are discussed in a number of this book's chapters. "Magic" consists of performing actions and/or speaking or writing words of power that are believed to cause change in the physical world. The Freemen's interpretation and use of law expressed in their unique system that they term "Common Law" is an example of the use of magic (see Rosenfeld's Freemen chapter). Ellwood analyzes the spectacular pageants staged by Hitler and the Nazis as magic rituals to create the millennial kingdom. The Native American Ghost Dance and

---

13. Thomas Robbins notes that the Russian Old Believers were not at first committed to revolutionary violence, but that their revolutionary violence evolved over several decades in response to persecutory opposition by the tsarist government. However, since religious pluralism was not permitted, or seen as desirable, in that era in Russia, the goal of the Old Believers had inherent revolutionary potential (personal communication).

the Xhosa Cattle-Killing can be seen as simultaneous "sacrifices" (offerings to propitiate powerful unseen beings) and magic rituals to eliminate the oppressors and bring protection and well-being. Both sacrifice and magic are features commonly found in religions, so it is not surprising to find them in millennial religions.

Ian Reader has coined the phrase "the pragmatics of failure" (personal communications from Reader and Jacqueline Stone) to indicate how a group may adopt a new method to achieve their ultimate concern when other methods fail. We can observe the pragmatics of failure operating in the Peoples Temple, the Solar Temple, Heaven's Gate, Aum Shinrikyō, and in a number of the revolutionary millennial movements. If peaceful methods are failing to achieve the religious goal, a group might resort to violent methods, and their violence may be directed inwardly against group members, or outwardly at enemies, or both. The pragmatics of failure also can work to move a group away from the use of violence. If a violent millennial movement experiences devastating defeat, a pacifist movement may arise from its ashes. Jacqueline Stone discusses this direction of the pragmatics of failure in her chapter on the relation of Nichiren's *Lotus Sutra* millennialism to both militant Japanese nationalism and subsequent peace movements.

In their chapters, the authors do not apply the word "cult" to the religions studied. "Cult" has become a pejorative word that tends to limit the objective study and understanding of religious groups. "Cult" has become a label for religions that people do not know much about and that they do not like. "Cult" as a pejorative label has the effect of dehumanizing people,[14] and thus supports the notion that it is socially acceptable to discriminate against them, persecute them, and even kill them (Wessinger 1995). Dehumanizing labels are a prerequisite to committing what is believed to be justified violence against people. The evidence indicates that if the Branch Davidians had not been labeled "cultists," those eighty men, women, and children would still be alive today and four law enforcement agents would not have died in an ill-conceived raid against the Davidian community (Tabor and Gallagher 1995; Wright 1995).

Although authors in this volume examine a number of religious groups and movements that have initiated violence or have the potential

14. In other languages, a version of the word *sect* is the pejorative term. The French *secte*, the Spanish *secta*, the German *Sekte*, and the Italian *setta* would be best translated with the English word *cult* in its pejorative connotations by society. I thank Massimo Introvigne for informing me of the pejorative word for *cults* in European languages.

to initiate violence, none of the authors wishes to demonize the members of these groups by labeling them "cultists."

Nor do the authors resort to "brainwashing" as an explanation for why people join millennial groups that may become involved in violence. Millennial thinking produces worldviews that function as other religions do to explain the human experience of evil and suffering. Millennialism offers hope that the experience of evil is not meaningless and that the righteous will be vindicated and included in a permanent condition of well-being. Millennial worldviews have their own internal logic that is appealing to believers (Underwood this volume; O'Leary 1994).

Charismatic leaders do not achieve authority without having followers willing to grant them authority. Charismatic leadership is not necessarily linked to violence and totalitarian control, but it sometimes is. Leaders claiming charisma cannot exercise coercive control over followers and unbelievers without having secondary leaders and followers willing to carry out violent actions they believe will build the millennial kingdom. Instead of blaming religious belief and activities on "brainwashing," it is best that individuals carefully consider to whom they grant authority and the types of actions required by particular religious commitments.

Some millennial movements may not have a single charismatic leader, but possess doctrines that may motivate believers to commit violence— the contemporary Euro-American nativist movement that includes Neo-Nazis and the Freemen is an example.

It is a normal, but regrettable, human characteristic to think in dualistic terms, good versus evil, God versus Satan, us versus them. Dualism is a prominent feature of catastrophic millennialism, whether the believers are the passive watchers for God's cataclysmic destruction, the armed survivalists prepared to protect their communities, or the aggressively violent revolutionaries. Radical dualism that dehumanizes opponents is a characteristic of the revolutionary progressive millennialism described in this volume by Ellwood, Lowe, and Salter.[15] A dualism that

---

15. The progressive millennialism that I studied in Annie Besant's thought was not characterized by a radical dualism that demonized and dehumanized opponents. Dualism was not absent in the thought of Annie Besant and her contemporary Theosophists, but the dominant emphasis in Theosophy is a monism that stresses the oneness of all beings and the shared divinity of all human beings. Annie Besant advocated social work and personal transformation to create what she termed the "New Civilization" (Wessinger 1988). More case studies of noncatastrophic progressive millennialism are needed for comparative purposes to more fully understand the typical characteristics of progressive millennialism and its relationship to what I am terming revolutionary progressive

demonizes and dehumanizes opponents is an ideology of conflict. People possessing a dualistic worldview are not surprised when conflict appears in the form of persecution and some may initiate violence.

Anticultists are not necessarily millennialists, but the antagonism against unconventional religions generated by the anticult movement is also a result of a radically dualistic worldview that has contributed to cases of tragic violence (see chapters by Moore and Gallagher in this volume).

Jeffrey Kaplan (in this volume and 1997a) suggests that the dualistic worldview expressed in "watchdog" organizations can have the unintended effect of exacerbating a mutually oppositional dualism. Watchdog organizations can promote the belief of some millennialists that they are being persecuted, and they can increase the probability that radical groups become more attractive to extremist and unstable individuals.

Religion is an expression of human nature's rebellion against finitude and is a product of human imagination. As an expression of human nature, religion is not necessarily "good."[16] Religion is used by humans to justify all types of behavior. People do bad things in the name of religion, because they are human (Wentz 1993), and evil acts committed in the name of religion are not restricted to unconventional religions. Some of the millennial groups involved in violence examined in this book were small alternative groups; others were socially dominant and their violence impacted entire nations and the world.

Some of the groups examined in this volume were assaulted; others initiated violence because of their fragility (often owing to their perception of being under attack); and many others possessed inherently revolutionary ideas that motivated people to commit violence. Nativist millennial groups can be found in all three of these categories.

### Assaulted Millennial Groups

The assaulted millennial groups treated in this volume are the Mormons, the Lakota Sioux at Wounded Knee, the Branch Davidians of

---

millennialism. I suspect that progressive millennialism that emphasizes nonviolent social work will stress the interconnectedness and unity of all beings as opposed to the dualism of revolutionary progressive millennialism that justifies violence. But being human, noncatastrophic progressive millennialists will retain the habit of thinking in dualistic categories, and these will become prominent if opposition is experienced.

16. I thank Ian Reader for emphasizing that religion is not "good" (personal communication).

Waco, Texas, the Dreads of Dominica, and the Israelites at Bulhoek, South Africa. The intentions of each of these religious groups were misunderstood and feared by the general public and law enforcement agents. They were not viewed as holding to valid religions worthy of respect. These groups were viewed as being dangerous to public order. Although some of these persecuted groups bear part of the responsibility for the violence that engulfed them, the primary responsibility for the violence rests upon law enforcement agents, members of the military, or members of the general public, who assaulted them.

In his chapter on the Mormons, Grant Underwood stresses that millennialists are not necessarily socially marginal misfits, and that millennialism provides a satisfying worldview, particularly to people experiencing persecution. Underwood demonstrates that catastrophic millennial beliefs intensify when a religious group is persecuted. When cultural opposition decreases and the group is permitted to build its institutions and to accommodate to society, the religion may retain its catastrophic millennial cosmology, but the intensity of the apocalyptic rhetoric will diminish.

The Mormons in nineteenth-century America were driven repeatedly from their homes. The governor of Missouri issued an extermination order against the Mormons in 1838. Their prophet, Joseph Smith, was murdered by a mob on June 27, 1844. The U.S. cavalry was dispatched against Mormons in Utah in 1857, and after the Civil War polygamous Mormon men were hunted down and imprisoned. As a result of these repeated assaults, Mormons armed themselves for self-defense. The Mormon record was not spotless. In the Mountain Meadows massacre, a Mormon militia detachment in southern Utah killed more than a hundred pioneers traveling to California. An intense oppositional context is conducive to violent outbursts.

Underwood stresses that it is essential to understand a group's millennial cosmology in its details to determine whether the believers see themselves as agents of the imminent catastrophic destruction. Underwood concludes that there is an "almost symbiotic relationship between persecution and millennialism." The dualistic worldview of many millennialists, especially of catastrophic millennialists, is validated and strengthened by their experience of opposition and persecution. As long as their ultimate concern is not endangered, persecution provides the assurance that prophecies are being fulfilled and that the suffering believers will ultimately receive their just reward from God. Underwood reports that the Mormons were strengthened by their persecution.

Underwood makes an important point relevant also to the ghost dancers and the Branch Davidians. Because the American Constitution guarantees freedom of religion, the threat to social order posed by "the Mormon Other had to be construed in such a way that its persecution was a manifestation of patriotism rather than bigotry." Therefore, the rhetoric of apostates and religious bigots demonized Mormons as incarnations of evil.

Once the persecution of the Mormons diminished, the Church of Jesus Christ of the Latter-day Saints, now a vast international church, became one of the greatest millennial success stories. The Mormon case teaches that, typically, if nonrevolutionary catastrophic millennialists are left alone, they will go about their business of routinizing their prophet's charisma into institutional structures and will become accommodated to mainstream society.

The Ghost Dance as described by Michelene E. Pesantubbee was a nativist movement expressing the reactions of some Native Americans to colonialism, defeat, removal from their land and traditional way of life, and confinement on reservations without adequate provision for survival. The ghost dancers expected divine intervention to remove the oppressing whites and restore their traditional lifestyle.

The massacre of a Lakota Sioux band at Wounded Knee on December 29, 1890, by federal soldiers bears numerous similarities to the Branch Davidian tragedy in 1993. In both cases, the religions were not accorded validity—the Ghost Dance was called "the Delusion" and the "Messiah Craze," the Branch Davidians were called "cultists"—thus the believers were regarded as irrational. Both persecuted groups were convinced that their freedom of religion was at issue. In both cases, exaggerated rumors of weapons stockpiling magnified the threat that each group was believed to pose to society. In both cases, federal agents misunderstood and discounted the group's religious beliefs and actions. In both cases, federal bureaucratic rivalry and jockeying for power created a context conducive to violence. In both cases, government officials refused to use qualified intermediaries to translate the conflicting worldviews to the two groups of opponents and thus de-escalate the tension, and the federal agents who did listen to the believers were regarded as becoming too sympathetic and were ordered to discontinue constructive dialogue. In both cases, the group's members knew that they were surrounded by overwhelming firepower; they preferred not to fight but were prepared to fight in self-defense. In both cases, the date of the predicted cataclysm was brought closer in response to the experience of persecution. In both cases, a crisis was precipitated by the unnecessary attempt to arrest a revered leader, that resulted in deaths of believers and law enforcement agents. In both cases, "an adversarial environment" (Pesantubbee this volume) was created by military deployment. Soldiers in both cases taunted and demeaned the besieged groups, indicating that they were pumped up for battle.[17] Rumors among the soldiers and misinformation given to the press and to Washington officials painted both groups as being dangerous to society. In both cases, the groups did not pose a threat to the public or to law enforcement agents.

Pesantubbee argues that if knowledgeable intermediaries had been used as bridges between the Lakota Sioux and law enforcement agents, the massacre at Wounded Knee might have been avoided. One hundred fifty-three Lakota were killed at Wounded Knee and forty-four were wounded. Twenty-five whites were killed and thirty-nine wounded. The soldiers, who were well armed and had four Hotchkiss cannons trained on the band, initiated the fighting. The massacre at Wounded Knee may also resemble the Branch Davidian tragedy in that there occurred a particularly vicious killing of children and unarmed men and women.[18] At Wounded Knee, twenty-six children under thirteen were killed.

In his chapter, Eugene V. Gallagher focuses on Branch Davidian theology. Gallagher's primary sources are audiotapes of David Koresh's Bible study sessions and transcripts of the Davidians' negotiations with FBI agents. Gallagher stresses that the Davidians were assaulted and fought in self-defense. The Davidians did not want to fight as evidenced by their frantic 911 calls in response to the BATF raid. In his theological teachings, Koresh reserved apocalyptic violence for God. The Davidians were armed, but they were not planning to attack members of society outside their community.

17. During the Branch Davidian siege, the personnel in the tanks mooned the Davidians, made obscene hand gestures, and verbally taunted the Davidians (Reavis 1995, 249–50). The tanks also made threatening maneuvers around the residence and destroyed Davidians' property.

18. It is difficult to sift through the multitude of facts and allegations of fact concerning the Branch Davidian tragedy, especially because federal agents dispute any allegation of wrongdoing. CS gas was inserted into the residence and possibly directly into the concrete-block room where the mothers and children were huddled, and a tank entering the building knocked concrete down upon them. Tanks also destroyed exit passageways. CS gas burns the skin and respiratory system and may cause asphyxiation. CS gas has an anesthetic effect and may have disoriented Davidians impairing their ability to escape (C. Moore 1995, 320, 345, 348, 351; House of Representatives 1996, 69–75).

The Davidians believed that Koresh was a messiah divinely inspired to interpret the Bible's prophecies and that he would participate in the events of the endtime bringing about God's judgment and his millennial kingdom. The assaults and persecution of the Branch Davidians in 1993 validated Koresh's interpretations of the Bible and therefore enhanced his status in the group.

Throughout the fifty-one-day siege, Koresh's interpretations of events in the light of the Bible remained flexible and responded to events. According to Koresh, the primary action required of believers was to study the Bible and wait for God's catastrophic destruction of the sinful world to be included in God's millennial kingdom. In order for the Davidians to be willing to exit their home, Mount Carmel Center, the scenario had to conform to the Davidians' understanding of the biblical prophecies, which was flexible until the very end—this is what FBI negotiators did not understand or take into account. Gallagher concludes:

> For the government forces, each individual act of physical or psychological violence, including establishing the perimeter blockade, preventing the Davidians from communicating with the outside world, assaulting the Davidians' aural and visual senses, and destroying their property with tanks, made it easier for other acts of violence to occur. On the inside of Mount Carmel, as the negotiation tapes clearly show, the government troops' actions reinforced the Davidians' perception that the BATF had meant to kill them all on February 28 and that the FBI might well decide to finish the job.

Koresh and the Davidians did not want to die, and they sought to negotiate their peaceful exit from Mount Carmel. All the persecutory actions taken against the Davidians by federal agents confirmed Koresh's prophecies and strengthened the cohesiveness of the group. This is why the Davidians were able to withstand fifty-one days of psychological warfare and physical deprivation.

I leave open the question of how the fire started—all of the facts and allegations are fiercely disputed. It is possible that the Davidians at the very last moment became a fragile millennial group and set the fire to preserve their ultimate concern of being obedient to God's commandments as revealed in the Bible so they would be included in God's millennial kingdom. The Davidians may have set the fire as a self-defensive measure to fight the tanks that were demolishing their home (Arnold 1994). Surviving Davidians claim that the fire ignited when the tanks knocked over kerosene lanterns. One thing is clear: The fire would not have started if tanks had not been inserting CS gas and demolishing the building.[19] Seventy-four Davidians, including twenty-three children, would not have died if the FBI assault had not occurred.

Because Gallagher's chapter focuses on analysis of Branch Davidian theology, I will recount briefly here the important events in 1993.[20]

On the morning of Sunday, February 28, 1993, Mount Carmel Center was assaulted by seventy-six armed BATF agents. In the ensuing shootout, five Davidians and four BATF agents died. Davidians allege that BATF agents shot at their residence from helicopters. That afternoon, a sixth Davidian was killed by BATF agents as he attempted to walk to Mount Carmel and rejoin his family.

The BATF raid was unnecessary. Undercover work by BATF agents had produced no evidence that the Davidians possessed illegal weapons. The affidavit for the warrant alleged child abuse, which does not come under BATF or federal jurisdiction. Texas social workers had investigated for child abuse and closed the case for lack of evidence. The affidavit also alleged that the Davidians were operating a methamphetamine lab. The House of Representatives majority report concluded that the methamphetamine lab allegation was a lie told by BATF commanders to obtain military support for the raid (House of Representatives 1996). David Koresh had a history of cooperating with official investigators, and he had extended an invitation to a BATF agent to visit Mount Carmel and inspect his guns, which was ignored. The BATF raid appears to have been carried out in an attempt to impress the new Clinton administration with an eye to obtaining the following headline: The BATF subdues a dangerous "cult."

FBI agents presided over the fifty-one-day siege during which fourteen adults and twenty-one children came out of Mount Carmel. Every time adult Davidians started coming out, FBI agents initiated or escalated physical deprivation and psychological warfare, which included turning off electricity and water, shining bright spotlights at night, blasting high decibel and irritating sounds, destruction of the Davidians' vehicles and property by tanks, threatening maneuvers by the tanks, and taunts by the tank personnel. If FBI agents believed that David Koresh

19. The United States in 1993 signed the Chemical Weapons Convention, which bans the use of CS gas in warfare (C. Moore 1995, 293).

20. For a fuller exposition of the events of the Branch Davidian tragedy, see Tabor and Gallagher 1995; Reavis 1995; Wright 1995; C. Moore 1995; House of Representatives 1996; Wessinger 1997c; and Wessinger 1999.

and the Davidians were psychologically unstable and likely to commit group suicide (Hall 1995), why were they subjected to psychological warfare and intense tactical pressure?

Religious studies scholar Dr. J. Phillip Arnold of Reunion Institute in Houston drove to Waco, and on March 7, 1993, offered his services to FBI agents, but he was ignored. On March 15 one of the Davidians, Steve Schneider, reported to FBI negotiators that the Davidians had heard Dr. Arnold discuss the Bible on a radio show. Schneider requested that Dr. Arnold be permitted to serve as mediator, or at the least be permitted to discuss the biblical prophecies with David Koresh. FBI agents did not respond to this request.

On April 1, 1993, Dr. Arnold and Dr. James Tabor of the University of North Carolina in Charlotte discussed the Bible in a radio broadcast as the Davidians listened. Arnold and Tabor suggested that the biblical prophecies, specifically the Seven Seals in the book of Revelation, did not predict that the Davidians would be martyred at that time; the Davidians could come out and be true to God's Word revealed in the Bible. They suggested that the prophecies indicated that God wanted Koresh to come out to spread his message to a broader audience. On April 2 Steve Schneider told negotiators that the Davidians would come out after Passover.

On April 14, 1993, Koresh sent out a letter stating that after he wrote his interpretation of the Seven Seals of the book of Revelation, he and the Davidians would come out. The negotiation tapes recorded the Davidians cheering at the prospect of the peaceful end of the siege. Attorney General Janet Reno was not informed about Koresh's promise to come out and she was led to believe that the negotiations were stalled. On April 16 the Davidians requested a battery-operated word processor to facilitate the production of Koresh's manuscript, and Koresh reported to negotiators that he had completed writing his interpretation of the First Seal. On April 17 the Davidians again requested a word processor. The word processor was delivered to the Davidians on April 18.

On the morning of April 19, 1993, the FBI assault began with tanks firing or spraying CS gas into the building. The tanks rammed the building, knocking down stairways and blocking exit routes, and knocking debris down upon the mothers and small children huddled in the concrete block room. Shortly after noon, fires ignited in areas where tanks had entered the building, which quickly flared into the memorable inferno. Fire trucks were held back until the building was consumed in flames. Shortly thereafter, the area was bulldozed.

The FBI assault against the Davidians was unnecessary. Arnold and Tabor had communicated respectfully with the Davidians concerning their religious beliefs, and they had persuaded Koresh that he could be taken into custody in a manner that conformed to biblical prophecy. David Koresh was a charismatic leader, a messiah, whom Davidians believed would participate in the events leading to the millennial kingdom. However, there was an ideological component to Koresh's authority, because the Davidians regarded the Bible as their ultimate authority. Steve Schneider told negotiators that he daily checked Koresh's assertions against the Bible (tape #201), and that if the Davidians could be shown from the Bible that God wanted them to exit Mount Carmel they would do so no matter what Koresh said (tape #129). One of the Davidians who escaped the fire carried out a disk on which was saved Koresh's interpretation of the First Seal. With the help of Arnold and Tabor, Koresh found a way to resolve the siege peacefully in a manner that conformed to biblical prophecies. David Koresh had informed FBI agents of his intention to come out soon.

On the Caribbean island of Dominica in 1974, Rastafarianism was declared an unlawful society, and a law was passed granting immunity from prosecution to anyone who killed members of unlawful societies. Dominican Dreads, that is, Rastafarians, had to seek places of refuge. Richard Salter reports that the Dreads who were catastrophic millennialists were less persecuted, because they awaited divine intervention, while the Dreads who were progressive millennialists and were creating their millennial kingdom were more persecuted because they threatened the established social order.

Salter's chapter provides an analysis of the different class resources Dreads used to cope with their persecution. The peasants, Nonm Tè (men of the earth), retreated to the bush. Nonm GCE (men with secondary degrees) were more likely to remain in the city. The Nonm GCE received financial help from relatives and they could express their views through radio and the press to persuade Dominicans that Rastafarianism was a legitimate religion. Violence was committed against the Dreads and by Dreads, including several gun battles with police. The Dread Act was repealed in 1981 and Dreads in the bush returned to Roseau, the capital city.

Contemporary Dreads are catastrophic millennialists, who focus on pure living to prepare for the millennial kingdom that will be established when "Babylon" is destroyed by Jah (God) or the Rastafarian messiah, Haile Selassie. The experience of persecution caused the Dreads to become less political. Their "pragmatics of failure" response to their persecution caused them to emphasize that their religion is a matter of personal lifestyle.

The Israelites of Bulhoek, South Africa, discussed in the chapter by Christine Steyn, were assaulted by police on May 24, 1921. Their prophet was Enoch Josiah Mgijima, who taught that blacks were the descendents of the biblical Israelites, and that Jehovah would deliver them from their bondage to whites. Like the Branch Davidians, the Israelites observed the Jewish Sabbath and celebrated Passover. Mgijima predicted war in which blacks would defeat whites, but the Israelites' role was to wait and watch.

In 1920 Mgijima's followers gathered at his residence in Bulhoek for Passover, but after Passover the three thousand Israelites refused to leave. The Israelites by their squatting on crown land were breaking a bylaw. Despite the use of intermediaries, the Israelites refused to leave. The mediation failed because civil agents did not recognize that the Bulhoek land was sacred to the Israelites, and that the Israelites were obeying God's orders. For the Israelites, God's authority outweighed the authority of civil laws. To be successful, negotiators had to be cognizant of the Israelites' ultimate concern and their religious worldview. It would have been wise if the police had not attempted to enforce an insignificant law on this millennial group obedient to Jehovah. The Israelites' commitment was expressed in their spokesman's statement: "God sent us to this place. We shall let you know when it is necessary that we go."

Eight hundred well-armed police surrounded the Israelites' village and set up a machine gun. Mgijima, like David Koresh, told his followers that they could choose to leave, but none of the Israelites did so. The police misinterpreted some of the Israelites' movements in worship (like the ghost dancers) as being threatening, and a battle ensued. The Israelites fought, but they were armed with spears, knives, sticks, and a few guns. After twenty minutes, 183 Israelites were dead, about 100 Israelites were wounded, and a policeman had a stab wound. The Israelites' village was razed and 150 were arrested. The demonization of the Israelites and their religion to the white public made the actions of the police appear to be reasonable.

Assaulted millennial groups contribute to conflictual situations by possessing arms and holding to a dualistic worldview that expects conflict. Their allegiance to God supersedes any obedience to governments, and this puts them in conflict with law enforcement agents. But the violence that engulfs assaulted groups, which often includes deaths of law enforcement agents, can be avoided if law enforcment agents learn to recognize the power of religious commitment and how millennial beliefs can contribute to violent scenarios. Law enforcment agents will be wise to use religion scholars with academic credentials as experts, instead of self-styled "cult experts," and if necessary, use religion scholars as "worldview translators" (personal communication from Jayne Seminare Docherty).[21] Law enforcement agents should avoid besieging a millennial group, which by definition is committed to a source of authority that transcends civil authority.

The plaque commemorating the Bulhoek massacre applies also to the other assaulted groups discussed in this volume:

> Because they chose the plan of God, the world did not have a place for them.

## Fragile Millennial Groups

A fragile millennial group initiates violence because of a complex combination of internal weaknesses and cultural opposition that threatens its religious goal. These factors may also threaten the leader's status within the group, but I wish to stress that believers become willing to kill or die to preserve their *ultimate concern*, the most important thing in the world to them, rather than have to admit that they were mistaken in holding to that goal. In the section on fragile millennial movements, the groups discussed are the Peoples Temple, the Solar Temple, Heaven's Gate, and Aum Shinrikyō. The separate chapter by Christine Steyn discusses the Xhosa Cattle-Killing movement, a case of an entire culture self-destructing in a millennial movement responding to colonialism.

Each of these fragile millennial groups viewed themselves as being persecuted, and they held to a conflictual dualistic view. Their actual persecution was variable. When members of these millennial groups committed violence against individuals who wanted to leave or against outsiders or both, the believers themselves were persecutors. The members of these groups held to the view that the end (their religious goal) justified their violent means.[22] The tragic outcomes of these fragile groups demonstrate that this is a very dangerous ethical approach.

Rebecca Moore's chapter on Peoples Temple describes the events that produced the mass suicide-murder at Jonestown, Guyana, on

---

21. Docherty derived the term from Lucas (1994).
22. The same is true of the revolutionary millennialists to be discussed below.

November 18, 1978, in which 918 members of Peoples Temple died including 294 children under eighteen. They died by either drinking punch laced with cyanide and tranquilizers, or by being injected with the deadly potion. Although the very young children, the very elderly, and some drugged dissidents were murdered, there is no evidence that the able-bodied adults and teenagers physically were forced to commit suicide. The group suicide had been discussed communally, planned, and practiced as a means to preserve their ultimate concern, which was to maintain the cohesiveness of their community. Immediately before the group suicide-murder, a few Jonestown residents opened fire upon Peoples Temple's enemies, the departing party of Congressman Leo Ryan, killing Ryan, three members of the news media, and a defector.

Peoples Temple members were catastrophic millennialists who had taken refuge in Jonestown, a socialist collective carved out of the Guyanese jungle. They expected that an imminent cataclysm would destroy capitalist society leaving the way open for communists to create the perfect society. More than 70 percent of Peoples Temple members were African Americans seeking relief from American ghettos, and the rest were whites (Maaga 1996, 9). They wanted to create a society free of racism, classism, sexism, and ageism. Their pessimistic view of existence summarized pithily by Jim Jones was that "Life is shit."

This pessimism was confirmed by the Peoples Temple's experience of persecution. Apostates formed a group called Concerned Relatives, who then orchestrated a campaign with multiple fronts to destroy Peoples Temple. Reporters were enlisted to publish sensationalized stories about Peoples Temple, and lawsuits were filed. Concerned Relatives sparked investigations by the Internal Revenue Service, the Social Security Administration, U.S. Customs, and the postal service. Peoples Temple members considered Congressman Leo Ryan's unwelcome visit to Jonestown an invasion by their enemies: the federal government, the news media, and Concerned Relatives. When Ryan's party departed Jonestown with sixteen defectors, Jim Jones and his community were convinced that their collective was being destroyed.

There were stresses internal to Jonestown, many of which were caused by Jim Jones himself. Jones, by virtue of his physical and mental decline owing to drug addiction, was in danger of failing to be the messiah that he claimed to be. Jones had set an impossible goal, the creation of a community in which there would be no problems, no dissent, and no lack of care. There were dissenters, some of whom were confined or drugged or both, while others managed to escape. Financial problems threatened the collective's survival and its ability to provide care. The relatively few able-bodied adults (about one-half of the residents) in relation to the seniors and children created a precarious economic situation in which the Jonestown leaders despaired of the collective's survival (Maaga 1996, 9). The survival of Jonestown was threatened, in part because of the composition of the community and the goals it set for itself, in part by the erratic behavior of Jim Jones, and in part by the actions of the American federal government and Concerned Relatives. Before the visit of Ryan and his party, the residents of Jonestown were already failing to achieve their religious goal. Congressman Ryan barged into a fragile situation and made it worse.

Moore explains that Peoples Temple members had become bonded to one another by their shared participation in rituals of violence, and that Peoples Temple's violence mirrored the violence endemic to American culture. In the end, Peoples Temple members used violence to preserve their ultimate concern. They perceived themselves as being persecuted by a coordinated conspiracy to destroy Peoples Temple, and they had evidence that the conspiracy existed. Peoples Temple's catastrophic millennialism involved a dualistic view of good versus evil, us versus them, and from their perspective it looked like the evil capitalists were succeeding in destroying their collective. As the title of Jeffrey Kaplan's chapter indicates, real paranoids have real enemies. A Jonestown publication stated: "We are not paranoid. We simply have found no other logical way to make sense of our experiences."

If federal agents, reporters, and Concerned Relatives had been less conflictual in their approach to Peoples Temple, the group suicide-murder may not have occurred. Peoples Temple needed some time to resolve its internal problems. If Jonestown had become an ongoing commune, Peoples Temple may have shifted toward a noncatastrophic progressive millennialism rather than continuing its catastrophic millennial and dualistic emphasis.

This is not to say that law enforcement agents should not investigate religious groups when crimes are suspected. Aum Shinrikyō discussed below demonstrates the violence that can result when the criminal activities of millennial groups are unchecked.

Massimo Introvigne's chapter discusses the Solar Temple, a small international religious group with primarily French-speaking members. The first Solar Temple deaths occurred in October 1994. Five people died in Quebec, and of these a couple and their baby were murdered. The Dutoit couple were defectors whom Solar Temple members identified as enemies, and their baby son, Emmanuel, was regarded as the Antichrist. In Switzerland about that time, forty-eight people were found dead at two locations. Solar Temple members made a "transit" to abandon this evil world for salvation on the star Sirius. Some of the dead were murdered, perhaps in an effort to help them make their transit, and others appear to have committed suicide. Several teenagers and some of the adults may not have chosen to make the transit. Gunshots, poison, and suffocation in plastic bags were the means.

In 1995 and 1997 more Solar Temple believers made their transit. On December 23, 1995, sixteen people including three children were found dead near Grenoble, France. All died of gunshots. On March 22, 1997, five adults were found dead in Quebec. One had been suffocated with a plastic bag, and the others died from smoke inhalation from the fire set to the residence. The second and third sets of Solar Temple deaths appear to have been imitations of the first transit. Introvigne focuses on the causes of the first set of Solar Temple murders-suicides.

The Solar Temple was a Neo-Templar organization participating in the Western occult tradition. At first the Solar Temple ideology appears to have harbored the progressive millennial hope that through ritual activity and spiritual transformation the New Age could be inaugurated on Earth. Solar Temple members believed that Masters guided evolution on earth, and their prophet, Joseph Di Mambro, claimed to speak for the Masters and had appearances of the Masters staged in his inner sanctum to impress believers.

Immediately before the first set of Solar Temple deaths, everything was unraveling. Members were defecting, including Di Mambro's son and the Dutoit couple, who could expose the holographic deceptions. By naming their son Emmanuel, the Dutoits threatened the status of Di Mambro's daughter, Emmanuelle, said to be the embodiment of the Cosmic Christ. Emmanuelle herself at twelve was becoming a messiah difficult to control (Palmer 1996). Di Mambro at seventy was seriously ill.

The stresses internal to the Solar Temple caused the group to be extremely vulnerable to cultural opposition. One apostate was very vocal in her criticisms in the media. Her opposition encouraged investigations by anticult groups and by police. In Quebec in 1993 Solar Temple members were arrested for buying illegal weapons, and sensationalized media coverage ensued. Solar Temple documents indicate that the transit to Sirius began to be considered at the time the members experienced what they considered persecution. There had been some earlier speculations about possible dates for the catastrophic end of the world, and in response to their experience of persecution, the date for the end was brought closer. Solar Temple believers concluded that humanity was refusing to evolve into the New Age and that the Masters had therefore abandoned planet Earth and ordered that the Solar Temple faithful should follow. Salvation would be experienced on another world.

Introvigne also discusses the Heaven's Gate group suicide of thirty-nine adults near San Diego in March 1997. They died by eating pudding or apple sauce mixed with phenobarbital, swigging vodka, and pulling plastic bags over their heads. The Heaven's Gate theology was a catastrophic millennialism that expected the imminent destruction of the earth. The group was a class training to overcome their humanness to graduate to The Level Above Human (Telah), or the Kingdom of Heaven. As Telah inhabitants, they would exist in eternal, neuter, extraterrestrial bodies, travel in spaceships, and they would guide evolution on various planets. The two messiahs, Bonnie Lu Nettles ("Ti") and Marshall Herff Applewhite ("Do"), set impossible goals for the group to achieve, setting dates for the flying saucers to pick them up, and the transformation of their human bodies into eternal extraterrestrial bodies. The flying saucers did not appear, and the promise of becoming eternal was disconfirmed by Ti's death in 1985. In 1997 Do felt his health was failing, and began to teach the group that they might have to abandon their human bodies to graduate to Telah. The perceived need to leave planet Earth was intensified by their belief that Earth very soon would be "spaded under." They concluded that the Hale-Bopp comet was the "marker," the sign it was time to exit Earth. They believed that Ti's spacecraft was following behind the comet and approaching Earth to pick them up. The Heaven's Gate class exited Earth to preserve their ultimate concern of transcending their humanness to gain eternal salvation.

The Heaven's Gate group had experienced cultural opposition in the mid-1970s from the media and relatives; however, the group minimized opposition by becoming secretive about their whereabouts (Balch 1982, 1995). Dualism was a prominent part of their catastrophic millennial worldview: the earth and human existence were evil, The Level Above Human was good. In the 1990s there was no actual persecution of the group, but their dualistic worldview and alienation from society made them *feel* persecuted by minor incidents such as receiving derisive email in response to their Internet postings.

Introvigne concludes that when internal stresses "are sufficiently strong, even moderate external opposition is easily translated into a narrative of cosmic persecution." A preexisting dualistic worldview of good pitted against evil is likely to enhance a group's sense of being persecuted. This was also the case with Aum Shinrikyō in Japan.

Aum Shinrikyō's guru, Asahara Shōkō, had a revolutionary vision of leading warfare to destroy the evil materialistic world to establish the Buddhist millennial kingdom, Shambhala. Asahara directed his inner circle of leaders and scientists to research, develop, and acquire weapons of mass destruction (Kaplan and Marshall 1996). But the release of sarin gas in the town of Matsumoto in 1994, which killed seven people and injured hundreds, and the release of sarin gas on the Tokyo subway in 1995, which killed twelve people and injured thousands, had the short-term aims of destroying Aum's enemies. Three judges in Matsumoto were scheduled to make a ruling in a land dispute involving Aum, and the Tokyo subway gas attack was intended to immobilize police, who were preparing to raid Aum's communes. As described by Ian Reader, Aum Shinrikyō was a fragile millennial group that repeatedly resorted to violence to preserve the group's religious goal of collective salvation. Some of Aum's members were preparing to wage war in the imminent armageddon that would establish the millennial kingdom, but in fact, the violence committed against Aum members, dissidents, defectors, and outside enemies was prompted by Aum's fragility and was aimed at preserving their ultimate concern from failure.

Asahara blended yoga, Hindu, and Buddhist ideas and practices with the predictions from the Christian book of Revelation and the prophecies of the European seer Nostradamus. He added to this syncretistic mix a dose of conspiratorial anti-Semitism. Asahara's combination of the absolute authority attributed to the guru in the Hindu and Buddhist *siddha* (perfected saint) tradition with Christian apocalypticism proved to be particularly deadly. Aum members meditated, practiced yoga and extreme forms of asceticism, but surrender to the guru was the primary means of salvation. The devotees strove to attune their thoughts to Asahara's, and underwent various initiations, including one in which Asahara's blood was ingested, to elevate their consciousness to Asahara's condition of enlightenment.

Asahara set impossible goals for his group, which contributed to the group's fragility. Asahara at first predicted catastrophic destruction in a nuclear war in 1999. He claimed that the nuclear catastrophe would be averted if two Aum centers were established in every country by 1993 and if thirty thousand people became Aum renunciates, goals that Aum did not come close to achieving. In response to cultural opposition and the weaknesses internal to Aum, Asahara brought the date for armageddon forward to 1995 and had his scientists work to develop weapons of mass destruction. They were successful in manufacturing sarin.

Reader argues that the stresses internal to Aum were primary in leading Aum down a path of increasing violence. Devotees were coerced and beaten to make them endure violent forms of asceticism. A devotee died from such ascetic practice in 1988, and another devotee who threatened to tell the police was murdered in 1989. About this time, Asahara began teaching his doctrine of *poa,* that a death ordered by the guru was of karmic benefit to the person murdered. The dualistic worldview of Aum Shinrikyō, which pitted the evil materialistic world against the spirituality of Aum, intensified. The leaders of Aum had criminal secrets and they could not permit any investigation. By 1990 Asahara was speaking of materialism as the devil *(akuma),* and armageddon would be a battle between the devil and those allied with truth *(shinri).* People who wanted to leave Aum were imprisoned, drugged, and tortured in rituals that were attempts to "brainwash" them.[23] Various enemies were targeted for murder—defectors, relatives of members, reporters. The attorney Sakamoto Tsutsumi proved to be particularly dangerous, because he threatened to make public evidence that Asahara's blood did not contain a special DNA that conveyed enlightenment to devotees who drank it. Sakamoto, his wife, and their baby son were murdered in 1989.

Reader notes that the first murders committed by Aum members occurred before cultural opposition was directed against the group. Aum's criminal secrets heightened the group's sensitivity to any criticism. The experience of opposition confirmed Aum's dualistic worldview. Asahara alleged that there was a conspiracy to destroy Aum, and picking up on international and Japanese anti-Semitic themes, Asahara alleged that the demonic conspirators were Jews, who were behind the Freemasons, the United States government, and the Japanese government (on Japanese

23. These individuals were damaged and some died, but the coerced indoctrination did not succeed in producing believers (Kaplan and Marshall 1996). Aum's efforts to brainwash people coercively demonstrate the pernicious effects that the popular belief in brainwashing can have when some organizations attempt to carry it out. On the other hand, Aum's social-influence processes, such as having members listen to repetitive audiotapes, were effective when devotees engaged in these practices voluntarily. The same is true of the ascetic disciplines practiced by Heaven's Gate members (see Balch 1995). The practices of Aum Shinrikyō and Heaven's Gate resemble the training within monastic orders and retreat centers in Christian, Hindu, and Buddhist traditions. My point here is that socialization methods are effective when people choose to be socialized, but not when the methods are coercive.

anti-Semitism see Goodman and Miyaza 1995). Police delayed investigating Aum to avoid appearing to persecute the group. The lack of official investigation permitted Aum to travel further on its murderous path that culminated in the Tokyo subway gas attack in 1995.

Reader concludes that a religious group can generate an "internally-created disposition toward violence," and that "a religious movement can, without serious provocation, develop the capacity for violence." Like members of Peoples Temple, Aum members' shared participation in rituals of violence, beginning with extreme and coerced asceticism, led them along a path of escalating violence against dissidents and outsiders.

The Xhosa discussed in the chapter by Christine Steyn are an entire culture that, because of its fragility, self-destructed in an orgy of violence that the Xhosa believed would bring about their collective salvation. The Xhosa of South Africa had been subjected to many years of warfare with white colonialists, first the Boers and then the British, over land. There had been a devastating smallpox epidemic, and their cattle suffered from lungsickness. The experience of these multiple disasters and persecution by the whites made the Xhosa long for the elimination of their white oppressors and restoration of their former prosperity.

In 1856 a girl, Nongqawuse, had visions that the Xhosa ancestors would return bringing with them powerful "new people," the Russians, who were believed to be black and the enemies of the British, as well as new cattle and possessions. All the existing cattle and possessions were said to be tainted by the evil magic practices of their owners. To bring the ancestors and the new people, the Xhosa must stop farming and kill all their cattle. The Xhosa king, Sarhili, became convinced of the truth of Nongqawuse's visions and ordered that the cattle be killed.

Several dates were set for the arrival of the ancestors and the new people, and when they did not appear, the king set a final date and ordered that all remaining cattle and farm animals be killed. The traditional Xhosa belief was that the sacrificial spilling of blood was necessary to induce the ancestors to intervene for their welfare (personal communication from Steyn).

In the Cattle-Killing movement, about four hundred thousand cattle were killed, and as a result of the Great Disappointment, about forty thousand Xhosa starved to death. Surviving Xhosa had no choice but to become indentured servants to whites, and their land was appropriated by whites.

The Xhosa undertook their violent actions in a desperate attempt to achieve their ultimate concern, their collective well-being, but like the other fragile groups considered in this volume, they succeeded only in destroying themselves and innocent bystanders.

## Revolutionary Millennial Movements

Members of revolutionary millennial movements obviously bear the responsibility for the violence they initiate, but the manner in which nonbelievers interact with them remains important. Revolutionary millennialists are motivated by a sense that they are persecuted. They believe that revolutionary violence is the means to become liberated from their persecutors and to set up the righteous government and society. Revolutionary millennial movements are numerous, and have caused death and suffering on a massive scale. The revolutionary millennial movements treated in this section include the Russian Old Believers, the Taiping revolution and Mao's Great Leap Forward in China, the German Nazis, the appropriation of Nichiren's *Lotus Sutra* millennialism by militant Japanese nationalism and subsequent Japanese religions devoted to peace, the Khmer Rouge in Cambodia, American Neo-Nazis, and the Montana Freemen and their religion known as Christian Identity.

The seventeenth-century Old Believers as described by Thomas Robbins were a nativist movement that aimed to restore the true worship of God in the Russian Orthodox Church and a righteous government. Their goal to purify the Orthodox Church and the tsar's government was revolutionary, because of the cultural and governmental intolerance of religious pluralism. The most radical of the Old Believers were convinced they were living in the endtime dominated by the Antichrist, often identified as the tsar or a regent. The government responded by arresting Old Believers, torturing them, and burning them at the stake. The persecution of the Old Believers pushed them increasingly to resort to revolutionary violence to achieve their goal. During the 1680s and 1690s, when groups of Old Believers found themselves besieged by government troops, or if they knew that troops were approaching, they would shut themselves in a church and set it afire. The radical Old Believers developed a theology that legitimated suicide by fire; immolation was a purifying second baptism that removed the Antichrist's influence and brought salvation. Thus, the extreme dualistic worldview of the Old Believers, their conviction they were living in the catastrophic endtime dominated by the Antichrist, and the opposition of the government prompted them to commit numerous immolative group suicides. Their experience of persecution intensified and confirmed their apocalyptic beliefs. The pragmatics of failure motivated radical Old Believers to commit group suicide again and again.

Robbins notes that moderate, nonsuicidal Old Believers survived to shape the ongoing movement. Because of the large size of Russia, Old Believers were able to build communities in remote areas. Most importantly, when the persecution decreased, the number of group immolations diminished.

China has given birth to numerous revolutionary millennial movements, and the chapter by Scott Lowe discusses two Chinese movements influenced by Western ideologies, Christianity and Marxism. Lowe's chapter describes the Taiping Revolution, 1850–64, led by Hong Xiuquan, and Mao Zedong's Great Leap Forward, 1958–62.

The Taiping Revolution was a nativist movement aimed at overthrowing the oppressive Manchu dynasty. Through warfare the Taipings gained control of one-third of China and established a capital at Nanjing. Hong Xiuquan, who claimed to be the younger brother of Jesus, was the messiah commissioned by the Heavenly Father to kill the demon Manchus and set up a righteous government. Hong was somewhat influenced by Christian scripture, but like the American Identity Christians (see Freemen chapter by Rosenfeld), the focus was not on loving and forgiving one's enemies, but passages in the Old Testament advocating the killing of God's enemies were stressed. Many thousands of lives were lost in the military campaigns and the sack of Nanjing by Manchu troops.

Mao Zedong's Great Leap Forward demonstrates the vast destruction that messiahs can cause when they set impossible goals. The millennial expectation was expressed in Great Leap rhetoric that "three years of struggle" would make "a thousand years of communist happiness." Mao set impossible production quotas for steel and rice. Officials colluded to make sure that Mao saw numerous small furnaces in the countryside and fields artificially packed with rice-bearing plants. Peasants melted down their farming implements to make steel, the land was deforested to provide fuel, and because of the falsely inflated rice production figures, the government exported rice for profit and taxed the peasants for rice they did not have. Millions of people starved to death. Mao blamed hidden enemies for the failure, and pragmatically launched the Great Proletarian Cultural Revolution in 1966 to maintain his power.

Robert Ellwood discusses the German Nazis as a revolutionary millennial movement that had the goal of establishing the Nazi millennial kingdom, the Third Reich, which was to last one thousand years. Hitler was the messiah, the true leader endowed by Nature with special gifts for his salvific role. National Socialism's idealization of a past German way of life close to the land made it a nativist movement. The German sense of persecution after defeat in World War I and widespread unemployment paved the way for Hitler's rise to power through electoral politics.

Nazi dualism demonized and dehumanized opponents, and identified Jews as vermin that had to be eradicated from the Aryan corporate body. The Holocaust demonstrates the massive genocide that results from dualistic beliefs. Unfortunately, anti-Semitism is a common characteristic of the dualistic attribution of evil in the thought of many contemporary millennialists as we learn from Aum Shinrikyō and the contemporary Euro-American nativist movement that includes Neo-Nazis, Freemen, Identity Christians, and others.

Jacqueline Stone's chapter on Japanese *Lotus Sutra* millennialism deriving from the Buddhist priest Nichiren (1222–82) illustrates how "millennial thinking need not be confined to individuals or fringe movements . . . but may represent particularly intense expressions of more widely held concerns." Stone discusses how *Lotus* millennialism was used by right-wing patriots and military men to legitimate Japan's expansionism in Asia, and also by a nationalistic socialist to undertake a government coup that failed. According to Stone, revolutionary millennial ideas "can serve to legitimize the actions of armies and politicians, and also give expression . . . to aspirations shared by a majority."

Stone notes that the pragmatics of failure can prompt millennialists to abandon violent methods for pacifist ones. After Japan's devastating defeat in World War II involving the atomic bombing of Hiroshima and Nagasaki, Nichiren's *Lotus Sutra* millennialism was used by pacifist religious organizations, Sōka Gakkai and Risshō Kōseikai, committed to working in peaceful ways to create the Buddhist millennial kingdom. The experience of devastating defeats has prompted other violent millennialists to become pacifists, notably the Anabaptists and the Babis, who evolved into the Baha'is (Waite 1995). Stone concludes that "violent millennialist energies are not necessarily integral to the millennial vision itself, but under different circumstances can be redirected in peaceful and constructive ways."

Richard Salter discusses the Khmer Rouge, which controlled Cambodia in the 1970s, as a communist millennial movement that succeeded in capturing the allegiance of some Cambodians because it possessed similarities to Buddhist concepts of time, ethics, and authority. The Khmer Rouge's "super great leap forward" that produced Cambodia's killing fields combined the goal of a fresh start in the year zero with a nativist reverence for past Cambodian glory in the Angkor kingdom. The Khmer people had been prepared for this communist revolutionary millennialism by their experiences of persecution at the hands of French colonialists, Cambodian rulers, and American bombing. The Khmer Rouge leadership, the Angkar, the "Organization," was the movement's messiah, which as the people's "dad-mom" *(pouk-me)* offered them collective salvation. Like other revolutionary millennial movements, killing was a means to create the millennial kingdom.

American Neo-Nazis discussed by Jeffrey Kaplan and the Montana Freemen discussed by Jean E. Rosenfeld are both part of a broader contemporary Euro-American nativist movement that is characterized by its virulent racism and anti-Semitism. These white people feel oppressed by the federal government, which they believe is controlled by Jews and is therefore called by them the "Zionist Occupation Government" (ZOG). They feel that whites are rapidly becoming a minority in relation to people of color in the United States. This Euro-American nativist movement is diffuse, but currently in America racist and anti-Semitic sentiments do not receive widespread social approval. This revolutionary millennial movement does not have a sufficient majority to make a concerted revolutionary effort, although federal agents are kept busy attempting to contain terrorists.

Kaplan reports that among Neo-Nazis, the attitudes toward violence range from the "just do it" approach to the warning expressed by George Eric Hawthorne not to commit foolish acts that result in incarceration: "Remember, this is a war and you are living behind enemy lines." The knowledge that they do not have a social majority prevents most Neo-Nazis from engaging in violence directed externally toward those whom they define as enemies. Indicative of the power of conflictual dualism, Neo-Nazis turn their hatred and violence against one another with remarkable ferocity.

In 1996 FBI agents consulted scholars of religion for advice about how to peacefully resolve a standoff with a group calling themselves Freemen residing on a Montana farm that they named Justus Township. The scholars consulted were Michael Barkun, Phillip Arnold, Jean Rosenfeld, and Catherine Wessinger. Jean Rosenfeld's chapter reflects the perspective of Arnold, Rosenfeld, and Wessinger, because we were in collaborative contact throughout the standoff.

As Identity Christians, the Freemen believe that the federal government is controlled by Jews (defined as the children of Satan), and that people of color are not human beings but are the "beasts of the field" mentioned in Genesis. White people are the true Israelites and Jews are satanic impostors. Only white people can be Christians, and Jesus was white/Aryan. They believe we are currently living in the violent tribulation period leading to the second coming of Christ. They believe that Christian Patriots are called by God to fight the "Second American Revolution" to establish true American republics obedient to Yahweh and his laws as given in the Old Testament. Before the standoff, the Freemen were waging paper warfare against the federal government by the magical use of their Common Law documents and bank drafts, but the Freemen also expressed a willingness to engage in a violent confrontation with law enforcement agents. The Freemen were willing to be martyred in a conflict that would prompt others on the radical right to fight the Second American Revolution.

The religion scholars advised FBI agents that they should avoid enhancing the Freemen's sense of being persecuted. This was achieved by keeping a low-key tactical presence, by permitting relatives and others to visit the Freemen, and by using intermediaries to induce the Freemen to negotiate face to face with FBI agents. The religion scholars also advised that the Freemen's religious worldview had to be factored into the negotiations and that the Freemen's ultimate concern—the destruction of the satanic federal government—had to be considered. The Freemen would exit Justus Township only under terms that permitted them to remain true to their religious goal.

Although some FBI agents deny that religion was a factor in peacefully resolving the Freemen standoff, Rosenfeld argues that the evidence indicates that the advice of the religion scholars was used. The Freemen were offered terms that assured them that they could carry on their fight against the government in the federal courtrooms. The pragmatics of failure prompted the Freemen to try to use a different method, that of arguing their case against the government in federal courts, after it became clear that the right-wing militias were not going to join with them in fighting the Second American Revolution.[24]

---

24. In fact, the Freemen were silenced in the federal courtrooms and were not permitted to articulate their understanding of the Common Law and the American Constitution. Four of the most highly committed Freemen (LeRoy Schweitzer, Daniel Petersen, Dale Jacobi, Russell Landers), who refused court-appointed lawyers and denied the jurisdiction of the federal courts, were convicted of conspiracy and bank fraud by a federal jury in July 1998 (Clair Johnson, *Billings Gazette Online*, July 9, 1998; James Brooke, *New York Times*, July 9, 1998). Others in this diffuse Euro-American nativist movement continue to use Freemen techniques of paper warfare against the government.

In her chapter on the Freemen, Rosenfeld concludes: "To assess whether or not catastrophic millennialists will resort to violence, one must determine from their writings, commentaries, and behavior what role they believe they are called to play at the end of time." Rosenfeld continues: "Because most millennial movements are not aggressive, we need to attain a level of knowledge about them that will enable us to identify with greater precision the few that promote violence and terror, keeping in mind that over time even the most threatening movements may become benign."

## Conclusions

This volume's final part, "Implications for Law Enforcement," contains an address given to the Los Angeles Police Department by Jean Rosenfeld in 1998. It is an introduction to the study of religion and millennialism, and it contains recommendations that highlight the ways in which religious standoffs (sieges) differ from hostage-taking incidents.

The British scholar Ian Reader has observed that Americans seem to specialize in sieges (personal communication). Obviously, the problem in the United States is that an overarmed public is in conflict with overarmed law enforcement agents. Both sides think in dualistic categories. Quite often retired police officers and military men become part of the contemporary Euro-American nativist movement; they simply reverse their dualism and redefine government agents as the bad guys.

Millennial movements of all types have implications for law enforcment. We have seen that there is great variety among millennial groups. There are those who peacefully await divine intervention; those who peacefully engage in social work to create the collective salvation; those who are armed for self-protection; those who are fragile and initiate violence; and those who commit revolutionary violence or wish to.

It is important that law enforcement agents be able to distinguish the differences. Given the complexities of millennial theologies and ideologies, it is best that law enforcement agents call on the expertise of scholars trained to study religious worldviews. Consulting academically trained scholars of religion will help law enforcement agents avoid unnecessarily assaulting a group, initiating a siege, or making a group feel persecuted.

It is very difficult to assess a millennial group's potential for violence from a distance, hence law enforcement agents should facilitate religious studies scholars' access to the group in question for interviews, dialogue, and observation. This approach was successfully used in 1998 when the Garland, Texas, police consulted Dr. Lonnie Kliever of Southern Methodist University about Chen Tao.

If necessary, scholars of religion can be used as intermediaries, that is, as translators of the religious worldview and its ultimate concern to law enforcement agents and vice versa.

If a religious group is suspected of crimes, ordinary law enforcement measures should be taken involving careful investigation and avoiding the excessive use of violence. I am not arguing that millennial groups should never be investigated. Aum Shinrikyō stands as a warning of the disastrous consequences that are possible when a millennial group's violence is left unchecked.

However, it is important that millennialists be viewed as human beings sincerely committed to their beliefs, even when their beliefs and practices are repugnant. Demonization and dehumanization of the believers (for instance, by labeling them "cultists") only increases the potential for conflict.

Millennialism addresses authentic human religious concerns and will always be with us. A sense of persecution strengthens conflictual millennial beliefs and impels some millennialists to take extreme actions. Law enforcement agents, members of the public, and the news media always should seek to interact with millennialists in a respectful manner and avoid making them feel persecuted. Potential and current believers should critically question the possible consequences of millennial beliefs, associations, and actions.

The chapters of *Millennialism, Persecution, and Violence* demonstrate that groups (including millennialists and law enforcement agents) that become bonded by their shared participation in rituals of violence travel a path that can lead to the escalation of violence to a massive scale.

# Part One

## Assaulted Millennial Groups

# 1

# Millennialism, Persecution, and Violence

## The Mormons

GRANT UNDERWOOD ⎯⎯⎯⎯⎯⎯⎯⎯⎯⎯⎯⎯⎯⎯⎯⎯⎯

Using the experience of the Church of Jesus Christ of Latter-day Saints (LDS) as a case study, this chapter seeks to advance five arguments regarding the relationship between persecution, millennialism, and violence. First, those who subscribe to an apocalyptic millenarian eschatology are not necessarily violence prone, psychologically maladjusted, or socioeconomically marginal. Second, apocalyptic millenarianism offers an ultimately satisfying worldview that makes particularly good sense to those who are persecuted. Third, oscillations in the intensity of apocalyptic millenarian rhetoric are directly related to the level of opposition the group receives. Fourth, an apocalyptic group's attitudes toward violence are also influenced by other traditions and philosophies. And fifth, when a group is allowed to live unmolested by the world around them, the likelihood of them interpreting their eschatological role in a violent manner is greatly reduced, even though they still maintain an apocalyptic cosmology.

## Millennialisms and Millennialists

*Millennialism*, it turns out, is far more than simply believing that the millennium, in the sense of a final, glorious conclusion to world history, is near. It is a comprehensive way of looking at the world and an integrated system of salvation. It is a type of *eschatology*—the term derived from Greek for "doctrine of the last things" or "end times" and used to refer broadly to people's ideas about the final events in individual human lives as well as the collective end of human history. Along the wide spectrum of thought created by a nearly universal fascination with the "end times" lies a kind of eschatological thinking denominated *apocalypticism*. Despite its popular usages in the late twentieth century, "apocalypse" (from the Greek root "to disclose" or "to reveal") is a technical term employed by scholars to refer to a type of Jewish and Christian literature that flourished between the years 200 B.C. and 150 A.D. Apocalypses disclose the future by predicting a coming cosmic transformation in which the suffering righteous will be vindicated and their evil opposers vanquished (Charles 1963; Collins 1979; Koch 1983; Hanson 1985).

Millennialism was a later, predominantly Christian, development growing out of Jewish apocalypticism. Its novelty was the expectation of a future "golden age" on earth *before* the final, apocalyptic transformation at the end of time. As various versions of the millennial dream developed over the centuries, some retained the vivid and dramatic spirit of their eschatological progenitor, lashing out against contemporary society and promising imminent vindication for the beleaguered faithful. Others drifted toward a more irenic view of the world around them and thought they saw in human progress evidence of either an imminent millennial kingdom or one that was already under way. By the nineteenth century there were two rival millennial visions of the future (Kromminga 1945; Ball 1975; Oliver 1978). What is often labeled *post-millennialism* but more revealingly may be called *progressive millennialism* constituted one approach. What most accurately should be called *apocalyptic millennialism* but more commonly is simply designated *millenarianism* or *pre-millennialism* (the two are often used interchangeably) represented the other.

"The millennial hope is a paradoxical one," explains James Moorhead, "and one can extrapolate a dismal or optimistic view of history, encompassing temporal disaster or progress, or both. . . . Efforts to seize the Kingdom by violence, passive withdrawal from corruption to await the Second Coming, or melioristic reform efforts—all these and other responses have been adduced from eschatological symbols" (Moorhead 1978, 8). Within the past generation, it has been shown that rather than a compensatory ideology for those on the fringe of social and economic progress, "millennialism is a natural, rational and sometimes normative force that can exert formative influence over all strata of society" (Sweet 1979, 513). That being the case, we "should be especially reluctant to conclude that prophetic and millennialist theorizing arose from tensions in the lives of individuals and in their society" (Oliver 1978, 14). Millennialists from all over the globe have held rather elaborate views about the future without necessarily being violence-prone misanthropes.

### But What about *Apocalyptic* Millenarians?

In Joseph Smith's earliest description of his first encounter with Deity in 1820, he recorded the words of the Lord thus:

> behold the world lieth in sin at this time and none doeth good no not one they have turned asside from the gospel and keep not my commandments they draw near to me with their lips while their hearts are far from me and mine anger is kindling against the inhabitants of the earth to visit them acording to th[e]ir ungodliness and to bring to pass that which hath been spoken by the mouth of the prophets and Apostles behold and lo I come quickly as it [is] written of me in the cloud clothed in the glory of my Father." (Jessee 1989, 6–7)

Such a stinging indictment of the present religious world along with the warning of an imminent visitation in judgment is standard fare among apocalyptic millenarians. As Ernest Sandeen has pointed out, they operate on "the assumption that an irreversible deterioration in religion and culture ha[s] now reached crisis proportions and that the final act in this era of world history ha[s] already begun" (Sandeen 1970, 22). From the LDS perspective, what inaugurated that act was foretold in John's Apocalypse (the New Testament book of Revelation): "And I saw another angel fly in the midst of heaven, having the everlasting gospel to preach unto them that dwell on the earth . . . saying with a loud voice, Fear God and give glory to him; for the hour of his judgment is come" (14:6–7). As Latter-day Saints understood it, this was not symbolic. The angel seen in vision actually visited Joseph Smith and delivered to him the Book of Mormon, which, by its presence, signaled that the end was nigh, and, by its contents, stood in judgment against the contemporary religious world (Underwood 1993).

Care must be taken that one does not resort to reductionism in seeking to understand apocalyptic millenarians. The tendency today, as Stephen Carter has shown so persuasively in *The Culture of Disbelief*

(1993), is to trivialize religious devotion, to see it as mere epiphenomenon for the things that really matter—money and political power. Yet, apocalyptic millenarians can certainly be understood as religious people who hold to a particular type of eschatology. They react strongly against the comfortable accommodation to the world evidenced by the dominant faiths. They call for a purification and a return to "old-time religion." They are fighting against attempts to make God present only in clerically mediated worship and in ordinary events of history. They want to free God to do the remarkable things he has done in the past. Their apocalypticism promises that he will do them again. It is the Kingdom of God rather than the corrupt kingdoms of this world that interests them. They are seeking the "riches of eternity" and the right to rule with Christ in the millennial kingdom, not for material profit or political power in "Babylon." At root, when apocalyptic millenarians wish to see the contemporary world replaced by the millennial world, it is because it has deprived them of spiritual, more than economic, opportunity. Only by adequately attending to the *religious* dimensions of apocalyptic millenarianism can these groups be fully understood.

Moreover, apocalyptic millenarians who see the world as corrupt and ready for transformation do not necessarily, or even commonly, see themselves as the agents of that change. Apocalypticism may be the dream of "the great reversal," but with that dream comes a certain realism. Power structures fully controlled by the adversary can hardly be expected to yield to the efforts of the godly. Therefore, apocalyptic millenarians tend to place little faith in human efforts. Only God can make the situation right, and such divine intervention is expected to come dramatically, even cataclysmically, as superhuman forces square off in the final showdown of good and evil. Such a faith engenders hope.

Confronted with the stark inadequacy of their efforts to thwart the onslaughts of persecution in Missouri in the 1830s, Mormons felt and expressed a heightened dependence upon God, realizing that nothing short of his supernatural intervention could defeat Satan's minions and usher in the long-desired millennial day of rest. Shortly after Missouri governor Lilburn Boggs issued his infamous Extermination Order in 1838 directing that the Saints "must be treated as enemies, and must be exterminated or driven from the State" (C. Johnson 1992, 34), Mormon apostle Parley Pratt composed a hymn that reflected typical apocalyptic yearnings:

How long, O Lord, wilt thou forsake
The Saints who tremble at Thy word?
Awake, O Arm, O God! Awake
And teach the nations Thou art God.
Descend with all Thy holy throng,
The year of Thy redeemed bring near,
Haste, haste the day of vengeance on,
Bid Zion's children dry their tear.

(Russell 1913, 19)


As the Saints fled Missouri, Joseph Smith and other leaders were taken captive and languished in jail for nearly six months in a Missouri town ironically named Liberty. From this crucible of adversity, Joseph Smith himself pled that the Lord would avenge the Saints of their wrongs, expressing at the same time abiding faith that "the time shall soon come when the Son of Man shall descend in the clouds of heaven" and shall "have our oppressors in derision" and "will laugh at their calamity, and mock [them] when their fear cometh" (Smith 1976, 3:291–92).

Nor were such sentiments restricted to the leadership. Apocalyptic millennialism offered a comprehensible way for ordinary Mormons to make sense of, and respond to, what was happening to them. This is well illustrated in a series of letters written to his family in the east by Albert P. Rockwood, who lived through the final months in Missouri. "Be not shaken at what I wrote in my last" letter, encouraged Rockwood, "but do even as we. Lift up your heads & rejoice knowing these things will precede the coming of our Saviour." In the context of a correct millennial eschatology, comfort could even be found in a world turned upside down. "The scenes which we have passed thro of late is a bright evidence that the work in which we have enlisted is of the Lord, for these things must all be before the comeing of Christ, Pestilence, Sword, Blood, Famine, & Fire" (Jessee and Whittaker 1988, 28–29, 30). As one scholar explains, the judgments to be poured out "were part of an immutable guarantee that no matter how much the wicked seemed to triumph in the present age, God would supernaturally set the scales of Justice aright at the Day of Judgment" (Davidson 1977, 83). Ultimately, God would issue his own extermination order against the Saints' oppressors: "The testimony of Judgements," wrote Rockwood, "have now commenced & like a whirlpool will sweep our inhabitants off the U. States." To bolster his point he cited the remarks of Joseph Smith's father: "The Patriarch observed last fast day that the time would soon come when a man should be considered of more value than a talent of gold [Isa. 13:12] for God would assuredly make the earth empty & waste by Judgements & but very few would be left [Isa. 24:6]" (Jessee and Whittaker 1988, 31).

If wicked oppressors and turncoat traitors would soon suffer God's vengeance, the Saints who remained faithful through it all would be refined in the process. "Do not let the Scourges of Zion weaken your faith," Rockwood admonished his family. "These things will all work out for the purifying of the church from dross & the ultimate Glory of God." The bottom line was that "if we hope to reign with Christ on earth with Abraham, Isac, & Jacob, Jeremiah, Daniel & others, who have come up out of much tribulation we must also be willing to come up thro tribulation that our garments may be washed in the blood of the Lamb [Rev. 7:14]" (Jessee and Whittaker 1988, 31).

What is obvious in this example and in numerous other episodes throughout nineteenth-century Mormon history is the almost symbiotic relationship between persecution and millennialism. The Saints often experienced severe persecution and crisis conditions. Although it is arguable that apocalyptic attitudes might have been partly responsible for provoking persecution, it is also clear that persecution reinforced their millenarianism by verifying the dualistic analysis of society central to apocalypticism. The Saints knew that as the Second Coming drew nigh, Satan would be waging a war of ever increasing intensity against them. Therefore, persecution became an assurance, albeit a painful one, that all was proceeding on prophetic schedule (Moorhead 1979, 421). Though physically destructive, such opposition, precisely because it fit into an eschatological drama with a predetermined victory for the Saints, was less than successful in daunting them. Their apocalyptic ideals provided strength in a world turned upside down, and allowed them to rationalize otherwise irrational behavior.

## As Persecution Increases, Millennialism Intensifies

Oscillations in the intensity of Mormon millenarianism corresponded closely to the treatment they received from their neighbors. The correlation between the experience of persecution and the expression of apocalyptic millennialism is pronounced. To plot the rise and fall of one is to identify the ebb and flow of the other. As Michael Barkun has written, "men cleave to hopes of imminent worldly salvation when the hammerblows of disaster destroy the world they have known" (Barkun 1974, 1).

After their expulsion from Missouri, the Saints sought refuge in Illinois and began to build their holy city again in Nauvoo. Within a half a dozen years, Joseph Smith had been murdered (on June 27, 1844), the Saints and their property were again at risk, and the prospect of another Mormon war was imminent (Godfrey 1965). This launched what is arguably the most famous exodus in American history. Future church president John Taylor spoke for many when he declared,

> We owe the United States nothing. We go out by force, as exiles from freedom. The government and people owe us millions for the destruction of life and property in Missouri and in Illinois. The blood of our best men stains the land, and the ashes of our property will preserve it till God comes out of his hiding place, and gives this nation a hotter place than he did Sodom and Gomorrah. "When they cease to spoil, they shall be spoiled," for the Lord hath spoken it [Isa. 33:1]. (*Times and Seasons* 1845, 1052)

The connection between injustices suffered and apocalyptic yearnings is pointed. Earlier a *Times and Seasons* editorial had endeavored to comfort the Saints with this thought: "He that said to the flood 'come' and make an end of wickedness, will say also 'go' to the elements, and sweep the earth with the besom of destruction till it is fit for Paradise again, and then my people shall inherit the kingdom" (1845, 952).

Utah offered less of an isolated oasis for these embattled millenarians than originally hoped. In the aftermath of the war with Mexico, the Great Basin became American territory and the United States government was determined to make the Mormons conform to certain national norms of behavior. In 1857 President James Buchanan dispatched A. Sidney Johnston at the head of twenty-five hundred army regulars to replace Brigham Young as territorial governor and quash the putative "Mormon rebellion" (Furniss 1960; Moorman and Sessions 1992). Buchanan sent no official communication of his action to Young so when the Saints first heard word, ironically during the annual celebration commemorating their safe arrival in the Salt Lake valley, they expected the worst. It seemed that armageddon was upon them, and they hunkered down. Brigham Young issued a call for all outlying Mormon colonies to be abandoned, for Mormon missionaries worldwide to return home, and for Utah territory to be placed under martial law. Fears were met by an intensification of apocalyptic rhetoric: "The greater its numbers [of the army], the greater and more complete its overthrow," responded apostle

Orson Hyde. "If the Red Sea be not the trap in which the enemy will be caught, there will be a snow of hail storm, a whirlwind, an earthquake, fire from above or from beneath, or the sword of the Lord and of Brigham" (Peterson 1989, 78).

Tragically, a portion of the Mormon militia in southern Utah was unable to distinguish the real "enemy" and, in response to minor provocation, slaughtered more than a hundred civilian emigrants en route to California. Fortunately, this isolated act of infamy, known as the Mountain Meadows Massacre, stands in sharp contrast with the predominant Mormon aversion to bloodletting. Brigham's stated order to the Mormon militia, and that only with regard to the "invading" army, was to "take no life, but destroy their trains, and stampede or drive away their animals, at every opportunity" (Arrington 1985, 255). To avoid full-scale war, Young even evacuated more than thirty thousand Saints from the Salt Lake valley for a season. As it turned out, near-starvation caused by Mormon guerrilla raids on the supply lines brought the U.S. Army to their knees and their commander to the conference table, not the clash of arms.

When the Civil War broke out a few years later, the Saints interpreted it as God's judgment upon a wicked and persecuting nation (Long 1981). For them, it fulfilled the word of the Lord: "I have sworn in my wrath, and decreed wars upon the face of the earth, and the wicked shall slay the wicked, and fear shall come upon every man" (D&C 63:33).[1] Again, it is noteworthy that the Saints did not see *themselves* as the agents of the apocalypse. In this case, their "wicked" persecutors would eventually turn on one another. The Saints would continue to practice what they called "the Mormon Creed"—"Mind your own business" (*Times and Seasons* 1844, 680).

The next surge in Mormon millennialism corresponded to the post-Civil War escalation of federal legal persecution in an attempt to eradicate polygamy (Firmage and Mangrum 1988). Just weeks after the United States Supreme Court ruled against the Saints in *Reynolds v. United States* (1879), Orson Pratt remarked that the Civil War "was nothing

1. Many of the revelations received during the early years of Mormonism have been compiled and canonized by the church as *The Doctrine and Covenants of the Church of Jesus Christ of Latter-day Saints*, or, more simply, *The Doctrine and Covenants*. Throughout the remainder of this chapter, the standard LDS convention of referring to this volume as D&C will be followed. First issued in 1835, the D&C has gone through numerous editions since. Unless the wording of the text has been modified significantly from the original, and so identified in these notes, any edition may be consulted with confidence.

compared to that which will eventually devastate [America]. The time is not very far distant in the future when the Lord God will lay his hand heavily upon that nation" (*Journal of Discourses* 1879, 20:151). The following year a revelation declared that the blood of martyred Mormons "cries from the ground for vengeance upon the nation which has shed their blood" and shall "speedily be avenged" for "the hour of God's judgment is fully come and shall be poured out without measure upon the wicked" (Kenney 1985, 7:619). With the passage of the Edmunds Act in 1882 and especially the Edmunds-Tucker Act in 1887, which legally dissolved the Corporation of the Church, apocalyptic millennialism deepened. Just before going on the underground to avoid prosecution for plural marriage, church president John Taylor declared, "You will see trouble, trouble, trouble enough in these United States. . . . I tell you in the name of God, Woe! to them that fight against Zion, for God will fight against them" (*Journal of Discourses* 1885, 26:156).

All of this began to gradually change in the 1890s after the cessation of plural marriage was announced and other concessions were made to achieve statehood for Utah in 1896 (Alexander 1986). What stands out in bold relief is that as public persecution thereafter declined, so did apocalyptic rhetoric among the Latter-day Saints (Shepherd and Shepherd 1984, 196). Looking back over the century that followed Joseph Smith's "First Vision" in 1820, it is clear that for the Mormons persecution and apocalyptic millennialism were essentially opposite sides of the same coin.

## Mormon Millennialism and Other Isms

Certainly in the world of the nineteenth-century dime novel (Miller 1881; Switzer 1882; Doyle 1888/1900), but even occasionally in more recent scholarly studies of Mormonism (Hansen 1967; Heinerman and Shupe 1985; Hill 1989; Brooke 1994), the Saints are portrayed as violent subversives. The myth of the mayhem-producing Danites—allegedly a secret vigilante force that committed murders under the direction of Mormon megalomaniac Brigham Young—and the specter of the Nauvoo Legion serving as shock troops in the Mormon quest to overthrow the United States government appear again and again as part of the popular construction of evil. Though more sober studies tend to dismiss these caricatures, what is often missed is the way in which other philosophies combined with the Saints' apocalyptic millennialism to condition their beliefs and behaviors.

First among these influences was a type of Christian pacifism. A famous verse of Mormon scripture exclaims "renounce war and proclaim peace" (D&C 98:16). Although the image of cheek-turning Christians who abstain from the use of force under any conditions is a popular pacifist stereotype, the majority position within Christianity historically has been to decry any war of aggression but to condone genuinely defensive wars conducted along "Christian principles." Mostly, members of the Church of Jesus Christ of Latter-day Saints have articulated their views and acted out their beliefs from within this mainstream Christian response. The revealed injunction cited above is embedded in a revelation explaining the conditions under which defensive war is permissible.

Joseph Smith's call for personal or private pacifism was clear:

> wise men ought to have understanding enough to conquer men with kindness . . . and it will be greatly to the credit of the Latter-day Saints to show the love of God, by now kindly treating those who may have, in an unconscious moment, done wrong; for truly said Jesus, Pray for thine enemies. Humanity towards all, reason and refinement to enforce virtue, and good for evil are so eminently designed to cure more disorders of society than an appeal to arms, or even argument untempered with friendship. (Smith 1976, 6:219–20)

The Prophet tried to practice what he preached. After one of many episodes of legal harassment, he told his friends,

> I have had the privilege of rewarding them good for evil. They took me unlawfully, treated me rigorously, strove to deprive me of my rights, and would have run with me into Missouri to have been murdered, if Providence had not interposed. But now they are in my hands; and I have taken them into my house, set them at the head of my table, and placed before them the best which my house afforded. (Smith 1976, 5:467)

To the degree that pacifism committed the Saints to loving their personal enemies, returning good for evil, praying for antagonists, turning the other cheek, and seeking peaceful solutions to interpersonal problems, LDS preaching was consistently pacifist. Smith, however, drew the pacifist line where life, liberty, or limb was at stake. The same Joseph Smith who taught long-suffering and love is also credited with declaring, after the Saints had suffered repeated depredations at the hands of mobs,

I call God and angels to witness that I have unsheathed my sword with a firm and unalterable determination that this people shall have their legal rights, and be protected from mob violence, or my blood shall be spilt upon the ground like water, and my body consigned to the silent tomb. While I live, I will never tamely submit to the dominion of cursed mobocracy. I would welcome death rather than submit to this oppression . . . any longer. (Smith 1976, 6:499).

In the words of a Mormon apostle later in the century, "We delight not in the shedding of blood, . . . we are for peace," but "we intend to have it, if we have to fight for it" (*Journal of Discourses* 1863, 10:153).

Years of persecution, including being forced by antagonists to abandon their homes on several prior occasions, finally brought this to a head in Missouri in 1838. The Saints' feelings were forcefully expressed by First Presidency member Sidney Rigdon in a Fourth of July oration that became known as the "Mormon Declaration of Independence." In rhetoric laced with biblical imagery, Rigdon declared,

Our cheeks have been given to the smiters—our heads to those who have plucked off the hair. We have not only, when smitten on one cheek, turned the other, but we have done it again and again, until we are wearied of being smitten, and tired of being trampled upon. We have proved the world with kindness, we have suffered their abuse, without cause, with patience and have endured without resentment until this day, and still their persecutions and violence do not cease. But from this day and this hour we will suffer it no more. We take God, and all the holy Angels to witness this day, that we warn all men, in the name of Jesus Christ, to come on us no more forever, for from this hour we will bear it no more, our rights shall no more be trampled upon with impunity, the man, or the set of men, who attempt it, do it at the expense of their lives. (*Rigdon* 1838, 54)

These lines are reminiscent of the revolutionary-era maxim "Don't tread on me." It should not be forgotten that Mormons were also Americans who were thoroughly steeped in the Lockean liberalism and classical republicanism that gave birth to the nation a mere sixty years earlier (Winn 1989). Their own revelations sanctified a respect for law and they were repeatedly enjoined to work within the country's legal system whenever possible. The hundreds of petitions for redress of grievances that the Saints submitted in the years after their wintertime banishment from Missouri offer ample testimonial to their respect for due process. The ideals expressed in their foundational document "Of Governments and Laws in General" could have been composed by any antebellum American:

> We believe that men should appeal to the civil law for redress of all wrongs and grievances, where personal abuse is inflicted or the right of property or character infringed, where such laws exist as will protect the same; but we believe that all men are justified in defending themselves, their friends, and property, and the government, from the unlawful assaults and encroachments of all persons in times of exigency, where immediate appeal cannot be made to the laws, and relief afforded. (D&C 134:11)

Arms were to be a last resort, and then only for preserving peace. Far from ever declaring a jihad, the Mormon *Millennial Star* editorialized:

> We wish it distinctly understood that the interpretation given . . . as to the Latter-day Saints drawing the sword against others who may differ from them in religious belief is without shadow of truth, being contrary to the whole spirit of the Christian religion, which they (the Saints) profess. . . . The Latter-day Saints never did draw the sword except in defence of their lives and of the institutions and laws of their country, and they never will. (1841, 2:43)

Apocalyptic millennialism assured the Saints that if due process did not produce justice, divine process soon would. "Let them importune at the feet of the judge," directed a revelation,

> and if he heed them not, let them importune at the feet of the governor; and if the governor heed them not, let them importune at the feet of the president; and if the president heed them not, then will the Lord arise and come forth out of his hiding place, and in his fury vex the nation; and in his hot displeasure, and in his fierce anger, in his time, will cut off those wicked, unfaithful, and unjust stewards, and appoint them their portion among hypocrites, and unbelievers; even in outer darkness, where there is weeping, and wailing, and gnashing of teeth. (D&C 101:86–91)

Later, after the requested petitions for redress fell on deaf ears, first in Missouri and ultimately in the White House (C. Johnson 1992), apocalyptic millennialism suggested to the Prophet, Joseph Smith, that a cataclysmic conclusion to history was inevitable. In an 1844 letter, Joseph Smith warned United States Sen. John C. Calhoun that

> if the Latter Day Saints are not restored to all their rights, and paid for all their losses, according to the known rules of justice and judgment, reciprocation and common honesty among men, that God will come out of his hiding place and vex this nation with a sore vexation—yea, the consuming wrath of an offended God shall smoke through the nation with as much distress and woe, as independence has blazed through with pleasure and delight." (*Times and Seasons* 1844, 5:395)

Persecution is indeed the incubator for apocalypticism.

Does this not prove that the Saints were fundamentally antagonistic to the United States government? Did they not wish to see a theocracy established? To be sure, early Mormon literature is replete with ringing affirmations of the reality of Christ's and the Saints' reign on earth, but they are almost always set in a millennial context. With many other Christians, the Mormons did expect the eventual fulfillment of scriptural promises that God would make a "full end of all nations" (Jer. 30:11) and that "the kingdoms of this world" would become the kingdom of "our Lord and of his Christ" (Rev. 11:15). The crucial question was *how* and *when*.

At times, LDS writers were not explicit, and this, combined with their definite anticipation of imminent fulfillment, has led some observers to think that Mormons expected to do more before Christ returned than merely be prepared to reign. Still, their fundamental eschatology was clear. The Saints would not be presenting the returning Lord with a kingdom to rule. Rather, it was the other way around, though they certainly felt they should do all they could to prepare themselves for that rule. Thus, it is just as likely that the legendary Mormon Council of Fifty, a nineteenth-century governing body set up in anticipation of managing the millennial kingdom and often considered the epitome of Mormon subversiveness, was a "symbolic formality" more than an actual revolutionary agency prepared to seize secular power (Quinn 1980; Ehat 1980).

Council of Fifty and First Presidency member Daniel Wells admitted that "it is the privilege of the Saints to take the kingdom and possess it as an everlasting inheritance," but "how is this to be done?" he asked.

> Is it to be by going forth in martial array, and taking it by force of arms? No. . . . It is to be brought about by observing the principles

of salvation which have been revealed from the heavens for the exaltation of the people; it is to be by uniting together that we may become a mighty phalanx against which the surges of iniquity may strike in vain. (*Journal of Discourses* 1861, 8:375)

Far from the Mormon Council of Fifty moving in to take over the world's citizenry, Christ himself would personally establish "a seat of government among them" that would "put an end to jarring creeds and political wranglings, by uniting the republics, states, provinces, territories, nations, tribes, kindreds, tongues, people, and sects of North and South America in one great and common bond of brotherhood." In the end, "truth and knowledge shall make them free, and love cement their union." Christ, not the Mormon prophet, would "be their king and their lawgiver; while wars shall cease and peace prevail for a thousand years" (*Proclamation* 1845, 9–10). This proclamation from the LDS apostles hardly sounds like a Mormon jihad or coup d'état. On the contrary, it predicts conversion, not coercion, to Christ's millennial standard. As Joseph Smith remarked, "I will not seek to compel any man to believe as I do, only by the force of reasoning, for truth will cut its own way" (Smith 1976, 5:499).

But what about Smith's candidacy for president of the United States in 1844? Was that not clear evidence of theocratic intent? Did it not raise the specter of an un-American marriage of church and state? "We . . . shrink from the idea of introducing any thing that would in the least deprive us of our freedom, or reduce us to a state of religious vassalage," replied the *Times and Seasons*.

> No one can be more opposed to an unhallowed alliance of this kind than ourselves, but while we would deprecate any alliance having a tendency to deprive the sons of liberty of their rights, we cannot but think that the course taken by many of our politicians is altogether culpable, that the division is extending too far, and that in our jealousy lest a union of this kind should take place, we have thrust out God from all of our political movements. . . . Certainly if any person ought to interfere in political matters it should be those whose minds and judgments are influenced by correct principles— religious as well as political. (1844, 5:470–71)

The issue for the Saints before Christ returned to set up the millennial monarchy was not the legitimacy of the government so much as the suitability of the governors. Mormons cherished the Constitution and saw it as part of that perfect primordium untainted by profane history. The same, however, could not be said of subsequent laws and leaders. Mormons consistently differentiated between the inspired Constitution and, in Brigham Young's words, "the damned rascals who administer the government" (Melville 1960, 47). This distinction is not unlike that held by most Americans dissatisfied with the current administration or party in power. They will fulminate, calumniate, and vituperate the opposition, but they rarely challenge the undergirding political principles upon which the country is built and even more rarely do they consider taking up arms to effect a change. Millenarian Mormons felt that soon enough a millennial kingdom would prevail. Meanwhile, they would follow the "Mormon Creed" and patiently do their part to prepare the way for the Lord's return and their millennial reign with him. From this perspective, they were more interested in the millennial bursting open of graves (the resurrection of the dead) than in the contemporary breaking down of institutions.

Part of the problem in fairly assessing the Mormon experience is that too few studies offer an adequate source criticism. Authors do little to help readers identify source biases or weigh their relative merits, and they tend to overlook what could be learned from social scientific studies of contemporary new religious movements (NRMs). Although they are sensitive to the liabilities of taking Mormon propaganda at face value, they seem less concerned about accepting statements from disaffected Mormons and acknowledged antagonists. Yet, students of NRMs have made important contributions to how apostates and the exposé literature they produce affects the social construction of evil. Common distortions include portraying church leaders as power-hungry despots who live above the law and are prone to violence and regarding churches as mere cover for economic and political pursuits. Sociologists Anson Shupe and David Bromley have identified a genre they call "atrocity stories," which are "constructed so as to portray . . . new religions themselves as vehicles for the personal, political, and economic aggrandizement of a few leaders at the expense of the well-being of members, their families, and the public at large" (1981, 198; see also Bromley 1998b).

An important new study by Terryl Givens explores representational patterns in nineteenth-century anti-Mormonism. It affirms "a proclivity to depict the Mormons as a violent and peculiar people" and seeks to analyze this construction. Givens argues that "the pressures of pluralism made it desirable to cast the objectionability of Mormonism in nonreligious terms." This is not to say "that the underlying hostilities were or were not really more religious than economic or political. It *is* to say that such hostilities, to be culturally sanctioned, had to take the form of political rather than denominational interests" (1997, 5–6, 7, 22). The rootedness of religious tolerance in America's ideological mythology made it virtually impossible to extirpate a *religion* from the body politic. Thus, the Mormon Other had to be constructed in such a way that its persecution was a manifestation of patriotism rather than bigotry. In this way specious claims about Mormonism being a social and political threat were reified. Anti-Mormonism illustrates "the necessary contortions that religion must be subjected to, the rhetorical strategies that must be deliberately and ingeniously applied, in order to maintain intact the underlying value system of pluralism and religious toleration while the aberrant group is proscribed." What this calls for is that scholars be just as cautious in using non-Mormon sources as they are in how they employ LDS sources. They should be aware of "the mechanisms by which ideology and acts of self-fashioning [by non-Mormons as well as Mormons] work to conceal inherent tensions and inconsistencies that arise when espoused values and political imperatives collide" (21–22, 45).

Unfortunately, this lack of source-critical sophistication often shows through in studies on Mormonism where authors, who may be wary of LDS sources, accept a little too readily the self-exculpating constructions of the Saints' antagonists. Too often the tropes of the old anti-Mormon literature appear in contemporary studies in only slightly revised form. Returning only to the Missouri conflict for a moment, many studies quote extensively from Missourian and apostate Mormon comments at the Court of Inquiry held in Richmond, Missouri, several weeks after the Saints surrendered in Far West, Missouri, to illustrate the totalitarian excesses and aggressive militarism of the Saints. Yet, they omit the reaction of faithful Mormons, such as Parley Pratt, who wrote to his family just after the hearings that "the apostates have sworn to murder and treason and almost everything against us which never entered our hearts to say or do" (Jessee and Whittaker 1988, 32).

As already pointed out, apocalyptic millennialism is *ultimately* subversive. In a sense, though, so is all religion. As Stephen Carter contends, "A religion is, at its heart, . . . a way of saying to fellow human beings and to the state those fellow humans have erected, 'No, I will *not* accede to your will.'" Religion provides an independent moral voice that prevents "the reduction of democracy to simple and tyrannical majoritarianism" (1993, 37, 41). Thus, it is true that the Mormons in the 1800s were subversive when they refused to be dictated to in their domestic arrangements, just as in the Civil Rights era of the 1960s the Southern Christian Leadership Conference was labeled subversive. Yet, both groups strove to be peaceful and nonviolent in acting out their ideals.

In the case of the Mormons, their millennialism compounded the propensity toward misperception. Explained future president Wilford Woodruff, "It startles men when they hear the Elders of Israel tell about the kingdoms of this world becoming the kingdom of our God and His Christ. They say it is treason for men to teach that the kingdom Daniel saw is going to be set up, and bear rule over the whole earth." As always, the key was *how* and *when*. "Is it treason for God Almighty to govern the earth? Who made it? . . . whose right is it to rule and reign over you and the earth? . . . It belongs solely to God and He is coming to rule and reign over it. When will that be? It may not be perfected until Christ comes in the clouds of heaven with power and great glory" (*Journal of Discourses* 1869, 13:164)

### Apocalypticism and Accommodation

In an 1889 "Official Declaration," the First Presidency and Quorum of Twelve Apostles "solemnly declare[d]" that

> this Church does not claim to be an independent, temporal kingdom of God, or to be an *imperium in imperio* aiming to overthrow the United States or any other civil government. It has been organized by divine revelation preparatory to the second advent of the Redeemer. It proclaims that "the kingdom of heaven is at hand." Its members are commanded of God to be subject unto the powers that be until Christ comes, whose right it is to reign.

Moreover, they added, "Notwithstanding the wrongs we consider we have suffered through the improper execution of national laws, we regard those wrongs as the acts of men and not of the Government; and we intend, by the help of Omnipotence, to remain firm in our fealty and steadfast in the maintenance of constitutional principles and the integrity of this Republic" (Clark 1966, 3:186).

That this document, both intentionally and inherently, had a propagandistic quality is acknowledged. Its significance lay in providing the groundwork for Mormonism's twentieth-century accommodation with the United States. As one historian has noted, "It is not too much to say that although the manifesto on plural marriage of September 1890 has received more attention, it was not as important as [this document] in laying the basis for the restructuring of Mormonism and its relationship with American society" (Alexander 1991, 259). Today, Mormons are widely regarded as quintessentially, even hyper, American. In a sense this validates the Mormon claim all along to have been fundamentally peaceful, law-abiding citizens, for once the persecution slowed, these aspects of their religious sensibilities became plainly manifest. Equally apparent is the corresponding decline in certain aspects of their apocalyptic rhetoric, which "diminished drastically after 1920" (Shepherd and Shepherd 1984, 196), about the same time that public persecution subsided.

This, however, should not be taken to mean that formal LDS eschatology has changed. Rather, it is that "even though an apocalyptic scenario [for] the last days is still a central Mormon doctrine, it is no longer enunciated by modern conference speakers with anything like the emphatic fervor of nineteenth-century leaders" (Shepherd and Shepherd 1984, 196). Though Latter-day Saints still talk about the end times, for many Mormons these doctrines have a detached and textbookish quality. The social ramifications of their eschatology are rarely if ever discussed today, and soteriological dualism is disparaged. The term "wicked," for instance, no longer refers to all unbelievers. Today, it is applied only to the morally corrupt, and the good and honorable of all religions are expected to be alive during the millennial kingdom. As people make their peace with the world, the dream of the "great reversal" diminishes. In short, the more abrasive features of millenarianism that served LDS needs in an earlier period have been quietly, perhaps unwittingly, laid aside in recent years.

On the other hand, inasmuch as apocalyptic millennialism sets forth certain distinctive expectations about the manner in which the millennial kingdom will be established as well as its nature and the way Christ will exercise control over it, little has changed for the Latter-day Saints. During the 1980s, LDS apostle and theologian Bruce R. McConkie published the longest work ever written by a Latter-day Saint on eschatological matters. What is striking is how little McConkie's millennial treatise differs from those written during Mormonism's first generation. The same supernatural biological and geological changes anticipated then for the millennium are expected today, including the abolishment of infant mortality, the herbivorization of carnivores, the unification of continental landmasses, and the comingling of mortals and resurrected immortals (McConkie 1982). That such views seemed plausible in the early nineteenth century is perhaps not surprising. That they are still maintained today provides dramatic testimony of the degree to which

LDS millenarianism in particular and Mormonism in general have resisted the encroachments of modernity. Then again, as Paul Boyer has shown, a sizeable number of Americans today, such as those who endorse the *Late Great Planet Earth* (Lindsey 1970), hold similar views under the rubric of "dispensationalism," a popular contemporary form of apocalyptic millennialism (Boyer 1992).

## Conclusion

What, then, does the Mormon case study show? First, the single greatest factor in propelling a movement to emphasize an apocalyptic rhetoric of judgment and vengeance seems to be the persecution they feel from those around them. Second, the rhetoric will at all points be in dialogue with and conditioned by other traditions and philosophies cherished by the group. Thus, a group like the Mormons may experience savage persecution without becoming inveterately violent because their version of apocalyptic millennialism is restrained by other equally powerful ideals. Third, a crucial factor in what might make a millennialist group violence-prone is the degree to which its eschatology emphasizes human agency in bringing about the millennium. What is often misunderstood by those who do not take eschatology seriously is that apocalyptic millenarians, despite their sometimes frightening and vindictive rhetoric, are historically *less* likely to see themselves as midwives to the millennial kingdom. On the contrary, they tend to be beleaguered minorities whose only hope for salvation is felt to be in the hands of the Almighty. Their predicament may cause them to verbally lash out against their persecutors in threatening, even hateful ways, and they may very well resist if attacked, but *if left alone* they are almost always nonviolent. In short, for a nation that avoids persecution of its religious minorities, even its rabidly apocalyptic ones, there is no need for "eschatophobia" and certainly no need to replay "Buchanan's blunder" or "Waco's wackiness" with each new group of apocalyptic millenarians who arise on the scene.

# 2

# From Vision to Violence

## The Wounded Knee Massacre

MICHELENE E. PESANTUBBEE

Early in the evening of December 29, 1890, William Fitch Kelley, general correspondent for the *Nebraska State Journal* (Lincoln), hurriedly handed his first account of the Wounded Knee massacre to a courier, who rode furiously through the night to the telegraph office at Rushville (Utley 1963, 229; Kelly 1971, 182). The next morning his story appeared in newspapers around the country. The public response was immediate and mixed. Some people lambasted government officials and soldiers for the senseless and brutal killing of unarmed men, women, and children; others praised the troops for their bravery in battle that had put an end to the Lakota[1] threat. Today, opinions regarding the massacre remain just as mixed. Reporters, scholars, and government agencies have studied civilian, military, missionary, and Lakota reports, and when their accounts are put together, they present a reasonably clear picture of the events that led up to the tragedy at Wounded Knee, but the causes for the massacre remain debatable.

For some who perceived the massacre at Wounded Knee as the culminating event of an uprising or outbreak by Lakota ghost dancers,

---

1. The Yanktonai and the Teton are two of seven major groups that are collectively known as the Sioux. The Teton are further divided into seven bands: Brule, Sans Arc, Blackfoot Sioux, Minneconjou, Two Kettles, Oglala, and Hunkpapa. Lakota is the Teton designation for themselves and is the term I use throughout the chapter to broadly refer to the Yanktonai and Teton people.

the causes for the Lakota response were many and justified. Although one would have to look at the entire history of Lakota/white relations to fully appreciate the dynamics leading to Wounded Knee, a brief look at conditions in 1890 as described by commissioner Thomas J. Morgan in his report of 1891 is telling. According to Morgan, the Lakota were experiencing great changes in their mode of life including loss of buffalo, confinement to land unfit for agriculture, crop failures, epidemics, cessions of land, and removal. In addition, the United States government had reduced appropriations and rations during a time of great need and had failed to honor certain treaty promises. Morgan also believed that the sudden appearance of the military at reservation agencies and the spreading of rumors about the dangers presented by ghost dancers inevitably led to a Lakota outbreak (Mooney 1896/1973, 329–31). For others who believed the military and the federal government were at fault, the disaster was attributed to a lack of leadership, a system of patronage, the inexperience of agents and cavalry, the failure to follow orders, and struggles over authority.

All of these were no doubt contributing factors, but I want to examine specifically the role of religious persecution, colonialism, and cultural ignorance in conjunction with struggles over jurisdictional authority and lack of mediation in creating a condition conducive to violence. All of these factors influenced decisions to suppress the Ghost Dance, and they supported a setting in which rumor and misinformation prevailed. The absence of effective coordination between agents, government and military officials, soldiers, and white civilians, and the absence of mediation between government agents and Lakota allowed misconceptions to inform attitudes toward the ghost dancers that eventuated in the massacre at Wounded Knee.

The chain of events leading up to the massacre began in November 1889 when two medicine men, Short Bull, a Rosebud Reservation Brule, and Kicking Bear, a Minniconjou from Cheyenne River Reservation, along with delegates from Pine Ridge and Rosebud, went to visit Wovoka, the Paiute prophet who had a vision about the dance. They returned in March 1890 and began teaching Lakota about Wovoka's vision. As told by Lakota dance leaders, in the spring of 1891 a great disaster would occur annihilating all whites. At the same time, the spirits of deceased Lakota relatives would return to populate the earth driving in front of them herds of buffalo and horses. The world as the Lakota once knew it would be restored. However, the Lakota had to dance to bring about these changes.[2] By dancing they also could ward off disease and heal the sick (Mooney 1896/1973, 786–89).

The Ghost Dance movement, or more accurately spirit dance, attracted a sizeable following among the Lakota. Even those who did not immediately embrace the new dance ritual attended or kept informed of the dances. That the Lakota were drawn to the dance is consistent with their religio-cultural history. Visions have always informed and shaped Lakota actions and culture. Visions, which could be spontaneous or induced, brought them knowledge, aid, and protection. In the light of their reservation status, Wovoka's vision had great appeal to them. His vision prophesied a time of apocalypse—a future time when the earth would be rocked by cataclysmic events that would annihilate the white race. After the great apocalypse, the Lakota world would be restored to its earlier state that supported their hunting and warrior culture.[3]

The colonialist attitude toward non-Christian cultures is evidenced by the response of whites on and around the Lakota reservations toward the ghost dancers. As pointed out by Raymond DeMallie in his cross-cultural study of the meanings attached to the Ghost Dance, "the dance itself, the actual ritual, became the focus of misunderstanding between Indian and whites. . . . For the Lakotas the dance was a symbol of religion, a ritual means to spiritual and physical betterment" (1982, 392).

Whites, however, did not perceive the Ghost Dance as a valid religious ceremony. Instead, they called it "the Delusion" and the "Messiah Craze." Agent James McLaughlin of the Standing Rock Agency referred to the dance as the "present craze" and the "excitement." Of the ghost dancers, he reported that "it would seem impossible that any person, no matter how ignorant, could be brought to such absurd nonsense" (Commissioner of Indian Affairs 1891, 123, 125).

2. Ceremonial dancing for the Lakota is performative prayer that evokes "a network of images related to sense experiences, moods, emotions, and values" (Gill 1987, 97), and may culminate in a vision experience as often happened to participants in the Ghost Dance. Dancing is also sacrificial prayer as one gives of oneself through exertion and oftentimes fasting. By dancing the Lakota are not only communicating with the supernatural beings but they are also reinforcing belief and strengthening community.

3. News of Wovoka's prophecy of the destruction of whites by supernatural intervention was known by all who participated in the Ghost Dance, but the Lakota were the only ones who were systematically depicted as instigating an outbreak to hasten the apocalypse. Although rumors also spread about the intentions of the southern Plains ghost dancers, they never reached the intensity of those about Lakota intentions. Thus, the symbols of violent resistance to religious suppression (threats, bullet-proof ghost shirts, waving of rifles) did not become characteristic Ghost Dance phenomena among southern nations.

This was a time when vast resources of money and human energy were being devoted toward the Christianization and acculturation of Lakota. As part of an ideology of manifest destiny, efforts were under way to suppress Sun Dance[4] and ghost-keeping[5] ceremonies and to encourage the Lakota to take up farming and ranching. The Ghost Dance movement laid all those efforts to waste, as it called for a return to the old ways. The frustration felt by agents and other whites as Lakota began ghost dancing is evidenced by their commentary. Agent McLaughlin scornfully noted that the "progressive and more intelligent, and many of our very best Indians" had submitted to the superstitious belief (Mooney 1896/1973, 787). He and Agent Gallagher at the Pine Ridge Agency felt the dance was demoralizing as well as indecent and disgusting (Commissioner of Indian Affairs 1891, 124–26).

Local whites and some acculturated Lakota, appalled by the return to non-Christian practices, misrepresented the Ghost Dance with their alarming descriptions to the public. For example, Mary Collins, a teacher at Standing Rock, described dancers as "screaming, dancing and wildly waving their arms" (Vestal 1934, 69). Mrs. Z. A. Parker characterized their prayers and songs as "the most fearful, heart-piercing wails I ever heard,— crying, moaning, groaning, and shrieking" (Folk-Lore Scrap-Book 1891, 161). Among the Lakota, Plenty Bear, a scout, reported that dancers at Porcupine Creek were dressed "in their devilish toggery" (Kelly 1971, 50).

The dance, in fact, was conducted with respect and reflected the prereservation-era beliefs of the Lakota. In preparation for the ceremony some of the dancers fasted before cleansing and purifying themselves in the sweat lodge. Purification was followed by painting of sacred symbols on their faces and donning of eagle feathers and ghost dance shirts. About noon the dancers, men and women, formed a circle facing the center of the dance ring where a sacred pole[6] stood. After a prayer by the

4. The Sun Dance is an annual ceremony when communities or nations come together to pray for the well-being of the world, and it involves fulfillment of vows through fasting, offerings of flesh by piercing or cutting, and dancing. In 1883 the commissioner of Indian Affairs declared the Sun Dance illegal.

5. The ghost-keeping ceremony, or more accurately keeping of the soul, was a way for families and communities to prepare the spirit of a beloved person for its journey to the spirit world and as a way of honoring the deceased person. The ceremony could last up to one year, which missionaries and reservation teachers found counterproductive to Western economic practices that they were trying to instill among the Lakota.

6. To use Mircea Eliade's well-known construct, the dance pole is the *axis mundi* where the sacred from the above and below and human beings come together and the mythic becomes the present.

dance leader, the dancers joined hands and began a slow, rhythmic, shuffling side step to the left. As the dance continued the dancers began to move faster and sing louder. At times someone would fall to the ground in a trance and receive a vision. Some of the dancers, in the same manner as in the Sun Dance, would offer small pieces of flesh to the creator (Utley 1963, 85–90; Eastman 1945, 32; Moorehead 1891, 162–63; Coates 1985, 91–93; W. F. Johnson 1891, 47).

Ghost dancing was perceived not only as a step backward toward barbarism but also as a challenge to white authority as reflected in Agent Perain P. Palmer's report to the commissioner of Indian Affairs. He described ghost dancers as "Hostile Indians" and said they were "preparing to defy the authority of the Department." In another instance, Daniel F. Royer, an inexperienced agent at Pine Ridge, tried to stop the ghost dancing. When the Lakota ignored his warning, he immediately requested troops. Clearly overreacting, Royer reported that the dances were damaging to the Lakota and "the only remedy for this matter is the use of military" (Utley 1963, 97, 103–5).

To put a stop to the ghost dancing, agents and military officials authorized force to suppress dance gatherings. The ghost dancers, rather than being seen primarily as devout religious people, were characterized as defiant and were referred to as "hostiles," "vicious savages," and "enemies" (Vestal 1934, 82; Coates 1985, 94; Kelly 1971, 182). In a *New York Times* article Gen. Nelson A. Miles warned readers that "when an ignorant race of people become religious fanatics it is hard to tell just what they will do" (Coates 1985, 91), thus creating an image of ghost dancers as irrational and unpredictable, and therefore dangerous.

Despite the frightening rumors about the ghost dancers, some Lakota and white, alike, recognized that suppression of the Ghost Dance constituted religious persecution. According to Elaine Goodale Eastman, supervisor of education for the Lakota, "Their followers insisted that this was their 'church,' which ought to be as safe from molestation as the scattered chapels of the Christian Dakotas" (1945, 31). When an army officer told Big Foot that he and his followers could not leave the reservation without a pass and that they must not dance, Big Foot replied, "My friend, do you get a paper from the Great Father at Washington when you pray to the white man's God?" (Walker 1992, 158). Sitting Bull expressed similar sentiments when he wrote Agent McLaughlin that his people prayed to God just as he did. One agent, Valentine T. McGillycuddy, wondered, "What right have we to dictate to them on a religious belief . . . ? If the Seventh Day Adventists get up on the roof of their houses, arrayed in their ascension robes, to meet the 'second coming,' the U.S. Army is not rushed into their field" (Vestal 1934, 89).

While religious persecution toward the ghost dancers continued, rumors began flying about the so-called war dances of the Lakota. According to James Boyd, "Older residents, and those acquainted with Indian warfare, knew well that an outbreak was always preceded by a series of dances" (1891, 180). Although dancers were urged not to carry anything metal in the dances, including weapons (Eastman 1945, 33; Sword 1892, 31; Mooney 1896/1973, 788), some of them began to carry rifles, partly for protection and partly as a symbol of status. They also needed their rifles for hunting to secure food for the many people who attended the dances, especially with the recent crop failures and reduction of rations. Some of the dancers also wore ghost shirts, which they believed would protect them from bullets. The presence of weapons and ghost shirts, however, fueled rumors about an impending Lakota outbreak.

Exaggerated reports of gun stockpiling by the Lakota spread quickly. On November 24, 1890, Kelly filed a story that read in part: "All settlers from the north for forty miles are rapidly congregating in Gordon [Nebraska, just south of the reservation] and are badly scared. Trains going east for the past two days have been crowded with women and children seeking a safe retreat in case of an outbreak" (Overholt 1978, 172–73). Brig. Gen. L. W. Colby of the Nebraska National Guard also spoke of the increasing "alarm and anxiety among settlers." He said this response existed not only on the borders of Pine Ridge but also as far north as Mandan, North Dakota (173).

The rumors about war dancing were also fueled by the response of ghost dancers to religious persecution. When Agent Hugh Gallagher at Pine Ridge, along with several police, tried to stop the dancing at No Water's Camp on White Clay Creek, several dancers responded to his demands by leveling their guns toward him and the police. They warned him that they were ready to defend their religion with their lives (Mooney 1896/1973, 846–47). A similar incident occurred at Cheyenne River when Perain P. Palmer, an inexperienced agent, tried to use police force to stop the dancing there. His Lakota officers met armed resistance, and many chose to resign rather than confront their people (Utley 1963, 96–97).

Wild rumors of agents losing control over the Lakota, of Lakota preparing to attack white villages surrounding the reservations, were followed by petitions from settlers calling for protection, mobilization of the state militia, and delivery of arms and ammunition. Newspaper stories began demanding military action against the Lakota (Vestal 1934, 74; Utley 1963, 109). Paranoia about the intent of the Lakota got so out of hand that all persons at Pine Ridge were cautioned about speaking near any Indians or allowing them near any building or store, or the soldiers' camp (Kelly 1971, 39).

Historian Robert M. Utley suggests that some of the reports may have been instigated by whites who were suffering the devastating effects of a drought. They knew "that large-scale military operations would restore a measure of prosperity" (1963, 110). At least six citizens of LaGrace, South Dakota, challenged the validity of the rumors when they prepared a petition asking that the Lakota be allowed to cross the river, that they "are always well-behaved & only evil disposed persons could have any reason to complain" (Vestal 1934, 75–76).

The Lakota themselves were badly frightened by the increasing presence of the military as well as the fears of white settlers (Vestal 1934, 10). In September when the Brule arrived at Rosebud Agency for their biweekly rations, a rumor quickly spread among them that soldiers were on the reservation and that they had come to put an end to the ghost dancing. Immediately, the men prepared for battle and rode out south from the agency to await the soldiers. Agent Wright had to convince them that the story was false (Utley 1963, 94).

In another instance, toward the end of November, some of Red Cloud's men spread rumors among the Lakota at Pine Ridge that "they were to be attacked at once and put under guard by the troops and Indian police" (Kelly 1971, 39). Their fears were exacerbated by some of their white friends who, hoping to persuade the Lakota to give up their dancing, warned them of terrible repercussions if they did not stop. For example, Mary Collins warned Sitting Bull that if the dances did not cease, "the soldiers will come and kill all of your people. Your best warriors and men will be shot and the families will go unprovided for" (Vestal 1934, 69).

Although there were agents present on the reservation who had years of experience working with the Lakota and who were capable of mediating between whites and ghost dancers, military and government officials often ignored their advice. Struggles for jurisdictional authority over the Lakota and a system of patronage contributed to the growing hostile attitude toward ghost dancers. Through the patronage system some of the experienced agents were replaced by others who, inexperienced, were drawn into the web of rumors and overreacted to the dances, often calling for troops to prevent an outbreak. Their actions, in turn, intensified fears among whites and the Lakota.

When McGillycuddy visited Red Cloud's camp in the Badlands on behalf of the governor of Dakota, he received valuable information that opened the door for alternative actions other than military force. McGillycuddy told Brig. Gen. John R. Brooke that Red Cloud wanted to know why soldiers had been brought to the reservation. He said, "It looks as if they have come to fight, and if it is so, we must fight, but we are tired of war, and we think of our women and children, and our property, our homes, our little farms, and our cattle we are raising" (Vestal 1934, 83). If McGillycuddy's report is accurate, it is clear that Red Cloud and his people were not spoiling for a fight; on the contrary, they had too much to lose. They were not willing to cease their religious activities, but neither were they planning to start a war. Rather than trying to negotiate a compromise or reason with the Lakota about the benefits of returning to their agencies, General Brooke issued ultimatums. Kelly reported that when various Lakota asked to meet with General Brooke he refused, saying that "unless they ceased dancing of their own accord they would be made to stop" (1971, 36). He and the other commanding officers and agents assumed that the presence of soldiers would intimidate the Lakota into compliance.

McGillycuddy, however, recognized that the nearness of troops constituted a threat to the Lakota. He suggested that the troops be moved behind the Nebraska line. He also knew from experience that the Lakota did not usually initiate warfare in wintertime. Brooke, however, refused to consider McGillycuddy's suggestion, which would have temporarily eased the situation. Instead, he became sarcastic and, as McGillicuddy put it, "went up in the air" over his suggestion. Rather than considering the advice of someone well acquainted with the Lakota, the Indian Office began investigating McGillycuddy on charges of "abusing the administration" and "inciting the Indians to disturbance" (Vestal 1934, 83–84).

In late November McGillycuddy persuaded General Brooke to talk to Little Wound, a war chief. During the meeting Little Wound asked why soldiers were brought to stop the dances if whites were so sure that the Messiah[7] was not coming. He said that he had already told his people, "If this is a good thing we should have it, if it is not, it will fall to the earth itself." McGillycuddy explained to General Brooke the import

---

7. Porcupine, a Cheyenne, told Little Wound that Wovoka had identified himself as the messiah. Little Wound made a distinction between the messiah as the son of God and the Lakota supernatural Wakan Tanka.

of Little Wound's words. He said the Lakota would dance through the winter, and in the spring, if the Messiah did not appear as predicted, the Ghost Dance would die out (Vestal 1934, 89). Despite Little Wound's and McGillycuddy's predictions, efforts continued to suppress the dancing.

The relentless pressure from agents and Indian police to end the Ghost Dances, as well as the increasing presence of soldiers, led to a pivotal change in the prophecy at Red Leaf's camp near Rosebud. Short Bull, the Brule medicine man, told Red Leaf's people that although he had said the great cataclysm would come in the spring, whites were interfering so much that he advanced the time to the end of one moon. He told them that for a full moon (the month of November)

> We must continue this dance. If the soldiers surround you four deep, three of you, on whom I have put holy shirts, will sing a song, which I have taught you, around them, when some of them will drop dead. Then the rest will start to run, but their horses will sink into the earth. The riders will jump from their horses, but they will sink into the earth also. Then you can do as you desire with them. Now, you must know this, that all the soldiers and that race will be dead. (Mooney 1896/1973, 788–89)

Pressure from nearby whites continued unabated in November. Responding to the fear and demands of Royer, private citizens, and journalists, General Miles instructed General Brooke to deploy troops at Pine Ridge and Rosebud. On November 20 Brooke arrived at Pine Ridge Agency with Agent Royer, Special Agent James A. Cooper, three troops of the Ninth Cavalry Regiment, four companies of the Second Regiment, one company of the Eighth Regiment, and a Hotchkiss cannon and Gatling gun. On the same day three companies of the Eighth Infantry, two troops of the Ninth Cavalry, and a Hotchkiss gun reached Rosebud Agency. Six days later the entire Seventh Cavalry under the command of Col. James W. Forsyth arrived at Pine Ridge (Utley 1963, 113–14, 118).

By November 23 hundreds of Lakota families who wished to be disassociated from the ghost dancers had set up camps at Pine Ridge Agency. Although they were considered "friendlies," sentries patrolled the agency streets, and one hundred children were kept locked inside the Oglala boarding school under twenty-four-hour guard (Utley 1963, 117). Meanwhile, the ghost dancers, fearing punishment, had fled to the Badlands (Eastman 1945, 33). There, they resumed their dances with more fervor. They told A. T. Lea, a census agent, that they had no intention of taking the offensive but vowed to defend themselves if attacked. At Rosebud a similar response occurred as about eleven hundred Brule headed west. Part of them traveled to Wounded Knee Creek and the other part eventually joined with Short Bull's people, who led them to the mouth of White Clay Creek where they united with the Oglala dancers (Utley 1963, 117–18).

At this time internal struggles for control between agents and army officers became apparent. McGillycuddy arrived at Pine Ridge and offered to meet with the Lakota in an attempt to persuade them to go to the agency. Although McGillycuddy had the respect of the Oglalas and Red Cloud had requested that he be sent to advise them, General Brooke refused his offer and instead sent Frank Merrivale, an interpreter, who returned after being warned off by rifle fire. A few days later, however, Little Wound and Big Road returned to the agency with their bands, which left Short Bull's and Two Strike's people still at large (McGillycuddy 1941, 262; Utley 1963, 121).

Meanwhile, at the Lower Brule Reservation, Agent A. P. Dixon and his police force arrested nine dance leaders on November 27. Within a few days he had arrested twenty-two dancers, seventeen of whom were taken to Fort Snelling, Minnesota, for confinement in the military prison. Dixon had acted without authorization and was ordered immediately to cease making arrests. However, he had impressed upon the Brule the terrible consequences that awaited them if they continued dancing (Utley 1963, 130–31).

Attention then turned to Short Bull and the Brule, who had taken refuge in an area of the Badlands called the Stronghold. Still not willing to wait for the Ghost Dance to die of its own accord, but not wanting to initiate warfare either, General Brooke met with a delegation of ghost dancers and urged them to surrender. He offered to employ some of the young men as scouts in return. Turning Bear replied that he did not understand how General Brooke could hire men as scouts when there was no enemy to watch. Although Brooke did not succeed in persuading the ghost dancers to return to the agency, he had temporarily eased the situation by listening to their concerns.

However, before Brooke had time to continue his negotiations, two unfortunate events occurred. General Miles, annoyed by Brooke's approach, directed him not to engage in further discussion of grievances with or favors for the Lakota, and a group of cowboys attacked several Brule as they returned to camp after visiting a trading store, killing one.

It took the combined efforts of a scout and thirty-two non-ghost-dancing Lakota to persuade all but about two hundred dancers, including Short Bull and Kicking Bear, to return to Pine Ridge (Utley 1963, 138–42).

Despite the return of most of the dancers, newspaper correspondents and nearby settlers bitterly condemned what they considered Brooke's conciliatory approach. Eager for a showdown, members of the South Dakota militia began harassing the Lakota. Col. H. M. Day with sixty-two ranchers and cowboys that he mustered into the militia patrolled the Cheyenne River and skirmished with Lakota several times during the week of December 14. The contradictory actions of Brooke and Day only divided the Lakota over whether to fight, return to the agency, or flee. General Miles added to the confusion by second-guessing the decisions of officers in the field. When Brooke decided it was time to force the Brule out of the Stronghold, Miles sent him a message to keep the Lakota bottled up until winter set in, letting the cold and snow aid the troops in removing them (Utley 1963, 143–45).

The situation at Standing Rock was just as confused. Earlier in the fall Brig. Gen. Thomas H. Ruger determined that Agent McLaughlin and Lt. Col. William F. Drum had the situation under control and could handle any trouble that might arise. On October 17 McLaughlin had written a letter to the commissioner of Indian Affairs expressing his confidence that he could control any trouble that might result from the dances. Despite this positive assessment, all three officials agreed that Sitting Bull should be arrested and confined to a military prison (Utley 1963, 100, 110). Although Sitting Bull did not present a threat as a ghost dance leader, McLaughlin wanted him arrested because Sitting Bull held a strong influence over his people and because he felt Sitting Bull challenged his authority at the agency (Vestal 1934, 285; Danker 1981, 159).

Agent McLaughlin, however, decided to wait until winter set in before attempting the arrest of Sitting Bull. He felt that by cutting off rations during the heart of winter, cold and hunger would force the Hunkpapa to come into the agency. However, his plans were blocked on two fronts. The Indian Bureau never approved the withholding of rations, and General Miles determined to keep McLaughlin out of the picture. He authorized William F. Cody to arrest Sitting Bull immediately.

Although the president had sent out a directive giving the War Department full responsibility for suppressing an outbreak, McLaughlin interfered with Miles's orders. He conspired with General Ruger and

Colonel Drum to prevent Cody from carrying out his mission. He then contacted the secretary of interior and asked that the order be rescinded. The secretary of interior met with the president and the secretary of war, after which the president suspended Cody's orders and deferred all attempts to arrest Sitting Bull (Utley 1963, 123–25).

Miles was furious over McLaughlin's and Drum's interference and determined to eliminate any further interference from agents. He wrote his superiors that the only way to end the Lakota problem was to place them "under absolute control and beyond the possibility of doing harm." He argued that "those large powerful warlike tribes, that have been for years a terror to the north-west States and Territories" must be placed under military control at once (Utley 1963, 126).

Miles deliberately characterized the dancers as "warlike" to garner support for total military control. He began telling reporters that the situation was grave, and he blamed the Indian Bureau for reducing rations, thus deepening the animosity between agencies. His exaggerated reports of warlike Indians also inflamed local citizens (Utley 1963, 127). Thus, the ghost dancers became pawns between the military and the Indian Bureau in their struggle for authority.

His actions, however, incited factionalism in the army. Several important officers under his command were annoyed by his comments to the press. One unidentified officer was quoted as saying: "He wants to create a scare and pose as the savior of the country." Another officer told a correspondent for the *Army and Navy Journal* that "it is pretty well understood in Army circles that private ambitions have had more or less to do with the present Indian situation" (Utley 1963, 129–30).

Miles's tactics were successful. On December 1 the secretary of the interior ordered all agents to "cooperate with and obey the orders of the military officer commanding on the reservation" with regard to any operations intended to suppress any outbreak by force. That was not enough, however. Miles wanted complete authority over the Lakota situation. He demanded that civil agents be replaced with army officers to avoid, as he put it, "interference with the plans of the military as there has been recently" (Utley 1963, 128, 144).

Agent McLaughlin was afraid that Miles would try another arrest without consulting him, so he conspired with Colonel Drum to send the Grand River police to arrest Sitting Bull. He was aware that on December 10 Miles had sent a confidential telegram to General Ruger ordering him to tell Colonel Drum to arrest Sitting Bull. McLaughlin planned to arrest Sitting Bull on ration day when many of his people would be away.

However, on December 14 he received a report from Lieutenant Bull Head that Sitting Bull was planning to leave for Pine Ridge, with or without permission. He and Drum decided to arrest Sitting Bull the next morning rather than wait for ration day (Utley 1963, 152, 154–55).

McLaughlin's plan to use Indian police to arrest Sitting Bull, however, presented difficulties. Some of the police had relatives among Sitting Bull's people, and they did not want to fight with them, perhaps killing some of them. They also knew that as a Hunkpapa leader, Sitting Bull would not allow Yanktonai and Blackfeet to remove him from his camp. As a result, Crazy Walking, captain of the police, and three other police resigned, and One Bull, a nephew of Sitting Bull, was discharged. When McLaughlin tried to recruit four men from Sitting Bull's camp, they too resigned. Lieutenant Bull Head was forced to recruit men from Grand River to assist in the arrest.

According to McLaughlin, many of the officers were eager to arrest Sitting Bull because the ghost dancers repeatedly insulted nondancers. The antagonism between ghost dancers and nondancers was complicated by the internalization of cultural racism as a result of colonization. Lieutenant Bull Head, according to McLaughlin, found the indifference displayed by Sitting Bull and his followers toward the federal government's magnanimous gestures particularly vexing (Vestal 1932, 293). Despite the animosity of the police toward Sitting Bull, McLaughlin determined to carry out his initial plan of action.

On December 15 Lieutenant Bull Head, thirty-nine police, and four volunteers arrested Sitting Bull in his home. When the police exited the house with Sitting Bull, his followers, confused and angry at the arrest of their leader, quickly surrounded the nervous police. Suddenly, Catch-the-Bear shot Lieutenant Bull Head in the side sending him sprawling to the ground. As he fell Bull Head shot the unarmed and restrained Sitting Bull in the chest at the same time that another officer shot Sitting Bull in the back of the head. Everyone began shooting immediately and when the smoke cleared there were eight dead Hunkpapa, four dead officers, and three wounded officers, two of whom later died (Utley 1963, 158–60, 162).

The news of Sitting Bull's death shocked the Lakota nation. When Big Foot, a Minneconjou leader, heard there were refugees from Sitting Bull's camp, he sent some of his men to help them. When they reached Hump's camp where the refugees were, Hump, a former ghost dancer turned scout, refused to let them take the Hunkpapa and urged his people to get their weapons and "fix them!" (Danker 1981, 181) He erroneously assumed that Big Foot was planning to fight the whites, which would endanger all Lakota.

In the meantime a dispatch had been sent to Lt. Col. E. V. Sumner advising Big Foot's arrest. General Miles, continuing his campaign to depict the ghost dancers as dangerous, warned General Brooke that Big Foot was defiant and threatening (Danker 1981, 163). On December 21 Sumner met Big Foot's band as they traveled toward Cheyenne River Agency to draw rations. Sumner told them they must go back to their village, to which Big Foot agreed. Early the next morning Sumner organized Big Foot's people for the march toward Fort Meade. To maximize control over the Lakota, he divided them into three groups, separating each group with a troop of cavalry and thus stringing them out over several miles (Utley 1963, 180; Danker 1981, 184). According to Dewey Beard, a Minneconjou, they became "uneasy for the safety of their people who had gone on ahead and were far away. The signs were threatening to the Indians." They were afraid because they believed that Hump had told Sumner that Big Foot wanted to fight. Their fears intensified when a fight nearly broke out between them and the soldiers over a minor incident (Danker 1981, 183–84).

As the band neared the village of Big Foot, he reported that his people did not want to travel further. They wanted to stay in their homes. Although Sumner knew that General Ruger expected him to arrest Big Foot, he decided to allow the Minneconjou to go to their homes if they promised to go to Camp Cheyenne the next day for a council (Utley 1963, 181). The troops then continued on to Camp Cheyenne. That evening Sumner received a note from Miles telling him to move his prisoners to Fort Meade quickly. Sumner recognized the position he was in, because he had not arrested Big Foot. He wanted to be sure that Big Foot kept his promise, so he sent John Dunn, a local rancher, to tell Big Foot's people they must go to the agency. After Dunn left, Sumner ordered his troops readied, and they began marching back toward Big Foot's camp.

Dunn, grossly distorting Sumner's message, frightened the Minneconjou when he told them soldiers were coming in the morning to carry them off and would shoot them if they refused to go. According to Joseph Horn Cloud, Dunn urged Big Foot to take his people and flee to Pine Ridge because a thousand soldiers were coming that night to take them prisoner, and he did not want to see their women and children killed. Horn Cloud's brother Beard recalled that Dunn also said they would take the men, not the women, to Fort Meade and from there to an island in the ocean in the east (Mooney 1896/1973, 865; Danker 1981, 163, 167, 185).

That night two scouts were sent out to see if soldiers were coming. They returned to verify Dunn's story. The already uneasy Lakota became frightened. Big Foot immediately began moving his people toward Pine Ridge and hopefully to safety. The older women and the children, who could not move quickly and trailed behind the main group, were so certain of death from the soldiers that they cried and sang death songs as they walked (Danker 1981, 185).

Although Sumner did not believe that Big Foot was a threat, General Miles was incensed at his escape. Big Foot's actions had not only challenged the authority of the United States but had also reflected negatively on his command. He had Sumner brought before a court of inquiry. He also sent an inflammatory telegram to General Brooke stating that: "Big Foot is cunning and his Indians are very bad" (Utley 1963, 186, 192). He thus gave the impression that the frightened Lakota were deceptive and dangerous.

Before Big Foot could reach Pine Ridge he became extremely sick. Aware that soldiers were on Wounded Knee Creek and that he could not elude them any longer, he decided to go directly to their camp. On December 28 his band reached Pine Creek where they met four troops with four Hotchkiss cannons. Although Big Foot displayed a white flag, Maj. Samuel M. Whitside "signaled his column into skirmish formation, gave the command to dismount, and ran the two cannons out in front of the line." The Lakota responded by tying up the tails of their ponies in preparation for a fight and waving rifles (Utley 1963, 193–95; Danker 1981, 169).

Whitside, rather than trying to ease the situation, sent word to General Brooke suggesting that Colonel Forsyth and the rest of the regiment be sent to Wounded Knee to help disarm the Lakota. His assumption that the Lakota wanted to fight led him to intensify his show of force. He later testified that he hoped "by their presence, we could overawe the Indians, and so they would submit quietly to be disarmed" (Utley 1963, 197).

That night, when the troops and their prisoners stopped near Wounded Knee Creek, Whitside immediately ordered two Hotchkiss guns placed on top of Cemetery Hill with their muzzles pointed directly at the Lakota camp. He also instructed Capt. Myles Moylan to station Troop A and Troop I as sentinels around the Lakota camp. Moylan completely encircled their camp with twenty posts and had patrols range back and forth between the posts. When Colonel Forsyth arrived with the Seventh Cavalry later that night, he sent two more Hotchkiss guns to the top of Cemetery Hill. The Lakota became increasingly uneasy as there were now more than 500 soldiers and scouts to escort 120 men and 250 women and children to Fort Meade (Utley 1963, 198–201; Mooney 1896/1973, 870).

Most reports of events of that day indicate that everyone was friendly—the troops provided the Minneconjou with rations and tents and provided medical help for the ailing Big Foot. However, it is more likely that the Minneconjou were putting on a show in the light of their situation. According to Beard, the Minneconjou "agreed together that we would not be afraid to go in among the soldiers. . . . The Indians feared from the position and actions of the soldiers that the latter were going to fire on them; but Big Foot had told them to go right up to the soldiers calmly and confidently, showing no fear; and they did so." The soldiers, however, responded by aiming their guns toward the Minneconjou, some of them laying down on the ground positioned as if to fire. Beard said they could hear their guns clicking as if cartridges were being inserted into the barrels. The Lakota became frightened and thought they were going to be killed" (Danker 1981, 188).

After this show of force the Lakota were uneasy the rest of the night. Just before sunrise Beard said his father came to him and his brothers and told them, "They say it is peace but I am sure there is going to be fighting today." He told his sons not to start trouble, not to follow any Lakota who might start trouble, but "if the white people start trouble first, then you can do what you want to—you can die among your own relations in defending them" (Danker 1981, 190). The Lakota, thus, were anticipating trouble.

The following day, December 29, Forsyth ordered the men separated from the women and seated in a circle. Troops were placed around the men, creating a barrier between them and the women (Utley 1963, 208). Separating the women and children from the men was an ominous sign to the Lakota men, because Dunn had previously warned them that the men were to be taken away. They became even more concerned when they were ordered to give up their weapons. When the Lakota did not turn over as many rifles as expected, orders were given to search their tepees for anything that could be used as a weapon including awls used for sewing. The Minneconjou, surrounded by soldiers, could not shake the fear that if they gave up their guns they would be slaughtered by the troops (Utley 1963, 205–6, 210).

Their fear was compounded by a show of force intended to humili-
ate the men. An officer, reportedly drunk, told the Minneconjou that he
wanted them to stand in a rank before his men. He said his soldiers
would place unloaded guns at their foreheads and pull the triggers. After
that they would be free to return to their camps. According to Richard
C. Stirk, a white man living on White River, "this loading in their faces
was calculated to set the Indians to reasoning and to make them uneasy
and fearful." Instead, according to Beard, "this offended and angered
them and they reasoned among themselves and said they were human
beings and not cattle to be used this way." Although the men were
incensed by this action, Big Foot and another man urged their people to
remain calm (Danker 1981, 172, 192, 222).

Alcohol may have played a part in this demeaning act. The night
before a trader had arrived at Wounded Knee with a barrel of whiskey.
The officers, passing from tent to tent, drank and congratulated Forsyth
on his capture of the Lakota until late in the night. Although witnesses
reported that the enlisted men did not participate in the revelry and that
the officers did not appear intoxicated the next morning" (Danker 1981,
222; Utley 1963, 199), their actions suggest otherwise.

While the soldiers were taking guns away from the men, one deaf
man, Black Coyote, perhaps not understanding what was going on, refused to turn over his gun. The soldiers tried to take it away from him,
and the rifle discharged into the air (Danker 1981, 173; 192). Unfortunately, most of the enlisted men had never been under fire, nearly one-
fifth being recruits, and almost half of those having joined the regiment
only two weeks earlier. They were under the command of Forsyth who
had very little command experience against Indians (Utley 1963, 202).

Thus, the stage was set. The inexperienced recruits had been hearing unfounded rumors of Lakota attacks on whites, they had been confined
to agency camps practicing drills in preparation for confrontation, and
they had either heard or joined in the celebration of what was billed as
the capture of the "cunning" Big Foot. An adversarial environment had
been created that affected their perception of events just before the
accidental discharge.

While the Lakota men were seated in a circle, Yellow Bird, a medicine person, attired in ghost dance dress, began dancing and singing.
Some of the whites believed that he was haranguing the Lakota to fight,
especially because they believed the Lakota were concealing weapons.
One eyewitness said, "He began to jump and dance backward and forward before the Indians and to sing a war chant. He stooped down to

the ground and took up a handful of dirt and made two signal motions—opened two fingers and threw up a part of the dirt, then made two steps sideways and threw up the balance over the heads of the Indians" (Danker 1981, 235; Utley 1963, 210).

The soldiers and officers were unfamiliar with ghost dance ritual and they assumed that the thrown dirt was a signal to attack. However, this was a ritual act of the Ghost Dance. According to Z. A. Parker, who observed ghost dancing at Pine Ridge, after the Lakota danced a few rounds, they took up handfuls of dust at their feet, washed their hands in it, and threw it over their heads while crying with grief. They then raised their eyes to the heavens and began praying (Folk-Lore Scrap-Book 1891, 161).

However, the soldiers thought otherwise. When Black Coyote's rifle discharged, the inexperienced soldiers, perceiving the Lakota as enemies, instantly fired en masse without orders (Eastman 1945, 41; Danker 1981, 193). In less than half an hour 153 Minneconjou were dead and 44 were wounded. Among the whites 25 were dead and 39 wounded (Utley 1963, 228). When news of the massacre reached the American public, demands for an investigation filled newspapers and bombarded government offices.

During a court inquiry officers explained the soldiers' actions, stating that men, women, and children were together in the ravines, and in the heat of the battle they could not tell combatants from noncombatants (Utley 1963, 246). The death of twenty-six children under thirteen including four babies with skulls crushed by the butt of a musket or some heavy club (Moorehead 1891, 166) and the pursuit and killing of women and children over a two-mile stretch (Mooney 1896/1973, 870) indicates otherwise.

From the beginning, rumors, misinformation, and cultural ignorance combined to create a psychological environment of fear and animosity toward the ghost dancers. These factors, in and of themselves, however, do not account for the violent end to the Ghost Dance. Other millennial movements invite speculation about the intentions of believers, but they do not all end in violence. In the case of the Ghost Dance, rumors and misinformation were allowed to spread on the reservation largely unchallenged, creating an image of the Lakota as dangerous enemies of whites.

The perception of Lakota as threatening to white society derived from a long history of whites relating to Lakota as enemies. However, by the time of the Ghost Dance their ability to challenge the authority and might of the United States had been greatly curtailed. Yet, certain whites were able to draw upon that history through rumors and cultural ignorance to create an atmosphere of fear and anger toward the Lakota. The resulting massacre might have been prevented by prompt intervention first between various agencies of the government and second between the U.S. government and the Lakota.

In the first case, during the Ghost Dance period, members of the Indian Office and the War Department engaged in a power struggle with each other using tactics that demonized the ghost dancers. For instance, General Miles used the press to convince the Department of Interior and the president that the military should have full responsibility for the Lakota situation. His comments to the press reinforced the fears of civilians and soldiers on the reservation. The competition between departments and the use of the Lakota as pawns might have been contained if an individual or agency separate from the Indian Office or War Department had been given responsibility for coordinating actions and disseminating information about the ghost dancers.

A separate agency with coordinating powers also could have directed the adoption of a unified policy in government dealings with the Lakota. As it were, each agent or officer who engaged in negotiations with the Lakota did so without coordinating their efforts with each other. Depending on the experiences and motivations of each negotiator, strategies ranged from threatening arrest of Lakota men (Dunn) to offering jobs as scouts (Brooke). These disparate approaches drew varied responses from the Lakota, providing more opportunities for rumors to develop. Coordinating strategies through one person or agency might have minimized confusion between the Lakota and the government.

In the second case, even if the government had provided a united front in its negotiations with the Lakota, the power of the government over the Lakota might have prevented a peaceful solution to the situation. Agents and officers represented the power of the United States and could threaten the Lakota with force or withdrawal of rations and appropriations. Pushed into a corner, the Lakota might have resisted rather than give in to religious persecution.

By introducing mediation, a process in which a disinterested or neutral party arbitrates between two or more parties, the effect of the leverage or power of the United States over the Lakota could have been minimized. At the same time, a mediator could have given the ghost dancers a sense of greater autonomy. Ideally, a mediator could have served as an equalizing force by filtering out threats or ultimatums by the more powerful United States, thus allowing greater opportunity for peaceful resolution.

In reality, finding a neutral third party in this particular case was extremely unlikely. However, identifying someone who was acceptable to both parties would have been difficult but not impossible. Considering the history of white/Lakota relations, the person needed to be someone known to the Lakota. They would not have had reason to trust any white person unknown to them. One possibility, for example, might have been McGillycuddy who had enough respect among the Lakota that he was able to convince Little Wound to talk to General Brooke. As an agent of the government, McGillycuddy was also potentially acceptable to the United States. In a case such as this, the more powerful United States needed to be willing to entertain with good faith those people who were acceptable to the Lakota.

In the absence of coordinated strategies and cooperation between agencies, rumors that drew on the fears of whites about Lakota enemies were allowed to go relatively unchecked. As a result, a situation was created in which inexperienced soldiers perceiving the Lakota as a threat acted with an intensity borne of fear toward a group that in reality posed little threat to them. They, in fact, defeated an enemy that existed only in their minds. Coordination and mediation, however, might have eased the situation long enough for the rumors and fears surrounding the Ghost Dance to subside or for ghost dancers to return to their agencies without incident.

# 3

# ✳"*Theology Is Life and Death*"✳

## David Koresh on Violence, Persecution, and the Millennium

EUGENE V. GALLAGHER————————————————

Surprised by the overwhelming firepower behind the "dynamic entry" of the Bureau of Alcohol, Tobacco, and Firearms (BATF) and fearful for their safety, members of the Branch Davidian community outside of Waco, Texas, placed an emergency 911 call on the morning of February 28, 1993. During the call, David Koresh, the group's leader and prophet, attempted to engage Lt. Larry Lynch of the Waco sheriff's department in a discussion of their beliefs (see Tabor and Gallagher 1995; S. Wright 1995). Thinking that such a theological conversation could be deferred until a more suitable time, Lynch endeavored to steer Koresh away from it. But Koresh responded, "Look, this is life, this is life and death . . . theology really is life and death" (*Nightline* June 4, 1993). Koresh's comments, delivered amid the chaos of a full-scale military attack on his home and church, offer a point of departure for examining how he understood both persecution and violence in the framework of his millennial theology. Although Koresh expected persecution, he devoted himself to bringing saving knowledge to as many as possible; he repudiated any retaliatory violence, and reserved eschatological violence for God alone. Koresh's teaching gives little reason for anticipating that either he or the Branch Davidians would lash out violently at anyone and indicates that the causes of the violence on February 28 and throughout the fifty-one-day siege at the Mount Carmel Center are not intrinsic to Koresh's millennial theology.

Like so many other Adventists,[1] Koresh and the Branch Davidians were convinced that they stood at the end of time. Fortified with prophetic insight into the Scriptures, they had come to the Mount Carmel Center to dedicate their lives to pursuing the truth of God's word and to prepare for his imminent judgment. Their study of the Bible revealed the terrible fate that awaited those who rejected God, but they also beheld the sparkling promise that they might be spared God's wrath through acceptance of his servant's message. In that sense the Branch Davidians' theological convictions were a matter of *eternal* life and death; they offered the possibility of escaping God's condemnation and embracing salvation (Negotiation tape #26, Mar. 3, 1993).

The rhetoric of a catastrophic millennialism like Koresh's is inherently violent, foreseeing as it does the cataclysmic end of the world with its attendant natural, social, and cosmic upheavals (Wessinger 1997a). In such worldviews God is the primary author of both the apocalyptic violence and the final judgment. But the role of the human faithful can vary from an anxious watchfulness to an eager cooperation in bringing about the end (Boyer 1992, 297–98). One of the primary tasks of an apocalyptic prophet is not only to declare the imminence of the end but also to chart an appropriate path of human response. Visions of the end, even in textual form, remain flexible in the hands of an interpreter who is sensitive to the nuances of context. When changes occur in the lives of an interpreter or the interpreter's community, the meaning that a given text has for them will also change. The millennial prophet always strives to read both text and context in terms of each other. Just as the interpreter can discern the hidden meaning of both history and the present by reading them through the lens of the prophetic text, so also changes in context challenge the interpreter to discover how the text

1. The roots of the Branch Davidians reach back to the Millerite movement of the early 1800s. When William Miller's predictions of the Second Coming of Christ went unfulfilled, the movement faded away. But out of its rubble the modern Seventh-day Adventist Church began to take shape, led by Ellen G. White. In 1929 Victor Houteff formed a dissident group of Davidian Adventists and in 1935 he moved his group to a site outside Waco, Texas. Houteff's death in 1955 sparked conflicts over leadership that were not settled until the ascendancy of Ben and Lois Roden in the mid-1960s. David Koresh, then known as Vernon Howell, joined the Branch Davidians in 1981. (In August 1990 Vernon Wayne Howell legally changed his name to David Koresh. For consistency I will refer to him by the latter name throughout; see Tabor and Gallagher 1993, 58–63). Throughout the early 1980s, Koresh gradually became more prominent in the group and he secured his leadership position in the late 1980s.

remains relevant. Though Koresh never wavered from a prophetic reading of Christian Scripture that focused on interpreting the message in
chapter five of the book of Revelation about the scroll sealed with Seven
Seals, his thinking about the end of the world had distinct moments
during his leadership of the Branch Davidians. In general, however, Koresh
exhorted the faithful to study and to wait for God to act. But his perception of betrayal could lead him to reframe his message to address new
and unsettling events. Over the years, Koresh's basic message was mal-
leable enough to serve as a recruiting tool in Seventh-day Adventist
communities throughout the world, a template for understanding indifference to his message, a model for interpreting the bitter division that
was occasioned by his promulgation of a "New Light" of revelation, and
a paradigm for understanding the situation of his community during the
fifty-one-day siege.

Koresh's preferred mode of communication was always the oral
"Bible study," given directly to a group of fellow students of the Seven
Seals of the book of Revelation or indirectly to the faithful outside
Mount Carmel through audiotapes. Much to the government negotiators' dismay, Koresh adopted a similar mode of presentation in his conversations with them during the siege. Only at its very end did Koresh
feel permitted by God to commit his teaching to writing. He was com-
posing his book on the Seven Seals when the Mount Carmel Center was
destroyed during the FBI assault on April 19, 1993. The only completed
section of his manuscript escaped the fire with one of the survivors.
Taken together, the Bible studies, Koresh's discussions with negotiators,
and his partial manuscript give a fairly complete account of his thinking
from 1985, when he had a profound revelatory experience while staying
in Israel, until his death in 1993. Koresh was very consistent in the
articulation of his apocalyptic theology, peacefully persistent in the face
of outside apathy and opposition, and only very rarely moved to violent
threats and condemnations.

Among Koresh's Bible studies, one in 1989, "The Foundation,"
stands out for the forthrightness and vehemence with which he addressed a recent schism in his community. In contrast to the outrage that
Koresh expressed over the apostasy of several who had long been "in the
message," Koresh's reaction to the BATF raid on February 28 appears
measured, patient, and restrained. So does an hour-long radio address
that was taped inside Mount Carmel and broadcast nationally on March
2, 1993, in which Koresh resolutely focused on the articulation of his
message and abstained from condemning his attackers. Even in what

turned out to be the final days of the harrowing standoff, Koresh consistently hoped for a peaceful exit from Mount Carmel.

## Bible Studies: 1985–1989

A high school dropout who was plagued by learning disabilities, David Koresh was never especially brief or direct in his teaching. Though he had no formal training in biblical studies, Koresh had committed large parts of the King James translation to memory and relished the opportunity to demonstrate his command of the text. As a result, his Bible studies, sometimes in marathon sessions that took up the better part of a day, could be alternately spellbinding and numbing. The shorter audiotapes that he distributed to followers throughout the world and that some Davidians made during sessions manifest the same characteristics. Despite their superficial difficulty, however, Koresh's Bible studies expressed a consistent message founded on clear principles of biblical interpretation and an unshakable sense of his own calling.

Koresh was convinced that for the first time in human history "we are entering into a period of time where the Bible is going to be understood by somebody" (Howell 1987a).[2] Portraying himself as the essential agent of that understanding, Koresh asserted that "It's true that what I teach is the true interpretation of the Bible. It's so true that people for the first time in their life can understand the complexity of scripture. That's my work and that's my mission" (Howell 1989a). That new understanding of the Bible will yield full information about the final judgment. Koresh preached that "There's a hidden secret. God today has a plan contrary to any human planning. It's a plan to destroy mankind in a way that they've never known, a way that he can save them, and we're privileged to break down the walls of human wisdom" (Howell 1987a). Furthermore, God's plan will be implemented in the very near future: "we're in this period of time now, aren't we? But any day it could be cut short in righteousness. No one knows when it will be. It could be today, it could be tomorrow, you see? It could be next week" (Howell 1987a).

---

2. While James Tabor and I were writing *Why Waco?* Mark Swett graciously made available to us several Bible studies recorded by David Bunds and transcribed by Swett, along with a wealth of other material. Mark Swett maintains a very useful Web site on the Branch Davidians at <http://home.maine.rr.com/waco>. I will quote from transcripts of Bible studies and speeches.

In Koresh's understanding, the Bible speaks in a single prophetic voice. He articulated the general principle that "as God has given each messenger a portion of the truth, we must harmonize each prophecy of the Bible that we may know the whole truth and be prepared to be delivered because we are written in the book" (Howell 1987b). Such harmonizing enables the Bible student to uncover God's intentions, because God has adopted the practice of "repeating, repeating, again and again His ultimate wisdom through many different facets. This is the way God teaches. As we've been learning the prophets over and over again, every different prophet is saying the same thing" (Howell 1989a). Koresh's Bible studies thus conformed to a divine model; as God taught in the Bible, so Koresh taught in his Bible studies.

Unfortunately for them, humans have never really understood the prophets, both because of their intransigent opposition to God and because the prophets spoke of things that would only be fulfilled in the last days. As Koresh put it, "These prophecies, which have been for so many years in discrepancy with one another were not designed ever to be fulfilled in the days of these prophets. . . . Today the prophecies remain dead because people of today are not honest with themselves to read a passage of scripture, and then come to the proper conclusion of what this prophet is saying" (Howell 1987a). Koresh justified his focus on the prophetic literature by asserting both that the biblical prophets all speak about the same thing and that "they were written for our time" (Howell 1987a). The prophets' message about God's final judgment reaches its ultimate expression in the New Testament book of Revelation. In Koresh's interpretation, it "contains all the books of the Bible. All the books of the Bible meet and end there" (Howell 1985a; see Koresh 1993c, 197). Koresh's task as a biblical interpreter was to unlock the secrets of Revelation by using the rest of the Bible as a commentary on it.

Koresh's fascination with biblical prophecy, the last days, and the book of Revelation places him squarely within the Adventist tradition and also within a broader American subculture that has long been fascinated with prophecy belief (O'Leary 1994, 93–133; Boyer 1992). What set him apart was Koresh's singular understanding of his role in the last days. Although Koresh could speak like an Adventist prophet, claiming, for example, that "the Bible truth is plain now that God [is] revealing it through his servant" (Howell 1987b), at other times he crossed the line from being a messenger to being the message himself. Koresh saw himself in the Bible, and the role he claimed was not a small one. For example, in a complex attempt to align kings of Israel with the seven angels of the book of Revelation and both of those groups with the leaders of the Adventists and Branch Davidians, Koresh identified himself as "Vernon Howell, the seventh angel's message" (Howell 1985a). The emphasis on "message" rather than "messenger" seems intentional, because he later exhorted his audience, saying, "Let's repeat this again so Branches you'll understand it. Now the seventh angel's message is speaking" (Howell 1985a).

Koresh's self-identification as the message of the seventh angel of Revelation included the proclamation that "the seventh angel is teaching this for the first time since the history of the world. No one has ever known this prophecy" (Howell 1985b). Indeed, Koresh claimed to have been commissioned directly by the Lord in a vision: "the Lord told me, 'You're going to intercede in behalf of the world'" (Howell 1985b). Koresh saw himself as a new Cyrus, who like the ancient Persian king hailed by Isaiah as God's anointed, would deliver God's people from the Babylonians (Isa. 45:1). Indeed, Vernon Howell's identification with the Cyrus of the Bible eventually led him to adopt the Hebrew form of the name, Koresh, as his surname. Along with the new first name, David, it gave him a doubly messianic identity. As he described his identity in compact form:

> The ones who believe the seventh seal believe in Cyrus to deliver them from captivity. The message of Cyrus, the angel that ascends from the east, that same person who is also compassed with iniquity and infirmity, that same person is going to be able to stand before Christ and explain to Christ why we are so bad the way we are. That's why in the message of Revelation 18:1, Babylon is fallen, is fallen. (Howell 1985b)

Koresh's urgent message was thus founded on the twin pillars of his interpretative insight into the Bible and his divine call. His role was not only to interpret and proclaim the biblical message about the last days but also to enact it. In his role as an anointed prophet or "Christ" for the last days, Koresh also anticipated his own death at the hands of an unbelieving world, but his emphasis was on the suffering he would experience and not on any suffering that he would inflict on others (Tabor and Gallagher 1995, 10).

Although Koresh did not envision universal acceptance of his message, he did expect those who glimpsed the truth to take certain steps.

During a 1987 Bible study, Koresh considered the lamentable necessity of his mission:

> VERNON: So we never needed Martin Luther. We never needed Martin Luther. We never needed John Knox. We never needed Wesley, Campbell, or Miller, or Ellen G. White because . . .
>
> MAN: Not if we were to study the Bible like we should.
>
> VERNON: Well then, maybe we need people to be risen up to make us study the Bible. Maybe that's what . . . maybe I'm a thorn in your flesh. Maybe I'm here to get you to start studying so you can all come together and say "Look what I found," we all harmonize, we speak the same thing. We know the same thing, same spirit, same baptism, one Lord. (Howell 1987c)

Koresh always remained firmly convinced that any individual's patient study of the Scriptures would bring that person to the same conclusions that he had reached. It would then become incumbent on one "to wait on the Lord and do nothing more and nothing less than what God requires of us though we don't feel like anything" (Howell 1985b). Hearkening to the message also involved adoption of a strict way of life[3] and an unwavering focus on the Lord. Koresh observed that "indifference sometimes has allowed many people to be lost. . . . Let's put the things of this world secondary now. Let's put them last. Let's make an effort to learn this truth no matter what cost. You have the evidence thus far given to you and all I can say is let's pick up the pieces and go forward in the power and the spirit of God's word" (Howell 1985b). Those who would receive Koresh's message in faith would become part of a select group. Koresh promised his audience that

> upon hearing these tapes and seeing this truth as written in the Bible you are being called to be part of a remnant of those who will uphold the Bible and the Bible only as the only rule of faith. Do you have faith that Joel was a true prophet? Do you have faith that John the Revelator saw that "in the days of the voice of the seventh angel the mystery of God should be finished as he declared to the proph-

---

3. Besides morning and evening Bible study sessions that could go on for many hours, life at Mount Carmel involved twice-daily communion services of bread and wine. Feeding the community, educating the children, and maintaining the property also took considerable time. After 1989 men and women lived in separate communal quarters.

ets? [Rev. 10:7]" If so, John states that in the prophecies is the mystery of God which will be finished in the last message to be given to the world, the seventh angel. (Howell 1987b)

The faithful remnant would be fortunate indeed because "the message of Cyrus reveals to us the executive judgment and it's better to have it revealed to us, than to have it actually happen to us" (Howell 1985b). Those who did not accept the message would be subject to what Joel and other prophets describe as the utter devastation of the day of the Lord (Howell 1987a; see Joel 2: 1–11; Zeph. 1:14–18; Amos 5:18–20: Mal. 4: 5–6).

Although the role that he saw for himself in the last days is highly unusual, Koresh's vision of the apocalypse, cobbled together out of scriptural bits and pieces and focused on the events described in the book of Revelation, shared much with the broad apocalyptic tradition of Western civilization. Like many other figures within that tradition, Koresh admonished his followers to wait, study, and prepare for God's judgment. Koresh's exhortations to his flock support Jeffrey Kaplan's observation that "watching is what millenarians do best" (Kaplan 1997a, 168). God is the primary actor in the events of the last days. Even though many of the texts on which Koresh focused, including Daniel 11 and Revelation, foresaw a climactic battle that attended the end of the world, Koresh pointedly dissuaded his followers from imagining that they would play an active role at Armageddon: "sometimes when you see yourself going to Israel what do you see yourself doing. [You're] over there like a soldier, huh? It's not that way at all. That's not how you will get the kingdom" (Howell 1987a).

As it is outlined in his Bible studies, Koresh's millennial theology focused on careful study of the Scriptures, acceptance of Koresh himself as God's anointed messenger, a sober rejection of worldly things, a dedicated striving to remain worthy of God's saving truth, and an anticipation of God's imminent judgment. Koresh had no doubt that the day of the Lord would hold terrible violence for those who have shunned the truth but that violence will be enacted by God alone.

On the basis of the Bible studies, the Branch Davidians appear to be a peaceful apocalyptic group. Living at some remove from the world and preoccupied with their own religious doctrines, they do not seem to have been likely candidates for outbursts of violence against the society in which they lived. In fact, there were few violent incidents during their sixty-year history in Texas (Tabor and Gallagher 1995, 33–51). Although it is true that there were many guns inside the Mount Carmel Center and that some Branch Davidians did fire at BATF agents on February 28, why they originally collected those weapons remains highly controversial. Prosecutors in the trial of the surviving Branch Davidians claimed that David Koresh preached "a theology of death" and that the attack on the BATF was premeditated (Tabor and Gallagher 1995, 113), and Rep. Charles Schumer (Democrat, New York) made similar charges while brandishing a rifle for the cameras during the 1995 congressional hearings (see Committee on the Judiciary 1996, 1: 11–14). But survivors paint a very different picture (Tabor and Gallagher 1995, 64–65). The discussions of violence in Koresh's Bible studies clearly support the position of the remaining Davidians. Those who wish to argue the contrary have yet to provide compelling evidence.

Amid the recurring pronouncements of apocalyptic judgment in Koresh's Bible studies, however, one session stands out for the vehemence expressed against specific individuals. Although he was conducting a typical class, Koresh also had in mind a group of defectors in Australia. Koresh remarked that he intended "to send this tape to Australia to remind those people [of] our foundation" (Howell 1989b). During his teaching, however, Koresh moved well beyond simple reminders. Noting that "we have a schism amongst us" (1989b), Koresh was driven to his most exaggerated claims of self-importance and his most pointed condemnations of those who have strayed from the truth. He depicted the split within his group as provoking a time of decision, even as he questioned the maturity of all of the Davidians' faith. Koresh declared that "I'm going to show you about a God that you haven't yet known. You've all been spoon fed, you've all been diaper padded. And now it's time for this cloak to be thrown off and you['re] going to go through the fires. You're going to see whether you believe this message. I'm ready to be delivered. I'm ready to go through the portals [of] darkness and you're not. Let's see if you believe the message after so many years" (Howell 1989b). Trying to make the consequences of apostasy as clear as possible, Koresh stated flatly that

> if you don't follow the truth you['re] going to hell! Psalms 90! You'd better start fearing God, 'cause he's going to burn you in the lowest hell! His love! He's trying to show you he's gonna kill you! If you don't listen! Listen to [the] Lord! You don't know his fear now. You don't know his terror yet! You haven't seen his anger. But

you go ahead and dare Him! . . . Do you hear?! Do you understand? It's war. These governments of this world are coming to an end. The minds of men are going to be focused on a fact! Go ahead and laugh! Go ahead and muse in your minds. And see what happens to you, fools! (1989b)

Koresh became so agitated during his jeremiad that he lapsed, like the prophets in the Hebrew Bible, into divine first-person address, proclaiming, "now go contrary to that revelation of truth, and I guarantee you I'll kill you one day" (1989b). That startling assertion needs to be read in tandem with Koresh's promise that "I'll prove who I am, by showing you who God is" (1989b).

Koresh's most violent language in his Bible studies was also his most personal. It suggests that his recourse to vehement condemnation of the Branch Davidian apostates was bound up with his sense of personal identity and his millennial mission. The schism within the group threatened not only the community's stability but also, at least in the heat of the moment, Koresh's identity. To leave the group is not simply to choose an alternative but to deny Koresh as a prophet and hence to deny God. As Stephen O'Leary has observed, "the story of the apocalyptic tradition is one of community building, in which human individuals and collectivities constitute their identities through shared mythic narratives" (O'Leary 1994, 6). The ultimacy of what was at stake in the defections led Koresh to employ the idiom of his beloved Hebrew prophets and to declare God's judgment. It was not persecution from the outside that called forth Koresh's most heated rhetoric, but betrayal from within the group. Koresh himself was at his most volatile when the Branch Davidian community was at its most fragile. The violence, however, remained solely rhetorical; it was targeted on the intimate enemies who had once been a part of the group and expressed in a controlled, ritual setting. As angry as David Koresh may have been with Marc Breault and the other defectors, the only weapons that he used against them were words. Thus, the anomaly of Koresh's violent verbal outburst during a Bible study gives little reason to suspect that he would move beyond rhetoric to an actual physical encounter with the apostates. Koresh's millennial theology, no matter how agitated he became, did not offer him a blueprint for that kind of action. Although Koresh could speak for God as his prophet, punishment of the wicked was still reserved for God alone.

## Negotiations and Communications
## February 28 to April 19, 1993

Throughout the prolonged and often tedious negotiations during the fifty-one-day siege presided over by the FBI at the Mount Carmel Center, Koresh never wavered in his desire to engage the negotiators in Bible study that would lead them to the truth. Besides those daily conversations, Koresh audiotaped a major statement of his beliefs that was broadcast on the radio on March 2. Later in the siege he sent out several letters and in the final days he was working hard on his written interpretation of the Seven Seals. Koresh's statements during the first and last weeks of the siege give a good indication of his thinking throughout the fifty-one days.

Despite the physical and psychological trauma that he suffered,[4] Koresh did not deviate from the central message that he had been preaching for the previous eight years. On March 4 Koresh gave a succinct account of his mission to negotiator Henry Garcia, claiming, "I'm supposed to teach this stuff so it don't happen. Prophecies, prophecies are given so that they can be avoided and instead a blessing can be given" (tape #47, Mar. 4). Yet, Koresh did not expect his message to win universal approval. On March 2 he told Garcia that "there's a test in latter days. And it's a test of human intelligence. And all that which is human is not going to use its intelligence" (tape #13, Mar. 2). In his conversations with Garcia, Koresh again invoked the principle of scriptural harmony as a proof of the truth of his message:

> DAVID: So today we, we have a truth, a Bible truth. But it's not going to overthrow just the papacy.
> HENRY: Um-hum.
> DAVID: It's going to, you know, bring all the world into a valley of decision. People are going to have to hear it. They're

4. Koresh suffered wounds to his right wrist, severing a nerve near his thumb, and the lower left side of his torso during the February 28 BATF raid. The second wound left him unable to walk for several days. In addition, the negotiators promised him appropriate medical care only if he would come out of Mount Carmel; his refusal and their intransigence only further delayed his recovery. Constant pressure from the FBI tactical forces, including the broadcasting of earsplitting music, sounds of rabbits being slaughtered, and other psychological tactics kept Koresh and everyone else within Mount Carmel from getting adequate sleep. Nutritional and sanitary conditions consistently declined during the fifty-one-day siege.

going to have to say to themselves well, you know, that's right. That is right. That is exactly what is being said in harmony. And that, that does agree. (tape #13, Mar. 2; see tape #27, Mar. 3; tape #43, Mar. 4).

The test, as Koresh so often proclaimed, would have extremely consequential results. Koresh told BATF negotiator Jim Kavanaugh on March 3 that "If we are not with the God that's foretold th[ese] things, then we're the ones who end up being destroyed" (tape #27, Mar. 3). In sum, as Koresh told Kavanaugh that same day, "It's a message of life and death" (tape #28, Mar. 3). Throughout the difficult first week of negotiations Koresh's apocalyptic message did not differ substantially from what he had been preaching since 1985. Nor did the BATF assault on the Mount Carmel Center change his mind about the exercise of violence. Although Koresh repeatedly mentioned that he feared an attempt by the BATF or other government forces to finish off the surviving Branch Davidians (see tapes #8, #9, #10A, #10B, Mar. 1; #11A, #11B, Mar. 2; #26, #27, #33, Mar. 3), he consistently rejected the option of using violence against his attackers and completely repudiated the notion that he was considering suicide (see tapes #9, #10B, Mar. 1; #13, Mar. 2; #31, Mar. 3; #36, #37, #38, #41, Mar. 4).

Koresh's March 2 radio address returned to similar themes. He reasserted to his listeners that "the importance of the seals is that if you do not listen, you are going to end up making the worst mistake you've ever made in all your lives" (Koresh 1993a). Despite his immediate circumstances Koresh remained hopeful, observing that "the Psalms are not written because Christ is desiring to destroy mankind. On the contrary. The warnings of Psalms 1, in the light of the Judgment, is so that men might fear, and receive redemption" (Koresh 1993a). One distinctive feature of the March 2 speech is that, probably in response to his recent experience, Koresh depicted the violence suffered by Jesus during his lifetime as paradigmatic for the fate of any prophet. Koresh observed that "It's kind of like people always like to build the sepulchers of the dead prophets, and garnish their tombs, but yet they hate and kill living prophets. Only God knows why that is. But nonetheless . . ." (1993a). As God's living prophet in the last days, Koresh clearly anticipated a similar fate for himself.

Throughout the week after the BATF's botched raid, there was only one instance when Koresh expressed a willingness to engage in physical violence. In a March 1 discussion with negotiator Jim Kavanaugh,

Koresh responded testily to the government forces' steady advance on his property.

> DAVID: I said come on, Jim. The perimeter is our property line, okay? We want these guys off our property line.
> JIM: Okay. Well, I'm, you know, I'm going to see what I can do. I can't —
> DAVID: If they want to fight, we'll fight.
> JIM: I can't make that promise, David.
> DAVID: Okay, they, they want to kill us, they've got the big guns now. (tape #8, Mar. 1)

Koresh's comments, made in the immediate aftermath of the previous day's BATF assault and the escalating pressure from the government troops, portray physical violence as a conditionally justified form of self-defense. Only after being assured by the negotiator that a government attack was not imminent did Koresh return to his familiar millennial frame of reference. Concerning his willingness to have young children leave the Mount Carmel Center, Koresh observed that "if that don't mean anything to you or these hotheads, then we'll have to deal with that later in the judgment, won't we?" (tape #8, Mar. 1). Koresh's promise to fight back in self-defense, however, remained only an unfulfilled threat. Also, in his mind his present difficulties were much less consequential than the imminent judgment.

The negotiations that unfolded over the final days before April 19 reveal a similar picture. Frustrated with the negotiators' lack of interest in his teachings and having received divine permission to document his teachings in writing for the first time, Koresh receded into the background. Steve Schneider then took over most of the discussions with the negotiators. On April 9 Schneider reemphasized how central the Scriptures were to Koresh's self-conception, affirming that Koresh would not honor the negotiators' desire that he focus on concrete plans for leaving Mount Carmel and refrain from discussing the Bible. Schneider asserted that "unless he can bring in what he is, and that's the Bible, [then he won't speak]. I mean he'll talk about that [leaving], but always in relation to the Bible so you can understand where and why" (tape #201, Apr. 9). Like Koresh, Schneider was convinced that the last days were at hand. On April 18, Schneider testified: "I believe what all the prophets had to say about this earth and it's, it's filled up its cup already. Judgments are impending soon. No, no question about it" (tape #242, Apr.

18). Later in the same conversation, when asked whether he sees a "good ending," Schneider replied, "oh, yeah, positively, but not for everybody, just as in the days of Noah, you know, not for everybody. Most people—those that want this life, that's all they're going to have. . . . That's what all the Bible writers have to say" (tape #242, Apr. 18). Schneider also tried to make it as clear as possible that the Branch Davidians had never considered violence a means to their goals. On April 18 he reassured the negotiator that "there never have been plans ever to ever harm or to go after anybody in this world, never. . . . Even though we've got a foe that is an avowed foe, that's Marc Breault who's now living in Australia" (tape #243, Apr. 18). Schneider's comments support the notion that Koresh was announcing God's judgment in the 1989 Bible study when he threatened to kill the Australian defectors.

Similarly, Koresh made no threats of violence in an April 14 letter to his attorney, Dick DeGuerin, in which he promised to come out of Mount Carmel as soon as he finished his manuscript on the Seven Seals. Koresh again anticipated a fate that has been suffered by other prophets before him, observing that "as soon as I am given over into the hands of man, I will be made a spectacle of" (Koresh 1993b). In that letter Koresh also reported a vision in which he "was shown a fault line running throughout the Lake Waco Area. An angel is standing in charge of this event" (1993b). Koresh understood the imminent earthquake as a part of the apocalyptic warnings that might yet get people to harken to the truth. He expressed the hope that "it will probably be 'the thing' needed to shake some sense into the people" (1993b).

Despite the meager results of his decade of missionary activity, the shattering effect of the defections and active opposition of Marc Breault and other former members, the gruesome deaths of six Branch Davidians during the February 28 raid, and the constant pressure from government troops for more than six weeks, Koresh remained buoyantly optimistic about the impact of his message of the Seven Seals. He wrote to DeGuerin that

> I want the people of this generation to be saved. I am working night and day to complete my final work of the writing out of "these Seals." I thank my Father; He has finally granted me the chance to do this. It will bring New Light and hope for many and they will not have to deal with me the person. . . . We are standing on the threshold of Great events! The Seven Seals, in written form are the most sacred information ever! (Koresh 1993b)

Except for the recently granted permission from his heavenly Father to commit his teaching to writing, Koresh's message in the April 14 letter hardly differs from what he had been preaching since 1985. Divinely authored apocalyptic violence stands in the very near future, as does a violent worldly reaction to God's chosen messenger, but there is no hint that Koresh saw himself as anything but a spectator at the battle of Armageddon.

That impression is confirmed by the opening passage of Koresh's abbreviated manuscript on the Seven Seals. After a poetic preface that speaks, among other things, of "the pending judgment of the King," Koresh begins his exposition with a quotation from the gospel according to John 18:33–38, in which Jesus proclaims that "my kingdom is not of this world; if my kingdom were of the world, then would my servants fight" (Koresh 1993c, 192). Given the extraordinary importance that Koresh attributed to his manuscript, there can be no clearer indication of his repudiation of violence in connection with his millennial theology. Because God's kingdom is not of this world,[5] Koresh indicates, God's servants will not fight. Indeed, they had not fought, except for what they understood as justified self-defense, during the entire siege at Mount Carmel. They surely anticipated violence in the last days, but it would be visited upon the wicked by God himself. Their role was to proclaim the message of the Seven Seals, search for its certification in the Scriptures, undertake a regimen of study and self-discipline, and hope that they would be found worthy. David Koresh and the Branch Davidians never saw themselves as agents of God's wrath in this world.

## Conclusions

One of the reasons that the BATF gave for the initial raid on the Mount Carmel Center was the fear that a group with a stockpile of weapons would turn to violence (see Tabor and Gallagher 1995, 100–3). The Branch Davidians themselves, however, vigorously disputed that contention, and the survivors of the fire still dispute it. Despite the indelible images of the February 28 gun battle at the Mount Carmel

5. *Why Waco?* emphasizes that Koresh expected his biological children, like the elders in Revelation 4, to rule in the Kingdom of God on earth (Tabor and Gallagher 1995, 75). I have emphasized in this chapter that Koresh was anticipating a "heavenly" kingdom. In either case, there would be total transformation of the status quo; the Kingdom of God, whatever its location, is a heavenly kingdom in the sense that this world will be so thoroughly transcended as to be a new creation.

Center and the April 19 inferno that consumed the residence and nearly all of its inhabitants, David Koresh's theology, which expressed both his self-understanding and the understanding of the Branch Davidians as a group, is remarkable for the absence of threatened violent reprisals against specific enemies or exhortations to take up arms in support of God's cause.[6] Koresh taught that all human beings would soon stand before God's judgment, and he feared that very few would take advantage of the truth that God had commissioned him to preach. But Koresh never assigned to himself or his followers an active role in divine judgment or the violence that accompanied it.[7] Immediate, targeted violence by Koresh or other members of the community was repeatedly repudiated, save for a few brief mentions of self-defense on the days immediately after the February 28 attack by the BATF. Far more often Koresh and the Branch Davidians portray themselves as being subject to either the violent hostility of an unbelieving world or the terrible eschatological violence that will result from God's wrathful judgment.

Unfortunately for all, the government strategy of "tightening the noose" around the Mount Carmel Center may have had the unintended consequence of increasing the potential for violence on both sides. For the government forces, each act of physical or psychological violence, including establishing the perimeter blockade, preventing the Davidians from communicating with the outside world, assaulting the Davidians' aural and visual senses, and destroying their property with tanks, made it easier for other acts of violence to occur. On the inside of Mount Carmel, as the negotiation tapes clearly show, the government troops' actions reinforced the Davidians' perception that the BATF had meant to kill them all on February 28 and that the FBI might well decide to finish the job. Koresh and the Davidians had certainly not anticipated anything like the siege at Mount Carmel, and it continued

---

6. I am aware that both Koresh's sanctioning of corporal punishment of small children and his sexual relations with young girls could be considered instances of violence. Those issues, while worth pursuing, lie outside of my focus on specifically millennial violence.

7. In *Why Waco?* James Tabor and I wrote that Koresh expected the events of the endtime to take place in Israel and that he expected that "the Davidians would stand with the Israelis" in a battle against American-led United Nations forces (1995, 76). It is clear that the siege of the Mount Carmel Center precipitated a rethinking of that apocalyptic scenario. The Davidians clearly thought that they would always "stand with" the forces of good, but I do not see evidence that they envisioned acting on behalf of God and those forces to bring about the final judgment.

to perplex them throughout its duration. But, aside from what they saw as self-defense on February 28, their response was not to lash out violently at their immediate enemies. It was, to the deepening frustration of all the negotiators, to try to draw their persecutors to the truth through exhortation, proclamation, and study of the Bible. The Davidians reacted to persecution by peacefully intensifying their efforts at evangelization. In fact, their reaction to the initial attack by the BATF and the progressively escalating pressure by the FBI-led tactical forces contrasts strikingly to their reaction to the schism that resulted within the group after Koresh articulated his "New Light" revelation in the summer of 1989.[8] The defection of several Davidians and especially the efforts of a group led by Marc Breault to unmask Koresh as a false prophet called forth the most violent condemnation ever spoken by Koresh. Schism proved to be much more deeply troubling than persecution; external opposition confirmed the group's understanding of itself as a persecuted elect while internal dissension threatened that understanding to its core.

Despite the conviction that he needed to bring the message of the Seven Seals to the entire world, Koresh always knew that he was gathering an elite group for salvation. Accordingly, Koresh's missionary efforts were almost exclusively devoted to members of the worldwide Adventist community. As part of the endtime scenario, he expected the disinterest, scorn, and direct opposition of most of the world. But betrayal by those who had salvation within their grasp severely challenged Koresh's understanding of himself, his message, and his community.

The role of the apostate Branch Davidians in eliciting David Koresh's most violent rhetoric shows clearly how internal and external factors influencing the turn to violence blend into each other (see Robbins and Anthony 1995; Anthony and Robbins 1997). The schismatics who provoked Koresh's apocalyptic fury were threatening to him precisely because they had crossed the boundary between the inside and the outside of the group. They directed their criticism back at Koresh not as perplexed or horrified outsiders but as former intimates who still considered themselves students of the Seven Seals but who no longer accepted

8. This "New Light" revelation was that married couples should live separately and cease sexual relations, and that all women at Mount Carmel Center became Koresh's wives with whom he could have sexual relations to produce children to be leaders in God's kingdom (Tabor and Gallagher 1995, 68, 81, 86).

Koresh as their prophet. The knowing opposition of the Branch Davidian apostates was far more problematic for Koresh because he believed they had once grasped the message of the Seven Seals. Defection of believers struck directly at the value of the Bible studies he had been conducting for so many years, the stability of the group, and Koresh's identity as a prophet. Thus, defection, which turns internal factors into external ones, seems to be particularly important in calling forth violent reaction (see Robbins and Palmer 1997b; Coser 1956).

Thomas Robbins and Dick Anthony identify "the intrinsic instability of charismatic leadership" as another factor that may promote violence by marginal religious and social groups (Anthony and Robbins 1997, 262). In Koresh's case, however, that instability was counterbalanced by the fixed nature of the biblical text. Time and again during the negotiations Koresh deflected the negotiators' attempts simply to take his word on the truth of his message. Aware both of the broad social controversy about "cults" and of the way that he had been portrayed in the "Sinful Messiah" series in the *Waco Tribune-Herald* (see tapes #7, #9, #10A, Mar. 1; #11B, #22, Mar. 2; #24, #26, #27, #28, Mar. 3; #36, #40, #47, Mar. 4), Koresh insisted that the negotiators embark on the same arduous program of scriptural study in which the Branch Davidians had been involved. The Scriptures provided both a context for and constraints on the construction of Koresh's charisma. If the Scriptures foresaw no active role for the faithful in executing God's final judgment, then Koresh could not overrule the Scriptures.

Finally, it is likely that Koresh and his followers had a sober appreciation of their difficult situation. As Jeffrey Kaplan remarks, the "self-perception as a tiny and powerless band of the faithful acts as a powerful check on the catalyzation of violence. Millenarians are no fools. They are canny judges of the prevailing balance of forces" (Kaplan 1997a, 171). After February 28, any Branch Davidian attack on the government forces would truly have been suicidal.

Koresh's millennial theology was certainly a matter of life and death for him and the Mount Carmel community. But it did not sanction violent acts committed by the Branch Davidians. Koresh's apocalyptic message was so consistently articulated, in such a diversity of contexts, that external factors, most notably the February 28 BATF raid and the subsequent relentless pressure exerted by government forces, offer the most compelling explanation of the violence that claimed so many lives at Mount Carmel. Unwittingly, the government agents played a role in the Branch Davidian's apocalyptic scenario that the opponents of the prophets had always played and were expected to play again at the end. Steve Schneider wondered on April 18, "now, if you look at the prophecies, it talks about a place in the last days that's plowed like a field. Do you think, perchance, that it could be this place. . . . It seems like it's being fulfilled. I would never have dreamed—" (tape #242, Apr. 18). On April 19 the Branch Davidians' dream of millennial perfection turned into a nightmarish conflagration that neither side wanted.

# 4

# Shooting Dreads on Sight

## Violence, Persecution, Millennialism, and Dominica's Dread Act

RICHARD C. SALTER

Most people think,
Great God will come from the Sky,
Take away everything,
And make everyone feel high,
But if you know what life is worth,
You will look for yours on Earth,
So now you see the light,
Get up, stand up for your Rights—Jah.

> —Bob Marley and Peter Tosh,
> "Get Up Stand Up" (1973)

Woman hold her head and cry . . .
Now she knows that the wages of sin is death,
Gift of Jah is life,
She cried . . .
Cause her son had been shot down in the street
and died,
Just because of the system

> —Bob Marley,
> "Johnny Was" (1976)

How long shall they kill our prophets,
While we stand aside and look,
Some say it's just a part of it,
We've got to fulfill the Book.

> —Bob Marley,
> "Redemption Song" (1980)

## Introduction

In 1974 the government of Dominica[1] passed *The Prohibited and Unlawful Societies and Associations Act*, also known as "The Dread Act." Dreadlocks,[2] a central symbol of Rastafarianism, were prohibited, and Rastas who had them could be "shot on sight" by the police as members of an unlawful society.

According to the way the act was usually read, *anyone* with dreadlocks could be considered a member of an unlawful society, "the Dreads," and could be prosecuted (Section 4). Any Dread could be arrested at any time without a warrant (Section 5). Once arrested Dreads were not entitled to bail (Section 6.1) and could be held without charge up to forty-eight hours before seeing a magistrate (Section 6.2). Even then provision was for a summary trial with no right of appeal. Police could enter any place not used as a dwelling and search for Dreads without a warrant (Section 10.2), and were immune from prosecution for any duties or activities under the provisions of the act (Section 10.3), thus eliminating police accountability. Moreover, Section 9 stated: "No proceedings either criminal or civil shall be brought or maintained against any person who kills or injures any member of an association or society designated unlawful, who shall be found any time of day or night inside a dwelling house." This section became infamous for making it legal to shoot Dreads on sight.

The Dread Act was not hyperbole. All sections were acted upon at one time or another, even the most draconian. For example, on at least one occasion, *The New Chronicle,* Dominica's leading newspaper, reported the discovery of an anonymous dreadlocked corpse, bullet hole in skull, decaying in the bush (December 5, 1981). Virtually all Rastas who lived through the time of the Dread Act give accounts of themselves or others being shot at in the bush (i.e., in the forest), beaten up by the

---

1. The ethnographic information in this chapter was collected during field research in Dominica from January to August 1994. Dominica is a small island in the eastern Caribbean (population about eighty thousand; about three hundred square miles). It gained full political independence from Great Britain in 1978. Since 1967 Dominica was a State in Association with Britain, but before 1967 Dominica was a colony in various forms of Great Britain, and in the nineteenth century of France. French influence has been decisive, leaving the island with a French-based Kweyol language and a very strong Roman Catholic influence.

2. Dreadlocks refers to hair that is not combed or cut, and thereby turns into long tangled strands.

police while in custody, having their hair forcibly cut or yanked out, and otherwise being persecuted. The evidence for this type of violence is anecdotal, but is reported by many Rastafarians and by others. As Gabriel Christian (1992) describes it, "It is commonly thought that many more dreads were slain in the woods, their deaths left unannounced" (32). Christian goes so far as to call the conflict between government forces and Dreads "a small, undeclared, and semi-secret war" (29).

What effect did the Dread Act persecution have on the Dominican Rastafarian movement? How did it affect Rastafarian ideology? One effect was to split the movement into factions with very different orientations toward the expected millennial kingdom. In short, the persecution forced some Rastas deeper into isolation in the bush, where they tried to live out their millennial vision of equality and natural purity. The Dread Act brought other Rastas back into Roseau, Dominica's capital, where they waited for a millennial kingdom that would be brought by Haile Selassie or "Jah" (God). This chapter explores those differences in detail, focusing especially on why class origins might have such a dramatic effect on how the millennial kingdom is conceived. I will argue that low-class Rastas were more heavily persecuted in Dominica, and this persecution had the effect of driving low-class Rastas into the forest, where they began to live out their millennial vision. Ironically, upper-class Rastas, who were most tolerated, were able to return to Roseau sooner, and ultimately accommodated much more peacefully to Dominican society. In this sense, then, persecution exaggerated the Rasta flight and alienation from the world, but the development of toleration allowed Rastas to create a niche for themselves within Dominican society, where they could await the millennial kingdom peacefully.

## Millennialism in Rastafarian Ideology

Rastafarianism is a fast-growing religious movement that began about seventy years ago in Jamaica. At its start, it was an outgrowth and development of already existing neo-African religions, and it was especially attractive to displaced young male Jamaicans who were migrating from rural to urban areas (Chevannes 1994). It has since spread far beyond Jamaica, and currently there are significant numbers of Rastafarians in North America, South America, Africa, Europe, and Oceania. Though it originally spread through West Indian out-migration, more recently it has spread through the popularity of reggae, a Jamaican pop musical style that was heavily influenced by Rastafarians (e.g., Bob Marley and the Wailers) and the attractive ideological message presented in reggae, especially its emphasis on the integrity of the self, or the "I," and its condemnation of oppression.

Like other world religions, Rastafarianism in general cannot be designated millennial, because it differs significantly from place to place and is only truly millennial in specific communities. What can be said about Rastafarianism is that at its start it had a decidedly millennial orientation. The movement received an ideological impetus from Marcus Garvey's cryptic message in 1916 to "Look to Africa for the crowning of a Black King, he shall be the Redeemer" (Barrett 1988, 67). When Haile Selassie was crowned emperor of Ethiopia, an as yet uncolonized African nation, unbeknownst to him he became this messianic figure. Rastafarians believed that in the near future Haile Selassie would send ships to Jamaica to repatriate Rastafarians from the African Diaspora back to Africa. There they would lead a life of equality in harmony with other people and with the natural world.[3] Rastafarians also widely believed that they ought to avoid the dead, that those who lived a pure and good life would not die, and that a pure life involved various food proscriptions (e.g., not eating pork, or not eating "flesh" at all), and menstrual taboos for women. The movement also promoted a general male superiority, especially in its earlier stages.

As the Rastafarian movement developed distinctive styles such as dreadlocked hair, and practices such as the extensive use of marijuana (ritually, recreationally, and medicinally), they continued to be marginalized from Jamaican mainstream society, whose norms they rejected and to which they appeared dirty and unrespectable. When some Rastafarian groups were linked with nationalist political groups, they were further persecuted by the police, and retreated to a more isolated existence often in Rasta communes.

In 1966 Haile Selassie paid a state visit to Jamaica, and to his surprise, throngs of Rastas greeted him at the airport expecting that it was the time when they would be repatriated. Because of this incident, and because of increased academic attention paid to Rastafarianism, the movement gained widespread attention in Jamaica. When the Jamaican reggae singer Bob Marley became popular and the movement spread from the lower classes to the middle and upper classes in Jamaica, the movement gained more respectability and began to have a more broad-based membership. Since Selassie's death after a communist takeover of

3. They would lead an "Ital" (i.e., vital) life, in harmony with all living things.

Ethiopia in 1975, some Rastafarians have given up the belief in Selassie's divinity. The eschatological belief in repatriation also appears to have become less prevalent with increasing attention paid to liberation at home.

At the same time, it is important to remember that the millennial expectations of diverse Rastafarian groups remain quite different. While some Rastafarian groups are quietist, patiently awaiting the fulfillment of Scripture (the Bible) and the time to come when they will have power, sometimes even secluding themselves from the world until this happens, other Rastafarian groups are more active in their pursuit of the millennial condition. Using Wessinger's terminology (1997a), we might say that those who await the fulfillment of Scripture are catastrophic millennialists, believing that the millennial kingdom will come after Selassie's wrath has destroyed a corrupt world so that Rastas will be elevated to rule. Those who consider themselves to have a more active role in bringing about the millennial kingdom might be considered progressive millennialists, for they believe that they participate in creating the millennial kingdom.

In the Dominican Rastafarian movement, there have been both catastrophic millennialists and progressive millennialists. A decisive factor in leading Rastafarians in one direction or the other is the interplay between the social composition of the specific Rastafarian group and persecution. In Dominica, the persecution promoted by the Dread Act exacerbated preexisting social differences between Rastafarians. The different social segments in the Dominican Rasta movement then often have affinities for different ideological orientations toward the millennial kingdom. At present, catastrophic millennialism has become dominant in the Dominican Rastafarian movement, because despite its predictions of cataclysm, it constitutes less of a real threat to the established order and is therefore less persecuted.

### Dominican Rastafarians: Social Composition

In contrast to the lower-class origins of Rastafarianism in Jamaica, Rastafarianism came to Dominica in the early 1970s by way of upper-class Dominican students who were studying abroad and were involved in the Black Power movement. For these students, Rastafarianism was not so much a break with the Dominican past, but a continuation of events that had already been set in motion. The Dominican Black Power movement, which was influenced by the Black Power movement in the

United States and in other parts of the Caribbean (e.g., Trinidad), had pointed out the inequalities of Dominican society. Moreover, since the 1960s, the Labor Government of E. O. Leblanc had emphasized education and local culture, so more young people than ever were going to university with a sense of local pride (H. Christian 1992, 36–37). But the economic situation of the island was tenuous and jobs were scarce. Educated young men returned to the island aware of social inequalities, ready to redress them, but also were unemployed. In a classic case of what Merton (1968) calls "relative deprivation," these youth felt deprived of what they had come to expect by virtue of their social position, but also were aware of the inequalities upon which Dominican society was built. Although these students had gotten educations, gone to university, and done all that their social position required of them, the system had failed them, and they lost the status usually accorded them. As Gabriel Christian (1992) has written, these Rastafarians "felt a need to go beyond what some considered mere mouthings of black nationalist jargon. A need was felt to go back to the land, to nature, to create an entirely new and pure social and economic alternative to Babylon [the secular world]" (30).

Rastafarianism addressed this problem by reversing social status and valuing African roots, local traditions, and agricultural production. Rastafarianism was a way for these youth to value and honor themselves outside the status system from which they felt cut off. It also allowed these students to condemn the inequalities of the system, but without necessarily requiring them to participate in the system to change it.

It was natural that groups of young unemployed men would congregate. When they did, Rastafarian ideas filtered down to mainstream Dominican youth. Thus, while the Jamaican Rasta movement began with the lower class and rose through the social ranks, the Dominican Rasta movement expanded in the other direction. In Dominica, the Rastafarian movement developed from an idiosyncracy of rich youth to a widespread male youth movement. In making this transition, Rastafarianism bridged the gap between classes and different status groups in the youth segment. Despite different positions in Dominican society, alienation in general brought young men together in the Rastafarian movement.

When the lower classes got involved with Rastafarianism, the movement became more frightening to Dominicans at large. After all, it was one thing when the children of the elites joined a fad, but it became dangerous when ordinary youth questioned class and status boundaries, dressed differently, and flaunted their parents' norms. The Rastafarians used drugs, did not comb their hair, despised priests and the Catholic Church; they denounced the mulatto elite (of which some upper-class Rastas were a part) and the legacies of slavery on the island; they denounced the concept of private property and flirted with the socialist ideologies of Cuba and Grenada. Ultimately, they denounced the racial roots of Dominica's ruling class and decried the Catholic Church's complicity in the social structure as being part of white, foreign imperialism. Under this type of ideological assault on the social status quo, the scope and severity of the Dread Act becomes more understandable.

Generally speaking, Rastafarian responses to the act reflected the different social positions Rastas came from and the corresponding different forms of power they could mobilize. As the act took effect, Rastas split into identifiable factions. Two groups were especially important and can serve as ideal types in the movement: Nonm Tè and Nonm GCE.

### Tè Ferme: Refracting the Movement

In 1977 the prime minister of Dominica, Patrick John, donated land for a Rasta commune in an area called Tè Ferme (hard earth). Tè Ferme was supposed to be open to everyone, and the shape it took reflected the movement as a whole.

From the start Tè Ferme reflected, instead of eliminated, class and status differences. The donation of the land reputedly was made possible because of the influence of a particular Rasta's father, an upper-echelon civil servant who wanted a safe place for his son while the Dread Act was in force. Other Rastas responsible for organizing Tè Ferme also had parents involved in the Civil Service.

Although Tè Ferme was open to everyone, it soon became apparent that the division of labor at the commune was unequal. It divided along class and status lines[4] and these were reflected in the names given to the factions: Nonm Tè and Nonm GCE. Nonm Tè ("men of the earth") had not gone to secondary school, but they possessed valuable knowledge of farming and peasant traditions. In general, they were accorded little or no honor in Dominica at large, but within the Rastafarian

---

4. It also divided along sex lines. I do not have space here to analyze the sex division of Rastas, except to say that, in general, Rastafarian gender roles conform to the ideal norms of the British and West Indian middle classes.

movement, their knowledge and background was valued. Nonm GCE referred to men who had the secondary school qualification, the GCE. They tended to be from high-standing families, and, consequently, held a higher status in general society than the Nonm Tè.

As time went on, Nonm Tè adopted the label as a badge of honor. Although Nonm Tè provide the agricultural knowledge and physical labor to get Tè Ferme off the ground, it was implied by my informants that Nonm GCE spent most of their time just smoking "ganja" (marijuana) and "reasoning."[5] Resentment began to build and fueled ideological changes by Nonm Tè, whose class and educational backgrounds presented them with choices of lifestyle that were completely different from those faced by the Nonm GCE. Nonm Tè and Nonm GCE shared many things, including a general alienation from Dominican society, symbols, practices, and elements of a worldview; but the two groups occupied completely different places in society, so the specifics of their alienation from society were different, and they had access to different types of power both within and outside the movement.[6]

In the first place, the two groups knew different sorts of people. Nonm GCE used their contacts to get the land at Tè Ferme, but they also were protected from the Dread Act because of their contacts, a protection the Nonm Tè did not have. Nonm GCE social contact enabled them to access newspapers, to move more freely in villages and towns, and even to speak on state-run radio. Nonm GCE were able to air their views and explain them, and therefore they were less mysterious. They also articulated their beliefs in ways that were less threatening to the status quo, engaged in dialogue with representatives of mainstream society (for example in radio debates with priests), and presented Rasta ideology more as religion than as radical politics or social critique. As "religion" Rastafarianism could be accommodated in Dominican society as a personal preference. These Rastas were also given respect and honor for their formal asceticism, for in the context of "religion" these practices denoted "seriousness" rather than extremism.

The ability to present Rastafarianism as a religion also involved other types of power that only Nonm GCE could fully mobilize. Edu-

---

5. "Reasoning" is a central Rastafarian ritual. At its most basic it means talking, thinking, and sharing ideas about the world. It is usually done while smoking marijuana.

6. The description of the types of power the two groups had is borrowed from Pierre Bourdieu's (1990) analysis of four types of capital: social, symbolic, cultural, and economic. The typology usefully connects social position to types of practice, but the jargon is too heavy for what are presented here as commonsense divisions.

cational qualifications, for example, were a form of power that Nonm GCE could translate into money through high-quality jobs (when available). Nonm GCE also could translate their educational qualifications into social contacts through friends made at school. The GCE further conferred educational qualifications on Nonm GCE, which qualified them to speak as experts in public contexts. Not only was the degree itself recognized but the content of the education itself granted access to power. For example, literacy and grammatically correct English is mandatory for media success. The literacy of Nonm GCE both reflected and contributed to their religious status.

Nonm GCE continued to be better regarded as the movement came to be considered a "religion" rather than a "style." In 1979, shortly after publishing his book on Rastafarianism, Joseph Owens visited Dominica for a few weeks. Several Nonm GCE suggested that it was important for him to speak, because he had published a book on Rastafarians, he was a Roman Catholic priest, and the seriousness with which he took Rastafarianism demonstrated the seriousness and religious nature of the movement. Several Nonm Tè disapproved of Owens for the same reasons. He did speak in Roseau to a full hall, but only Nonm GCE and Rastas *pwe kay* (Rastas who stayed close to home) were able to attend, because police persecution was too brutal for Nomn Tè to risk coming openly into the city. The Nonm GCE were able to capitalize on Owens's visit, his book, and his status as a scholar/priest to portray Rastafarianism as a legitimate religion and themselves as the true adherents of that religion.

Both Nonm Tè and Nonm GCE were competent in culturally important practices and knowledge, but the Nonm GCE competency was an upper-class/elite status competency. They knew, even if unconsciously, what was needed to be taken seriously, and one sees this in their election of officers and formal organization. The organizational principles favored by the Nonm GCE dovetailed with the hierarchical principles of West Indian respectability and elite status, and mirrored the structure of the Civil Service. Taken together this promoted Rastafarianism as a legitimate "private" religion.

Perhaps most importantly, Nonm GCE also had money or access to money. Their families were wealthy and able to sustain them with groceries when the bush life was not producing food, and their contacts and educations translated into jobs and opportunities when they returned from the bush. These opportunities facilitated the reabsorption of Nonm GCE into the mainstream once Rastas were acceptable to a portion of the Dominican general public.

The situation of the Nonm Tè was entirely different. Not only did they lack the money the Nonm GCE had but the power they had was valued differently inside and outside the movement. Nonm Tè knew the practical competencies for living in the bush; this knowledge was useful for them when persecuted, but did nothing for their public status. When the Dread Act was passed the only social contacts Nonm Tè had were their peasant contacts, which they used to help build Tè Ferme, including arranging for Koudleman ("lend a hand") sessions in which work was donated from surrounding peasants to get large projects accomplished. Because they had no one to protect then, it was easier to persecute Nonm Tè, and some legislation seemed specifically directed at them.[7] They also did not have access to newspaper or radio, except through their Nonm GCE cohorts, so their story was not told. They were frequently looked down upon and labeled either "country bookies" (i.e., bumpkins) or "criminals."

Nonm Tè lacked most school education and the benefits that brought. They were schooled, in the main, by experience in peasant agriculture, a socially despised occupation. At Tè Ferme, agricultural skills were important, so Nonm Tè were indispensable. But it was only within the movement that agricultural skills were honored and translatable to status. Outside the movement they were denigrated. This status gap further alienated Nonm Tè from general society. Because the state did not recognize the competence of the Nonm Tè, and the recognition the state did give (in the form of the GCE) had nothing to do with practical knowledge, the Nonm Tè repudiated and mocked the state. The GCE was rejected as worthless, and the Nonm GCE were ridiculed behind their backs for their lack of skills.

Nonm Tè origins made them natural masters of peasant traditions. Many Rastas, both Nonm Tè and Nonm GCE, spoke *patois* in the bush, but it was the first language of many Nonm Tè, and frequently their English was spoken with the cadence and structure of *patios*—an immediate clue to class and status and a detriment outside the movement. But again, within Rasta circles, Nonm Tè commanded the indigenous language, which was valued. Peasant knowledge of agriculture to some extent could be translated into money, for example, with the knowledge of how to make charcoal from the trees that were cleared from the Tè Ferme land. Not least among the crops grown was marijuana. Again,

7. Honychurch (1995, 250) reports legislation that restricted the wearing of grass skirts and other fibrous material—something specifically done by Nonm Tè.

even if marijuana cultivation was honored within the movement, it left Rastas dishonored in the eyes of the wider community and legitimated police raids.

The Nonm GCE and the Nonm Tè were from different class and status orders, and they at first had coexisted peacefully through a shared inversion of typical Dominican notions of status. But under the persecution of the Dread Act, these shared notions of status were not able to hold Rastafarians together as one group. The Dread Act radicalized the ideology of the Nonm Tè, while the Nonm GCE continued to establish themselves in the eyes of the public as a nonthreatening and legitimate religion.

Interestingly, most violence against the government security forces was not committed by the Nonm Tè, whose more radical beliefs made them all the more anxious to escape from "Babylon." The most notorious acts of Rastafarian violence were committed by small groups led by relatively upper-class Rastas who fit into neither of these ideal types. Yet, the brunt of police persecution fell on the Nonm Tè.

Eventually, many of the Nonm GCE left the bush to return to the city, tired of a hard life that for them was essentially just one option, not the only option. This was not a choice for most Nonm Tè.

Most Nonm Tè did not reintegrate into society. They faced too much persecution, and because they were able to live in the forest on their own, they frequently did so as squatters. They "reasoned" on their own, and became more self-sufficient, retreating deeper into the forest to live more pure lives. The debacle of inequality at Tè Ferme convinced some Nonm Tè not to trust anything associated with the dominant order, even Nonm GCE. Because Nonm GCE had attended schools run by whites, and especially by white priests and nuns, they must have gotten their ideas from or been distorted by the colonizers. Nonm GCE were distrusted as were others from "Babylon." Book knowledge itself was distrusted. The Bible was a written source of authority, but it had been distorted so much by the "downpressers," the colonizers, and the Roman Catholic Church, that it could only be understood correctly through mystical revelation.

Ganja production continued to be important to the Nonm Tè, and as the popularity of drugs spread on the island, the Nonm Tè became more active in selling. That, too, lent itself to persecution. But the ganja trade was one of the few ways the Nonm Tè could earn cash during this time. In 1978, when the government of Dominica faced a succession crisis, the ganja trade became even more important because it became a way for some Rastas living in the bush, including some Nonm Tè, to get weapons for both protection and for antigovernment activities. Trades of ganja for guns took place between Rastas and members of Dominica's Defense Forces. Crimes involving guns further frightened mainstream Dominicans, and the Nonm Tè, whether involved with these crimes or not, were further alienated from society.[8]

Nonm Tè not connected to society fled deeper into the bush. They advocated an even more natural life living off the land. For some groups, not only was meat to be avoided but processed food in general was shunned. For others, it was reported that food was mainly eaten raw, and at times improperly washed.

The emphasis on natural living also affected Nonm Tè ideology. One informant told me about a Nonm Tè group who frequently ate pig in opposition to general Rasta doctrine forbidding pork, because they could catch wild boars in the bush. Everything was roasted over an open fire because that was the most natural way to cook. Bowls and utensils were fashioned from coconuts and calabashes. Even clothes were made from grass and bark, and natural style became a qualification for speaking at Nonm Tè reasoning sessions, where it was said by some, *"Nonm ki pa pote jip, paka dabout"* (A man cannot speak unless wearing a grass skirt).

Further, Nonm Tè reported that their highly individualistic lifestyles and distrust of authority made them question the status of Haile Selassi as Creator. Left on their own, Nonm Tè refocused their ideology more on their relationship with the earth and nature. Some Nonm Tè developed rituals of their own, like the "fire bath"—which led more mainstream Rastas to denounce them for "worshipping fire," "worshipping creation," or "worshipping the earth."[9]

8. Many crimes throughout the 1970s were attributed to Rastafarians. In general, the most severe of these crimes were attributed to a small group of Rastas, many of whom were upper class. Charges against Rastas included more than one murder, kidnapping, and many counts of predial larceny. Some of these crimes were considered retaliation for persecution under the Dread Act (G. Christian, 1992, 32). There were also several gun battles between state security forces and Rastafarians who were living in the bush, and several Rastafarians and a few security force members were killed in these battles.

9. The "fire bath" as it has been described to me developed among some Nonm Tè who lived in the bush in the late 1970s. It involved placing one's body as close as possible to a fire, one limb at a time, until vapor rose from the skin in an effort to purify the body. The ritual started spontaneously on a cold night while some Nonm Tè were reasoning in front of a fire. It was later modified to fit a similar ritual, which one of the Nonm Tè had seen in a kung fu film. The fire bath was practiced only by a small group of Nonm Tè, and it is not practiced at all anymore.

The net effect of Dread Act persecution on the Nonm Tè was to push them further from society, but also to refocus their millennial expectations on their own lives in the here and now. Ironically, persecution brought the millennial kingdom closer, not by convincing them that the apocalypse was near, or that Selassie would soon send ships, but by forcing them to live out their millennial expectations in the forest in isolation from the world. They were progressive millennialists insofar as they believed that their actions even if carried out apart from "Babylon" would usher in the millennium.

In the end, however, most Nonm Tè either did not survive, or they returned from the bush and assimilated into the mainstream Rasta movement. Some Nonm Tè groups were said to have suffered from bad health and malnutrition. An informant told me that the members of the group who ate pig all died of malnutrition, and other reports circulated about Nonm Tè who died from improperly washing the food they ate.

Most importantly, whether accurate or not, the fate attributed to Nonm Tè retroactively abolished what they stood for and heightened the difference between them and other Rastas who lived closer to society. As one Nonm GCE active in Tè Ferme said, "Where are they now?" In other words, if the "wages of sin is death," then the fate of the Nonm Tè proved the sinfulness of their lives. Not only did their lifestyles lead them to eat pig and live like animals but they questioned the status of Selassie and began to worship creation. Their faith in their own ability to escape Babylon and create a new life in "Zion" was misplaced. The time was not right for Rastas to rule the world.

### Millennial Expectations in the Newtown Nyahbinghi

The Dread Act continues to shape the Rastafarian movement in Dominica today even though it was officially repealed in 1981.[10] There are few Nonm Tè left who continue to refer to themselves by that name.[11] Some former Nonm Tè are still Rastafarians, but have given up

10. It is important to note that though the act was repealed, it was replaced at the same time with another act, the Anti-Terrorist Act, which served many of the same purposes. The main difference was that the Anti-Terrorist Act did not specifically direct itself to Rastafarians.

11. There are a significant number of dreadlock-wearing men who refer to themselves as "Dreads," and whose social characteristics and beliefs are like those of the Nonm Tè, but who do not appear to have any chronological links to the Nonm Tè. They do sometimes link themselves in spirit to the Nonm Tè.

the idea of living purely in the forest. Some of these Rastas now live in Roseau and practice their religion with other Rastas under the auspices of the Newtown Nyahbinghi. Many of the Nonm GCE are still Rastafarians., and those who live in or near Roseau (as most do) also gather to worship at the Newtown Nyahbinghi.

In the ceremonies of the Newtown Nyahbinghi, the current millennial understanding of most Dominican Rastas becomes clear. Therefore, in the remainder of this chapter, I present a brief ethnographic description of a Nyahbinghi meeting and an analysis of the millennial vision contained within the symbolism of the meeting.

### Symbols of the Millennial Vision

The Nyahbinghi ceremony begins with the members of the group arriving of Wah's yard. Wah is one of the leaders of this group, although there are other prominent members and there is no formal leader. Unlike the other leaders, Wah is from a low-class background, was a Nonm Tè, and lived in the bush starting early in the 1970s. By his account, he suffered severe persecution living "seven years in solitary confinement" in Dominica's prison for "stabbing a white man."

To start the ceremony, everyone steps outside of Wah's yard to a small flat area where dry wood is stacked for a fire. By the time stragglers arrive, there are thirty people at the meeting, only four of whom are women.

According to the Order of the Nyahbinghi, the fire that opens the ceremony represents His Imperial Majesty Haile Selassie's burning consumption of wickedness and sin. There are numerous references and exclamations about the burning of "Babylon" and the Pope, especially when the fire cracks and spits. Symbolically, this is significant, for it shows Selassie as the agent in cleansing the world of impurity.

After the fire is lit, everyone faces it standing in a circle and chants the appropriate Psalms. The Psalms to be chanted are authorized by the Order of the Nyahbinghi, a written document that the Newtown Nyahbinghi uses to organize itself.

After the Psalms, everyone moves back into Wah's yard. The left side of his yard is marked by a corrugated tin fence that separates us from the rest of Newtown. Such fences are common in Dominica, but also are symbolically significant in this case for insuring the separation of the Nyahbinghi from the village.

On the outside wall on one small building in the yard, there is a life-size painting of Wah wearing a grass skirt. This is a painting of a photo Wah has of himself during his time living in the forest as a Nonm Tè—a time he now understands as a time of "purification." According to Wah, a time of purification in the forest occurs about every hundred years in Dominica, and he cites the widespread maroon movement in Dominica as the past example.[12] In previous conversations with me, Wah has referred to himself as the first Nonm Tè.

As we enter Wah's yard from the fire ceremony, everyone moves to the back section of the yard and sits down in a circle on rough boards supported by cinder blocks. The circular seating arrangement gives no spatial recognition to anyone in the group, and it facilitates drumming and conversation by all. Symbolically, the circle is significant for representing the equality that Rastafarians desire within their community. But this equality does not necessarily extend beyond the circle of the Nyahbinghi, for some upper-class Rastas here will go back to jobs as lawyers or engineers, while other members will return to working small plots of land they squat on or to selling incense in the market. It should also be noted that although the seating is equal, it is not random, for I am directed where to sit and all women sit together in one area of the circle.

After a few minutes of chit-chat, prayers and Psalms again are sung. After these, the bowls of two or three large "chalices" (water pipes), about one and a half feet long, are filled with marijuana. Once lit, the chalices are passed around, clockwise, to everyone except the women, who generally smoke "spliffs" (marijuana cigarettes). Again, within the circle of male Rastafarians there is a symbolic equality. But the equality is dependent upon one's purity. For example, I am warned not to smoke chalice because I eat "flesh" and am therefore impure. The smoke of the chalice is sacred, and if it comes in contact with impurities, it destroys them (a homology to how Selassie's sacred fire burns out wickedness and sin). Thus, smoking chalice will harm my body unless I am pure. This appears to be the reason women do not generally smoke chalice, for women in general are considered in this group to be impure.

12. Maroons were escaped slaves who set up communities in the forest. They were widespread in several parts of the Americas, and they were especially strong in Dominica at the end of the eighteenth and beginning of the nineteenth centuries. In linking himself to the maroons, Wah links himself symbolically to heroic figures in Dominica's past.

## Chanting

After the chalices have been passed around the full circle, drumming and chanting begins. The chants themselves are a combination of well-known Rasta chants and those written by Wah himself. The well-known chants include "Rastaman, dry up your tears," which recognizes the oppression Rastafarians suffer, but optimistically points to a future without oppression. Wah's lyrics generally emphasize ethical behavior and the belief that personal ethical behavior will bring its own rewards, or will bring rewards from Haile Selassie. For example, one simple chant emphasizes the value of living a personally pure life in contrast to engaging in violent protest:

> You can't get to heaven with an M-16;
> Your life must be pure and clean.

Another chant simply refrains "Do good, do good." A third emphasizes what it might mean to be good and the relation that bears to life in the here and now: "Rasta don't want no carnal man." And a fourth simply proclaims "Few are chosen." At other sessions one might hear "Babylon must run, Babylon must die." Implicit in this chant is the belief that Selassie makes Babylon run and punishes Babylon. Rastas are chosen to rule, and they must prepare themselves for ruling by purifying their lives, not by destroying Babylon. Only if they are strong and pure will they survive Selassie's wrath and rule in the future.

The remainder of the Nyahbinghi alternates between chanting/drumming and reasoning. Reasoning is perhaps the most significant religious activity of Rastafarians. At its simplest level, reasoning is simply talking and having a conversation. It is symbolically crucial to understanding Rastafarians because in reasoning sessions any Rasta can speak and any topic can be discussed. Thus, it is in reasoning that Rastafarians are officially recognized as equal selves with equal share in divinity. It is through these sessions that Rasta beliefs undergo reformulation as they are discussed, questioned, and new "overstandings" are reached.[13] It is important to note that Rasta beliefs are not based in any way on consensus, but through reasoning what is True emerges.

13. In the Rastafarian cosmology, things that are low or down are not good, while things that are up or high are good. Words are changed to reflect this cosmology. Thus, through reasoning we do not reach "understandings," which would imply some sort of subterfuge, but we reach "overstandings" in which both parties reach a higher level of consciousness.

### Reasoning: Why Political Organization Is Unnecessary

During this particular Nyahbinghi, I am not the only outsider present; there is also a non-Rastafarian Dominican. He first speaks when Wah is speaking—itself a violation of the Rasta norms—and argues that Rastas need to organize politically to fight oppression. Wah cuts off his reasoning telling him that he is not allowed to speak, for this is the Nyahbinghi Order and at spiritual meetings (i.e., at Nyahbinghis versus "house reasoning" meetings) one needs to be recognized to be permitted to speak. Later Wah relents, recognizes him, and says he can speak. It is clear Wah wants an opportunity to respond to him.

Wah responds to the call of this "baldhead" (i.e., no dreadlocks) for political organization by saying that Rastas do not need to organize politically, for Rastas are already organized by Selassie and are here on earth to rule—and Rasta rule is coming with the "New Dispensation," which Wah implies is imminent. Wah continues that Rastas are here now to make life better, but better life comes through lifestyle choices—such as following the Order. Wah emphasizes the power that comes through lifestyle, and in reasoning about other issues, such as the problems in Haiti. He suggests that lack of power, suffering, and even death itself come from Selassie as punishment for bad lifestyle choices.

### Personal Purity, Preparation, and Patience: Awaiting Haile Selassie

In this ceremony and reasoning we see the most recent transformation of Dominican Rastafarians' millennial expectation. The Nyahbinghi rituals emphasize the power of Selassie to eliminate corruption and impurity, while the task for the individual Rasta is to prepare himself for the millennial kingdom that will be brought by Selassie. Wah, a self-proclaimed former Nonm Tè, does not think that the millennial kingdom can be brought about through organizations and political action, and like the Nonm GCE in the Newtown Nyahbinghi, he argues that personal lifestyle ultimately leads to salvation. The power to bring about the millennial kingdom is in Selassie's hands alone, and to challenge that is to invite death. Because of this emphasis, the Dominican Rastafarian movement at large is less political and more traditionally religious than it was twenty years ago, when it was still motivated to a large extent by the overtly political Black Power movement.

## Conclusion: Persecution and Social Composition

The persecution promoted by the Dread Act amplified preexisting social differences between various segments of Rastafarians and split the movement into parts that reflected the class and status structure of Dominican society at large. An upper-class segment developed into a quieter movement that fit within bounds commonly accepted as "religious." Dominican society at large accepted Rastafarians who presented their religion as a private affair focused on purifying the self and living a personally pure life. At the same time, this quieter group of Rastafarians relinquished its active orientation to accomplishing the millennial kingdom or "New Dispensation," and became oriented instead toward an imminent millennial condition that would be brought about catastrophically solely by Haile Selassie.

At the time of the Dread Act, the lower-class segment of Rastafarians in Dominica was forced by the persecution into the forest, where some of them radicalized under the ongoing threat of violence, became outlaws, and tried to set up enclaves in which they lived out their millennial vision.[14] This active orientation to accomplishing the millennial condition shows in the disregard this group had for the norms of Dominican society, especially the laws of private property, and the belief implicit in their actions that they could, through activity, create the millennial community that they anticipated. I have collectively labeled this group "Nonm Tè," and have suggested that they exemplified a progressive millennialism.

But many Nonm Tè died for their efforts. Others, such as Wah, returned to the city with changed millennial views. Aware that they could not bring about the millennial kingdom, they put their hopes in Jah, and rejoined with the Nonm GCE, with whom they now participate in the Newtown Nyahbinghi. Despite their different pasts, both groups now participate together trying to live the "pure and clean life" that will prepare them for rule in the New Dispensation.

---

14. Nonm Tè were, in fact, outlaws, given the formulation of the Dread Act. In addition, they often did not respect laws of private property, so they were accused of stealing crops and food from farmers and other peasants, and were accused of more serious crimes. The most serious crimes appear to have included the activities of upper-class Rastas, including some who, according to the oral histories I collected, were somewhat opportunistic in their approach to Rastafarianism. Because these Rastas were ultimately shot by security forces, I have no firsthand way of confirming this appraisal.

*Part Two*

# Fragile Millennial Groups

# 5

# "American as Cherry Pie"

## Peoples Temple and Violence in America

REBECCA MOORE ───────────────────────

When H. Rap Brown observed in 1967 that violence was as American as cherry pie, he was justifying the civil rebellions erupting in black ghettos across the nation, and criticizing the institutional racism that caused them. The 1960s and 1970s witnessed state-sanctioned violence in Vietnam, in Central America, and in the United States. Americans could watch sheriffs' deputies beating up Freedom Riders in the South, U.S. troops dropping bombs and napalm on Vietnamese villagers, or police attacking demonstrators in Chicago, Berkeley, or on almost any American campus—all on the nightly news.

This is the historical context in which Peoples Temple developed.[1] Jim Jones (1931–78), its charismatic leader, established Peoples Temple in Indianapolis in the 1950s as a protest against a racially segregated church and community. He moved the Temple to Redwood Valley, California, in the 1960s seeking safety from what seemed like imminent nuclear war. It branched into San Francisco and Los Angeles in the 1970s seeking new members from the ranks of the urban poor, many of whom were African Americans. It moved again in mid-1977 to a remote jungle in western Guyana on the north coast of South America, to escape the violence, poverty, and racism of life in America. And on November

I want to thank the following readers for commenting on this paper: Fielding McGehee, III; John and Barbara Moore; Mary Sawyer; Scott Lowe; and Catherine Wessinger.

1. One of the most complete histories of Peoples Temple is John R. Hall, *Gone from the Promised Land*, 1987.

18, 1978, the people living in Jonestown, Guyana, killed their children and took their own lives.[2]

Theology married ideology in Peoples Temple in a radical interpretation of the Gospel imperative to care for the poor, the hungry, the sick, the imprisoned (Matt. 25:35–40). The Temple opened its doors in the heart of black neighborhoods in San Francisco and Los Angeles, where members offered a variety of social programs, which, in turn, attracted new recruits. Some joined because of the Gospel of Jesus Christ, others because of the Gospel of Karl Marx. In both cases the Temple's activism appeared to offer a vigorous challenge to the culture of racism and classism that marked American society. It is important to remember that the optimism of liberation movements in the 1960s gave way to pessimism, rage, and despair in the 1970s, and thus Peoples Temple provided an alternative to mainstream American culture *and* to a moribund counterculture.

It is no exaggeration to claim that Peoples Temple and the violence surrounding it were as American as cherry pie. But Peoples Temple also belonged to a prophetic religious tradition that was utterly American as well. This tradition included abolitionism, social gospel progressivism, and civil rights activism. To suggest that Peoples Temple, or even Jim Jones, is anomalous in American culture is to misread and ignore history. America produced Peoples Temple and the tragedy at Jonestown, just as it produced the nineteenth-century slave trade and the twentieth-century civil rights movement. America created the Vietnam War and the peace movement; Ronald Reagan and Robert Kennedy; Rush Limbaugh and Martin Luther King, Jr. Attempts to distance ourselves from what happened are therefore misplaced and misguided (Chidester 1988, 24–46).

To understand why more than nine hundred people died in a jungle thousands of miles from their places of birth, it is necessary to examine the growth of injustice *against* Peoples Temple and the rise of injustice *within* Peoples Temple. In this essay I argue that increasing external threats, which were quite real and well documented, escalated the vio-

2. According to the Staff Investigative Group (SIG) to the Committee on Foreign Affairs of the U.S. House of Representatives (May 15, 1979), 909 people died in Jonestown. I add to that figure Sharon Amos, who killed her three children and herself in Georgetown, Guyana; and the five people murdered at the Port Kaituma airstrip as they attempted to leave Jonestown. This brings the total to 918 who died that day. According to a report filed with the SIG by the Department of Health, Education, and Welfare, 188 Social Security beneficiaries died in Jonestown. A General Accounting Office audit states that 294 children under eighteen died (Moore 1985, 363).

lence internal to the organization. The result triggered assaults on Temple members leaving Jonestown with Congressman Leo Ryan on November 18, 1978; the assassination of the congressman, members of the news media, and a defector at the Port Kaituma, Guyana, airstrip; and the mass murders-suicides of members of the Jonestown community.

## Violence and Peoples Temple:
## A Reconsideration

In the twenty years since my sisters Carolyn Layton and Annie Moore and my nephew Jim-Jon Prokes died in Jonestown, my thinking about what happened in Peoples Temple and at Jonestown has changed. I wrote *A Sympathetic History of Jonestown* (1985) as a counterweight to the mass of quickie anticult books that popped up after the suicides (Kilduff and Javers 1978; Kern and Wead 1979; Krause 1978; Mills 1979; Nugent 1979). I tried to explain and interpret the actions of the members of Peoples Temple in a way that would make sense of what had happened, both to the reading public and to myself. In the process, I downplayed the violence internal to the institution. This is most apparent in the chapter "For Every Good Thing, Something Bad."

Evidence seems conclusive, however, that (1) beatings and public humiliation sessions regularly occurred as part of the Temple's means of controlling its members; (2) individuals were privately threatened or intimidated; (3) suicide drills were practiced as a way to test loyalty and to prepare members for the "real thing"; (4) some individuals were controlled with drugs in Jonestown and an atmosphere of repression grew there as Jim Jones's health deteriorated; and (5) violence broke out against Congressman Ryan and against the community itself. In 1985 I tried to contextualize these facts by calling them "paradoxes," "double standards," or "ironies." There are several reasons why I am no longer willing to do that.

First, the credibility of the anticult movement (ACM) has been demolished and I no longer need to try to balance their biased accounts. The coercive tactics of deprogrammers have been exposed, the threat to the free exercise of religion by the ACM has been recognized, and perhaps most importantly, the crucial and negative role anticultists played in shaping government action toward the Branch Davidians in Waco, Texas, has been documented (S. Wright 1995; Tabor and Gallagher 1995). Second, books and articles by scholars of religion have critically assessed the accounts given by apostates, or "defectors" as they were called in 1985 (Hall and Schuyler 1998; Shupe and Bromley 1994; Shupe, Bromley, and Breschel 1989), and similarly eliminated the need to put things in perspective. Third, the voice of Jim Jones's biological son, Stephan Jones, has begun to emerge in articles (L. Wright 1993), books (Maaga 1996), and in personal conversations. His reports of what happened in Jonestown confirm the worst, yet appear neither self-serving nor judgmental. Finally, time has allowed me to face the fact that my sisters were involved, either explicitly or implicitly, in planning *some* of the violence that occurred in Peoples Temple. Maaga cites a letter Annie wrote in which she argues for the suicide of the community (1996, 119–21).

How did Peoples Temple members rationalize their internal violence? Carolyn defended the security gate and armed guards at the Temple buildings in Redwood Valley by saying that local townspeople had fired shots into the area (R. Moore 1985, 115).[3] Racial incidents in the predominantly white towns of northern California persuaded members that they were not safe. *Peoples Forum,* the newspaper of Peoples Temple, reported frequent harassment of members. The group excused the guards at the Temple on Geary Street in San Francisco because of conflicts with Neo-Nazis and the Nation of Islam.

Disciplinary actions against members came under the rubric "catharsis." Catharsis sessions comprised confession and humiliation before the entire community. True catharsis required a change in behavior, such as repenting of an elitist attitude, or giving more time to the cause. Some of the behaviors requiring repentance included resenting decisions made by the Temple Planning Council (the decision-making body for the group), or calling someone names. It is clear that church members, not just Jim Jones or the Planning Council, vigorously participated in the discipline. One Temple woman kept a diary, which noted that: "Glenn Hennington was on the floor for driving without a license for six months. He got a ticket. He had to fight with a girl who knocked him out, which exhilarated the feminine portion of the audience (R. Moore 1985, 127). Complicity in discipline, catharsis, fake faith healings, and other questionable, unethical, or illegal activities bound Temple members to one another.

3. In December 1979 Chuck Beikman, a Temple member, told my father, John Moore, that he went outside after the shooting incident and found that another Temple member had fired the shots.

Jim Jones mediated the news for members in the United States, but with the move to Guyana his control of information became virtually absolute. In Jonestown he could blow up a border skirmish between China and the Soviet Union into a major war. He could claim that America was herding blacks into concentration camps. The outside world, already threatening and hostile, became forbidding, dangerous, and closed. It became apparent to Peoples Temple that its enemies were successfully persuading the news media and agencies of the United States government to investigate the organization in ways that threatened its livelihood.

A dualistic worldview pitted the good guys—Peoples Temple— against the bad guys—a racist and classist society that epitomized the greed and selfishness that Peoples Temple members categorically rejected (Wessinger 1997b, 282). Those who joined the group sought to create a new society, a utopia, which my sister Annie described in her last letter to the world:

> There were no ugly, mean policemen wanting to beat our heads in, no more racist tears from whites and others who thought they were better. No one was made fun of for their appearance—something no one had control over.
>
> Meanness and making fun were not allowed. Maybe this is why all the lies were started. Besides this fact, no one was allowed to live higher than anyone else (R. Moore 1986, 285–86).

Coupled with the egalitarian sentiments expressed by Annie, was an apocalyptic expectation that dominated Jim Jones and ultimately the entire community. Whether the end of life in the United States came by fascist take-over or nuclear annihilation, it *was* coming. The group shared and promoted Jim's apocalyptic expectation in plays, in speeches, in confessions, and in songs. The night Leo Ryan stayed in Jonestown a young woman sang a song titled "1981":

> You will stand in line
> With your passport to sign
> And the government says "no" to your kind.
> (R. Moore 1985, 157–58)

A journal by a Peoples Temple member declared that "Nuclear war is made certain" after Jim gave a discouraging, and biased, news report on the Middle East (158). Current events seemed to confirm the imminent end of the world.[4] Aggression against Peoples Temple itself, however, also validated apocalyptic fears and expectations.

## Violence Against Peoples Temple

A body of literature about apostates from New Religious Movements (NRMs) and their influence upon government and the news media has arisen in the past decade (Hall and Schuyler 1998; Shupe and Bromley 1994; Tabor and Gallagher 1995).[5] The fiery end of the Branch Davidians in Waco, Texas, in 1993 also focused attention on the undue credibility that apostates received from government agencies handling the siege (Tabor and Gallagher 1995; S. Wright 1995). A critical approach to apostates did not exist at the time of Jonestown, however, and so a group calling itself the Concerned Relatives, comprised of former Temple members and relatives of current members, had virtually unchallenged access to the media and to the government.

The Concerned Relatives began to organize as early as 1976, but did not go public until an August 1977 article in *New West Magazine* presented its allegations against the Temple without much critical analysis. Spearheading the movement were Timothy and Grace Stoen. The couple sought to regain custody of their six-year-old son, John Victor, whom they had legally entrusted to Jim Jones. Tim, a lawyer and top leader in the Temple, had assigned custody to Jones when Grace fled the Temple in 1976. When Tim defected a year later, he and Grace joined forces to try to get John Victor out of Jonestown. The custody issue was complicated by the fact that Tim had signed an affidavit that said that Jones was the biological father of John Victor. In January 1978 the Stoens traveled to Guyana to try to exert personal pressure on the U.S. Embassy, the government of Guyana, and on Jonestown. When they returned without having seen their son, they began to lobby members of

4. Catherine Wessinger differentiates between catastrophic millennialism and progressive millennialism. The former "involves a pessimistic view of humanity and society"; the latter, more optimistic, sees "humans engaging in social work in harmony with the divine will" to progressively create a new kingdom on earth (Wessinger 1997b, 282–83). She identifies Peoples Temple as a catastrophic group, and I tend to agree.

5. Much of the information for this section is drawn from chapter 11, "The Vise," in *A Sympathetic History of Jonestown*. Written in a journalistic rather than scholarly style, the book's sources can nevertheless be documented in the Moore Family Collection of the "Peoples Temple Archives" in the Schubert Hall Library of the California Historical Society.

Congress, including Congressman Leo Ryan, whose own daughter was a member of the Rajneesh religious commune in Oregon.

The next major offensive from the Concerned Relatives came in April 1978 with the release of an "Accusation of Human Rights Violations by [the] Rev. James Warren Jones Against Our Children and Relatives at the Peoples Temple Jungle Encampment in Guyana, South America." The group sent the document to the media, members of Congress, the U.S. State Department, and to Peoples Temple. They listed a number of grievances, such as denial of access to relatives, censorship of mail, and prevention of travel by family members. The "Accusation" also included affidavits from Steven Katsaris that related his failed attempt to see his adult daughter, Maria, and from former member Yolanda Crawford, who lived in Jonestown for three months in 1977.

After the publicity surrounding the "Accusation" died down, a new strategy emerged: intensified legal action against Peoples Temple. Tim Stoen filed lawsuits seeking damages against Peoples Temple and Jim Jones on behalf of three other disgruntled relatives. Despite a countersuit filed against Tim Stoen in the summer of 1978, Peoples Temple still faced these three suits as well as the Stoen custody suit in November.

Most damaging, and ultimately most persuasive to U.S. government agencies and to Congress, was an affidavit Tim Stoen helped Deborah Layton Blakey prepare after her defection from Peoples Temple in Guyana in May 1978. Besides describing the rough living conditions that prevailed in the community, Deborah reported that Temple members had conducted suicide rehearsals. Deborah's affidavit and personal communication with Congressman Leo Ryan persuaded him to travel to Jonestown.

The access the Concerned Relatives had to the media and to government agencies helped create a hydra of federal, state, and local investigations into the activities of Peoples Temple. If these investigations had found any evidence of fraud or illegal activities, Peoples Temple would have seen many of its financial resources dry up. The threat to the very existence of Jonestown from several agencies, including the U.S. Customs Service, the Federal Communications Commission, the Social Security Administration, and the Internal Revenue Service, was quite real.

The U.S. Customs investigation began in February 1977 at the instigation of former members and continued into 1978. The year-long investigation included surveillance of Peoples Temple property in Redwood Valley and San Francisco; lookouts posted in Houston, New Orleans, and Miami; and cargo searches. Nevertheless, the Customs

Service failed to turn up any signs of smuggling or contraband. "At no time was there any evidence of a substantial enough nature to justify an affidavit for either a search warrant or a presentation to the U.S. Attorney for Federal Grand Jury Action," a Customs agent reported to the House Foreign Affairs Committee investigating the Jonestown deaths (R. Moore 1985, 279–80). Nevertheless, U.S. Customs forwarded a report made in August 1977 to Interpol and to the State Department, which Peoples Temple members then received from the government of Guyana.

Aside from inaccuracies in the report, the most intriguing statement follows: "As a result of this action [Customs' surveillance], a continuing series of magazine, newspaper, radio and television articles and coverage has been given to JONES and the Church. Subsequently, investigations have been initiated by San Francisco and Mendocino counties" (281). In other words, a concerted and planned effort existed to discredit and dismantle Peoples Temple. Peoples Temple members were concerned not only about the delay of needed items shipped from the United States to Guyana but more importantly, about the effect the report would have on their relationship with officials in the government of Guyana. After all, they were in Guyana only at the pleasure of Prime Minister Forbes Burnham's ruling party. Any unfavorable publicity or damaging incidents, they felt, could jeopardize that.

The custody case waged by Tim and Grace Stoen also threatened the delicate balance between the Temple and its supporters in the highest levels of the Guyanese government. A visit to Jonestown in September 1977 by the Stoens' attorney from America, coupled with the absence from the country of some members of Guyana's ruling party sent the community into a panic. The group threatened to commit mass suicide if John Victor were removed, according to Charles Garry, the Temple's San Francisco attorney (R. Moore 1985, 285). My sister Carolyn later explained the political significance of the case. "From the political perspective we know that if we do not get backing on this issue, how could we ever have confidence in the government backing us on far more controversial issues" (286).

Further evidence of the coordinated attack on Peoples Temple came in the form of a Federal Communications Commission (FCC) investigation into the group's use of the amateur radio waves. The FCC began monitoring Temple communications in April 1977 after receiving a tip from a ham radio operator. The chief of the FCC's Enforcement Division urged the San Francisco office of the FCC to continue daily coverage between 1977 and 1978. By November 1978 the agency had logged between forty and sixty hours of conversation.

The major communications link Jonestown had with Peoples Temple in San Francisco, and with the outside world, was through its ham radios. Radio conversations ranged in topics from continuing education and agricultural training to T-shirts and tractor parts. Sometimes members read political statements over the air. The biggest problem, as far as the FCC was concerned, was that the Temple seemed to be conducting private business over the public airwaves, and was going out-of-band to do so. "We haven't found anything wrong other than the business-type traffic," complained one FCC engineer. "It's the out-of-band bit we need to hang them" (R. Moore 1985, 293).[6] In August 1978 the FCC warned Elton Adams, a Temple licensee, that revocation of his license, as well as fines, might occur if he continued to use his station to facilitate the administration of Peoples Temple.

Transcripts of the FCC's communications show that the investigation was influenced by the negative publicity generated by the Concerned Relatives. One engineer told another about a television talk show that aired charges against the Temple. "Make it an official observation," was the response. Mirroring the crimes listed in the Customs Service report, an FCC report from August 1977 said that "the Peoples Temple may be engaged in nefarious acts on an international level" (R. Moore 1985, 294). The "nefarious acts" purportedly included gunrunning, narcotics smuggling, and illegal transfers of funds out of the country.[7]

6. Ham radio operators are required to operate within certain designated bandwidths. Peoples Temple members were conducting business on unauthorized wavelengths.

7. A two-year probe by the U.S. Customs Service failed to uncover any evidence of gunrunning. The government of Guyana recovered thirty-two weapons from Jonestown: seven shotguns, fourteen small-caliber rifles, ten pistols, and a flare launcher. Three additional pistols were taken from Peoples Temple members fleeing Jonestown. The U.S. Bureau of Alcohol, Tobacco, and Firearms ran a trace on the weapons and found that twenty-five of them came from a rifle shop in Ukiah, California. All but three of the weapons had been purchased before March 1975, while thirteen were bought before 1970. "Hardly an arsenal," Skip Roberts, Guyana's chief of police, told us (R. Moore 1985, 372–73).

Drugs had been shipped to Jonestown, but they seemed to be primarily for medicinal purposes, except the tranquilizers and potassium cyanide, which were used to control, and eventually kill, people. These kinds of drugs were not what the Customs Service was worried about.

Clearly U.S. dollars had been smuggled out of the country, given the fact that foreign bank accounts existed in Panama and Switzerland. Some of the Panamanian accounts were in my sister Carolyn's name.

The FCC's revocation threat of August 1978, coupled with a re-iterated threat in November 1978, came on top of a new communications problem. The Maritime Mobile Net refused to carry phone patches from Peoples Temple, claiming that the FCC told it the calls were illegal (R. Moore 1985, 299). What this meant was that calls from Jonestown, Guyana, had to be routed through the Temple's San Francisco office. Direct calls could no longer be made.

The possibility of financial disaster from two sources overshadowed the potential disruption of the flow of supplies and communications. The Social Security Administration (SSA) office in San Francisco in the summer of 1977 asked postal officials to alert it immediately to any address changes marked Guyana. The Postal Service went a step further and, according to a USPS routing slip, ordered *all* U.S. Treasury checks destined for Guyana returned to Treasury. Not until the late Congressman Phillip Burton (Democrat, California) wrote several times, appending the Postal Service note, did the SSA finally resolve the problem in December 1977. Normally, all SSA and SSI (Supplemental Security Income) checks are forwarded, and the Treasury Department notified (R. Moore 1985, 299). In the spring of 1978 more checks were misrouted. Letters poured in from Peoples Temple, and SSA quickly resolved the problem. But an SSA interim report detailed the "extraordinary lengths" it followed to prevent any sort of fraud by Peoples Temple.

As of June 1978, about $37,000 worth of Social Security checks went to Temple beneficiaries each month. Repeated investigations by the U.S. Embassy staff in Guyana verified that those receiving the checks were in fact alive. Then-Health, Education and Welfare Secretary Joseph Califano reported that handwriting analysis confirmed the endorsements of Peoples Temple members that were made on checks dated November 3, 1978 (R. Moore 1985, 365–66). Although one woman, Lisa Layton, died of cancer at the end of October, her checks were returned to the government, unsigned and uncashed.

The second threat to the Temple's financial security came from the Internal Revenue Service. In February 1978 the IRS informed the organization that it was conducting an examination to determine if the Temple were receiving income from any activity subject to income tax. In other words, the agency was investigating, and had been investigating for two years, whether the Temple was adequately reporting unrelated business income, which was taxable (Hall 1987, 197–98). In the February letter the IRS district director asked for organizational documents, financial statements, payroll tax returns, and copies of licenses and permits to operate commercial activities. The lawyer handling the IRS case for the Temple quickly determined that it was not an official audit and learned that it was negative publicity about Peoples Temple that prompted the most immediate IRS move against the church. Despite the ad hoc nature of the IRS request, its investigation was still pending on November 18, 1978. The IRS finally revoked the Temple's tax-exempt status after its demise, and sought back taxes for the last thirty months of the church's existence from the Peoples Temple receiver.

A number of events occurred in the summer and fall of 1978 that compounded the insecurity the community felt. On top of Deborah Layton's defection in May, Terri Buford, another trusted financial officer in Jonestown, left in October. The departure of these two women, who had access to and control of millions of dollars of Temple assets, required a mad scramble by Jones and his leadership group to protect the Temple's holdings in various foreign banks.

The defections of Buford and Layton seemed evidence enough of a conspiracy against Peoples Temple. Mark Lane and Don Freed provided definitive proof. Don Freed, a writer whose credentials included political thrillers such as *Executive Action*, visited Jonestown in August 1978 and encouraged Lane to visit in September. As far as Peoples Temple was concerned, Lane had impeccable credentials as a long-time supporter of liberal causes. The group hired the conspiracy buff to uncover plots against it, and that he did. "Mom and Dad have probably shown you the latest about the conspiracy information that Mark Lane, the famous attorney in the ML King case and Don Freed the other famous author in the Kennedy case have come up with regarding activities planned against us—Peoples Temple," Annie wrote in October 1978 (R. Moore 1986, 282). Carolyn wrote that Don Freed told them that "anything this drug out could be nothing less than conspiracy" (272).

The conspiracy that Lane and Freed exposed involved a private detective named Joe Mazor whom the Concerned Relatives had hired. Mazor confessed his sins to the community in Jonestown in September, explaining that he had had a change of heart when he realized that the Concerned Relatives had lied to him. Lane perhaps had persuaded Mazor to come clean. The lawyer announced in Guyana on September 20 that "We have also concluded without question that there has been a massive conspiracy to destroy the Peoples Temple and a massive conspiracy to destroy the Reverend Jim Jones" (R. Moore 1985, 305). Lane repeated the charges in San Francisco on October 3. Temple documents show that Lane promised to file a lawsuit against various Concerned Relatives that would reveal details of a conspiracy against the Temple during discovery proceedings. Lane, in short, verified what Peoples Temple members had suspected all along.

## Violence Within Peoples Temple

The concerted and well-organized effort of the Concerned Relatives to harass Peoples Temple had a devastating effect on the people in Jonestown. Between the time of the mass immigration of Peoples Temple members into Jonestown in summer 1977, and November 1978, internal dissent escalated, and along with it, repression and inner-directed violence. The Special Care Unit in Jonestown housed dissidents rather than rule-breakers. If someone broke the rules, he or she was assigned more work. If individuals dissented, however, they were assigned to Special Care, where the Jonestown medical staff administered and monitored intensive sedation. Charles Garry, the Temple's long-time attorney, believes that Eugene Chaikin, a Temple member who was also a lawyer, might have been housed in Special Care. Garry was unable to see Chaikin during his November 1978 visit despite repeated attempts to do so (R. Moore 1985, 220).

The workload increased, as a relatively few able-bodied adults tried to farm and support children and the seniors (Maaga 1996, 138). With about a third of the Jonestown community under eighteen, and another third over the age of retirement, all of the daily chores fell on the same group of people. Field workers never knew when their breaks would be scheduled; they never knew in advance when they might have a day off. The security force was ordered to patrol constantly. Eventually, it got out of hand: one security officer cocked his gun and aimed it at people, presumably to intimidate them (Moore 1985, 309).

Tommy Bogue made one of the more dramatic escape attempts late in 1978. Caught by the security force, he and his friends were shackled in chains for three weeks and forced to chop wood for eighteen hours a day. Bogue said that others who tried to escape were placed in a coffinlike box for several days (R. Moore 1985, 309).

Meanwhile, the suicide drills increased in frequency and intensity. At these drills, participants would drink fruit punch and pretend to fall down dead. It was a test, they were told afterward, to prove their loyalty to Jim Jones, to the community, and to the cause.

It is clear now that the group rehearsed suicide many times. Members of the Jonestown community were mentally and physically ready to die. Carolyn and Annie had both told my family in letters that they were "prepared" to die. We interpreted their remarks as statements of their willingness to die for what they believed, not a willingness to kill themselves. But the rehearsals served a ritualistic purpose: everyone knew what was expected and what to do. During an earlier drill one person testified that: "Life is shit. What Dad [Jim Jones] says is true, life outside this collective is shit. . . . I want to die a revolutionary death" (R. Moore 1985, 333).

In the eyes of Jones, the enemies within threatened to subvert the entire organization. The enemies without—hostile government agencies, a skeptical press, angry relatives, disloyal apostates—remained distant. But the forces converged when Congressman Ryan announced on November 1, 1978, that he would visit Jonestown.

Ryan knew the trip could be dangerous. He had been warned by Deborah Layton and believed that mass suicide was a real possibility. On November 13, the U.S. State Department told him of the presence of weapons in the community. Ryan knew of alleged illegal activities because the Los Angeles district attorney asked him to interview some Temple members about an extortion complaint. Moreover, in the briefcase he took with him to Jonestown, Ryan had notes concerning Jim Jones's lewd conduct arrest in 1973. Nevertheless, Ryan was determined to go at any cost.

Equally threatening as Ryan's trip itself was the congressman's choice of traveling companions. Despite warnings from the State Department and the U.S. Embassy, Ryan took with him every enemy of Peoples Temple. Tim and Grace Stoen, other opponents of Peoples Temple, hostile reporters, and people who had sued the Temple or had threatened to retrieve their children by force, made up Ryan's entourage.

When Jones learned that the congressman's plane was en route to Jonestown on November 17, he announced over the loudspeaker: "Alert, alert! We're being invaded!" (R. Moore 1985, 319). Ryan's visit fulfilled Jones's prophecies and verified his interpretation of the truth.[8] Had Ryan not gone to Jonestown, or had he stage-managed his visit otherwise, the results might have been different (Hall and Schuyler 1998). Maaga's study of the organizational structure of the Jonestown community indicates that Jim Jones may have been facing a coup led by trusted female leaders, which would have made him a powerless figurehead

8. This also seemed to be one of the lessons of Waco: the government's actions demonstrated the validity of David Koresh's prophecies.

(1996, 97–103). Stephan Jones claims that he and his brothers were ready to kill their father because of his destructive influence on the community (L. Wright 1993, 78; personal conversation). Carlton Goodlett, Jones's doctor in San Francisco, believed he would have been dead from drug abuse and illness within a few months (R. Moore 1985, 221). Instead, Leo Ryan's arrival reestablished the credibility of the faltering leader.

After Ryan left for the airstrip, taking sixteen defectors with him, Jones sent security forces to kill the congressman and reporters. He then gathered the community into the central pavilion for instructions.

An audiotape of the final discussion indicates how well prepared the community was. "We're all ready to go," declared one man. "If you tell us we have to give our lives now, we're ready. All the rest of the sisters and brothers are with me" (Maaga 1996, 149). A woman reassured the group that: "This is nothing to cry about. This is something we could all rejoice about. We could be happy about this. They always told us that we could cry when you're coming into this world. So we're leaving it, and we're leaving it peaceful" (153). This woman's comments indicate that members of the Jonestown community did not see themselves as participating in a violent act. On the contrary, they saw themselves taking their leave quietly, peacefully, and yet as an act of protest. Jim's final recorded words demonstrate this: "Take our life from us. We laid it down. We got tired. We didn't commit suicide. We committed an act of revolutionary suicide protesting the conditions of an inhumane world" (157).

Maaga argues that members of the Jonestown community saw their choice as being between loyalty to the group, which meant death; or betrayal, which meant survival (Maaga 1996, 121–23). Although the violence in Peoples Temple did burst forth against outsiders, it was primarily directed at insiders, at individuals *within* the group. Although violence served as a form of social control, it also created bonds within the new family and new society Jim and his followers were trying to create. When people suffer together they either feel closer as a result or they become alienated. People in Jonestown had suffered together, and some were alienated by that suffering. But most drew closer together.[9] In other words, violence—from disciplinary sessions to suicide drills—served as the glue that held people together. It was by practicing com-

9. In a personal conversation (1997) Mary Sawyer notes that shared suffering describes, in part, the black experience in America. The suffering that Peoples Temple members endured strengthened rather than weakened their bonds of commitment.

mon rituals, not by receiving death threats that Temple members made suicide possible.

## Conclusions

"We are not paranoid," a *Peoples Forum* editorial declared. "We simply have found no other logical way to make sense of our experiences" (R. Moore 1985, 273). The *Forum* explained that a conspiracy against the Temple existed. Mark Lane, like Dr. Frankenstein, gave life to the monster. Paranoia existed within Peoples Temple, as evidenced by public and private confession, community security forces, and conspiracy discussions. But the group found its conspiracy theories validated in negative news accounts that uncritically reported the views of Concerned Relatives. The Temple's perception that the U.S. government was involved in the persecution was also correct. In this essay I have tried to demonstrate that the Temple's perception of being persecuted was not mere fantasy, but was a correct reading of a well-orchestrated effort that was mounted against Peoples Temple to destroy the institution. The intention was surely not to destroy the members of the organization, but that is what happened.

Relatives, the news media, and the government perpetuated violence against the group even after its death. News accounts sensationalized the rumors, innuendoes, and gossip provided by apostates and relatives. The media demonized Peoples Temple members by showing them over and over again in death, rather than in life. *Time* and *Newsweek* would have been guilty of libel had not my sisters been dead, but libel laws do not cover the dead and so anything, and everything, was said about them, including the accusation that my sister Carolyn was a member of a death squad seeking opponents of Peoples Temple. The U.S. government wanted to bury the bodies in Guyana, but when the Guyanese government loudly protested, shipped them to Dover Air Force Base, two thousand miles from the Temple's home base in San Francisco.

The most egregious violence in my mind was the government's failure to perform even the most rudimentary of medical examinations on the bodies. No blood, tissue, or urine samples were obtained. An autopsy is the very least society owes the victims of violent death, but neither the U.S. nor the Guyana governments conducted these in any meaningful way. This means that the real cause of the deaths in Jonestown is ultimately unknown, as the autopsy report on Carolyn prepared by the Armed Forces Institute of Pathology indicates:

Cause of Death: Probably cyanide poisoning.
Manner of Death: Undetermined (R. Moore 1985, 45).

The injury Peoples Temple did to itself is obvious. The injury done against Peoples Temple is equally obvious, but nowhere have I heard any words of remorse from those involved in the actions against Peoples Temple. In fact, members of the Concerned Relatives criticized my parents in January 1979 for not joining them. As recently as 1996 a Temple apostate, seeing my mother for the first time in twenty years, said, "You could have prevented it!"

All of us who had relatives in Peoples Temple are involved in varying degrees with the tragic outcome. My parents, John and Barbara Moore, chose to affirm the good that they saw in Peoples Temple and in my sisters. They questioned the Temple's secrecy and its adulation of Jim Jones. They chose not to side with either the enemies of Peoples Temple or with Peoples Temple itself, but with my sisters. Although we do not know how this stance factored into the final equation, we admit that undoubtedly we played some role. I have never heard any of the Concerned Relatives make even a partial admission of responsibility for accelerating the conflict that exacerbated the tension in Jonestown, or for instigating the persecution of Peoples Temple.

It took almost ten years for a scholar to link the actions of the Concerned Relatives with the apocalypse in Jonestown, which Hall did in *Gone from the Promised Land*. "The key to understanding Jonestown," he wrote, "thus lies in the dynamics of conflict between a religious community and an external political order" (Hall 1987, 296). Twenty years after Jonestown, Bromley put together *The Politics of Religious Apostasy: The Role of Apostates in the Transformation of Religious Movements*, which further explored the role apostates play in affecting the internal dynamics of New Religious Movements (1998a). The essays in Bromley's book document the effect former members have in shaping public perceptions of nontraditional—or, as he calls them, contestant and subversive—religions.

Despite Hall's earlier work, scholars of NRMs still have failed to take the Temple's complaints against the government seriously, dismissing them as Temple rhetoric or conspiracy theorizing. The actions by Temple members on their final day seem to encourage a spirit of condemnation or indifference. The sympathy that scholars had for the Branch Davidians reflects a critical attitude toward apostates that did not extend retroactively toward the Concerned Relatives. In addition, scholars were critical of how the government handled the situation at Waco. I have yet to see outrage over government handling of Peoples Temple either before, during, or after November 18, 1978, and a full examination of what the U.S. government did, and did not do, has never been completed. The Staff Investigative Report on Ryan's assassination may have information on this, but because much of the document is classified, it is impossible to tell what the committee may have learned.

The violence of society and government both molded Peoples Temple and later turned on the Temple itself. That violence exists today just as surely as it did in 1952, 1965, and 1978. Although Peoples Temple at first rejected the injustice of its culture, it eventually embraced injustice as a social necessity. It went further, however, in adopting self-directed violence as a means of political change. While those in the group saw themselves as martyrs sending a message to capitalist America with their revolutionary suicide, the group actually eliminated its own radical foot soldiers. Given the society that spawned the movement, Peoples Temple's adoption of violence as a way to redirect the course of human events is utterly American and seems almost inevitable.

# 6

# *The Magic of Death*

## The Suicides of the Solar Temple

MASSIMO INTROVIGNE —————————————————————

The three incidents of suicides and homicides involving the Order of the Solar Temple (in French, Ordre du Temple Solaire, OTS)—an esoteric new religious movement based in Switzerland and Quebec— elude easy comparisons with Jonestown and Waco (Hall and Schuyler 1997). They are much more like the 1997 group suicide of Heaven's Gate in Rancho Santa Fe, California. The OTS did not belong to any catastrophic millennial tradition, and was part of a larger religious subculture in which apocalypticism is not widespread. Additionally, OTS members did not fit the stereotype of the desperate "cult" member. Most of them were solid, respectable, middle-age citizens, some with considerable financial means.

On the other hand, when more closely examined, a number of elements in the bizarre history of the OTS offer material for comparison with other recent violent incidents involving new religious movements. To situate the OTS in this larger picture, I will, first, discuss the religious subculture in which it was born (a subculture largely ignored in the English-speaking world). Second, I will briefly review the history of the OTS focusing on the crucial months before the first homicide-suicide of October 1994. Third, I will discuss the different causes cooperating to produce the extreme results of multiple homicides and suicides committed by OTS members. I will argue that factors both internal and external to the group should be taken into account to understand why the tragedies occurred.

138

## The Magical Milieu

Within the larger milieu of those interested in alternative spirituality (Campbell 1972), a specific magical milieu can be identified. Although some interaction with other segments of the larger alternative milieu exists, in fact members of the magical milieu have a sense of their own distinctiveness. They regard themselves as part of elite movements as contemporary representatives of an "ancient wisdom" older than any organized religion; they regard religion as a lesser form of spirituality. Their social background, from lower- to upper-middle class, is also normally higher than in other parts of the larger alternative milieu. They have absorbed—mostly through the influence of the modern Theosophical tradition—Eastern ideas and terminology, including karma, reincarnation, and chakras (centers of consciousness in spiritual bodies). However, they do not regard themselves as part of the Theosophical milieu, because they feel that the Western esoteric tradition is older and deeper than its Eastern counterpart.

In the magical milieu, movements flourish with different foundational mythologies connected to the Grail, Egypt, gnosticism, the Rosicrucians (a mythical brotherhood of supposedly remote antiquity first mentioned in early seventeenth-century documents), and the medieval Knights Templar (a Catholic religious order suppressed by the Church and the French king Philip the Fair in 1312, whose secret survival to modern times is unanimously rejected by academic historians, yet vigorously affirmed by a variety of esoteric movements). Within the magical milieu, each group selects a preferred foundational myth, and it is possible to distinguish between neo-Templar, neo-Rosicrucian, neo-gnostic, and other subtypes of magical new religious movements (or new magical movements; see Introvigne 1990). Dual and multiple membership (unlike in other new religious movements) is the rule rather than the exception, and the same individual often belongs to a variety of different groups.

The magical milieu also entertains a complicated relationship with Freemasonry and with the Christian churches of the liturgical tradition (Roman Catholic and Anglican). Participants in the milieu widely believe that both these churches and Freemasonry were once part of a valid esoteric chain, but have in the latest centuries lost their legitimacy, becoming too mundane and rationalist. Members of the magical milieu frequently try to obtain a Masonic initiation, often from splinter lodges or "fringe Masonry." Also, it is not unusual for some of them to be ordained as priests or consecrated as bishops in one of the many small splinter churches led by "wandering bishops," who claim a more or less remote and genuine Catholic or Anglican succession. On the other hand, magical milieu participants remain largely critical of all contemporary mainline forms of the Christian Church and of Freemasonry (the more so in the French-speaking world, where the largest Masonic groups parted company from the English-speaking lodges in the nineteenth century to proclaim a more rationalist, and occasionally atheistic, worldview).

The ancient wisdom of the new magical movements is not usually apocalyptic. Their worldview seems much more preoccupied with the individual "ascension" of each initiate to a higher state of existence or awareness than with the future of the world at large. On the other hand, this ancient wisdom is almost invariably dualistic. It claims a radical distinction between this world of darkness and the world of light accessible to initiates only. As the history of gnosticism shows (Cohn 1957), radical dualism can verge toward apocalypticism. Whether or not actual apocalyptic thought develops may depend upon a number of factors including the prevailing social conditions and the relationship between each dualistic movement and society. Apocalypticism does not prevail in most of the modern families of new magical movements. This observation applies, although exceptions exist, to the neo-Templar groups and to the Rosicrucian tradition, of which the largest international body is AMORC, the Ancient and Mystical Order Rosae Crucis founded by an American, Harvey Spencer Lewis (1883–1939), and headquartered in San Jose, California, but dozens of other movements are also active (Introvigne 1990, 184–215).

Although Templar rituals, based upon the mythical underground survival of the medieval Order of the Temple, existed in European Freemasonry since the eighteenth century (Le Forestier 1987), most modern neo-Templar movements trace their origin to the Order of the Temple founded in 1805 by Bernard-Raymond Fabré-Palaprat (1777–1838). This French physician and Freemason claimed to represent an uninterrupted succession of Templar "Grand Masters" operating secretly since the suppression of the medieval Order in the fourteenth century. After Fabré-Palaprat's death in 1838, the neo-Templar movement went through a number of schisms, a usual phenomenon in the magical milieu.

After World War II, more than one hundred small neo-Templar bodies were in existence throughout the world (Introvigne 1995a). The Sovereign and Military Order of the Temple of Jerusalem (OSMTJ) probably had the best claim to a succession from Fabré-Palaprat. On the other hand, its French and Italian branches were infiltrated in the 1970s by organizations with dubious political aims, such as the Service d'Action Civique [SAC], a Gaullist private police in France, and the infamous Lodge P2 founded by Licio Gelli in Italy, and lost a number of members. Other international groups emerged, claiming an alleged succession from other branches of the medieval Order of the Temple preserved outside of France independently from the lineage leading to Fabré-Palaprat. They also referred to mystical experiences in which their founders (in a vein originally popularized by the early Theosophical Society) were directly initiated (occasionally from the spirit world) by secret "Masters of the Temple."

Jacques Breyer (1922–96), a prolific French esoteric author, claimed to have had precisely that initiatory experience with two companions on June 12, 1952, in the ruins of Arginy Castle in France. He was contacted by the Masters of the Temple and asked to establish a "Templar Renaissance." In 1953 he claimed to have obtained the "apostolic" succession (an allegedly uninterrupted chain from the medieval Knights Templar) by associating to his enterprise Maxime de Roquemaure. The latter, a French nobleman, claimed to have inherited the mantle of a Catalunian branch of the Order of the Temple kept underground for centuries in faraway Ethiopia. These events led to the establishment of the Sovereign Order of the Solar Temple (OSTS). The OSTS was formally established on June 24, 1966. Breyer selected as Grand Master a Monaco socialite, Jean-Louis Marsan (1923–82), a friend of Prince Ranier III. Marsan incorporated the OSTS under Monaco law in 1967.

In the 1960s both Raymond Bernard (b. 1923) and Julien Origas (1920–83) came into contact with the Arginy movement. Origas had been an interpreter and perhaps a minor agent for the Nazi police during the German occupation of France. He had served three years in jail for these activities.[1] Bernard was the second highest ranking officer in the international hierarchy of the Rosicrucian order AMORC and the leader of AMORC's extremely successful French-speaking branch. After meeting Breyer, Bernard decided that it would be wise to establish a Templar order controlled by himself in order to keep within the fold members of the French chapter of AMORC seeking a parallel neo-Templar initiation.

1. In sensationalist accounts of the Solar Temple, these rather minor activities of Origas as a Nazi collaborator were elevated to the mythical status of leader of the whole Gestapo in Brest.

In 1969 Bernard circulated a photocopied text relating his meeting in Rome with "Jean," a French gentleman "connected with a royal family." "Jean" led Bernard to the "crypt" of the Catholic abbey of St. Nilus in nearby Grottaferrata. Here Bernard was created a Knight Templar by a mysterious "White Cardinal," associated with the true Order of the Temple (Caillet 1997, 41–43; Bernard 1970, 180–83). Later (see Bernard 1976), Bernard added references to a council of twelve secret Masters ruling the world whose leader was called Maha. Bernard ultimately admitted (1997, 167) that the Grottaferrata episode, "Jean," the White Cardinal, the Council of the Twelve, and Maha were all "purely fictional" figments of his own imagination. They were, however, he claimed, based upon deeply moving personal mystical experiences including one during a visit to St. Nilus—where, by the way, there is no crypt.

What is true is that claiming authority from the secret Masters, Bernard had initiated in 1968 two trusted AMORC associates, Robert Devaux and Julien Origas, as Knights Templar in the Cathedral of Chartres (Caillet 1997, 47–49). In 1970 Bernard incorporated a new neo-Templar organization under French law, the Renewed Order of the Temple (ORT) and became its first president. In 1971 he asked Origas to replace him as president of the ORT. Origas accepted with a letter in which he told Bernard that "I will only be your straw man" (56). During 1971–72, the ORT flourished with hundreds of members under a double structure. Origas was formally the president, but he reported to a "Secret Grand Master," who was the real leader of the ORT—Bernard (60–61). The double structure was needed to keep the ORT clearly separated from, yet ultimately controlled by, the French branch of AMORC. The arrangement was at first accepted by Ralph M. Lewis (1904–87), the American Imperator (world leader) of AMORC. In October 1972, however, with Lewis increasingly concerned about the possible detrimental effect on the international AMORC of ORT's increasing success, Bernard decided to leave the ORT. Although maintaining a good personal relationship with Origas, Bernard started discouraging AMORC members from joining the neo-Templar order.[2]

---

2. In 1988 Bernard finally left AMORC, and revived, in connection with his new organization CIRCES (International Center for Cultural and Spiritual Research), another neo-Templar organization he had asked Origas to establish in 1971, the Sovereign Order of the Initiatic Temple (OSTI). OSTI had remained largely dormant before 1988. For a fictionalized (and ferocious, often frankly unfair) hostile account of the esoteric career of Bernard, barely disguised under a pseudonym, see Damotte 1996.

Origas was thus left on his own and became the real Grand Master. Origas continued to rely upon secret Masters. He also reconstructed the ORT's doctrine based on the teachings of the I AM Religious Activity of the United States.[3] Origas first received these teachings from a splinter group led in southern France by Angela von Bast. After his break with von Bast in 1977, Origas came into contact with the parent I AM, whose European headquarters are in Switzerland (130).

Origas was a difficult man, and personality conflicts led to half a dozen schisms.[4] On the other hand, although distinct from OSTS, Origas's ORT kept excellent relations with Breyer and recognized the primacy of the founding experience at Arginy (Mayer 1997, 23).

On March 21, 1981, the leaders of OSTS and ORT converged in a ceremony in Geneva to swear allegiance to a "once and future" supreme secret Master of the Temple (Delaforge 1987, 136; Mayer 1997, 22). They met on the premises of a third organization, also associated with the ceremony and recognized by Breyer as part of the Arginy movement: the Golden Way Foundation established by Joseph Di Mambro (1924–94). The ceremony of March 21, 1981, was—according to Di Mambro (Mayer 1997, 22)—at least as important as the Arginy experience, and was later cited as the founding date of the Order of the Solar Temple.[5]

## The Order of the Solar Temple

Di Mambro was born in Pont-Saint-Esprit (Gard, France) in 1924. A jeweler by trade, in 1956 he joined AMORC (Mayer 1997, 13). He

---

3. The I AM Religious Activity was established by Guy W. Ballard (1878–1939), who in 1930 reported an encounter with Ascended Master Saint Germain on Mount Shasta in California. In 1932 Ballard incorporated in Chicago the Saint Germain Foundation. I AM teaches that regular contact with the Masters may be established through special techniques. With the appropriate training, human beings may eventually ascend to the exalted state of Masters immediately after death.

4. Among those alienated by Origas was Patrick Truchemotte (1929–86), who in 1973 had ordained Origas as a priest in his small Catholic splinter group, the Gallican Catholic Church. Truchemotte then sponsored the schismatic Order of the Knights of the Holy Temple, also known as Resurrected Order of the Temple (ORT) (Caillet 1997, 107–8, 135).

5. The ceremony did not imply any merger between the OSTS, the ORT, and the Golden Way Foundation. Although the OSTS leaders Breyer and Marsan kept in touch with Di Mambro and Origas, they kept their organization strictly separate. This point is

had some responsibilities in the Rosicrucian organization and left it about 1970. Di Mambro displayed considerable skill as a spiritualist medium channeling discarnate Masters, and he was looking for experiences stronger than AMORC. He joined the Arginy movement and traveled to Egypt and Israel (where he allegedly conceived his son Elie [1969–94] on Mount Carmel, a mountain associated with the biblical prophet Elias). After a minor skirmish with French justice in 1971 for writing bad checks, Di Mambro moved to Annemasse near the Swiss border, and later to Switzerland. There he started in 1973 a full-time career as a teacher of yoga and occult philosophy. From that time on, Di Mambro established an astonishing number of secret (and not so secret) societies, organizations, and associations, whose names may easily confuse both the initiates and the scholars. His main venture in the 1970s was La Pyramide (1976–78) in which his closest students lived communally.

In 1977 Nicole Koymans (1928–94), a yoga teacher in Geneva and a member of Di Mambro's inner circle, brought to La Pyramide her student Christine Meylan (1944–94) and Meylan's husband, Michel Tabachnik, already well known in musical circles as a promising young conductor. In 1978 Tabachnik joined Di Mambro's new venture, the Golden Way Foundation. Tabachnik moved to an apartment within the Golden Way property in Saconnex-d'Arve near Geneva with his second wife, Sabine, a student of Di Mambro, who had divorced Christian Pechot (1945–94). Christian Pechot later married Tabachnik's former wife, Christine Meylan, and both died in the 1994 tragedy. In 1979 Tabachnik became the president of the Golden Way Foundation, whose real leader remained Di Mambro (Tabachnik 1997, 62).

---

worth noting, for Marsan's friendship with both Prince Ranier III of Monaco and Di Mambro led in 1997 to the extraordinary claim by news media that Princess Grace was a member of the Order of the Solar Temple (Carr-Brown and Cohen 1997). There is no evidence that Prince Ranier III and Princess Grace were members of OSTS. Princess Grace died in 1982, whereas the Order of the Solar Temple (OTS) was established in 1984. The name of Princess Grace was not mentioned in any of the surviving OTS papers found in Switzerland. The story about Princess Grace was sold to the British television network Channel Four and other media by one "Georges Leroux," allegedly a former member of the OTS. In fact "Leroux," whose real name is Guy Mouyrin, is not mentioned in any of the (fairly complete) existing lists of OTS members. Mouyrin, on the other hand, is well known to the Swiss and French police as a former convict and professional con artist (personal communication from Jean-François Mayer, Jan. 1998).

At this stage Di Mambro's ideas were still largely derived from AMORC with little emphasis on Knights Templar or neo-Templarism (although he knew Origas since their AMORC years). The core membership of Di Mambro's group was composed of the "brotherhood" living communally in Saconnex-d'Arve (Tabachnik 1997, 65–66; 76–77).

In 1982 the Golden Way was joined by Luc Jouret (1947–94), a Belgian homeopathic doctor who had established a practice in Annemasse. Jouret was born in 1947 in Kikwit, Belgian Congo (present-day Zaire), to Belgian parents. After graduation as a medical doctor in Brussels in 1974 and military service as a paratrooper, his interests had focused on alternative and New Age medicine, particularly homeopathy. He also had contacts with a number of Belgian New Age, Masonic, and occult groups, and had visited the Far East. In 1977 Jouret and his wife-to-be Christine Pertué (1952–94) became affiliated with the World Teacher Trust (WTT), an organization established in 1971 in India by Ekkirala Krishnamacharya (1926–84) called "Master E. K." The WTT combines ideas about the Masters derived from the Theosophical Society and the theosophical author Alice Bailey with a strong emphasis on homeopathic medicine. Jouret and Pertué visited Master E. K. in India and were instrumental in promoting the WTT throughout French-speaking Europe. After his meeting with Di Mambro in 1982 and Master E. K.'s death in 1984, Jouret did not keep in contact with the WTT (personal communication, WTT Europe, December 1997). Jouret divorced Pertué after five years of marriage in 1985. However, she remained in the OTS and died in the Swiss tragedy in 1994. In the 1980s, Jouret's reputation as a homeopathic doctor became remarkable to the point of becoming international, but Jouret also established himself as a respected lecturer on naturopathy and ecological topics in the wider New Age circuit. In 1981 he established the Amenta Club to manage his speaking engagements. After 1982, the Amenta Club (later renamed Atlanta) became a vehicle to disseminate Di Mambro's ideas about secret Masters. In Jouret, Di Mambro not only gained a trusted associate but also a charismatic and popular speaker, much younger and energetic than the sixty-year-old Di Mambro. Di Mambro introduced Jouret to Origas, and the Belgian doctor quickly ascended to a leadership position in the ORT.

Documentary evidence exists indicating that before his death in 1983 Origas designated Jouret as his heir and future Grand Master of the ORT. Jouret's claims originally were not disputed by ORT's members; however, it soon became clear that Jouret was introducing into the ORT new teachings inspired by Di Mambro that were quite foreign to Origas's ideas. The Origas family and the Grand Prior of the ORT, the Italian Gregorio Baccolini (1913–97),[6] reacted. They took advantage of the fact that Jouret had never been consecrated as Grand Master in a formal ceremony (a matter of considerable importance in esoteric circles). Nor was Jouret an officer of the legal ORT structure incorporated under French law. Jouret, thus, was excluded from the ORT in September 1984. The ORT went on under the leadership of Origas's widow, Germaine, and Gregorio Baccolini. It maintained in 1997 some five-hundred members (Caillet 1997, 147–49).

Jouret, who had no legal right to the name ORT, had to create with Di Mambro a new splinter organization called in 1984 ORT-Solar Tradition and later International Order of Chivalry-Solar Tradition, or Order of the Solar Temple. Asked to mediate, Breyer suggested that ORT and OTS separate amicably, seeing no harm in multiplying the movements recognizing the Arginy Renaissance (Mayer 1997, 27). Breyer, however, could not prevent the development of bitter feelings between the two orders. Breyer strongly suggested that Jouret's and Di Mambro's branch resettle in Canada. Both OSTS and ORT had some members there, and Tabachnik had moved to Toronto for professional reasons. Breyer hoped that his brand of neo-Templarism would thus eventually spread to the United States and the whole of the Americas.

Di Mambro and his wife, Jocelyne (1949–94), settled in Toronto in 1984. In 1987 a book was published in English under a pseudonym with the aim of disseminating Templar ideas into the United States (Delaforge 1987). By this time, Di Mambro's movement was like a system of Chinese boxes. People at first attended Jouret's speeches organized by the Amenta and Atlanta Clubs. Those most interested were invited to join the Archédia Club, an occult (but not truly secret) organization with a quasi-Masonic initiation ceremony. The most dedicated members of the Archédia Club were eventually invited to join the

6. As a young Catholic Benedictine priest, Baccolini was a chaplain in the fascist Republic of Salò at the end of World War II (journalistic accounts of the OTS later made him out to be Mussolini's confessor, an entirely fantastic claim). After the war he joined the Moscow Patriarchate of the Eastern Orthodox Church, and then a number of (noncanonical) Orthodox splinter churches: the Church of the True Believers of Greece, the Autocephalous Ukraine Church, and the independent Kiev Patriarchate. Besides his association with Origas's ORT, Baccolini was the Grand Master of the Order of the Poor Knights of the Temple of Solomon, still another neo-Templar order headquartered in his hometown, Torino, Italy.

true secret Templar organization, the OTS. Contrary to Breyer's prophecy, very little recruiting success was obtained in the English-speaking world.

In 1989 (possibly the year of its maximum success) the OTS had, according to Swiss historian Jean-François Mayer, 442 members. Ninety were in Switzerland, 187 in France, 53 in Martinique (in the French-speaking Antilles), 10 in Spain, 86 in Canada (mostly in Quebec), and only 16 in the United States (Mayer 1997, 31–32). Quebec became, on the other hand, a focus of OTS activities, and by 1984 a number of members were living communally in Sainte-Anne-de-la-Pérade. Jouret had considerable success in French-speaking Canada as a motivational speaker, especially at Hydro-Quebec, the public hydroelectric utility of the Province of Quebec. There he recruited fifteen executives and managers for the OTS between 1987 and 1989. By this time, an apocalyptic element was a central part of OTS teaching.

The theme of the "end of the world" had been introduced into the neo-Templar tradition by Breyer (1959). His book on esotericism, *Arcanes Solaires, ou les Sécrets du Temple Solaire,* ended with a study of the "secret of the Solar Temple," presented as an "alchemical" chronology of humanity. The human race had passed through six ages, each dominated by a different religion, and Christianity was "the last religion." The end of the age of Christianity would be "the end of the world" for us. Humanity would move to "the New Earth, a celestial extension of humanity" (not another planet but a transformed planet Earth) (Breyer 1959, 250). For the end of Christianity and thus the end of the world, Breyer proposed three speculative and alternative dates: 1999, 2147 (or 2156), and 2666. He noted, however, that although these three dates were the most probable, a number of other dates could be proposed (257). At any rate, dates were less important than an appropriate spiritual preparation.

Jouret combined Breyer's doctrine with New Age fears about destruction of our planet by pollution and ecological resource mismanagement. The OTS was also influenced by a number of survivalist themes. In 1986 the OTS published two volumes of *Survivre à l'an 2000* (How to survive the year 2000), which included both occult doctrine and practical advice in the style of American survivalist literature. Although Breyer was originally responsible for indicating that catastrophic events were threatening Europe, and that Canada might eventually become an ark of salvation, he was not enthusiastic about OTS date-setting. In the 1990s, Breyer increasingly kept his distances from the OTS.

According to Mayer, the OTS, in turn, distanced itself from Breyer by de-Christianizing its message and de-Catholicizing its ritual. OTS rites included a mass, because Jouret had in 1984 been ordained a priest by Jean Laborie (1919–96), bishop of a small fringe Catholic splinter group, the Latin Old Catholic Church (Caillet 1997, 108). By comparing similar OSTS and OTS rituals, Mayer concluded that Jouret and Di Mambro had de-catholicized both the mass and other neo-Templar rites (Mayer 1997, 28–30), and had included references to non-Christian occult traditions.[7] These references included UFO and extraterrestrial lore, a feature already present (but certainly less important) in Breyer's OSTS.

When the public discovered the OTS apocalyptic worldview behind the facade of Jouret's motivational speeches, the group started to experience strong and organized opposition.

### The Tragedy

In the French-speaking world, the anticult movement is much more prominent than elsewhere. It has experienced (well before the first Solar Temple deaths in 1994, which added fuel to the fire) a degree of governmental support unknown in the English-speaking world (Introvigne and Melton 1996). The OTS, however, barely caught the attention of the French anticult organizations in the 1980s, although it was occasionally mentioned.

The situation changed in 1991. In that year, the Martinique branch of ADFI (Association pour la défense des familles et de l'individu, the largest French anticult organization), ADFI-Martinique, denounced the conversion of wealthy Martinicans to the OTS and their eventual move to Quebec. ADFI-Martinique was able to join forces with the Swiss Rose-Marie Klaus, a disgruntled OTS former member. Her husband, Bruno (1947–97), had left her within the frame of "cosmic" marriage rearrangements allegedly dictated by the secret Masters. Rose-Marie Klaus contacted the Canadian anticult association, Info-Secte, Quebec's branch

---

7. Although Hall and Schuyler (1997) emphasize the cultural continuity between OTS and Roman Catholicism, it is perhaps useful to note that in the French-speaking magical milieu (and in the OTS) we do not find only persons with a strong Catholic background. There are also those raised according to the canons of the French "laïcité" with quite anti-Catholic (if not anti-Christian) feelings, that are particularly widespread in some segments of the upper classes in France, Belgium, and French-speaking Switzerland.

of a larger international anticult network, and was eventually invited to speak in Martinique at the end of 1992 (Hall and Schuyler 1997, 299). Eventually, Klaus's determined opposition made inroads, and Jouret found it increasingly difficult to be invited as a motivational speaker.

In November 1992 members of the Canadian Parliament received death threats from a mysterious terrorist group, Q-37 (allegedly including 37 members from Quebec). Q-37 announced the intended murder of Quebec's minister of the interior, Claude Ryan, considered guilty of adopting a political line too favorable to the claims of Native Americans. Although it was later admitted that Q-37 most probably never existed, the Quebec police suspected a possible involvement of the OTS. Although Jouret occasionally expressed views hostile to the claims of Native Americans in Quebec, this was by no means an important concern for the OTS. There were many right-wing organizations more likely to be associated with Q-37.

It was, as a consequence, probable that the information leading to the opening of an investigation of the OTS on February 2, 1993 (Mayer 1997, 45), came from the anticult milieu. Within the frame of this investigation, two OTS members, Jean-Pierre Vinet (1939–94) and Hermann Delorme, were arrested on March 8, 1993, as they attempted to buy three semiautomatic guns with silencers, illegal weapons in Quebec. An arrest warrant was also issued against Luc Jouret, who was at that time in Europe. In fact, the arms deal had been arranged by a police informant engaged in a sting operation. The prosecution ended with a "suspended acquittal" and a minor fine for Jouret, Vinet, and Delorme. Delorme left the OTS after the incident (Delorme 1996, 19–24).

Jumping on the news about OTS, Rose-Marie Klaus managed to have lurid accounts of the "cult of the end of the world" published in a number of daily newspapers and tabloid magazines (Introvigne 1995a; Hall and Schuyler 1997, 301). Vinet was fired from his position at Hydro-Québec, and police investigations were launched in France and Australia, where Di Mambro had some financial interests, later grossly exaggerated by sensationalist accounts in the press.

It is not easy to determine whether the preparation for a "transit" of the core members of the OTS to another planet was started before or after the first Canadian police actions in 1993. According to Mayer, who has participated in the Swiss official police investigation and has studied the files left on OTS computers in Switzerland, dates of creation of documents show that the first versions of the texts about the "transit" were written almost at the same time when the Canadian investigation was started in February 1993 (Mayer 1997, 45). By that time, Rose-Marie Klaus had already launched her public campaign (Hall and Schuyler 1997, 299).

In the same year, the OTS was confronted by two major factors of internal stress. In Quebec, Jouret had proved not as effective as a manager of the different Templar activities than as a public speaker. Dissension erupted, and Robert Falardeau (1947–94), an officer with the Quebec Ministry of Finances, replaced him as Grand Master. Jouret founded a new organization called ARCHS (Academy for the Research and Knowledge of Higher Science). Jacques Rochelle, the lawyer of the defendants in the Canadian case, first called the separation a "schism" in a 1993 press conference (Pelchat 1993).

Although Rochelle was understandably attempting to protect his clients, things were—as usual in the magical milieu (and in the Arginy tradition)—more complicated. According to Delorme (1996, 94), although the new organization had a distinctive style, several persons remained members of both ARCHS and OTS. Both groups acknowledged the ultimate authority of Di Mambro. Di Mambro, however, was experiencing problems with his personal dignity and his leadership based upon charismatic claims to revelation from the Masters. He had serious health problems and was compelled to wear diapers. A number of French and Swiss members had left the OTS in 1993, wondering whether their money had not mostly been spent to support the leader's rather luxurious lifestyle. Worst, dating to 1990, rumors were circulating that the most secret and sacred experience of the OTS—visible manifestations of the Masters of the Temple—were, in fact, electronic tricks stage-managed on behalf of Di Mambro by Tony Dutoit (1958–94). These rumors led Di Mambro's son, Elie, to quit the OTS. Dutoit and his wife eventually confirmed the rumors, distanced themselves from Di Mambro, and in 1994 named their newborn baby Christopher Emmanuel. The naming was particularly intolerable to Di Mambro, who regarded the name Emmanuel reserved for his daughter Emmanuelle, but addressed in the OTS as "Emmanuel" as if she were a male. Emmanuelle (1982–94)—allegedly conceived by Dominique Bellaton (1958–94), Di Mambro's mistress, through cosmic intercourse with a discarnate Master—was regarded as the embodiment of the Cosmic Christ. As a consequence, Di Mambro become persuaded that the infant Christopher Emmanuel Dutoit was the Antichrist. In the 1990s, while some members—through a cognitive dissonance phenomenon not unusual in the magical tradition—explained away the stage-managed apparitions of the Masters as an unfortunate but necessary way to keep weaker souls within the fold, others left the OTS.

Di Mambro's threatened loss of charisma within the OTS explains his paranoid reaction to the different police investigations. In 1994 his lawyer informed him that, owing to a number of "political and legal" reasons connected to "a pending criminal investigation," the passport of his wife, Jocelyne, might not be renewed. Di Mambro reacted with a document concluding that "all the polices in the world are focused on us. Our file is secret, nobody could access it but the leaders." He claimed that OTS was "the hottest file in the planet, the most important of the decade if not of the century" (Mayer 1997, 59–61). Di Mambro concluded that "the game is afoot, and the concentration of hate against us will supply the energy needed for our departure."

The departure, as we know, took place in October 1994. It is unclear exactly when messages from the Masters and from a "Heavenly Lady" channeled by Di Mambro and by Camille Pilet (1926–94), the most prominent and wealthy businessman in the OTS and the alleged reincarnation of Joseph of Arimathea, started preparing the Templars for a "transit" outside this world (probably about 1990). It is also unclear when exactly (probably in late 1993) at least an inner core of members learned that the "transit" would not involve a spaceship or other extraterrestrial vehicles but a mystical suicide.

On October 4, 1994, fire destroyed Joseph Di Mambro's villa in Morin Heights, Quebec. Among the ruins, the police found five charred bodies. Three of these people—the Dutoit couple and their "Antichrist" baby son—had been stabbed to death before the fire was started. Two Swiss members of the OTS, Gerry Genoud (1955–94) and his wife, Colette Rochat (1931–94), ignited the villa and voluntarily died in the fire. Having perpetrated or at least supervised the murders in Morin Heights—which probably took place on September 30—Joel Egger (1959–94) and Dominique Bellaton (the mother of the "cosmic child" Emmanuelle Di Mambro) joined fifty-one members and children of members of the OTS in Switzerland.

In the early morning of October 5, the police found all of them dead in two OTS centers, one in Cheiry (canton of Fribourg) and one in Granges-sur-Salvan (canton Valais). Twenty-three bodies were found at Cheiry and twenty-five at Granges-sur-Salvan along with the remains of devices set to start the fires that almost destroyed both centers. Among the victims at the Cheiry farm was its owner, Albert Giacobino (1932–94). Regarded as a traitor, he was suffocated to death with a plastic bag.

Renée Pfaehler (1914–94) and Camille Pilet appear also to have died by suffocation in plastic bags. Both were faithful members of the OTS and their deaths were probably voluntary. The other victims in Cheiry were killed by pistol shots. Those dead in Salvan were poisoned—or poisoned themselves—with a lethal mixture of drugs, with the possible exceptions of two teenagers—the cosmic child Emmanuelle Di Mambro and Aude Séverino (1979–94)—and three adults (Elie, the apostate son of Joseph Di Mambro, Madeleine Brot [1956–94], and Pauline Lemonde [1938–94]), who may have died in the fire without first having been poisoned. The lengthy investigation by the Swiss police and judiciary confirmed that most of those dead at Cheiry were murdered, while at least a good half of those found at Granges-sur-Salvan committed suicide.

The dichotomy between suicide and murder is only part of the story, if we believe four documents sent by the OTS to the press, to former members, and to scholars through Patrick Vuarnet (1968–95) (a member of the OTS and the son of French former skiing champion turned industrialist Jean Vuarnet). The documents were accompanied, in some cases, by videos and by a fifth document in which Di Mambro deplored "the barbarous, incompetent and aberrant conduct of Doctor Luc Jouret," who had transformed in a "veritable carnage" what should have been a glorious transit. The documents, collectively referred to as "the Testament," mentioned that some "traitors" had been "executed." However, they also suggested that together with the killed traitors (including the Dutoits in Quebec, Di Mambro's son Elie, and possibly Falardeau) and the core members strong enough to understand the full implications of the transit, there were also weaker Templars. The latter did not disagree with the idea of the transit (although they may have figured it as something different from a suicide), but needed some "help" to accomplish it. The Testament's description of the different types of deaths was consistent with the findings of the Swiss official investigation (Mayer 1997; Introvigne 1995b).

Interestingly, very few former OTS members reinterpreted the OTS within the frame of the anticult worldview. Those few included Thierry Huguénin (1995), who barely escaped the Swiss killings. Most of the former Templars continued to express sympathy for the OTS, and some explicitly told the Swiss judges that they regretted not having been "called" by Di Mambro to participate in the transit (Mayer 1997, 74).

In fact, it seemed that Di Mambro had planned the survival of some "witnesses" by establishing in Avignon on September 24, 1994, yet another organization, the ARC. ARC stood for Association for Cultural Research for the external world, and Alliance Rosy-Cross for initiates. The idea of having both a "public" and a "secret" name for the same organization was consistent with Di Mambro's style and his paranoid need for secrecy.

One of the speakers at the Avignon meeting founding ARC was Michel Tabachnik. Despite his personal dislike for Luc Jouret that, he now says, prevented him from formally joining the OTS (Tabachnik 1997, 75, 91), Tabachnik had been an occasional speaker for the movement in Quebec and had kept in touch with Di Mambro. The only public figure to survive the 1994 tragedy, Tabachnik subsequently was accused by the anticult movement and by some media of being the hidden leader of the OTS or at least the successor of Di Mambro. His musical career was compromised. In 1996 a criminal action was started in Grenoble, France, against Tabachnik regarded as a possible ideological source of the tragedies through his speeches and writings. He insisted that he never approved the suicides and homicides, and regarded himself, rather, as a "scapegoat" (Tabachnik 1997).

Notwithstanding the continued police interest in what was left of the OTS, a second tragedy happened in 1995. On December 23, sixteen members of the OTS—including Patrick Vuarnet and his mother—and three children of the members were found dead in the Vercors mountains near Grenoble. The first findings of the French investigation concluded that at least some of the dead (and certainly the children) were murdered. At any rate, all died by pistol shots. The organizer of the tragedy, and the leader of what was left of the OTS in Europe after Di Mambro's death, appeared to have been Swiss psychotherapist Christiane Bonet (1945–95), seconded by two French policemen in active duty, Jean-Pierre Lardanchet (1959–95) and Patrick Rostan (1966–95). French investigators think that the victims were killed by Lardanchet and by a Swiss OTS member, André Friedli (1956–95), who finally shot themselves.

In a third incident discovered on the evening of March 22, 1997, in Saint-Casimir, Quebec, five members of the OTS committed suicide. These were Bruno Klaus, the former husband of vocal apostate Rose-Marie, Pauline Riou (1942–97), Didier Quèze (1957–97), his wife, Chantal (1955–97), and his mother-in-law, Suzanne Druau (1931–97). Druau was suffocated by a plastic bag (a trademark of OTS deaths) while the others were asphyxiated from smoke before being reached by the fire set to the Quèze home. There was no evidence of violence or poisoning although the victims had consumed significant doses of tranquilizers. The three children of the Quèze couple, two boys (13 and 16) and a girl (14) (Séguin 1997), discovered a first aborted attempt to set fire to the home during the night between March 20 and 21. This led to a discussion between the adults and the children, and the children were permitted to choose whether they would participate in the suicide. On the night of March 21 the children were still undecided and debating among themselves. Based upon the children's testimony, the Quèzes had the impression that the children were ready to "leave" with them, and in the night between March 21 and 22 suffocated, with her consent, the grandmother, Suzanne Druau. Didier Quèze then tried to set in motion the machinery intended to cause the fire, but he was ultimately stopped by the children, who still wanted to discuss the question of their deaths. In the early morning of March 22 the children finally decided that they did not want to die. They were mildly drugged and helped their father set fire to the house, then left with some personal possessions and "some mementos of their parents" (Naud 1997, 3–4).

Although only a handful of persons who regard themselves as members of the OTS—or the ARC—remain alive in Europe or Quebec after the third tragedy, further suicides cannot be excluded, as long as even one single person still shares the OTS's ideology and thus regards the transit as both reasonable and desirable.

### Why the Tragedies?

Why exactly, among hundreds of groups in the magical milieu (more than a hundred in the neo-Templar subfamily alone), only the OTS evolved toward suicide and murder is not an easily answered question.

The anticult movement and some journalists closely associated with French and Swiss anticult organizations at first suggested the usual model of brainwashing. When, however, they took a closer look at the personalities of those who died, they had to recognize that most of the Templars did not fit the usual profile of "brainwashed cultists." As mentioned earlier, the Templars were not college students but solid middle-class citizens (and, in some cases, they were members of the Geneva jet set). The brainwashing explanation was, thus, converted into the claim that the OTS was not what it claimed to be, but a facade to hide a different kind of conspiracy involving secret services of different countries, organized crime, and large-scale money-laundering operations (Campiche

1995; Introvigne 1997b).[8] Although entire books have been devoted by militant anticult journalists to these issues, no hard evidence has emerged, and these theories have been dismissed by both the Canadian and the Swiss investigators. Once sensationalist pseudofactors are discarded, a number of concomitant factors, both internal and external, contributing to the tragedies emerge.

External factors include the campaign started by ADFI-Martinique and Rose-Marie Klaus, and the subsequent police investigations in Quebec, Australia, and France. There is little doubt that this was interpreted by Di Mambro and his closest associates as intolerable persecution. Indeed, the fourth document of the Testament was entirely devoted to accusing those organizing the "systematic persecution" of the OTS, including the government and the police of Quebec, of "mass homicide." Should we, as a consequence, interpret the transit as a response to the opposition? As Hall and Schuyler (1998) remark, "whether the deaths would have been orchestrated absent the opposition and ensuing scandals is a counterfactual experiment that cannot be completed." As we have seen, the dates when the first documents clearly hinting at a radical transit were created on the Swiss computer of the OTS more or less coincide with the first police investigations of the group. The question remains why the OTS reacted to the perceived persecution as it did, while many other new religious (and magical) movements have endured a much larger amount of ridicule, anticult opposition, and police harassment (particularly recently in continental Europe) without any violent reaction.

In this regard, internal factors should also be considered. The perverse effects of Di Mambro's threatened loss of charisma have been emphasized by Susan Palmer (1996), and were indeed a key factor. Similar problems seem to have affected Jim Jones, Asahara Shōkō, and Marshall Herff Applewhite (known as "Do" in Heaven's Gate). All had health problems coupled with disconfirmed prophecies or claims. Not only may they have reinterpreted their loss of health and charisma as a cosmic tragedy, but the group itself may have collectively read the problems of the leader as a metaphor for planetary illness.

Additionally, one is forced to recognize that there are ideologies and doctrines more prone than others to propel a group into violence

8. Scholars, including myself and Jean-François Mayer (who, as I mentioned earlier, participated in the Swiss official investigation), who dismissed these theories from the very beginning were simply regarded by the anticult journalists as part of the conspiracy.

(Introvigne 1995b, 1998; Mayer 1998, 1999; Rosenfeld 1999). The choice of exiting this world becomes rational if the world is regarded as doomed, about to be "recycled" or "spaded under" to use the terms of Marshall Applewhite's Heaven's Gate internet manifestos (Introvigne 1997a).

A number of date-setting movements quietly await the end of the world without resorting to violence. However, unlike the OTS and Heaven's Gate (or the Peoples Temple at Jonestown), most of these groups do not produce narratives in which suicide can be interpreted as something else. The Testament claimed that what the OTS was about to do was not suicide, but something radically different. The Templars—as explained in more detail in three videos sent to a French Templar together with the written documents—through the force of the Blue Star (connected to Sirius) were expected to reach Jupiter where they could eventually become secret Masters themselves. A very similar ideology (although with a different background) was present in Heaven's Gate. The members of Heaven's Gate who committed suicide near San Diego in March 1997 (probably the same day, between March 22 and 23, when the third suicide of the OTS occurred in Quebec) were persuaded to leave Earth simply to reach the interplanetary Kingdom of Heaven. Such narratives are by no means impossible, but less easy to produce in a contemporary Christian context, where there is a strong taboo concerning self-inflicted death. Certainly, in the cosmic vision of the OTS or of Heaven's Gate it makes more sense to become a Master on Jupiter or a god on the planet called Kingdom of Heaven than to remain on planet Earth about to be destroyed.

Other factors may have played a role, including a possible copycat effect connecting one "cult suicide" sensationalized in the media to another. Mayer (1997, 10) mentions a disturbing tape found by the Swiss police in Granges-sur-Salvan, on which Jouret and Di Mambro discuss their plans in spring 1994. Jouret complains that "we have been anticipated by Waco," and Di Mambro replies that in fact "it would have been preferable to leave six months before them." But, at any rate, "what we would do will be more spectacular." It seems that the media have become so important that "making headlines" is the only way for a suicidal movement to find a confirmation that, far from being marginal, it has an important role in this world. In a similar vein, Heaven's Gate mentioned Waco, the OTS, and Aum Shinrikyō in a World Wide Web posting of September 20, 1996 (Introvigne 1997a, 60).

The most astute scholarly speculations notwithstanding, probably we will never know whether the OTS members would have caused the deaths without what they perceived as their systematic persecution. The external factors did play a crucial role according to Hall and Schuyler (1997), while Mayer (1997, 1999) regards the factors internal to the group as primary. A comparison with Heaven's Gate—which, in one of its "exit videos" described as "persecution" the "mixture of ridicule and hostility" experienced when the group started posting its apocalyptic messages on the Internet—seems to confirm that, when internal factors are sufficiently strong, even moderate external opposition is easily translated into a narrative of cosmic persecution. On the other hand, the opposition experienced by the OTS—while not as obviously harsh as that directed against the Branch Davidians—was not exactly moderate. An international police action seems, after all, more serious than a number of jokes posted on the Internet.

# 7

# *Imagined Persecution*

## Aum Shinrikyō, Millennialism, and the Legitimation of Violence

IAN READER _____

### Introduction

The gas attack on the Tokyo subway system on March 20, 1995, was the most extreme in a series of criminal activities carried out by the Japanese new religious movement, Aum Shinrikyō (also known under its English name Aum Supreme Truth). Aum was a small (by Japanese standards) new religious movement founded by the charismatic Asahara Shōkō[1] as a yoga group in 1984. It took under the name Aum Shinsen no Kai in 1986. The organization's name was changed to Aum Shinrikyō in 1987. In 1995 Aum probably had some ten thousand members in Japan of whom over more than eleven hundred were renunciates (*shukkesha*), who had renounced the world and their families, regarded themselves as Buddhist nuns and monks, assumed Buddhist holy names, lived in Aum's communes, and dedicated themselves completely to the religion. Aum had gained a foothold in Russia with estimates of some thirty thousand followers there (although it

---

1. All names are in Japanese style with the family name first followed by the given name. Asahara officially renounced his leadership of Aum in June 1996 in favor of his two sons. This move was designed to draw a line between Asahara (who, although not convicted yet, is officially regarded as the architect of its murderous behavior) and the extant group, so as to assist the organization in its efforts to stop being proscribed under Japanese law. Succession through the family line is very common in Japanese religious movements. For expanded discussion on the themes in this chapter, see Reader 2000.

was banned subsequently),[2] and had made largely unsuccessful attempts to gain converts in Europe and the United States.

The subway attack was a hastily organized affair ordered by Asahara on March 18, 1995, to forestall imminent police raids related to Aum's suspected illegal activities. These included the abduction (and, as it later was discovered, murder) of a property dealer, Kariya Kiyoshi, who was in dispute with Aum concerning his elderly sister, who was a member wanting to leave, and an earlier nerve gas attack in June 1994 in the town of Matsumoto that killed seven and injured hundreds of people.[3]

Under Asahara's orders, members who were chemists manufactured quantities of the nerve gas sarin, which was then placed in plastic bags and carried onto the Tokyo subway by five Aum members who punctured the bags with sharpened umbrella tips releasing the gas into crowded rush-hour trains, killing twelve and injuring thousands of people. If a primary intent of the attack was to forestall police raids, it failed. Because of hasty preparation, the poison gas was impure, and hence did not cause the destruction that otherwise might have occurred. The police raids were not stopped, but took place with increased force starting on March 22, 1995, and continued for several weeks under the full glare of media publicity and with emphatic backing from the government and general public. The police uncovered extensive evidence of wrongdoing over several years. During the investigation, hundreds of Aum officials and members were arrested, including Asahara on May 16, 1995, and many have been charged with crimes ranging from murder and kidnapping to the manufacture of illegal drugs and weapons.

The criminal trials resulting from the "Aum affair" (*Oumu jiken*) will continue for an appreciable amount of time. Estimates suggest that

2. Information on Aum in Russia remains rather scarce. Hints have been made that, as a result of its largesse, it developed good contacts with and the protection of highly placed officials in the Russian system. Aum also certainly benefited from the uncertainties created by the postcommunist upheavals, and the rapid growth of new religions in Russia in this period. On Aum in Russia, I have relied upon Japanese media reports as well as the valuable recent paper by Yulia Mihailova (1996).

3. See Reader 1996 for a fuller description of the events leading up to the raids, including the widespread foreknowledge among the Japanese media and elsewhere about the imminent raids. An immense amount of literature in Japanese outlines in varying degrees of accuracy the sequential details of Aum's criminal activities. Among the more balanced are Fujita 1995; Tōkyō Shinbun Shakaibu 1995; and Kyōdō Tsūshinsha Shakaibu 1997. In English the journalistic account of Kaplan and Marshall 1996, though overly sensationalized, provides information on Aum's activities, although it is weak on the reasons for these activities.

Asahara's trial alone, in which he faces some seventeen charges of conspiracy to murder and to illegally manufacture weapons and drugs, will take at least ten and possibly as many as twenty years to complete. However, the evidence uncovered so far coupled with confessions made by some of the accused (although not by Asahara, who has admitted that Aum was responsible for the crimes but has largely denied personal involvement)[4] enable us to make some fairly accurate statements about Aum's criminality.

Thus, it is clear that Aum Shinrikyō was responsible for a series of criminal activities dating to the autumn of 1988. These activities began in Aum with the coercion of devotees to make them perform spiritual austerities that were believed to be vital for their salvation.[5] Aum's coercive asceticism produced unexpected results with the accidental death of a devotee during practice, which led Aum's leaders to cover up that death (a criminal act in Japan) so as to protect the organization from investigation, and later caused them to extend the cover-up by killing a dissident who threatened to go public with details of the accidental death and cover-up. This initial excursion into criminality in 1988–89 later extended into an escalating cycle of violence directed against those in the wider world whom Aum's leaders perceived to be enemies and to be threats to Aum's mission. These first cases of violence directed outside Aum included the murder in November 1989 of a lawyer, Sakamoto Tsutsumi, and his wife and child. Sakamoto, who was acting as the representative of a group of parents and former members who had made complaints against Aum, had begun an investigation of Aum and believed he had uncovered evidence to take Aum to court on charges of fraud and deceit against its members. While Aum thus resorted to violence and murder against individual opponents, it also shortly afterward,

4. As of late 1997 Asahara has admitted to being present when one dissident member was murdered, ordering the deaths of the Sakamoto family, and has accepted that as leader of the organization he bears some responsibility for the events, but he has not yet made a full admission of his role in the affair. Fuller details of the proceedings of Asahara's trial are found in Kyōdō Tsūshinsha Shakaibu 1997 and on the Asahi Shinbun's Web site, <http://www. asahi.com/paper/aum/aum.html>.

5. These included performing meditations, chanting, and prostrations, very often for extended periods of time, and often in seclusion. Seclusion in spartan cells to perform such practices for long periods was also common, as were extended cold water immersions, believed to "cool down" the mind and reduce mental turbulence, and hot water immersions, believed to raise psychic energy and internal heat, somewhat in the manner of the raising of internal heat in shamanic practices. The use of physical beatings also occurred

in 1990, took the first steps toward acquiring more generalized means of violence, engaging in attempts to produce biological weapons to be used against the public. After these experiments failed to produce results, Aum began, from 1993, to manufacture chemical weapons such as poison gases, a process that culminated in Aum's use of such weapons between June 1994 and the summer of 1995 in a series of attacks on the general public. In all, close to thirty people are known to have been murdered by Aum members (and perhaps several more), as well as thousands more injured, while innumerable other crimes were committed ranging from illicit manufacture of chemical weapons and extortion to various breaches of fiscal law.

These criminal activities were restricted to a relatively small group (perhaps 150 or so) of highly placed and trusted disciples surrounding Asahara. Even at the highest ranks, there were those who were not implicated in criminal activities. Most of the followers appear not to have been aware of their leaders' murderous activities even if they might have been aware of some of the violence and coercion that occurred in the group's commune at Kamikuishiki in Yamanashi prefecture, and even if they hardly can have failed to have been aware of the doctrinal legitimations of violence in Asahara's teachings. The general membership was taken aback at the police raids,[6] and many at first refused to believe that their religion had anything to do with the subway attack, rather believing (as the organization's own rhetoric had been telling them) that Aum was the target of a vast conspiracy aimed at its destruction. Immediately after the subway attack, Aum publications vigorously asserted Aum's innocence and complained of conspiracies against it (*Vajrayāna Sacca*, no. 9, April 1995). As evidence of wrongdoing emerged, however, most of the members left the organization. Of about

occasionally (see below) based apparently on the notion that the beatings exorcised impure thoughts and pollutions. Such activities can be found in various forms in Japanese religious culture: exoricistic beatings occur occasionally in Japanese shamanic healing practices, seclusions *(komori)* in caves to perform meditations and the like are done in the mountain ascetic traditions, cold water immersions *(misogi, mizugori)* occur in Shinto asceticism and purification rituals, and standing under cold waterfalls *(takigyō)* and other cold water immersions are performed in the mountain ascetic traditions. Hot water immersion is also found in the old varieties of the *yudate* ritual of mountain asceticism. A variety of cold water asceticism caused the death of Majima Terayuki (see below).

6. Members' shock when the police raided was recorded (Takahashi 1995, 3) and was related to me by former and current Aum members during interviews in Tokyo in October 1997.

ten thousand members in Japan in March 1995, fewer than a thousand now remain members.[7]

The Aum affair, which was perhaps the first case of the use of chemical weapons by a private organization, has raised numerous questions about the relations between religion and the state in Japan, and about legal issues relating to religions' registration, regulation, and functioning in a democratic society (see Itagaki 1995; Kisala 1996; Mullins 1997; Kure, Hashizume et al. 1996; Takimoto and Fukushima 1996; Watanabe 1997). Questions have also been asked as to how a religious organization could perpetrate what is widely termed in Japan "indiscriminate terrorism" (*musabetsu tero*), and many commentators, particularly in the media but also in the academic world, have questioned whether Aum was really a religion given its criminality and its apparent political ambitions.[8] (Aum briefly in 1989–90 created a political party and ran candidates for office in elections, and according to some reports had vague plans for a coup in late 1995.) However, as previous academic analyses (Reader 1996; Shimazono 1995a, 1995b, 1997) have emphasized, Aum in its practices and orientations displayed salient religious characteristics that were central to the organization's violence.

## Millennialism, Prophecy, Conflict, and the Legitimation of Violence

Aum's millennialism, its world-rejectionist communal nature, and its intense focus on ascetic practice, which together produced a sense of hierarchic elitism, intensified the group's rejection of worldly mores, led it into an increasingly catastrophic vision of the future, and Asahara into an increasing spiral of cataclysmic prophecies concerning the coming of the millennial kingdom. These increasingly catastrophic millennialist visions

7. I base this comment on my interviews with members of Aum in October 1997 and January 1998, and on the figures supplied by Araki Hiroshi, an Aum official. Some of the current members remain unconvinced by the public disclosures about Aum and appear to think that other forces produced the violence of which Aum is accused.

8. It has been the tendency in the Japanese media and public discussions about Aum and in the masses of books that have appeared in the Japanese press on Aum to regard Aum solely through criminal and terrorist lenses, viewing it as a deviant political group or as a manipulative extortionist organization with Asahara pictured largely as a maniacal and power-mad fraud. Even some notable scholars of religion have questioned whether Aum can be seen as a religion (e.g., Yamaori 1995). Kaplan and Marshall (1996) also present Aum simply as a scheming political or criminal terror group.

were linked to Aum's failure to achieve the growth and recruitment to which Asahara and other Aum leaders aspired, and to Aum's increasingly bitter conflicts with mainstream society, which created within Aum what one member later called a "persecution complex" (*higai mōsō*)[9] that intensified Aum's antagonistic stance toward society and stimulated its readiness to use violence (Reader 1996).

Shimazono Susumu (1995a, 1995b, 1997), while emphasizing the interactions of Aum's millennialism, prophecy, and world-rejectionism, has extended the analysis of the affair by examining the Aum belief world. In so doing, Shimazono has drawn attention to Aum's extreme emphasis on the spiritual powers of its leader, and its concomitant doctrinal underpinnings gleaned from Asahara's readings of esoteric Buddhist literature. As Shimazono demonstrates, an emphasis on the absolute authority and power of the guru (a term used within Aum), and, ultimately, of his close disciples produced a doctrinal stance that legitimated and sanctioned violence (1997, 21–68, 88–100). At first, such violence was internal to the organization and was used to enforce ascetic practices upon disciples to spiritually purify them; austerities were considered crucial to the attainment of enlightenment and salvation in the face of the imminent apocalypse. However, such internal violence eventually spread outward underpinned by doctrinal legitimations based in notions of spiritual elitism, eventually extending as far as justifying the killing of spiritually "inferior" beings if the guru and his disciples considered this necessary.

To understand how Aum's violence was produced, it is necessary to recognize the roles played by Aum's shifting concepts of millennialism and its legitimation of violence, which were related to elitism and to perceptions of Aum's relationship with the outside world—a relationship increasingly viewed through a lens of conspiracy and persecution—and to understand how these interacted with events in Aum's development to produce the violence that ensued.

In this chapter, I focus on a critical period in Aum's development between 1988 and early 1990 when Aum moved from internalized violence based upon faith in asceticism and the powers and rights of its spiritual leader to murders of enemies and the first attempts to manufacture weapons. In this period Aum lost the struggle over cultural legitimacy (to use Hall and Schuyler's concept [1997] ), crossed the borderline

9. This comment was made by Noda Naruhito, an official of Aum, in an interview in *Shūkan Asahi*, Oct. 13, 1995: 25.

into illegality, and became engaged in conflicts with the parents of members, the media, and neighbors, which produced an increasingly sharp gulf between Aum and the rest of Japanese society and convinced Aum members that a massive conspiracy existed aimed at destroying Aum. Through this lens of perception formed in this period, Aum began to develop its "persecution complex"—a complex that was largely self-created, and which emerged alongside Aum's developing doctrinal framework that provided legitimation for acts of violence. As it did so, Aum's millennialist orientation, which was originally of a more optimistic and progressive nature, turned increasingly catastrophic and linked to Aum's rejection of contemporary materialist civilization, which would be swept away to be replaced by a more spiritually aware culture. Drastic visions of cataclysm came to dominate Asahara's public discourses as he prophesied the imminence of a cataclysmic war. Although this cataclysm would begin a new spiritual age, it would destroy much of humanity; the numbers who would survive were quite limited. This shift to an *overtly* catastrophic millennialism is the concern of this chapter. I emphasize "overtly," because, while recognizing the validity of Catherine Wessinger's terms "progressive millennialism" and "catastrophic millennialism" (1997a), it is important to note the nuanced interactions between the two, and that progressive millennialism may at times be innately catastrophic, manifesting overtly catastrophic forms as a result of specific circumstances. This was the case with Aum, whose millennialism, even in its earlier optimistic and progressive phases, had a catastrophic undertone that became manifest toward the end of the 1980s when various, originally internal, problems caused that catastrophic element to emerge as the dominant form of Aum's millennialism. As such, I consider that the division between progressive and catastrophic millennialism is not always as clear as the terminology implies, and that we need to indicate that sometimes progressive millennialism can have inherently catastrophic undertones, which can, owing to circumstances, be transformed into overtly catastrophic expressions.

In the case of Aum, we see what I would term a progressive catastrophization of millennialism. In the following discussion, we will see how a religious group can, through internal and largely self-created crises, move down a path in which it views its relations with the outside world through a lens of persecution and constructs legitimating doctrines that enable members to engage in violence.

To make sense of these issues and of this critical period in Aum's history, it is first necessary to outline some of the important elements in Aum's background, structure, and belief system.

## Aum Shinrikyō: Structures and Beliefs

From its early status as a yoga and meditation group to the present day, Aum has emphasized personal spiritual liberation and the attainment of superhuman powers such as levitation. Indeed, his claim to have the power to levitate (and photographs showing him in midair published in various alternative religious magazines in the mid-1980s) first brought Asahara to public notice.[10]

From its beginning, Aum was world-rejecting in that it critiqued contemporary materialism. Converts were taught that withdrawal from the world into Aum's communes to perform asceticism under the guidance of the guru was vital to true spiritual development. Despite Aum's emphasis on withdrawal from the wider world, the world was regarded as the place where spiritual fulfillment was to be obtained. It was in this world that Aum's millennial aspiration for the construction of a new, spiritually based, future civilization was focused.

Aum's main appeal was to people alienated from the pressures and the materialistic orientation of Japanese life in the 1980s and the 1990s.[11] Many of Aum's themes were found in other Japanese new religions of the time—promises to provide followers with superhuman powers, a preoccupation with the direction in which the world was heading, and a general dissatisfaction with contemporary Japanese scientific rationalist culture, which placed enormous emphasis on success in the hierarchic education system and which appeared to limit individuality and self-expression.

The notion of a potential cataclysm that would engulf the world was an idea that resonated in much of Japanese popular culture from the 1970s onward, especially after 1973, when the prophecies of the

10. Asahara claimed to have experienced the "miracle of levitation" in February 1985 ("The Tracks of Salvation, Part 1," 1989a, 46). Asahara denied this was a "jump" (an accusation made against him by many critics), but an experience of flying (Asahara 1986a, 16–21).

11. This sense of alienation came through in the interviews I conducted with current and former Aum members (Tokyo, Oct. 1997 and Jan. 1998) and is expressed in two autobiographies by former members (Takahashi 1995; Kajima 1996), both of whom experienced estrangement, Takahashi because of feeling anonymous in a faceless society, and Kajima because, as the abandoned daughter of an American-Japanese relationship who was adopted and brought up in Japan, she was constantly discriminated against because of her ethnicity—a theme that quite possibly was true of others in Aum, some of whom were from groups such as the Korean minority that have suffered discrimination in Japanese society.

sixteenth-century French seer Nostradamus, with their seeming predictions of an end-of-the-world scenario at the end of the twentieth century and (at least in the popular Japanese translation of the time) the implication that a savior would appear from the East to save the world, became available in a popular Japanese translation. The prophecies of Nostradamus were considered highly relevant by many of the new religions that developed in Japan from this period on, notably Kōfuku no Kagaku, Agonshū, and Aum (Shimada 1995, 103–16). Many general and genuine concerns especially about nuclear proliferation and environmental destruction underlaid the ready acceptance of Nostradamus's prophecies, and the articulation of millennial end-of-time scenarios proved to be highly popular and effective in attracting followers in the 1980s. Such scenarios revolved around a mixture of human-created and natural disasters such as nuclear wars, earthquakes (a familiar fear in Japan), and environmental disasters, but also tended to contain an underlying message of hope, at least for the Japanese—the promised "savior from the East" through whose efforts and religious movement the world would be saved. Thus, for example, Agonshū's millennialist predictions of doom were balanced by the hope, indeed the promise, of salvation through the spiritual leadership of Kiriyama Seiyū and his teachings (Reader 1988, 1991; Kiriyama 1995a). This promise of salvation was linked to the emergence of a new and more spiritual era in which contemporary materialistic (and, by implication, Western) civilization would be swept away. At times, the rhetoric that underpinned this belief had distinctly nationalist themes as in the proclamations of Ōkawa Ryūhō, the founder and leader of Kōfuku no Kagaku, that with the coming of the new age Japan would shine forth like the sun. Ōkawa predicted large-scale destruction in the United States with California sliding into the sea (Ōkawa 1990a, 1990b, 1990c, 1990d).

Aum shared many similarities with the other new religions of the time, notably Agonshū, of which Asahara was a member in the early 1980s. While Agonshū sources have disputed the extent to which Asahara was a committed member (Kiriyama 1995b), many Agonshū themes found their way into Aum, most notably the emphasis on esoteric, and especially Tibetan, Buddhism, interest in yoga and meditation, an emphasis on the potential for gaining superhuman powers (chōnōryoku), an interest in Nostradamus's prophecies, and a belief in the potential for world destruction at the end of the twentieth century coupled with a promise and mission of world salvation (Shimazono 1997, 124–38).

Probably the aspiration to enlightenment (associated with super-human powers) proved the most attractive aspect of Aum for many of its followers, although Aum's articulation of concerns about the future, and the offering of salvation in the face of this apparent crisis, also proved attractive.[12]

Linking these themes and providing the focus of the movement was the charismatic Asahara. Born partially blind in southern Japan in 1955 to an impoverished family, Asahara moved to Tokyo in 1977, married and raised a family there. From the late 1970s, he began to be interested in herbal medicines, yoga, and religious practices, eventually joining Agonshū, but leaving it in 1984 apparently dissatisfied because of its lack of ascetic practice. In 1984 he established a small yoga and meditation group in Tokyo, performed various austerities, began giving initiations to his small but growing band of followers, and subsequently claimed to have attained full enlightenment during a visit to India in 1986.

Asahara's claims to have attained enlightenment, to possess the power of initiating his followers into higher levels of spirituality, and to be able to lead them into the millennial kingdom were attractive to followers, many of whom have testified to Asahara's ability as a teacher and spiritual guide and to his possession of a potent spiritual charisma.[13] Asahara's earliest publications after establishing Aum were primarily concerned with emphasizing the importance of undergoing spiritual training and practicing austerities, and with affirming the potential for acquiring superhuman powers through such exercises (Asahara 1986a, 1986b), and include substantial sections recording his experiences and those of his followers involving their ability to levitate, to acquire powers of wish fulfilment and telepathy (Asahara 1986a, 245–300), to have enlightenment experiences and to attain various stages of awakening (Asahara 1986a, 302–65; 1986b 151–297; 1987, 149–301). He also apparently became ill while ministering to his disciples, most particularly through initiation rituals in which he as guru took on their karmic ills, a process

12. In interviews conducted in Tokyo in October 1997, two leading Aum officials stated that it was the aspiration to enlightenment and their belief in the ability of Asahara to lead them there that brought them into the movement. They believe also that members who joined for such reasons have been the most likely to stay in the aftermath of the exposure of Aum's criminality.

13. In October 1997 both current and former members testified in interviews to Asahara's prowess as a teacher. A Japanese researcher, Maekawa Michiko, who has been researching post-sarin Aum has also reiterated to me that many of those who have left Aum continue to emphasize these qualities of Asahara.

that caused him to become tired and sick on numerous occasions (Asahara 1989a, 2; "The Tracks of Salvation, Part 2" 1989b, 46; *Mahayana News Letter* no. 14, 1989, 2–3, 24–25).

Aum exhibited an extreme form of guru veneration and was innately hierarchic. There were numerous levels of spiritual attainment, which were matched by a hierarchy of titles that reflected each member's rank and that created an inner elite. The former member Takahashi Hidetoshi has commented on this elitism noting that lay members were not regarded highly by Aum's leadership, that only when one became a renunciate (*shukkesha*) did real asceticism began in Aum, and that admission to the rank of *shukkesha* was highly controlled (1995, 52–53). Even here Aum possessed a hierarchy with the highest practitioner being known as *bosatsu* (Bodhisattva), topped by Asahara himself, who received a number of titles including *saishū gedatsusha* (the attainer of ultimate liberation).

Besides the hierarchy within Aum (and the implied lack of status of those outside it), the Aum worldview included belief imbibed from Buddhism that there were various realms of existence and of spiritual transmigration in which progression occurred toward supreme liberation. Crucially, it was considered that karmic merits and demerits created in this existence determined one's future spiritual progress or regress. In particular, according to Aum doctrines, one's spiritual level depended upon ascetic practice and upon spiritual empowerment from the guru, who was able to help his followers in their spiritual ascent by his teachings and initiations.

The importance of initiations was a theme assimilated from esoteric Buddhism, and in Aum a number of initiation rituals were used for which followers paid considerable sums of money, and through which, it was believed, the powers of Asahara were passed to his followers. Such initiations (most notoriously the imbibing of Asahara's blood) eventually created problems for Aum, and became a prominent element in the media exposés by the *Sunday Mainichi* magazine in October 1989, which portrayed Aum as a manipulative group extracting large sums of money from followers for bizarre rituals, and led to the investigation by the lawyer Sakamoto Tsutsumi.

## Millennialism and Mission

The mission of salvation and of constructing the new world was entrusted to Asahara by a deity (probably Shiva, who was regarded by

Asahara as a personal guiding spirit)[14] that manifested to him while he was performing austerities on a beach in Japan in 1985 ("The Tracks of Salvation, Part 1" 1989a, 47; Shimazono 1995a, 13–14; 1995b, 388). Asahara was commissioned by the deity to create an ideal spiritual kingdom on earth by transforming first Japan and then the rest of the world into the Buddhist paradise of Shambhala (Shimazono 1995b, 393–98). The creator of Shambhala, according to the esoteric Buddhist tradition, would be an ideal king who would be reborn as a savior to defeat unbelievers in a final war and establish the supremacy of Buddhism (388). Thus, Asahara identified himself simultaneously with the savior prophesied by Nostradamus and the king ordained to restore Buddhism and triumph over infidels. This he saw as a military mission, for the vision he received told him he would be "the central figure of the war" ("The Tracks of Salvation, Part 1" 1989a, 47). In other words, Aum's original and generally optimistic vision of the realization of a spiritual kingdom on earth and of world salvation was interwoven with darker images of a religious war against unbelievers.

This millennialism also contained an undertone of the potential for disaster. In 1987, for example, Asahara gave a talk entitled "Prediction and Salvation" (*yogen to kyūsai*) (Asahara 1987, 106–17; English trans. in 1988, 87–94) in which he mentioned the possibility of nuclear war, and suggested that internal troubles would cause Japan to rearm, and that as a result nuclear war would break out around 1999. However, Asahara stated that if Aum was able to open two branches or more in every country of the world by 1993, such cataclysmic events would not

14. In "The Tracks of Salvation, Part 1," (1989a, 47), it was simply reported that a deity manifested itself to Asahara. Shimazono (1995a, 13–14) stated that this deity was Shiva. I consider this likely given that Asahara reported frequent spiritual interventions from Shiva to guide him at various stages in his life; Shiva was the normal transmitter of spiritual messages to him. In "The Tracks of Salvation, Parts 1–3" (1989a, b, c), there were reported various cases of these interventions, such as one in which Asahara received a message to go to Dharamsala in India (the home of the Dalai Lama), and it was noted that "Lord Shiva's suggestion always comes out of the blue and this time was no exception" (1989c, 49). In various of his books and sermons, Asahara referred to the messages he received from Lord Shiva, and to how Shiva guided his life. Asahara appeared to have seen Shiva not simply as a Hindu deity, but as a powerful spiritual force transcending religious boundaries and appearing in different manifestations. He regarded Shiva as having several Japanese Buddhist manifestations, such as the deities Fudō Myōō and Daikokuten (Asahara 1986a, 56–59). It was likely that Asahara became fascinated with Shiva as a result of his travels in India, because of Shiva's importance as a destroyer and creator in the tantric and esoteric Hindu traditions and in various yoga practices (see Asahara 1986a).

happen (1987, 106–7; 1988, 87–88). He even suggested that if Aum could spread its word across the world his own mission would be over (1987, 109; 1988, 90). This introduction of possible disasters that could be averted by Aum's successful growth was repeated elsewhere in Asahara's talks in which he stated that the disasters he predicted for 1999 would not occur if Aum could produce thirty thousand enlightened beings (Mainichi Shinbun Shūkyō Shuzaihan, ed., 1993, 131).[15] However, Asahara also exhibited signs in his early books (e.g., Asahara 1987) of the paranoia and concern over persecution that became a common feature of Aum subsequently, by articulating his fear that Aum would face oppression from the state—a fear that became an obsession contributing to Aum's eventual "persecution complex."

## The Advent of Armageddon
## and of Pessimistic Millennial Views

In 1988 a new term was added to Asahara's vocabulary: Armageddon. His visions of a war between good and evil were reaffirmed when at this time he read the book of Revelation of Saint John, which he encountered when a disciple brought him the Bible to read while he lay sick in bed, a situation caused, according to Asahara, by having performed too many initiations (Asahara 1989a, 2). Identifying with many of the images in the Bible, notably the dualistic imagery of the religious leader as savior or sacrificial victim for the truth, Asahara subsequently produced two books identifying himself with Christ and using this imagery of salvation and sacrifice (1991a, 1991b; published in English as Asahara 1992). However, in his book *Metsubō no hi* (with the English subtitle "Doomsday") written at the end of 1988 and published in February 1989 (1989a) and its sequel *Metsubō kara kokū e* (From doomsday to the empty sky) (1989b), in which he claimed to fully explain the prophecies of Nostradamus and to interpret the Seven Seals of the book of Revelation, Asahara first openly expressed and developed his increasingly pessimistic millennialism predicting the advent of a final war, Armageddon.

In *Metsubō no hi*, Asahara, stating that he had been ill and exhausted from giving too many initiations (2–3), voiced doubts about his ability to save the world alone and spoke of the inevitability of a final

15. In an October 22, 1997, interview with an Aum member in Tokyo, he stated that he had heard Asahara talk about the need to create thirty thousand enlightened people, and that the desire to be one of these had been a major spur to his joining Aum.

cataclysmic war, which he stated would occur between the United States and Russia. Although he still offered some hope for salvation, Asahara no longer thought Aum could save all of humanity. From this publication on, indeed, Asahara's predictions became increasingly severe in the scope of the destruction that would come, not only through war but also through pestilences, earthquakes, and eruptions, and in terms of the numbers who could survive. The publication of these two books signaled a shift toward a more pessimistic and destructive millennialism, which manifested itself increasingly in the tone of Asahara's unpublished talks to higher level initiates that commenced in autumn 1988 and continued until 1994 (n.d.). From this point on, Asahara displayed an interest in the means with which the coming Armageddon would be fought, and an interest in weapons began to be expressed in his sermons.

Elsewhere I have described Asahara's later prophecies relating to armageddon, in which Armageddon became increasingly imminent, its scale of destruction enhanced, and the nature of the weaponry used became increasingly extreme. In the 1995 publication *Hiizuru kuni wazawaichikashi* (Asahara 1995a; later trans. into English as *Disaster Approaches the Land of the Rising Sun* [1995b]), Asahara predicted that the final war would start in 1995 and that all would die except sincere Aum believers (Reader 1996, 55–65). In this escalation of prophecies, there was a remarkable shift in the position Aum occupied in the scenario of coming disasters, a point noted by Serizawa Shunsuke (1995, 33–34). In *Metsubō no hi* (1989a), the focus was on a potential war between Russia and the United States, and Aum stood on the sidelines retaining the potential to ameliorate matters and to save its members and at least some others. In the prophecies of 1995, Aum was at the center of events, the focus of pernicious attacks by American and Japanese government forces using poison gases, and the target of a worldwide conspiracy of Jews and Freemasons, and Aum could only save its core of faithful renunciates—everyone else was doomed. In effect, Aum's focus and the implicit meaning of its message changed from the dangers facing the world at large to the dangers Aum was confronting as evidence of its criminality became known to law enforcement agencies.

## Internal Crisis and the Development and Legitimation of Violence

This progression in Asahara's prophetic utterances, and the development of his concept of the "conspiracy" against Aum cannot be dealt

with here (see Reader 1996, 54–70; Fujita 1995, 60–64). What concerns
us in this chapter is how and why this overt and increasingly catastrophic
view emerged in the period before the publication of *Metsubō no hi*
(1989a), for in this period Aum members first engaged in violence. I
draw attention to two primary factors in this process, both of which were
related to the focus on asceticism.

First was the failure to achieve the institutional growth desired by
Aum leaders (Reader 1996). Aum had developed a rhetoric that linked
salvation and the avoidance of disaster to Aum's success and growth. This
was a disastrous link given that Aum's growth was not particularly fast. By
1989 it had recruited fewer than five hundred renunciates, a total far
short of its aim of thirty thousand before the prophesied cataclysm of
1999 (29, 42–43). Aum had barely advanced out of Japan, and showed
no sign of being capable of opening two branches in every country in the
years to come. This failure to achieve goals set by the leader provoked not
only an increasing antipathy to the world that appeared to be ignoring
Asahara's message but also an increased pessimism about the organization's
ability to carry out its mission of world salvation. This sense of failure in
relation to the external world contributed to the raising of tension inside
Aum, and played a part in producing the concern with conspiracy and
persecution, which thus served as "explanations" of the failure to grow.

In raising tensions inside Aum, the sense of failure encouraged the
second crucial factor: the turning to violence and criminality inside the
organization and the doctrinal legitimation formulated for such behavior.
From 1988 Asahara began to coerce believers to engage in or increase
their asceticism. The continuing emphasis on physical austerities to produce higher states of consciousness was at the root of this development,
but in addition it is clear that in believing in the value of physical austerities to eradicate pollution and to purify the spirit, Asahara regarded
physical beatings as having an exorcistic effect.[16] From about 1988 coercion was used to force some Aum practitioners to engage in severe
austerities, while beatings were given to others, especially those who
proved reluctant ascetics, such as Asahara's wife, Matsumoto Tomoko.[17]

16. The concept of physically beating out spiritual impurities is found in the Japanese folk and shamanic traditions as well.

17. Tomoko has spoken in a number of interviews about having been beaten to
make her perform meditation (Arita 1995, 68). Although she previously implied that this
enforced discipline was good for her by getting her to embark on a valuable spiritual path,
in a recent court appearance, she has claimed that she, too, was a victim of her husband's
brutality (*Asahi Shinbun* and Asahi Internet Service, Oct. 28, 1997).

The legitimations for such beatings came from Aum's hierarchic nature, its focus on the all-powerful nature of the guru, and from Asahara's doctrine of violence based upon his belief that the spiritually advanced have the right, and, indeed, the duty, to coerce the spiritually backward to lead them to higher states of being. Coercion, thus, in his view was a compassionate act aimed at helping those who were beaten to attain salvation.

Asahara expressed these notions frequently in his public talks, although more frequently in the private internal seminars for the benefit of high-level initiates (Asahara n.d.). In one such talk given on August 20, 1989, Asahara spoke of how if A beat B, normally A would acquire bad karmic demerit; however, if A (the guru) beat B (the spiritually lower disciple) to save B from falling into hell as result of lack of spiritual endeavor, then that beating was, while a sin against conventional morality, in fact the only way that the guru, following the Vajrayāna path of Buddhism, could act (67). In a talk on March 3, 1990, Asahara spoke of how he had to beat various of his disciples at different times to encourage their practice—including his wife and his teenage daughter (109). He repeated frequently that the guru, and the higher path of Buddhism he considered that he followed, were not bound by conventional morality (e.g., 63).

It is clear from these talks that Asahara had imbibed the image of the harsh guru who cared so deeply about the enlightenment of his disciples that he pushed them beyond ordinary endurance. Asahara gained this image of the harsh guru from reading Tibetan Buddhist (Vajrayāna) stories relating to great gurus such as Marpa and Milarepa in which such gurus appeared to be portrayed as existing beyond the normal realm of conventional morality, capable of commanding absolute obedience from their disciples and of ordering them to perform seemingly immoral acts in the furtherance of the Buddhist path (see Asahara n.d., 65, for his discussion of such stories, which reflected his belief that this was how a guru *should* behave).

These doctrinal formulations aimed at encouraging practice and at disciplining those who did not meet the necessary standard required for salvation provided Aum with a legitimation for violence, which first was directed internally against members, but later was directed externally. This legitimation of violence because of one's position in the spiritual hierarchy became a critical issue when linked to another concept Asahara had imbibed from Tibetan Buddhism, which was expressed in the term *poa*. This term referred to the notion (found throughout Buddhism but certainly prominent in Tibetan Buddhism) that the souls of the dead could be helped toward better rebirths through the spiritual intervention of a spiritually advanced figure; this notion motivated the various rituals and services performed for the dead by, for example, Tibetan Buddhist priests. In Aum, the notion of the guru being able to intercede on behalf of the spirits of the dead to stop them from falling into hell and to allow them to receive a better rebirth was, indeed, part of the promise of salvation Asahara made to his disciples (Aum Translation Committee 1992, 154–57).

The term *poa* and this underlying concept apparently was first used in a talk Asahara gave on January 4, 1987, to the movement's faithful. However, Asahara's interpretation went beyond mere intercession after death to a virtual legitimation of murder. It was permitted, Asahara proclaimed, for a guru to *order* the death of another person if it was karmically beneficial for that person so as to stop him or her from living a bad life and accumulating karmic demerits. If a guru told a disciple to kill someone, he averred, this would be the right time for that person to die and hence would be a karmically good death—this action Asahara termed *poa*. *Poa* was, he believed, legitimated in the teachings of Tibetan Vajrayana Buddhism, which, he considered, expressed a morality different from that of the ordinary world. What in the human relativistic world would appear to be wrong, from the Vajrayana perspective was a splendid act of "transformation" *(poa)* (Kyōdō Tsūshinsha Shakaibu 1997, 233).

While Asahara claimed to speak only speculatively here, this line of reasoning, which appeared to allow the guru to order the deaths of others and made the carrying out of such an order a good and compassionate deed by the disciple, was reiterated in powerful terms in Asahara's internal teachings to his high-ranking disciples, particularly in a talk on April 7, 1989, in which he underlined the legitimate nature of *poa*, which term, he stated, meant to "change in order to give someone salvation" (Kyōdō Tsūshinsha Shakaibu 1997, 32–33). This concept—killing to save—became a legitimating motive for Aum's subsequent murders, used, for example, to justify the killing of the Sakamoto family (who would have otherwise fallen into the hells after death because of the father's "persecution" of Aum).

## Crossing the Boundary of Legality: The Deaths of Majima and Taguchi

These legitimations of violence rooted in Aum's hierarchy and power of the guru provided the framework within which the harsh enforcement of ascetic practice and the subsequent killings would occur. However, there was a further, more immediate, reason why Asahara in his talks in 1989 began to emphasize the power, or indeed the duty, of the guru to order killings. It was a reason that might have produced the *necessity* to extend the doctrinal formulation of *poa* as a way of helping souls after death into one of helping them leave this world. This was the unexpected and accidental death of a disciple named Majima Terayuki in autumn 1988 while undergoing enforced cold water ascetic practices ordered by Asahara. The repercussions of this incident pushed Aum across the boundary of legality.

The death of Majima was an intense shock to Asahara and his associates, and called into question the guru's capacity for good judgment, given that he had ordered the asceticism. More immediately, however, it brought into question the whole existence of the organization. Aum was planning to apply for legal recognition under the Religious Corporations Law in Japan in the following year. (Registration confers various privileges and protections to religious institutions and is a normal step once a group has attained a number of followers.) News of Majima's death certainly would have prevented Aum's application from being approved. More crucially, a death under dubious circumstances could well have been used by the media to discredit Aum and Asahara entirely, and cause Aum's activities to be curtailed.

Fearing such exposure that threatened Aum's mission of world salvation, Asahara ordered a cover-up in which Majima's body was secretly destroyed. This in itself was a criminal act. To defend its mission and the reputation of its guru, then, Aum engaged in its first clear breach of Japanese law. Indeed, one might suggest that at this point Aum placed itself above the law, and showed that its mission was regarded as more important than the law of the land. This set a pattern for the future behavior of Aum members with a recurrent tendency to regard laws as inapplicable to them.

The disregard within Aum for the law and the desperate concern to protect Aum's mission came to the fore shortly after Majima's death. In early 1989 another follower, Taguchi Shūji, who had been present at Majima's death and who had subsequently lost faith in Asahara, threatened to go public with an account of Majima's death. Recognizing that this would be an even greater calamity for the organization than Majima's death, Asahara ordered the murder of Taguchi (in other words, it was necessary to *poa* him), and thus Aum's first deliberate murder was carried out by close disciples in February 1989. It was perhaps no coincidence that the teachings about *poa* as a means of saving a soul, about the right and power of the guru to order deaths under certain circumstances, of the duty of disciples to carry out such orders, and of the karmic merits that thereby would accrue to them appeared shortly after this in April 1989.

As a consequence of the Majima and Taguchi affairs undertaken to protect Aum's mission, Aum had crossed a line and contained a deadly secret, which meant that any serious attempt to investigate the organization had the capability to totally destroy it. In such terms, the earlier hostile attitude within Aum toward the outside world became increasingly strong, thereby heightening the capacity for conflict with the outside world. It was in such terms that Aum reacted with hostility in spring 1989 to the objections made by the parents of some of its *shukkesha* when Aum applied for legal recognition under the Religious Corporations Law, and to subsequent investigations by the mass media and by Sakamoto Tsutsumi. Sakamoto, an attorney hired to represent a group of citizens with grievances against Aum, uncovered fraud connected to Aum's initiations. In an Aum pamphlet it was claimed that Asahara's blood had been tested by a well-known university laboratory and was found to contain a unique form of DNA, which could be passed to disciples through the initiation. Sakamoto found that no such test had been carried out by the laboratory, and he informed Aum's lawyers that he could make a case against Aum for fraud. As a result of this threatened exposure (and Asahara's fear that it would jeopardize a planned election campaign; see below), the Sakamotos were killed by Aum disciples acting upon Asahara's orders to *poa* Sakamoto.

The Sakamoto murders occurred just after the *Sunday Mainichi* ran a series in October 1989 attacking Aum (much as it and other media had attacked other new religions in the past) for being fraudulent and acquisitive. The Sakamoto murders occurred also in the run-up to the February 1990 election in which Aum participated by establishing its own political party, the Shinri party, under the leadership of Asahara. The negative publicity from the *Sunday Mainichi* articles and the Sakamoto affair (although no charges were brought against Aum at the time, there was much suspicion in Japan in late 1989 and early 1990 that Aum was somehow involved in the disappearance of the family), and the bizarre election campaign Aum fought (in which followers wearing Asahara masks chanted his name repeatedly), provoked a negative public reaction and led to a humiliating defeat. All the Aum candidates lost heavily, and afterward the campaign, as well as the organization itself, were immensely ridiculed in the press. This event, coming after the disasters of the previous twelve months or so, provided the final straw in Aum's alienation from society. Rejection at the polls, and the resulting humiliation in the press, coming on top of Aum's failure to attract enough followers, its conflicts with Sakamoto and others, its desperate and illegal endeavors to cover up internal problems, and the alienation produced by recourse to murder had transformed Aum's path completely. Not only had Aum lost the struggle for legitimacy but also it had become an organization with criminal secrets—and an increasing predisposition to criminality, both to shield the earlier events and because of its social alienation.

In April 1990 Asahara summoned his disciples to a seminar on the island of Ishigaki far to the south of the mainland where he indicated that Aum would abandon its mission of saving the world (which had shown itself to be beyond redemption), and would henceforth only endeavor to save members. During this period the first preparations for war with society were made involving a failed attempt to create biological weapons—the precursor of later and more coordinated schemes to create chemical weapons such as the nerve gas sarin.

## Persecution, Conspiracies, and the Evil of the World

During the turmoil that enveloped Aum from late 1988 until mid-1990 (a period that included the Sakamoto murders and the election debacle, but which also saw Aum applying for registration as a religious organization and becoming the focus of complaints from parents and criticisms from the media), attitudes within Aum became hardened and began to become obsessed with what was seen as a devilish plot against Aum, and with the concern of surviving this plot and the cataclysmic war that was approaching (Shimazono 1997, 33). Thus, the earlier vision of a war between good and evil forces catalyzed into a clear understanding that the world outside of Aum was that evil force. Indeed, contemporary society was sustained by evil, for by 1990 Asahara in his sermons began to equate materialism with the devil (*akuma*) and to describe the present age as one in which ordinary people were crushed by evil—an evil also sustained and spread by a conspiracy of Freemasons and Jews to undermine Aum. This notion of a conspiracy against Aum appears to have been articulated at first during an interview with Asahara in Aum's *Mahayana News Letter* published in July 1990 (29), and it became intimately connected with the expectation of Armageddon. According to Asahara, evil forces were dragging people downward karmically in a matrix

of struggle and conflict in which the forces of evil (the devil, *akuma*)
were engaged in battling against those of truth (*shinri*) (32). (The term
*shinri* not only meant "truth" but also referred to Asahara's organization.) The conflict of good and evil in Asahara's earlier vision thus became a battle between Aum (the truth) and the devil of the material
world, who became the enemy or foe (*teki*) against whom Aum must
struggle in war. The notion of such a war provided a legitimation of
violent action against an evil foe (33)—a foe that was rapidly becoming
the whole of society outside Aum.

## Conflict and Persecution

Thus, the period during which Aum irrevocably crossed the border
of legality was the period when its legitimation of violence was developed, when its millennialism became increasingly pessimistic and catastrophic, and when it became increasingly locked into a worldview of
conflict between itself and the "evil" world of mainstream society. In this
period, too, there were increasing claims that Aum was being persecuted—claims that culminated in the imagined conspiracies against it and
the assertion that Aum was the target of poison gas attacks by its enemies
(Reader 1996, 66–69).

Aum did encounter growing opposition in this period. Complaints
about its initiatory and monetary demands upon its followers, especially
by parents whose offspring were below the legal age of adulthood (twenty
in Japan) and thus should have had their parents' approval before becoming *shukkesha,* did lead to opposition to Aum's application for incor-
poration under the Religious Corporations Law, to media attacks, and to
the investigation by Sakamoto. Aum did receive a barrage of media
ridicule after its election debacle in 1990 as well as many hints in the
media that it was responsible for the disappearance of the Sakamotos.
Moreover, when in 1990 Aum bought land at Namino in the southern
island of Kyushu and began to build a commune there, it encountered
resistance from the local villagers, some of whose attempts to hinder the
commune's development (including the refusal to accept the residential
applications of commune residents) were illegal (Kumamoto Nichinichi
Shinbun 1992).

In all these cases, Aum resorted to complaints of persecution. When
its officers were arrested in 1990 for violations connected with the purchase of the Namino commune land (the identity of Aum was concealed
when purchasing the land and the intention for the land was not revealed

prior to purchase), there was a vehement reaction within Aum to these arrests even though they had been carried out in strict accordance with the law and because of violations of the law. The arrests were, Asahara alleged, "persecution," drawing parallels to the oppression of Tibetan lamas by the Chinese authorities, and were parts of a state "plot" to destroy Aum (Asahara 1991c, 1–2, 4). Asahara was also dismissive of the right of the state to arrest those who had broken its laws; it had used the Land Development Law and "slight suspicions on false entries in a Notary Document . . . as an excuse for their compulsory investigation and illegal arrests" (5), and he predicted that the police who had arrested Aum members would fall into the hells after death (6).

The obsession within Aum with persecution was expressed also by several of those who were arrested in this affair. Maha Khema (the holy name of one of Aum's leading disciples, Ishii Hisako), who spent fifty days in prison for violation of the Land Development Law, talked of her time in a cell and of how "dire persecutions are inflicted on the truth" and made predictions of karmic retribution that would come to the persecutors: "I think the rage of gods who observe good and evil of this human world is reaching its culmination. Volcanic eruptions must be one of the symbols of the rage of gods . . . when the fury of the gods has reached its acme, what kind of retribution will be brought on them . . . this isn't hard to imagine" (Maha Khema 1991, 100). Another Aum official jailed in the affair, the lawyer Aoyama Yoshinobu, also wrote extensively on this matter, placing his arrest not in the context of illegal actions he had committed but of religious persecution (Aoyama 1991).

However, one can hardly regard any of these cases as worthy of the term "persecution" or even of unreasonable external pressure. Given that Aum had already caused one death and one murder before any unfavorable words appeared in the press, before it was investigated by Sakamoto, and before it received any opposition from unhappy villagers, one might suggest the cries of "persecution" were fabricated to protect Aum from closer scrutiny that might uncover more unpalatable truths than just the allegations about costly initiations and the like. Nor can excessive external pressures be seen as a serious contributory element in the violence that erupted given that Aum had resorted to murder before any external conflicts. The external pressures Aum received were hardly extreme— media investigations of religious movements are, for example, common in Japan (Morioka 1994).

Indeed, the irony might be that Aum benefited from Japanese concerns with religious persecution. Even though there were some strong arguments raised against Aum's application for affiliation under the Religious Corporations Law, which held up the application for four months, Aum was able to appeal, complaining as it did of religious persecution, and as a result the authorities granted the application (Reader 1996, 36–37). The Japanese historical awareness of the suppression of religious movements by a Shinto-backed fascist nationalist government in the earlier part of the twentieth century was a factor in the creation of a constitution in 1946 that guaranteed religious freedom. Given that historical background, the police in contemporary Japan have been very cautious in dealing with or investigating religious organizations, and it is probable (although it has never been publicly stated as such) that the reluctance of the police to examine Aum more closely after incidents such as the Sakamoto murders was a result of this historical legacy. Rather than actual persecution being a factor in pushing Aum into violence, it is quite possible that the police's *fear* of appearing to engage in persecution may have allowed Aum to evade proper investigation and allowed it to travel further along the path of violence.

## Conclusions

In this chapter, I dealt with the beginnings of Aum's trajectory toward the extreme violence of its latter period and with the early transformations in its millennialism. These beginnings are crucial to understand Aum's subsequent development as an increasingly catastrophic millennial religion—a catastrophic millennialism that was a prime factor in bringing Aum to the point of war with Japanese society in 1995—and to show how a religious movement can, without serious external provocation, develop the capability for violence and the conditions that produce a subsequent (and in Aum's case highly lethal) explosion of violence. In many respects this latter theme is most striking about Aum's violence. While its increasing catastrophic millennialism certainly intensified Aum's readiness to produce weapons and resort to violence, the internally created disposition toward violence as an acceptable course of action whenever the organization's mission was endangered was most crucial in what happened.

This disposition toward violence was certainly rooted within Asahara's personality, but it began to be expressed in earnest after the death of Majima with the shift to an increasingly pessimistic millennialism and a growing legitimation of violence. The doctrinal legitimations of violence were underpinned by an innate sense of superiority based upon Aum's truth claims and mission, and were fueled also by Aum's alienation from society and conflicts with those in society, conflicts that from the Aum viewpoint confirmed that the material world was corrupt, and hence further affirmed the legitimacy of violence. The process in which violence came to be accepted as a reasonable and necessary course of action was impelled also by the perception within Aum that it was being persecuted—a perception that was elevated into an assumption of a conspiracy directed against Aum to prevent it from accomplishing its mission.

A persecution complex was created within Aum born out of its nature as a closed, hierarchic, communal, and world-rejecting religious organization believing in the imminence of a world catastrophe and the coming of a new order. In the mind-set of that persecution complex, the doctrinal notions of the legitimation of violence, precipitated as they were by events that developed as a result of Aum's emphasis on asceticism, were able to flourish and provided the justifications for Aum to make weapons for its "defense" that readily translated into outbursts of violence. Although Aum's acts of violence were not part of a sequence of coordinated events, they were produced within a matrix of thoughts conditioned by circumstances rooted in Aum's nature as a religious movement that affirmed the right of someone higher in the spiritual hierarchy to use force if necessary to encourage (or "save") those in subordinant positions. In introducing violent coercion into the movement and legitimating such acts not simply as correct religious acts but as duties of the guru, Asahara sowed the seeds that grew into the Tokyo subway attack, and that allowed Aum to embark on its "defensive" actions, which were in fact explicit acts of aggression against an outside world and against subway travelers who were not, within Aum's reading of the world, innocent victims of indiscriminate terrorism so much as legitimate targets in the war against evil that Aum was fighting.

The levels of Aum's violence—from internal beatings and murders, to the eradication of a whole family, to the horrors of chemical warfare— are quite extraordinary in the field of new religions. Although the number of deaths it caused is nowhere as high as that at Jonestown or Waco, for sheer extended violence and for the potential horrors it could have caused, Aum stands virtually in a category of its own. The duration and extent of the movement's criminal activities from 1988 until 1995 and their potential for mass destruction with the public use of chemical weapons are of an unprecedented scale. This does not, however, mean that Aum can be set aside from analysis in the context of other new religions. As I have shown elsewhere, there are some distinct parallels in

Aum's evolution to those of the Rajneesh movement, which also espoused a communally based form of millennialism, engaged in hostile
disputes with its local surrounding community, and plotted to make and
use toxic weapons (Reader 1996, 97–107).

Thomas Robbins (1997) has recently critiqued what he terms the
"interpretive approach" to the study of religious movements and violence, suggesting that this may cause scholars to overemphasize the extent to which violence is produced in religious movements as a response
to external provocation. He cites Aum as a case in which external provocation appears not to have been a major element in producing its trajectory toward violence. This chapter reiterates Robbins's view; Aum's
violence was internally created, not externally provoked, and while Aum
members saw provocation and persecution all around them, these were
largely self-created images of a worldview that depended upon a sense of
persecution to sustain its own internal logic. Indeed, as evidence from
the beatings of devotees to the concealment of deaths has shown, the
criticisms its opponents made at the time were quite legitimate in that
they raised questions about a religious organization that, no matter how
potent its spiritual messages and the individual quests of its members
might have been, was from early on engaging in violence that eventually
endangered the lives of thousands of people.

In assessing how religious groups become involved in violence, we
have to recognize, as the Aum case demonstrates, that although external
provocation and persecution may play a role in some cases, attention also
needs to be paid to the ways in which movements can themselves create
these very themes from within their own thought-worlds. As this chapter
has indicated, Aum leaders and members created the conditions for externally directed violence from within the Aum system of thought and
practices, that beginning with the drive to enlightenment, renunciation,
and world salvation, became suffused with a sense of spiritual superiority
that affirmed that violent actions were legitimate, and generated both a
set of real conflicts and a mind-set of imagined persecution, all of which
impelled Aum toward the horrors of the Matsumoto and Tokyo gas
attacks in June 1994 and March 1995. After embarking on a mission to
save the world, Aum by March 1995 had arrived at a position in which
destruction appeared to be the most viable form of salvation.

*Part Three*

## Two Nativist Millennial Movements

# 8

# Millenarian Tragedies in South Africa

## The Xhosa Cattle-Killing Movement and the Bulhoek Massacre

CHRISTINE STEYN ⎯⎯⎯⎯⎯⎯⎯⎯⎯⎯⎯⎯⎯⎯⎯⎯⎯⎯⎯⎯

Millenarian movements occur in all areas of the world and often in the wake of European colonial rule, and in South Africa it was no different. In this chapter, two little-known South African millenarian movements that ended in tragedy will be introduced. The similarities, differences, and unique characteristics of the two groups will be discussed in the light of Barkun's work on millenarianism as response to the experience of multiple disasters (1974). It will be shown that both these movements conform in all respects to the characteristics as specified by Barkun.

## The Xhosa Cattle-Killing Movement

Toward the end of the eighteenth century, white farmers (trekboers) in search of new pastures and land entered the eastern Cape, an area still referred to as "Border." Here they encountered the Xhosa[1] with whom they at first intermingled peacefully—trading in iron, copper, and trinkets

---

1. Today the term "Xhosa" is used to refer to any Nguni-speaking person from the Eastern Cape. However, it used to refer to only one national entity under the rule of King Sarhili (sometimes referred to as Kreili), but divided into various chiefdoms. There was the Gcaleka Xhosa under the immediate rule of Sarhili, the Ngqika Xhosa under Sandile, the Ndlambe Xhosa under Mhala, and a number of lesser chiefdoms, the most important of which was the Gqunukhwebe Xhosa under Phatho (Peires 1989, xii).

for cattle. The trekboers, used to dealing with the vulnerable Khoisan (an indigenous people whose culture disintegrated in the face of colonial forces), did not expect any conflict with the Xhosa people. Soon, however, these two proud groups, who probably both regarded themselves as superior to the other, clashed. Escalation of skirmishes followed, and in 1788 the governor of the Cape, Baron Joachim van Plettenberg, met with some Xhosa chiefs at which time the Great Fish River was established as the colony's eastern border. The white farmers would stay to the west and the Xhosa to the east of the river to keep the peace. However, what the governor did not understand was that according to Xhosa law, the agreement was only binding upon the people who made it, and the Xhosa people who were not involved did not consider themselves bound by it. By 1781 there were a number of chiefdoms still west of the river and it was decided to evict them. The evictions, killings, and cattle plundering that consequently took place came to be known as the First Frontier War. During the next one hundred years, eight more Frontier Wars would be fought, the only changes being that the colonizers switched from being Dutch to British in 1805, the new border moved ever eastward, and the number of white settlers increased dramatically (despite some of the Boers [Afrikaner farmers] leaving the area in the Great Trek into the interior in search of more land—free from the British and Xhosa—during 1835–38).

The Eighth Frontier War (1850–53) was the longest and most brutal of all these wars, and at the end of it an estimated sixteen thousand Xhosa had been killed or had died of starvation. In a meeting between the governor, Sir George Cathcart, and the Xhosa chiefs, it was agreed that the chiefs would henceforth be allowed to govern their people according to their own laws. No sooner had this been agreed upon, when Cathcart was recalled and the new governor, Sir George Grey, rescinded the agreement and installed magistrates to "assist" the chiefs and their counselors in judging legal cases. Politically and economically, the Xhosa people were defeated by many years of war, but the yearning for precolonial days could not be stilled.

On the spiritual side, Xhosa religion was being influenced by Christianity through its missionaries who had been active in Xhosaland since 1817 (Peires 1989, 134). Traditional Xhosa religion had a monistic worldview in which all was seen as one and pervaded by divinity. Human beings and their animals had emerged from the underground caverns where they previously existed through a hole in the ground (or alternatively through a marsh overgrown with reeds). There was no clearly defined belief or system of worship, but the duty of human beings was to maintain harmonious relations within the cosmos. Traditional practices focused on the ancestors who were believed to be present both in this world as well as in the spirit world, below the ground or water (Hodgson 1982, 17ff). In contact with the indigenous Khoi people's religion, the concept of God and the Devil had developed in Xhosa religion, but it was the Christian concept of resurrection that captured the Xhosa imagination because it filled a lacuna in traditional thinking. Death, in Xhosa religion, was regarded with deep ambivalence. On the one hand, death was regarded as a natural transition from one form of life to another (as an ancestor), but on the other hand, death was viewed with fear and terror. The latter view was greatly enforced by a smallpox epidemic that struck about 1770. Before this blight, the dead were buried, but now people refused to touch corpses and the dying were carried outside and left to die in the bush. Surviving relatives had to undergo elaborate purification rituals before entering the community again. The Christian message that death was not final and that the dead would arise was thus received with "joyful misunderstanding": "When . . . [the missionary James Read] told them that woman and all mankind would rise again from the dead, it caused uncommon joy among the [Xhosa].[2] They said they should like to see their grandfathers, and others whom they mentioned. Congo inquired when it would happen, and if it would be soon, but Mr Read could not gratify his wishes on that point" (quoted in Peires 1987, 68).

Two prominent and influential diviners, Nxele (d. 1820) and Ntsikana (d. 1821) contributed to the assimilation of Christian ideas into Xhosa religion. Nxele grew up in the Cape Colony where he was in contact with Christian thinking, but when he returned to his people as a diviner to one of the chiefs, he had developed his own synthesis. He claimed divine power and even summoned the people to witness the resurrection of the dead from beneath a rock and the damnation of witches to the underground. He taught that the whites and the blacks

---

2. I have followed the lead of historian J. B. Peires, who substitutes the term "Kaffir" with "Xhosa" in brackets. The term Kaffir (Kafir, Caffre) comes from the Arabic word for unbeliever and was commonly used when referring to black people. The country where the Xhosa lived was called Kaffirland or Kaffreria. In time, however, the term has accumulated so much derogatory connotations that today it is viciously insulting to use it.

each had their own God and that these two were in opposition against each other. The whites had killed the son of their God and had therefore been expelled from their land, and that is why they were now looking for new land. Mdalidiphu, the god of the blacks, was the stronger and would eventually prevail in the battle between the two. Nxele, the supreme "wardoctor" (adviser in matters of war), led the Xhosa armies in an abortive attack against Grahamstown in 1819. He died trying to escape from Robben Island to which he was banned by the colonial authorities. His followers refused to believe that he was dead, and his return was eagerly awaited long after his death (Peires 1987, 69ff).

Ntsikana, a diviner to a rival Xhosa chief, taught the opposite to Nxele. His theology was one of submission and peace. He agreed that there were two gods, but they were not in opposition to each other, rather they were father and son. He urged people to humbly submit to the will of God. Although his teachings were not appreciated at the time, after the catastrophe of the cattle killings, the Xhosa were more open to the ideas that he had propagated so many years previously (Peires 1987, 69ff).

The most vital factor in events leading to the Cattle-Killing movement was the appearance and spread of lungsickness in the Xhosa's immense herds of cattle. This is a highly infectious, fast spreading, and fatal disease that could be halted only by killing off all infected animals. In the Xhosa worldview, health is the normal state and disease must therefore have a cause. The cause may either be a dereliction of duty toward the ancestors or the influence of malevolent forces. Either way, it was the responsibility of the people to rectify the imbalance, both by propitiating the ancestors and eradicating the evil.

In 1856 there was thus a combination of influences that set the stage for the tragic events that were to follow. The Xhosa had been subjugated by many years of war, their land had been systematically taken from them, their traditional religion had been infiltrated by foreign elements, and their much loved and highly prized cattle herds had been infected with a virulently infectious and fatal disease.

Into this arena stepped a young orphan girl, Nongqawuse. She was cared for by her uncle, Mhlakaza, who was an influential Xhosa diviner. Mhlakaza had obviously spent quite some time in the Colony, for he spoke fluent Dutch and in April 1850 he had become the first Xhosa to be confirmed as an Anglican (Peires 1989, 35). His dearest wish was to be a full-time "Gospel Man," who could evangelize the Xhosa. However, this hope was cruelly dashed by the archdeacon in Grahamstown, who, together with his household, continued to regard Mhlakaza as a servant. Eventually, after being dismissed by the archdeacon, he returned to Xhosaland where he began preaching a gospel of his own. When the teenage Nongqawuse began seeing visions of strangers coming from the sea and hearing messages, she informed her uncle, who realized the importance of the visions and straightaway conveyed the information to the chiefs and the Xhosa people. The gist of the message was that the whole community of ancestors would arise from the dead and return to the land together with "new people." Before this could take place, all cattle should be slaughtered because they had been reared by contaminated hands of people who had dealt in witchcraft. No one should cultivate, but great new grain pits should be dug, new houses should be built, and great strong cattle enclosures should be erected, for the ancestors and new people would bring with them new healthy cattle and new grain: "So says the chief Napakade, the descendant of Sifuba-sibanzi"[3] (quoted in Peires 1989, 79).

To a people close to despair, this message made immediate sense. Everything they owned, their dearest possessions, their cattle, their homes, their food, their implements and utensils were all bewitched and unclean and had to be destroyed. The new people, whom Nongqawuse had seen and spoken to, were waiting to come and to bring with them everything everyone could wish for—beautiful strong new cattle, new corn, new clothes, health, youth, and most of all, the ancestors would return with the new people. As to the identity of the new people, the Xhosa had heard rumors that the much despised Governor Cathcart had been killed by the Russians (in the Crimean War) and assumed that these Russians had to be particularly strong, and, of course, black, if they were fighting the English. These new people would therefore be Russians and also ancestors of the Xhosa.

Had it not been for the support of Sarhili, their highly esteemed and much loved king, the catastrophe might have been averted. But Sarhili had investigated the matter personally by traveling to Mhlakaza's

---

3. Peires quotes Gqoba, who speaks of Napakade, the son of Sifuba-sibanzi (1989, 137). Today Napakade (the Eternal One) refers to God the Father and Sifuba-sibanzi (the Broad-Breasted One) to Jesus Christ. In this quote, however, the names are reversed and according to Peires, this probably reflects the uncertainty regarding the status between God and Christ at the time of the cattle killings.

home where what he saw convinced him of the truth and the authenticity of Nongqawuse's prophecies. He returned to his Great Place and ceremoniously commenced the slaughter by killing his favorite ox and ordering the nation to obey the prophetess's instructions.

Many Xhosa people proceeded to Gxarha to investigate the matter for themselves, and though many were convinced, there were also many unbelievers. Despite these, the killings began in earnest. Hundreds of cattle were slaughtered each day and corn was dug out of the grain pits and thrown away. Rumor had it that the resurrection would take place on the full moon of June 1856, but when this date passed without the hoped-for events, Mhlakaza was pressured into naming another date and that was the full moon of August 1856. When this date too passed without consequence, the killings floundered and the movement seemed to collapse. However, within weeks of the First Disappointment, Sarhili reiterated the order to kill. Mhlakaza had convinced him that because some people had sold their cattle, the ancestors were not appeased. The ancestors loved cattle and without the spilling of blood they could not be propitiated. This seemed perfectly logical, given the emphasis in Xhosa culture on sacrifice as the only appropriate method of communication with the spirit world.

After the First Disappointment, Mhlakaza even attempted, quite unsuccessfully, to convert white farmers to the movement despite the general belief among Xhosa people that the whites were an entirely different species of humanity and therefore were not included in the prophecies. The prophet did, however, increase his assault on unbelievers (which now included white farmers) with dire warnings of terrible punishment that would be inflicted on unbelievers when the new people came. It became generally accepted that the whites together with all other evil things would be swept to sea in a great storm that would precede the resurrection of the dead.

Meanwhile, back in the Cape, Governor Grey was less interested in curbing the killing of cattle than in imposing his new administrative system on the reluctant Xhosa (Peires 1989, 112). He sent a blunt and threatening letter to Sarhili in which he demanded that the killings stop immediately, to which Sarhili replied curtly that Grey should not meddle in Xhosa affairs. Grey decided to send a ship to the mouth of the Kei River near Gxarha to survey the land and see if it was possible to land men and supplies there should it in the future become necessary. When the Xhosa saw the ship, they gathered in great numbers ready for war, which they were certain would follow. Not knowing that the ship was only sent on a surveying expedition, they were fascinated when it calmly turned around and sailed away. Rumors were soon flying that the new people under leadership of Sarhili's dead father had destroyed the ship. This event gave new life to the faltering Cattle-Killing movement.

Toward the end of 1856, the people were beginning to experience the results of their actions. People were going hungry and were beginning to look longingly at the corn and cattle of the unbelievers. It was rumored that the ancestors of the unbelievers had interceded with the new people lest the unbelievers be damned for refusing to kill their cattle. The pressure on the unbelievers became unbearable, for they were being held responsible for the continued postponement of the resurrection. Instead of facing the real possibility that they were mistaken, believers continued in a blind frenzy to kill and destroy, because turning back was no longer seen as an option—all their bridges had been burnt behind them and there was only the way forward into more destruction and the hope that with the next feat their actions would be rewarded. At this stage, believers understood that the only reason the prophecies had not come to pass was that there were still some animals that had not been destroyed, and lest it should be their actions that further delayed the resurrection, people went ahead and slaughtered even the milk cows that they had held back for fear of starvation.

In the first week of February, Sarhili, after a visit to Mhlakaza and Nongqawuse, announced that the new people would arise within eight days of his return to his Great Place. Certainly before the end of the ninth day the new people would arrive. On the day of the arrival, the sun would rise late, blood red, and then set again and it would become pitch dark. A great storm with thunder, lightning, and strong wind would follow, and then the dead would arise. During the following days there was much activity with people sewing milk sacks, cleaning homesteads, killing off the last goats, chickens, and dogs, and generally getting ready for the return of their loved ones and the new people. Some built signal fires to indicate the position of their homesteads lest they be passed by, and others climbed on to rooftops to watch for the new arrivals.

> On the appointed day, the sun rose and progressed as normal. The people sat in quiet desolation. One believer recalled: "I sat outside my hut and saw the sun rise, so did all the people. We watched until midday, yet the sun continued its course. We still watched until the afternoon and yet it did not return, and the people began to despair because they saw this thing was not true" (Peires 1989, 158).

Disillusioned and hungry, the believers had nowhere to turn but against
the few unbelievers who still had some food and cattle. These peoples'
lives were in grave danger because the government accorded them no
protection against believers. Killing, thieving, looting, and petty crimes
flourished as believers went about scrounging for food, and eventually
one magistrate, Major Gawler, established his own police force of Xhosa
unbelievers to police his district.

In the aftermath of the Great Disappointment when people were
scavenging, thieving, and even killing to stay alive, Governor Grey saw
the opportunity of pushing through his master plan for the Xhosa. It
had always been his vision "to make them part of ourselves, with a
common faith and common interests," which in fact meant to make
them "useful servants, consumers of our goods, contributors to our
revenue" (Peires 1989, 318). The problems of severe labor shortage in
the British colony and the demand for more land by white farmers could
be solved by pushing the starving Xhosa into labor contracts.[4] The
authorities did all in their power to prevent Xhosa people from hanging
on to their land. They provided famine relief only in exchange for labor
in the Colony, and even refused to provide the remaining Xhosa with
seedcorn, for they had no money to pay for it. If Xhosa wished to
purchase seed they would first have to sign labor contracts (for three to
five years) and earn the necessary money. Having vacated their land,
however, the Xhosa would not have land to which they could return
after the contracts expired.

It is estimated that forty thousand Xhosa starved (including
Mhlakaza) in the aftermath of the cattle killings. About four hundred
thousand head of cattle were slaughtered, and the amount of land lost
as a direct result of the catastrophe was more than six hundred thousand
acres (Peires 1989, 319). Xhosaland vanished. Many of its chiefs were
imprisoned on Robben Island on petty charges, and the Xhosa who did

4. The labor contract read as follows: "I the undersigned a [Xhosa] of . . . of the
kraal . . . hereby of my own free will undertake to proceed to any part of the Colony of the
Cape of Good Hope, and in such fashion and in such manner and mode as I shall be
ordered by the Chief Commissioner, and I further undertake faithfully and truly to perform
such contract of service as the Resident Magistrate of . . . [the district to which sent] shall
enter into on my behalf, it being understood that such contract shall not exceed the term
of three or five years from the day of agreement entered into on my behalf and that he
will fix at his discretion the wages and food to be allowed me during the continuance of
the said contract to which I willingly consent." The five-year limit did not apply to juveniles
who were "apprenticed" and "naturally" had to stay on longer.

not die of famine-related diseases or took up labor contracts were concentrated into villages which eventually degenerated into slums and migrant labor pools.

Thus, the millenarian visions of a young girl led to the subjugation of a nation by a colonial power, which was indecently quick to capitalize on the suffering and anguish of a people in the throes of a great tragedy. In later years, there was much speculation about a "Chief's Plot" and "Grey's Plot" to place blame on each other for the events, but careful scrutiny of both theories proved that both were unsubstantiated. The tragedy was born out of the anguished suffering of the Xhosa people's disintegrating society, military defeat, the encroachment on their land and belief system, and the fatal cattle lungsickness disease. In retrospect, the lungsickness seems pivotal, and without it the tragic events might never have occurred.

### The Bulhoek Massacre

There is a mass grave where 183 people[5] lie buried at a place called Bulhoek about fifteen miles outside Queenstown in the Eastern Cape. A tombstone carries an inscription, "Because they chose the plan of God, the world did not have a place for them." These mournful words describe plainly how the "Israelites" experienced the events that took place there on May 24, 1921, when a millenarian group was forcefully subdued by government forces.

The history starts with Enoch Josiah Mgijima, who was born at Bulhoek in 1858 into a prosperous family who belonged to the Wesleyan Methodist Church. Enoch's father was a Mfengu peasant, who as a child had fled Natal with his family when they were terrorized by Chaka, the great Zulu warrior. The term "Mfengu" means "we are wanderers who seek help" (Edgar 1988, 3) and it refers to the refugees who had sought help from the Gcaleka Xhosa during the Zulu wars. Many of the Mfengu eventually turned against their benefactors when they fought a war against the British army in 1834–35. The Mfengu were rewarded by the British through gifts of land, which accounted for the Mgijima family wealth when Enoch was born. This was, however, to be eroded during the

5. Different sources give different numbers. Edgar (1988) and *The Reader's Digest Illustrated History of South Africa* (1988) claim 183 dead; Sundkler (1976, 72) maintains that 117 were killed; and the *Daily Dispatch,* an East London-based newspaper (in Millard 1997 and Cameron 1994), declared that 163 died.

ensuing years. Owing to ill-health, Enoch, in contrast with his brothers who all went on to higher education, completed only five years of schooling and became a farmer and Methodist lay preacher (4).

In April 1907 Mgijima had a vision in which an angel took him to heaven and told him that he had a mission to lead people to the Old Testament tradition in their worship of God. He was also told that there would be war and that the end of the world was near and only those who worshiped God faithfully would be saved (Edgar 1988, 7). Although he felt unworthy, Mgijima started preaching and soon gained a sizable following. When Halley's comet appeared in the sky in April 1910, Mgijima interpreted it as a sign of God and felt vindicated in his call to turn to the religion of the Old Testament. In 1912 he parted ways with the Methodists and aligned himself and his followers with a small church, the Church of God and Saints of Christ, founded in the United States by an African American, William Crowdy, who taught that black people were descended from the lost tribes of Israel and were therefore Jews.

Mgijima's visions continued to the dismay of his church. In 1912 he predicted that the world would end before Christmas Day, and his followers responded by not planting their fields. When the end did not occur, the followers were much poorer, but not at all disillusioned by their prophet. He then predicted a catastrophic war that was going to destroy all sinners, and when World War I broke out, he interpreted this as the fulfillment of his vision. In time, his visions became more violent and he predicted a great war between blacks and whites, and although the Israelites would not participate, the blacks would vanquish the whites. By 1919 the leaders of the Church of God and Saints of Christ were sufficiently disturbed to ask him to renounce his visions, and when he refused, they excommunicated him. Mgijima and his followers now took the name "Israelites," and became one of a growing number of African Independent Churches[6] (Edgar 1988, 11). He taught that the New Testament was a fiction written by white people, the Israelites were Jehovah's elect, and Jehovah would deliver them from the bondage of the Europeans in the same way he delivered the original Israelites from

6. Today the term "African Initiated Churches" is used and it refers to the Christian Churches that give a unique African expression to Christianity. They are autonomous and unaffiliated to any mission or mainline church. It is estimated that there are at least six thousand of these churches today and they have a total membership of about 8.5 million people (Anderson 1992, 47).

Egypt. The Sabbath was kept and the annual Passover festival was observed at Bulhoek (Sundkler 1976, 72).

Most important of the teachings was the celebration of the annual Passover at Mgijima's home, Ntabelanga (in the Bulhoek area). In 1920 Mgijima called on all his followers to join him for Passover and they arrived in large numbers. He had applied to the authorities for the usual permission for his followers to come to the Passover earlier that year and explained that many people were coming from far away. Because there were rumors that some of his followers were settling in permanently, the authorities were reluctant to give the necessary permission, but Mgijima assured them that his followers would not be staying. Finally, the authorities agreed. But instead of leaving, ever more followers arrived and settled. The new arrivals were all in contravention of a location bylaw that regulated the number of huts that could be built in certain areas, and many of the Israelites were now squatting illegally on Crown Land.

The lot of the black people had deteriorated dramatically over the previous two decades. The Land Act of 1913 had effectively divided South Africa into black and white areas and had delivered the best land into the hands of whites. Many African sharecroppers were forced off white farms by this law. The periodic harsh droughts that South Africa suffers and the Rinderpest, a cattle disease that swept through the land at the end of the previous century, had left many black farmers destitute, and as a result many were laboring on white farms or in mines. Added to this, the 1918 flu epidemic had killed nearly a thousand in Mgijima's region (Edgar 1988, 12). Higher taxes were imposed, and the political frustration of blacks surged, when those who having served in the war received no reward for their service after the war. The lot of the people was going from bad to worse, and Mgijima's promise of dramatic change and salvation gave hope and solace to helpless and desperate people. They were with their prophet awaiting the last days, and they were adamant that no one was going to remove them from this land.

Government officials issued warnings, and Mgijima promised that his followers would leave after a service on June 18, 1920, but this did not happen. Instead new arrivals were erecting more shacks and houses, and there were about three-thousand Israelites congregated at Bulhoek. A village had sprung up with streets and brick houses around the central tabernacle where worship took place four times a day. The people tried to be self-sufficient, and had their own skilled workers and even a nursing brigade and police force. A school for Bible study was established, and the village elders presided over a court that tried people for religious violations. Their cattle and sheep, however, grazed on land owned by nearby farmers and this led to much conflict.

A pattern developed over the following year: summonses were issued by the authorities, promises to comply were made, promises were broken, and new summonses and warnings were issued. Frustration reigned. In the meantime, some Israelites had begun to arm themselves, and when officials tried to approach the encampment, they were turned away by the armed men. This prompted police to send a force of a hundred men to camp outside the settlement in December 1920. The Israelites were offered rations and train tickets if they would leave, but the offer was met with disdain. The police observed the Israelites marching in the distance, and not realizing that this formed part of one of their church services, they became alarmed and fled when a large group advanced toward them. In their haste, they left behind all their supplies and tents. This event was to have dire consequences. Rumors soon spread that the Israelites had defeated the police, and that the bullets of the police had turned to water. The Israelites were the children of God and invincible.

The government then sent out a delegation of Africans, who were perceived as moderates, to reason with the Israelites, but they were unsuccessful. Next, a delegation that included army and police officials and the secretary of Native Affairs met with the Israelites, but their reasoning was also fruitless. The Israelites requested that the prime minister, Jan Smuts, meet with them and the officials agreed to convey the request. However, on their departure, the official spokesperson for Mgijima, his brother Charles (a well-educated man and one-time court interpreter), told them "God sent us to this place. We shall let you know when it is necessary that we go" (Edgar 1988, 20).

It was now apparent that neither side would give in. Neighboring white and black farmers were pressuring the government to take action against the Israelites and hostilities between Israelites and non-Israelites led to skirmishes and even one case in which a farmer shot and killed an Israelite. White farmers accused the Israelites of stealing cattle and sheep, and black farmers feared that the government might use the crisis to confiscate everyone's land, and both asked for official intervention. The Israelites no longer paid any taxes, they refused an official request that they make a list of the names of all the Israelites, and no European was allowed near the camp. The prime minister was engaged in an election campaign and declined to meet with the Israelites, but sent a delegation of the Native Affairs Commission in his stead. However, this meeting took place only in April 1921. The delegation offered to consider making Ntabelanga an Israelite center of worship (but not a center for permanent residence), but this was rejected. Charles Mgijima's parting words when negotiations broke down were: "We thank you for your patience. Now it will be a matter between the Lord and the Government" (Edgar 1988, 26).

The commission members recommended that a force be sent to move the Israelites, but urged that it should be "sufficiently strong to overawe [them] and so prevent unnecessary bloodshed" (Cameron 1994, 89). In early May 1921, a police force of eight hundred men under the leadership of the commissioner of police was deployed at Bulhoek. Mgijima told his followers that he foresaw bloodshed and that anyone who wanted to leave was free to do so. No one left.

On May 24 the police moved into position on the slopes overlooking the village. The Israelites were armed with broad-bladed spears, sticks, and knives, and they also had a few guns. The police, on the other hand, were well armed and their weapons included a machine gun (Millard 1997, 425). The Israelites marched outside as part of their morning service, but this was interpreted as a war dance by the police. The police asked for one more discussion in which they asked the Israelites to lay down their arms and allow them to enter the village, but this was rejected. A colonel tried one last time to persuade the Israelites to surrender, but he was told by an elder that "If it is to be a fight, I warn you that Jehovah will fight with us and for us" (Edgar 1988, 32).

In subsequent reports, each side blamed the other for the massacre that ensued. The Israelites claimed that police shot first; the police maintained that the Israelites started running into battle and they had to defend themselves. The result, however, was a fierce confrontation in which the Israelites in their white robes were easy targets. Despite being mowed down, they kept charging and twenty minutes later 183 lay dead and nearly 100 were wounded. One policeman suffered a stab wound (Edgar 1988, 33). Police arrested Mgijima in the tabernacle where he was praying with the women and children as well as 150 Israelites, and then demolished the illegal huts. Transportation was arranged for the women and children to return to their homes. At a trial six months later, Mgijima and his brother Charles were sentenced to six years hard labor and the other followers between twelve and eighteen months imprisonment.

## Conclusions

In considering these two events, we see that both conform to Barkun's broad description of millenarian movements as "those instances in which human beings band together and actually act upon a belief in imminent and total transformation" (1974, 2), as well as Wessinger's definition of a catastrophic millenarian group: a group with a pessimistic view of humanity, society, and history that believes that, to eliminate evil, the world or existing order has to be destroyed and created anew by God or a superhuman power (1997a). Both movements provided their members with explanations for their suffering and hardships, and both offered a vision of redemption.

Virtually every characteristic of millenarian movements as recounted by Barkun are present in these two groups despite the differences between them: association with periods of disaster; change and social upheaval; claims to esoteric knowledge; dependence upon charismatic leadership; blanket condemnation of the existing social and political order; and intense emotional expression (1974, 18–19).

In comparing the two movements, there are a number of interesting differences. The first is a difference of scale. The Cattle-Killing movement was a national disaster and is still, in some quarters, referred to as "the national suicide of the Xhosa." An estimated 40,000 Xhosa died in the aftermath of the cattle killings, and most who survived had to leave their land as contract laborers. Surely this must count as one of the most devastating millenarian catastrophes of all time. The Israelites, on the other hand, never numbered more than 3,000 of whom 183 died in the massacre. In one case, a nation was nearly wiped out; in the other, a relatively small religious group was persecuted and dispersed.

Second, there is a difference in the activity in the groups. In the Cattle-Killing disaster, people were active in bringing about the new dispensation. Thousands upon thousands of beasts were slaughtered and enormous amounts of grain were destroyed, while many preparations were made for the arrival of the new cattle, grain, and people. The isolated group of Israelites, on the other hand, waited upon the Lord in prayer and worship to liberate them into a new life. Their sin was that they were doing so on Crown Land.

A third difference concerns the charismatic leader. The figure of Mgijima was pivotal in the Israelite movement. He was the linchpin around which the movement revolved. Without his visions and leadership there would not have been an Israelite movement. Nongqawuse, on the other hand, was a teenage girl, who had no power or influence in a patriarchal society. That her visions became the spark that set the flame ablaze was due to her uncle, Mhlakaza the diviner, who convinced the king and chiefs of the authenticity of her visions.

Superficially viewed, there seems to be similarities between the groups as far as sociopolitical causes of the movements are concerned, but upon closer inspection the conditions were notably different. The Cattle-Killing movement grew from a nation on the edge of full-scale despair; the circumstances of the Israelites, while bad, were no worse than that of millions of other blacks in the country. Clearly, the sociopolitical circumstances did not play the same role in the two movements.

Barkun points out that multiple disasters are necessary for such movements to form. In the case of the Cattle-Killing, there had been almost continual war for about a hundred years, but the last of the Frontier Wars was the worst and had taken place only three years previously. Sixteen thousand people had died, many cattle had been carried away, and the traditional land of the Xhosa had decreased even more. The clash between the two cultures had led to the breakdown of Xhosa tradition. Clearly, Barkun's colonial hypothesis that asserts that contact between technologically unequal cultures produces social changes that can give rise to millenarian movements is applicable (1974, 34); so is the theory of decremental deprivation. The Xhosa were not tempted by the lifestyle of the whites—they longed for their own unspoiled existence before the colonizers arrived, but with the loss of land and cattle this was becoming increasingly difficult. To exacerbate matters, disaster struck again in the form of the fatal lungsickness. When Nongqawuse prophesied the resurrection of the dead on condition that all the cattle be slaughtered, that was the catalyst that drew all the other factors together and led to the onset of this movement. Consecutive disasters, the infiltration of millenarian ideas in the Xhosa worldview, and a final disaster in the lungsickness disease created a fertile field in which Nongqawuse's prophecies could grow into a catastrophic millenarian movement.

As far as the Israelites were concerned, they came into being only fifty years after the Cattle-Killing and in the area just north of what previously had been Xhosaland, and thus could not have been unaware and untouched by the earlier events. During Mgijima's lifetime, the lot of the Africans (even those who had received land from the British) had been steadily deteriorating. Soil erosion, drought, cattle disease, high taxes, the Land Act, and the new pass laws left the people impoverished and frustrated. However, many of these conditions affected all the people of the country and millions of black people were equally hard hit as the people in the Queenstown district. The role of Enoch Mgijima in the development of the movement must therefore weigh more heavily than the adverse sociopolitical conditions that the people were experiencing. The mere existence of the group, however, did not imply that violence or disaster would necessarily follow. For that, this group had to come into conflict with the authorities, who insisted (at the behest of local farmers) on enforcing an insignificant location bylaw, and Mgijima had to resist acquiescence.

Both movements confirm Barkun's view that millenarian movements "inhabit that border area where the religious and political fuse and interpenetrate" (1974, 44–45). Both rejected the legitimacy of the authorities. Sarhili curtly told Grey not to meddle in Xhosa affairs when he tried to stop the cattle-killings, and Mgijima and his followers repeatedly told the authorities that they were following God's will and recognized no other authority. The procrastination of the authorities in taking a stand against the Israelites seemed to have confirmed in their minds that they were protected by God and that the laws of the land did not apply to them.

The scandal of the Cattle-Killing movement lies in the haste with which the colonial government acted to exploit the tragedy for sociopolitical gain. Grey succeeded beyond his wildest expectations to procure all the cheap labor the colony needed and all the farmland necessary for white colonial farmers. In the case of the Bulhoek massacre, it is generally acknowledged that this was not a purely religious movement, but that it had strong political overtones. Mgijima and his followers simply would not accept the law that stated that they could not live in their "Holy Place." This aspect was cited by political leaders as a milestone in the long liberation struggle. Thus, Nelson Mandela could speak about the incident some forty years later and ignore completely its religious aspect:

> South Africa is known throughout the world as a country where the most fierce forms of colour discrimination are practised, and where peaceful struggles of the African people for freedom are violently suppressed. It is a country torn from top to bottom by

fierce racial strife and where the blood of African patriots frequently flows.

Almost every African household in South Africa knows about
the massacre of our people at Bulhoek in the Queenstown district
where detachments of the army and police, armed with artillery,
machine guns, and rifles, opened fire on unarmed Africans. (quoted
in Edgar 1988, 39)

The debacle led to a government inquiry into the role and nature
of the independent churches,[7] but oddly enough, not to an inquiry into
the massacre itself. From all the evidence, it seems clear that the government was sincere in its desire not to have a violent confrontation, and
it was widely thought to have dealt with the Israelites with leniency. One
should, however, not overlook the fact that the government could not
afford to be seen as caving in to the Israelite demands. White South
Africans especially felt strongly that the Israelites should be dealt with
harshly in order to set an example to black would-be rebels who might
be contemplating insurrection.

With regard to the last characteristic of millenarian movements,
namely intense emotional expression, very little is known. Nevertheless,
it is probably safe to say that the orgy of cattle-killing in Xhosaland was
accompanied by intense emotions, and the Israelites were certainly engaged in almost continuous religious activities.

It is clear that when compared with other millenarian groups worldwide, the Cattle-Killing movement shows remarkable similarity to the
Ghost Dance of the American Indians inasmuch as both tried to bring
about a millennial condition with the resurrection of the dead ancestors
and restoration of land and cattle or buffalo through a demonstration of
devotion through dance or sacrifice. The effect for both was to strengthen
the hold of the invaders and to break the back of native resistance to
white encroachment (Thorpe 1982, 140). The tragedies of the Bulhoek
massacre and the massacre of Lakota Sioux at Wounded Knee (see chapter by Pesantubbee in this volume) were both a result of government
agents misunderstanding the religious cultures of people viewed as "other"

---

7. The Commission of Inquiry's report recommended that "so long as the movement is not mischievous it should be tolerated and where it springs from a worthy motive
and is working in harmony with the Government it should be encouraged" (Sundkler
1976, 73). The strict conditions for recognition that were approved led to the situation
that of eight hundred known independent churches in 1948, only eight have been recognized officially.

and as dangerous. The Bulhoek massacre also calls to mind the recent events involving the Branch Davidians near Waco, Texas (see chapter by Gallagher in this volume). Both groups were besieged by government forces who showed little to no comprehension of or respect for what they were dealing with, and both groups were eventually forcefully subdued by the authorities with tragic consequences. Both groups were demonized to such an extent that the actions of the authorities seemed justified to the general public. Considering how long millennial movements have been around, it is astounding that authorities are apparently still at a loss about how to deal with them.

*Part Four*

# Revolutionary Millennial Movements

# 9

# Apocalypse, Persecution, and Self-Immolation

## Mass Suicides among the Old Believers in Late-Seventeenth-Century Russia

THOMAS ROBBINS _____

Collective suicide perpetrated by deviant religious "cults" has recently been in the news. The Branch Davidians in Waco, Texas, in 1993, the Order of the Solar Temple in Quebec, France, and Switzerland in several incidents from 1994 through 1997, and the Heaven's Gate UFO group in 1997 are alleged to have perpetrated collective suicides or murder-suicides in which considerably more than a handful of lives were extinguished.

These episodes are dwarfed in magnitude by the 1978 mass suicide at Jonestown, Guyana, associated with the Peoples Temple church in which more than nine hundred persons perished (Hall 1987). However, as I pointed out more than a decade ago (1986), the Jonestown holocaust may itself have been significantly exceeded in its scope by mass suicides associated with the schismatic "Old Believers" at the end of the seventeenth century in Russia. The Old Believers were persecuted, and their early leader, Avvakum, was burned alive at the order of Tsar Feodor in 1682. "During a six-year period from 1688 to 1694, 20,000 Old Believers voluntarily followed their leader into the flames, preferring martyrdom to accepting the religion of Antichrist" (Massie 1980, 66; see also Miliukov 1942, 59; Vernadsky 1969, 716). These suicides transpired in several discrete events, some of which may have cost between a thousand and twenty-five hundred lives (Crummey 1970, 39–57).

The existence of collective suicides or murder-suicides in the more recent events associated with the Peoples Temple (Hall 1987; Chidester 1988), the Order of the Solar Temple (Introvigne 1995a; Palmer 1996; Hall and Schuyler 1997), and the Heaven's Gate group is more or less uncontested. This is not the case with regard to the Branch Davidian tragedy at Waco (Lewis 1994; S. Wright 1995).[1] On the other hand, Hall and Schuyler (1998) argue that even when the existence of suicides seemingly perpetrated by a deviant sect is clear, the violence cannot be properly understood as a simple event created by a sinister "cult," but should be viewed as the emergent outcome of an escalating conflict between a stigmatized apocalyptic sect and an "oppositional coalition" that includes state authorities. In the escalation the heterodox apocalyptic sect is destabilized, which results in desperate or despairing violence.[2]

The provocative Hall-Schuyler model cannot be fitted in all its details to the late-seventeenth-century Old Believer events. The dynamic roles of governmental persecution and sectarian conflict with state authorities are more more conspicuous in the Russian Old Believer episodes compared with recent Euro-American events. This reflects the tsarist "Caesaropapist" context of sect-state conflicts, which contrasts sharply with modern Euro-American religious pluralism. In this paper I will briefly summarize and analyze the events (or what Hall and Schuyler would call "apocalyptic religious conflict") leading up to the mass suicide episodes at the end of the seventeenth century.[3] It appears that an apocalyptic spiritual climate, a culture of monolithic church-state integration, church schism, and social unrest led to the increasing politicization of a growing religious protest movement, which in turn led to intense persecution, apocalyptic expectations of the imminence of Antichrist, and finally to large-scale, eschatologically rationalized mass suicides. Finally, I will

---

1. In a recent paper (Robbins 1997) I tentatively accepted the dominant view that David Koresh et al. "suicidally" lit the fire that destroyed Mount Carmel Center and claimed the lives of most of the besieged Branch Davidians. C. Moore (1995) has registered one of a number of strong dissents. The issue has not been definitely settled.

2. Hall and Schuyler (1998) compare murder-suicides associated with three movements: the Peoples Temple, the Branch Davidians, and the Order of the Solar Temple.

3. My factual account will be somewhat abbreviated related to an earlier paper (Robbins 1986), which compared the Old Believer mass immolations to the (nonincendiary) suicide of about nine hundred persons at the Peoples Temple settlement at Jonestown, Guyana, in November 1978 (see also Robbins 1989). However, several new sources are used (e.g., Scheffel 1991; Hughes 1990), which were unknown or unavailable to me earlier.

suggest some limited convergences between the fiery Old Believer suicides and the incendiary (and possibly suicidal) deaths of David Koresh and his followers at the Branch Davidian "Mount Carmel" settlement near Waco in 1993.

## Religious Crisis in Seventeenth-Century Russia

The Great Dissent, or Raskol, was set off by Nikon, appointed by Tsar Alexis as Orthodox patriarch of Moscow. During 1652–54 Nikon decreed alterations in Orthodox liturgy and ritual. These changes included making the sign of the cross with three instead of the traditional two fingers, plus other liturgical modifications that broke with Muscovite tradition. Intended to bring Muscovite practices into conformity with older Greek and Ukrainian usages, these changes provoked fierce clerical dissent, but were forced through by means of several church councils during 1654–56. Led by Archpriest Avvakum, the dissenters, who were exiled and disciplined in 1656, maintained that the traditional Muscovite church "was sacred and nothing in its practice or doctrine could be suppressed or altered. . . . They regarded any modification of the church service as a sin that obstructed the way to salvation" (Zenkovsky 1957a, 42). From the Avvakumist perspective, Nikon and the tsar had led the holy Orthodox Church into apostasy!

It should be noted *that there was no legitimation for religious pluralism in Muscovite tradition,* and neither Nikonians nor Avvakumists would countenance pluralism or any separation of church and state. Both Nikonians and dissenters accepted the doctrine of "Moscow the Third Rome," according to which Moscow had succeeded Rome and Constantinople to become the third and final spiritual capital of mankind. The holy church of Moscow was the exclusive vehicle of Christian truth. Muscovite Orthodoxy "was the only currency in the economy of salvation. If Moscow was to fall from grace, betray the faith as had the first two Romes, it would mean not only the fall of Moscow as a state, as a divine punishment, but the end of the whole world. . . . Moscow's fall would signify the end of the possibility of salvation for all men, and the coming of the last days" (Cherniavsky 1970, 146). This doctrine had two key implications for the Raskol: (1) The initial aim of the dissenters was not obtain "religious freedom" to practice their own traditional rituals—to be left alone—but to reverse the Nikonian reforms and restore the traditional liturgy to the One True Orthodox Church. Avvakumist religious dissent was thus implicitly *political* from the outset.

(2) Persistence of the Nikonian liturgical revisions and thus of the perceived apostasy of the Orthodox Church necessarily had *apocalyptic* implications. Dissenters would be tempted to conclude that "the end was at hand" in terms of the "last days" of the world and the dreaded coming of Antichrist (Cherniavsky 1970).

## Growth of the Movement

According to some scholars, opposition to the Nikonian reforms was at first centered in monastic institutions. Many respectable abbots and senior monks "were convinced that they were defending the only true traditionalistic orthodox values and were willing to fight to martyrdom" (Murvar 1971, 290); moreover, "the Russian monks enthusiastically welcomed the opportunity for personal charisma and innovation which was so dramatically offered them in the Raskol and denied them by their state church" (291).

However, as the Raskol grew, it attracted many peasants for whom religious restorationism may have partly functioned as a symbolic expression of antagonism toward the consolidation of serfdom and the bureaucratic centralization of the state.[4] As harsh repression forced dissent to go underground, the "opponents of reform underwent a gradual transformation from a relatively small clerical faction to a popular movement which combined religious and social dissent" (Scheffel 1991, 37). The backward-looking traditionalism of the movement tended to associate it in the eyes of discontented peasants both with religious authenticity and social justice. "This perceived connection assured its popularity but also persuaded state authorities to draw an indelible parallel between *raskolniki* and political dissidents. Henceforth they were to be persecuted as enemies of both church *and* state" (38).

In 1667 there was a confrontation between authorities and the monks of the Solevetskii Monastery, who not only refused to accept liturgical reforms but also ceased to pray for the tsar and took up arms

---

4. As Crummey (1970, 9) points out, the peasants were illiterate such that for them "ritual, gesture and doctrine were inseparable" and liturgical alterations therefore appeared to transform the faith. Serfdom was legally institutionalized in 1649 while political centralization was proceeding. Antichrist became a symbol of new and oppressive religious, political, and socioeconomic tendencies. Old Belief thus became a diversified protest movement that attracted monks, peasants, townspeople, and Cossacks. "What united its adherents was their opposition to everything new and oppressive in Russian life—to the power of Antichrist" (Crummey 1970, 25).

to resist soldiers sent from Moscow to chastise them. A final onslaught in 1675 produced a bloodbath with almost two hundred defenders slain.

## Climate of Apocalyptic Expectation

The growth of the Raskol was affected by the fact that "in the middle decades of the seventeenth century, the cultural atmosphere of Russia was charged with tension born of apocalyptic expectations" (Crummey 1970, 7). This mood was stimulated in part by the publication by the state printing office in 1644 of the *Book of Cyrill*, a collection of Ukranian and south Slavic apocalyptic writings, which compiled an incredible sales record (five hundred copies in one month) for its time and influenced popular culture. "By the 1640s . . . there was a certain mood or ideology of insecurity, of rejection, in which men associated the evil they were rejecting or fleeing from, with the Tsar. And the ideology of the early Raskol intersected with if it did not draw upon, this mood" (Cherniavsky 1970, 152–53).[5]

The apocalyptic milieu of seventeenth-century Russia tended to focus largely on the dreaded coming of Antichrist, with less attention devoted to the subsequent second Advent of Christ and the millennial kingdom. One sect, led by the mysterious, ascetic hermit Kapiton, maintained that "the end of the world was at hand and that Antichrist already ruled the world" (Crummey 1970, 7). Kapiton's devotees were encouraged to prepare for the End through fasting, prayer, and other ascetic practices. But some Kapitonists "longed to follow the example of the saints of the early church and suffer martyrdom for their faith. . . . Small groups of the sect's members quenched their thirst for martyrdom by burning themselves to death in 1665 and 1666 in scattered locations of northern Russia. Their example was contagious" (45). The immolative apotheosis of the Kapitonists was designated by the participants as "purification by fire" (Vernadsky 1969, 698). The self-immolation of the Kapitonists was on a far smaller scale than subsequent Old Believer mass suicides. Nevertheless, the Kapitonovschina, which transpired after the beginnings of the Raskol, may have influenced later Old Believer self-immolations.

5. A similar apocalyptic mood might be said to characterize late-twentieth-century America (Robbins 1986). In particular one might compare the subculture of anti-tsar, antireligious innovation and agrarian protest to which the Old Believers were assimilated and in which demonic Antichrist was thematized with the contemporary rural, antistate, paramilitarist subculture in which a demonic "New World Order" is evoked (Lamy 1996).

## Further Politicization and Escalation of the Conflict

We have noted above that religious and social protest tended to fuse as the Raskol eventually attracted many peasants. Avvakumist religious restorationism gradually became a central element of a general underground subculture of anti-tsar, antinobility (antiserfdom), and sometimes ethnic protest in which the tsar or the institution of tsardom was seen to be associated with Antichrist (Cherniavsky 1970). The besieged traditionalists at the Solevetskii Monastery (see above) reportedly welcomed fleeing participants in the failed peasant rising of Stepan (Sten'ka) Razin, and later Old Believers contributed a contingent to the revolt of Pugachev against Catherine the Great in the late eighteenth century.

Perhaps even more important for the escalation of tension between state authorities and religious dissidents and the increasing politicization of the dissidents was the participation of *raskolniki* in palace intrigues and attempted coups. At various points over several decades, Avvakumist religious restorationism appeared to be on the verge of triumphing and destroying the hated Nikonian reforms, but the dissidents always managed to snatch defeat from the jaws of victory with the result that the stigma of political subversion gradually became more securely fixed to religious restorationism while the restorationists became more alienated and volatile.

The reforming patriarch Nikon, who appears to have wanted to create something like a Russian papacy, lost the support of Tsar Alexis and was deposed. The tsar recalled Avvakum from exile and some boyars (nobility) began to patronize him. But Avvakum, whose views on church and state were also incompatible with tsarist Caesaropapism, was reexiled in 1664. In 1666–67 a council of bishops deposed Nikon but also endorsed his liturgical revisions and anathematized the Avvakumists. The inclusion of "666" in the date of the fateful council did not escape the notice of the dissidents.

In 1676 Tsar Alexis died. The government, which acted for Alexis's sickly son and successor, Feodor, exiled Mateev, a powerful "westernizing" official who had been a conspicuous foe of the liturgical traditionalists. "For a moment the Old Believers had hopes that the wheel of history was turning and that the government would take a more conciliatory attitude toward them. These hopes did not materialize" (Vernadsky 1969, 709) perhaps because Tsar Feodor's tutor had been fiercely anti-Avvakumist. As desperation spread among the faithful, many of them came to believe "that the kingdom of Antichrist was about to come.

These [extremist] trends developing among the Old Believers worried even Avvakum" (709).[6] In 1679 troops were sent to apprehend the leaders of a hermitage on the Berezorka River where Old Believers were said to have gone into a state of religious ecstasy. "When the soldiers arrived they found only smoldering ruins; the Old Believers had burned the buildings and themselves. Seventeen hundred men and women perished in the holocaust" (710).

Punitive measures against the Old Believers were intensified after a traditionalist demonstration by the Strel'tsy ("musketeers"), or Moscow garrison, in 1681 and after the suppression of an abortive political conspiracy that Avvakum had supported. In 1682 Avvakum and two associates were burned at the stake.

The year 1682 also saw the passing away of Tsar Feodor. Mateev returned to power in alliance with the family of Tsarevich Peter (later Peter the Great), whose impaired stepbrother, Ivan, was shunted aside. Exploiting discontent among the Strel'tsy, Feodor's sister Sophia instigated a riot. The Strel'tsy seized the palace, murdered Mateev, and installed Sophia as regent for Ivan and Peter. But the traditionalist forces in the Strel'tsy became overbearing and overplayed their hand. They compelled the new regent to sponsor a tumultuous public debate on Nikon's revisions. Bullied and treated with discourtesy, the regent perceived that acceptance of the restorationist agenda would stigmatize her father (Alexis) and brother (Feodor) as heretics and deprive her regime of legitimacy. Sophia exclaimed: "If Afansy and Nikon were heretics, then so were our father and brother. This means that the reigning tsars are not tsars, the patriarchs not patriarchs and the prelates are not prelates. We refuse to listen to such blasphemy" (Hughes 1990, 77).

Subsequently, Sophia mobilized a detachment of gentry cavalry, which proceeded to overpower the guard of Prince Khovanskii, commander of the Strel'tsy and an Old Believer sympathizer, who was promptly executed. The crisis of 1682 "showed that the Old Believers were prepared to support any rebellion that offered hope for the restoration of the old faith. There could be no doubt that the Old Believers were a threat to the tranquility of the state as well as to the Church. Sophia

6. Up to his immolative execution, Avvakum resisted the idea that the tsar was Antichrist *in person*, although he told Tsar Alexis's son that Alexis "sits in torment, I have heard from the Savior" (Crummey 1970, 15). Avvakum leaned less toward apocalyptic speculation than did many of this disciples, but his letters praising early suicides were extrapolated to support later episodes after his death (15).

understandably became their implacable enemy" (Crummey 1970, 40). Horrific persecution ensued (see below).

Many Old Believers now fled to the hinterlands where they sometimes joined forces with dissident ethno-political groups and clashed violently with authorities loyal to the regime. "In the Don area, a party consisting of Old Believers and defenders of traditional Cossack autonomy overthrew the Orthodox and pro-Moscow hetman [chief] . . . at the end of 1686" (Crummey 1970, 42). In 1707 Old Believers fought with the Cossack insurgent Bulavin against the armies of Tsar Peter.

The series of "near miss" attempts to use coercion and political intrigue to restore the old practices tantalized the Old Believers, but ultimately left them increasingly frustrated and embittered and ready to believe that Antichrist had arrived or was very imminent. Simultaneously, the tsarist regime was increasingly led to perceive the militant religious restorationists as a serious political threat, and thus to strengthen repressive measures. The sociological model of "deviance amplification," which has sometimes been employed to explain the escalation of conflict between a deviant religious minority and public authorities, seems to apply here. Concerned with mutual interpretive feedback processes that interrelate concurrent increases in sectarian alienation and official social control, the deviance amplification model has been applied to tensions involving the Church of Scientology (Wallis 1977), the Branch Davidians at Waco (Palmer 1994), and contemporary Christian Identity paramilitarists (Barkun 1997).[7]

## Climactic Mass Suicide Events and De-Amplification

In 1684 the regent's government promulgated severe repressive measures aimed at the Old Believers. They were to be tortured and then burned at the stake if they refused to recant. "For many adherents to the old faith, the new situation seemed so incomprehensible that they sought solace in radical apocalyptic beliefs which explained Raskol as the first

7. It should be noted that the deviance amplification model can be applied in a short-term time frame as in Palmer's application of the model to events immediately preceding the fiery destruction of the Davidian residence at Waco (Palmer 1994), or in a longer time frame, for example, the escalating tensions between the Old Believers and the tsarist state over several decades leading to several mass-suicide episodes. In any case, the model implies that neither party to an escalating conflict is exclusively responsible for a catastrophic outcome at the end of the process, but both parties become trapped in interpretive feedback loops.

sign of the Antichrist's impending arrival" (Scheffel 1990, 45). "In their religious ecstasy many of the Old Believers sought the solution of their plight in self-immolation. . . . It is estimated that between 1684 and 1691 no less than twenty thousand men and women burned themselves" (Vernadsky 1969, 716). The eschatological rationale that accompanied many of these immolations has been described by Murvar (1971, 295).

> The basic religious doctrine, professed repeatedly in various periods by [Russian] religious virtuosi, was that the true believers' commitment calls for baptism by fire, *gar,* through which the seal of Antichrist is finally broken. . . . The favorite way of practicing *gar* was to lock themselves up and perish together by setting fire to the building during the religious ceremony.

According to Zenkovsky (1957b, 51), some incidents of *gar* among Old Believers may have taken "the lives of two and three thousand persons at once." From the account of Crummey (1970, 39–57), there were episodes such as the two Paleostrovskii Monastery incidents of 1687 and 1688 in which peasants led by religious restorationists seized an Orthodox monastery and thus deliberately provoked a punitive military expedition and siege. When government forces were on the verge of breaking through, the defenders would set the buildings on fire and they as well their prisoners (Orthodox monks) would perish. Crummey (51) writes:

> The Old Believers wanted martyrdom and were willing to go to great lengths to organize suitable circumstances. It was not enough to take one's life. One had to be convinced that one was a victim of persecution. . . . Therefore, the Old Believers provoked a crisis which they knew would force counter-measures and then prepared to kill themselves when they should be overpowered. This urge for passive suffering was complemented by a . . . hunger to fight back against those who had destroyed true religion. Real social and economic grievances of a local nature intensified this spirit of resistance.

There were other incidents, however, in which soldiers would be sent to burn down a hermitage at which Old Believers had gathered and to arrest the heretics. Before the troops could accomplish their mission Old Believers would burn themselves to death. "Whenever a community of Old Believers was in extreme danger the members would turn to suicide as the last resort and begin ritualistic preparations for the final sacrifice" (Crummey 1970, 57).

"Many thousands came to regard death by fire as a second baptism which would cleanse them of the Antichrist's influence, and entire parishes chose collective self-immolation during the 1680s and 1690s" (Scheffel 1991, 46). Yet, many Old Believers such as Abbot Dosifei and his disciple, Evfrosin, vehemently opposed suicide, which Evfrosin denounced in an influential pamphlet. Prosuicide militants were accused by Evfrosin of lack of faith (if flight was unavailing, the true Christian should submit to torture and trust God) and also of manipulating devotees through deception (e.g., lying about the approach of soldiers), coercion, and the use of hallucinogens (Crummey 1970, 56). Some of these accusations resemble the claims about "brainwashing" in contemporary "cults." "Time," Crummey (56) notes, "was on the side of the moderates," in part because the world did not end and also because the suicidal radicals tended to depart the earthly realm. Surviving Old Believer leaders "came to see that they would simply have to adjust to continued existence in Antichrist's world" (56). Collective suicide was condemned at a meeting of Old Believer leaders in 1691.

The "de-amplification" phase of the conflict of Old Believers with the state was facilitated by the early policies of Peter the Great, who, having overthrown his stepsister Sophia in 1689, mitigated the persecution somewhat. Peter's attempt to distinguish between the Old Believers who actively opposed his regime and those who merely sought to preserve their faith "cut the ground from under the militant position" (Crummey 1970, 57). Moderate religious dissidents paid a double poll tax, engaged in mining and other profitable ventures, and collaborated with the state in building projects. Later, Peter's policies became somewhat more repressive, and persecution further intensified under Empress Anna in the 1730s. Old Believers were obliged to revisit issues that had been debated in the reigns of Peter's predecessors, such as whether the tsar was Antichrist in person or merely beguiled by Antichrist's spirit, and whether Old Believers could legitimately pray for the ruler. A second, smaller-scale wave of immolative suicides erupted during Anna's reign and continued under the reign of Peter the Great's relatively disinterested daughter, Tsarina Elizabeth, in the 1640s. Her successors Peter III and Catherine II (Catherine the Great) pursued more liberal policies, but sporadic immolations continued down through the mid-nineteenth century.

It should be noted that the Regent Sophia's horrendous persecution merely stimulated more extreme behavior by the Old Believers, and, moreover, did not effectively suppress the movement. Her statutes made adherence to the Raskol a state crime and provided that persons who incited others to burn themselves would themselves be burned, "but this and other measures simply prompted a further round of self-immolation, as whole communities sought to save their souls before the world ended" (Hughes 1990, 123). But "moderates" who rejected suicide could take refuge in the heavily wooded wilderness and establish a secret community, which might escape detection. Or they could flee to the frontier areas that were partly dominated by groups, such as the Cossacks, who were resisting the central government. Many dissidents, however, were neither antisuicide "moderates" nor "extremists." They were conflicted, "caught between apocalyptic visions of martyrdom and the desire to retreat from the lost world and build a firmly established community in which the old faith could be preserved" (Crummey 1970, 55). When persecution was slightly mitigated, the retreatist desire became dominant.

The examples of the late-medieval French Cathars and the incipient Protestant movements in early modern Spain and Italy indicate that fierce repression can sometimes effectively suppress dissident faiths. In Russia, however, the vast size, expanse of wilderness, and ethnic pluralism of the young nation undercut the effect of atrocious persecution.

## Conclusion

The "Third Rome" consensus and the illegitimacy of religious pluralism made Avvakumist religious restorationism inherently political from the outset and, moreover, suggested to the dissidents the possibility that the apostasy of the state church heralded the coming of Antichrist. The conviction that the advent of Antichrist was either imminent or already here was strengthened by continually increasing tsarist persecution, which was intensified in response to the merging of religious and social protest in a climate of unrest and also to the involvement of the restorationists in palace intrigues and political subversion. Over three decades, the mutual perceptions of the religious dissidents and the tsarist regime became increasingly hostile and alarmist. Persecution and sectarian alienation continually intensified and mutually "amplified" each other. However, it required the combination of intense persecution, fervent expectations of the imminent end of the world, continuing Orthodox liturgical revisionism (perceived apostasy), and social grievances felt by the peasantry to sustain the radical response of collective suicide. When the End tarried and the regime backed off from the extreme measures of Regent Sophia, the enthusiasm for immolation waned and implicit accommodations evolved. The Old Believers ultimately splintered into a profusion of sects, some of which practiced (smaller-scale) collective suicide or other extreme practices such as castration (Murvar 1971).[8] A sort of counterculture of agrarian and anti-tsar protest evolved in which religious restorationism played a significant role, and the authoritarian modernizing ruler Peter I provided an ideal symbolic model for the demonic tsar-Antichrist (Cherniavsky 1970). This is ironic considering the role of Peter's initial relative moderation in promoting the stability of Old Believer communities.

### Postscript: Old Believers and Branch Davidians

Like the Old Believers in several episodes, the Branch Davidians at Waco met their end in a raging fire in the context of a military siege. They had not sought the confrontation with federal agents, and thus they cannot really be compared with the most extreme Old Believers who twice seized the Paleostrovskii Monastery in 1687–88. However, if it is assumed that the followers of David Koresh *did* set the fire that destroyed the Davidian compound on April 19, 1993, then possibly the doomed Davidians may somewhat resemble "most Old Believers," for whom "suicide came to be viewed as an extreme step to be taken only if all else failed" (Crummey 1970, 57).

There is a tradition, particularly marked in Byzantine and Muscovite history, of collective, immolative suicides by sectarians in a context of fierce persecution. Under Emperor Justinian in the sixth century, the severely persecuted peasant residue of the once widespread apocalyptic Montanist heresy "locked themselves into their churches and burned themselves to death rather than fall into the hands of their fellow Christians" (Dodds 1965, 67).

A contributing factor in some of these tragedies has been a scriptural tradition involving the eschatological and millenarian role of *fire* as a precipitant of the final Apocalypse. It is a tradition with which David Koresh, the messianic leader of the Branch Davidians, who was known for his prodigious memorizing of biblical passages pertaining to eschatology (Kelley 1995), would surely have been familiar.

---

8. Murvar (1971) sees the Old Believers and Kapitonists as early theistic exemplars of a tradition of Russian messianism, which later included "secular" movements such as the populists (Narodnikii) and Marxist-Leninist Bolshevikii.

The Davidian community at Mount Carmel near Waco, Texas, was, like various Old Believer settlements, under siege. An attempted "dynamic entry" by federal agents from the Bureau of Alcohol, Tobacco and Firearms (BATF) in February 1993 was botched, and a shootout erupted in which four agents and six Davidians perished. The FBI then replaced the BATF, and there was a fifty-one-day standoff with negotiations culminating on April 19 in what appeared to be an assault by the FBI with tanklike rams and gas (Kelley 1995). After several hours, the communal building was consumed in flames. The fire was allegedly set by Koresh et al. as a mode of collective suicide, although counter-allegations trace the fire to flammable gas employed by the FBI. "Either way, most church members went to their deaths believing that their enemies were destroying them on schedule as prophesied in Revelation 6:11" (Arnold 1994, 27).

Dr. Phillip Arnold, an expert on religion who indirectly negotiated with Koresh, is critical of the FBI.[9] He is agnostic on the question of who did set the fire. Yet, he is "certain that the Davidians were familiar with numerous biblical references to the role that fire would play in God's final judgement—'fervent heat,' 'flaming fire,' 'ashes' are well-known images in apocalyptic passages. Many of these passages confirm that fire would be the means that God would melt away the old order and usher in the new" (Arnold 1994, 28). Arnold further comments:

> Given the important role that eschatological fire plays in scripture and in Davidian exegesis, it is likely that David Koresh and the church members considered the burning of their sacred center as the prophesied fire which would immediately precede the opening of the sixth seal. For them the burning of Mt. Carmel could be the spark which would ignite the worldwide conflagration ushering in the "Day of the Lord" when "Earth shall be burned up." (2 Pet. 3:10)

It is therefore quite possible, notes Arnold (29) that "Koresh saw himself as a Davidic messiah who brings in the final conflagration." Like the Old

9. Whether or not Koresh's associates set the fire, federal agents of the BATF and FBI have been criticized for provoking apocalyptic zealots who were volatile but retreatist and not originally aggressive, though well-armed; see many of the essays in collections edited by Lewis (1994) and Wright (1995). Somewhat similarly Crummey (1970, 25) notes that the dynamic persecutory action of the officials, through their policies, "determined in which direction Old Belief would develop and which of its varied elements would predominate."

Believers, Kapitonists, and late Montanists, he might have refused "to surrender to the enemies of God's people." Arnold (29) asks, "did Koresh repeat King David's last words and proceed 'in flaming fire' to take 'vengeance on them that know not God?' (2 Thess. 1:7,8)?"

In their book *Prophets of the Apocalypse* (Samples et al. 1994), four Christian opponents of cults are also undecided as to who lit the climactic fire, but they lean more heavily than does Arnold toward the view that Koresh arranged for the setting of a "cleansing fire," which Koresh viewed as an eschatological sparkplug.[10] In the authors' view, the Davidians originally opposed suicide, which did not fit into Koresh's endtime scenario involving a "battle or violent confrontation during which he and many of his followers would die" (78). But what observers would consider "suicide" was permissible in the context of an overwhelming attack by demonic "Babylonians," who intended to slaughter "The Lamb" and his entire flock. Quoting from notes entered in the Bible of a former Davidian, Samples et al. suggest that the FBI assault involving armored vehicles shooting gas into punctures in the compound walls made by rams was interpreted by Koresh in terms of a prophecy in Nahum 2:3–4, in which "Chariots shall be with flaming torches in the day of his preparation." If the events at Waco were closely following a biblical script, then perhaps "All that remained was for the Lord (Koresh himself) to 'kindle a fire' that would 'devour all around him'" (81; see Jer. 50:24,32).

By launching an apparent assault on April 19, the FBI may have made possible an acceptance by the Davidians of "suicidal" acts to which they had been opposed. But even if the fire was *not* lit by Koresh's followers, they refused to surrender to overwhelming force mobilized by the state. The Davidians "believed that God did not want them to surrender to their enemies" (Arnold 1994, 30). In this respect they did somewhat resemble the more unambiguously suicidal Old Believers and the Kapitonists and Montanists before them.

---

10. The Old Believer suicides might be considered a classic instance of *eschatological or millenarian suicide,* a model that the Davidian immolations may possibly fit (see above). Although Robbins (1986) compares the mass suicides of the Old Believers to the (nonincendiary) mass suicides of Jim Jones's followers in Jonestown, Guyana, in 1978, Hall (1987, 130–38) argues that in some respects, the Jonestown holocaust did *not* continue the tradition of Christian millenarian suicide. Hall argues that the deaths in Guyana really evoke an earlier militant Jewish suicide tradition (exemplified by the siege of Masada in the first century) in which collective suicide is envisioned as a moral vindication of the dead and as a rebuke to their enemies *but not as an eschatological event* (see also Robbins 1989).

The Old Believer suicides as well as earlier Russian and Byzantine episodes differ from recent Western events involving the Peoples Temple, the Branch Davidians, the Solar Temple, and the Heaven's Gate UFO group in one key respect: the earlier violence transpired in a religious and cultural setting characterized by Caesaropapism and official intolerance of religious pluralism. Salvation was possible only through the official Church, and religious dissidents were often severely persecuted and easily became alienated and apocalyptic. It may appear ominous that some of the wild sectarian behavior once associated with persecuted sects in a religiously monolithic state is now transpiring in the relatively libertarian and pluralistic culture of North America.[11]

11. It is worth noting that recent provocative state action that has contributed to contemporary sectarian violence ranges from a quasi-military raid (Waco), through an unarmed congressman's site visit (Jonestown), to some investigation in a context of anticult agitation (the Solar Temple), to practically no state or public involvement (Heaven's Gate). Heaven's Gate may represent a limiting case for Hall and Schuyler's model of sectarian mass suicide as a function of "apocalyptic religious conflict."

# 10

# Western Millennial Ideology Goes East

## The Taiping Revolution and Mao's Great Leap Forward

SCOTT LOWE

### Introduction

The Taiping (Great Peace) Revolution of 1850–64 violently announced the arrival of a tumultuous new force in Chinese rebellion: Christian millennial expectation.[1] Roughly a hundred years later, a Marxist variant of this same millennial impulse was to have equally devastating impact on Chinese society in the form of "Mao Zedong Thought" and its practical expressions: the "Great Leap Forward" and the subsequent "Great Proletarian Cultural Revolution."[2] Both the Taiping Revolution and Mao's

---

1. The Chinese term *Taiping qiyi* is usually (and correctly) translated "Taiping Rebellion." I have chosen to view the Taipings as a *revolutionary* force because their aims were far more sweeping than the mere change in leadership implied by "rebellion."

Given its venerable history in Chinese literature, *Taiping* is a curious name for a movement seeking to destroy much of traditional Chinese culture. The compound *Taiping* (Great Peace) is first found in the "Taoist" *Zhuangzi* where it refers to a golden age. "Taiping Dao" (The Way of Great Peace) is the name of a Taoist religious movement that rebelled in C.E. 184, successfully establishing a theocratic state.

2. This essay will focus on the Taiping Revolution and the Great Leap. Although the Cultural Revolution provides perhaps the most unequivocal evidence of Mao's deification and the fundamentally millennial nature of his movement, the roots of the later extremes are first clearly visible in the Great Leap, so it is there that we shall look.

ambitious experiments have been studied in exacting detail by dozens of specialists. In this essay I will focus narrowly on selected aspects of these powerful movements' histories and millennial ideologies.

Catastrophic millennialism has a long history in China. It can clearly be seen in so-called White Lotus groups dating back at least four hundred years. Using an apocalyptic theology developed, in part, from Buddhist teaching, White Lotus leaders taught that the *kalpa* (a Sanskrit term meaning "eon") was about to turn, ushering in a new age. However, before the new world could emerge, a "black wind" would blow, annihilating all but the true believers, who would then inherit a transformed earthly paradise. White Lotus leaders convinced their followers that their personal efforts, manifested as violent revolt, would serve as the catalyst needed to bring on the supernatural forces of global destruction (example Naquin 1976, 56–61). Scholars have been tempted to see Manichean influences in these groups but now tend to downplay the likely impact of this "Western" tradition.

In any case, only in the past 150 years have unambiguously Western influences led directly to Chinese revolutionary movements, movements of unprecedented ideological scope and unparalleled destruction. The Taiping Revolution alone is estimated to have led to the loss of at least 20 million lives, while the cost of Mao's radical social restructuring may be even larger. Though very different in motivation and goals, these two movements drew their inspiration from Western millennial ideologies. Each produced cataclysmic devastation comparable to that of a major world war.

Though immensely destructive, as we shall see, neither the Taiping Revolution nor Mao's "permanent revolution" perfectly fit the definition of catastrophic millennialism developed in Wessinger's essay (1997a), for they both relied on human effort with little or no faith in direct divine intervention. Neither expected the world to be destroyed and renewed by superhuman forces. The Taiping Revolution was, however, marked by the extreme dualism characteristic of catastrophic millennial groups. Maoism can best be understood as an atheistic variant of progressive millennialism.

## The Taiping Revolution

Historians agree on a number of causes for the enormous social unrest roiling south China in the middle of the nineteenth century. Resentment of the incompetent political rule of the Manchu Qing dynasty, unequal and crippling land distribution patterns, the burgeoning opium trade, inflation, overpopulation, and recurring famines are just a few of the factors underlying the breakdown of social stability and the rule of law in Guangdong and Guangxi provinces in the years preceding the Taiping Revolution. Any combination of these factors might account for the rise of armed rebellion, and there were certainly many popular movements that found sufficient cause for revolt in the conditions of the time. For the Taiping Revolution these factors were unquestionably important, but not primary; the Taiping Revolution found its ultimate concern in the visions and divine mission of its founder, Hong Xiuquan.

## The "Sovereign"

Hong Xiuquan was born of Hakka parents in Guangdong province in 1814. The Hakka (Mandarin: *kejia*, "guest people") had migrated to south China from the north many generations earlier, yet despite their long residence in the south they were not fully assimilated into the local society and tended to live in their own villages, where they could band together for mutual support and defense.

As a child, Hong was distinguished by his obvious intelligence. His clan pooled its resources to give him a solid education in the Confucian classics, hoping that he would eventually pass the imperial exams, the key to gaining a lucrative and prestigious career as a government official. Hong's success in the exams was certain to provide both status and considerable economic benefits for his extended family. However, despite his talent and diligence, Hong failed repeatedly to pass at the higher levels. The pressure to succeed was enormous, but by design only a tiny percentage of candidates ever managed to pass the artificially difficult exams. Hong's failures left him increasingly bitter and distraught.

In 1837 Hong once again failed the provincial exam in Canton. Shaky and unable to walk, he was carried in a sedan chair back to his home, where he appeared to enter a coma. For forty days he was delirious, alternating between periods of manic wakefulness and deep lethargy.[3] His family feared first that he might die and later that he had become insane. At times Hong flailed out wildly, his strange and cryptic utterances suggesting that he was fighting demons. A few months later, Hong seemed miraculously cured and spiritually transformed. His com-

---

3. Scholars doubt that Hong was "sick" for exactly forty days; they assume he chose the figure for its biblical resonance.

manding, charismatic presence now attracted the honest and upright, while repelling the dissolute and immoral (Hamberg 1854, 14; Michael 1971a, 63).

Hong talked openly to his friends about his "sickness" and discussed his strange visions. Over time, Hong's descriptions of his visions grew increasingly formalized, as he elaborated their symbolic content in rather obvious ways; however, even the simplest outline of his experiences reveals the sources of inspiration for his later revolutionary career (see Hamberg 1854, 9-13 and Michael 1971a, 52–63, for descriptions of the visions).

As Hong remembered it, after falling in a swoon on his bed he was visited by a band of angelic beings, both human and animal-like in form, who carried him up to heaven in a sedan chair. Upon his arrival in the radiant, dazzling celestial realms he was washed both externally and internally, his soiled viscera pulled out and replaced with new organs. Once cleansed of worldly contamination, Hong was led before the throne of the "Heavenly Father." The Heavenly Father told Hong of his disappointment with the humans he had created, for they no longer followed his law or showed him proper reverence, perversely preferring to worship demons instead. The Heavenly Father also introduced Hong to the "Elder Brother," the Father's other son, who had evidently been sent down to earth at a previous time.

Hong spent what seemed to be ages in heaven—though he was gone only forty days in human time—before reluctantly returning to his earthly home. During his celestial sojourn, Hong fought great battles with the hordes of demons that had infiltrated all the levels of hell and heaven, even sneaking into the court of the Heavenly Father. After Hong proved his mettle as a demon slayer, the Heavenly Father gave him his commission, recorded years later in an official Taiping document: "the Heavenly Father, the Supreme Lord and Great God, also ordered the Sovereign [Hong] not to take them [the demons] captive, but to wait until they had gone down to that level of heaven which is the world, and then decapitate them" (Michael 1971a, 58–59). Hong took his charge to kill earthly demons very seriously, as we shall see.

Confucius also came under severe attack in Hong's visions. Though at first part of the heavenly retinue, Confucius fled with the demons when he realized that the corrupt and misleading lessons he had given on earth more than two thousand years earlier were about to be exposed before the Heavenly Father. Hong, by now a frustrated and failed scholar of Confucian teachings, was assigned the psychologically gratifying task of hunting down the "Master" and dragging him back in disgrace to the heavenly court, where God ordered Confucius caned for his meddlesome ignorance.

The visions ended when Hong reluctantly returned to earth with the instruction that he would "sleep" for several years before awakening to his true destiny.

Scholars have speculated at great length about the possible causes of Hong's "sickness," generally concluding that he must have experienced a psychotic episode. The most obvious explanation of his visions has never been noted, so far as I can tell, and that is that Hong experienced a spontaneous "shamanic initiation." The major components of Hong's experience—falling deathly ill, seeing angelic beings, traveling into the heavens, having his internal organs washed and replaced, meeting with a supreme spirit, and eventually recovering robust health—are the standard features of shamanic initiation, as attested by a great wealth of ethnographic reports from diverse cultures worldwide (Eliade 1964, 34). Only one aspect of a textbook perfect shamanic initiation was missing from Hong's psychic adventures. As Eliade notes, "Naturally, this type of ecstatic experience is always and everywhere followed by theoretical and practical instruction at the hands of the old masters" (33). Unfortunately, Hong was living in a culture without strong shamanic traditions. No teachers were available to place his experiences in their proper context.[4] Left to interpret the visions on his own, Hong drew self-aggrandizing conclusions that would later lead to an orgy of destruction and incalculable human suffering.

Back "on earth" Hong did indeed slumber for several years. While in Canton for an earlier attempt at the provincial exams, he had been given a pioneering collection of Christian booklets, *Quan Shi Liang Yan,* "Good Words to Admonish the Age." Christian missionaries had long been barred from China and had just recently been allowed limited access to the main treaty ports. The collection Hong received was one of the first publications written by a Chinese Christian convert. Hong later maintained that he had not read the work at the time he received it but had merely glanced through several of the pamphlets, before shelv-

---

4. The Hakka culture had long experience with possession, and mediums soon grew powerful within the Taiping leadership. Hong's visions differed fundamentally from the familiar mediumistic trance and seemed bafflingly new to his contemporaries. Ironically, a thousand years earlier shamanic flights had been a common feature in the religions of south China.

ing them and forgetting all about their strange contents. Six years after his recovery, in 1843, a relative drew Hong's attention to the volumes, which Hong read with growing amazement and recognition, as he finally understood the true meaning of his visions. Later, in 1847, Hong studied briefly with Issachar Roberts, an American Evangelical missionary, presumably gaining greater familiarity with orthodox Protestant Christianity, but the initial Taiping teachings seem to have been drawn entirely from Hong's visions and the contents of "Good Words to Admonish the Age" (Boardman 1952, 109–10).

The Bible passages and commentaries that compose "Good Words to Admonish the Age" spoke directly to Hong. He now understood that he was Jesus's younger brother, God's Chinese son,[5] sent down to earth to destroy pagan idols and bring the deluded masses of China back to the worship of the one true God, the God of Adam, Noah, Abraham, Moses, Jesus, and Hong. By acknowledging Hong as his son, God was declaring himself the Father of the Chinese people. This paternity clearly implied to Hong that the spiritual status of the Chinese people must, at the very least, equal that of the white imperialist forces threatening the Middle Kingdom. The demons in Hong's vision were the Manchu barbarians, whose corrupt Qing dynasty had brought so much suffering to the Han people.[6] Hong had been appointed by God himself to overthrow the Manchu demons and lead the Chinese with a stern new teaching drawn from the Bible and his visions, not the hated Confucian classics. Nothing less than a total revolution—political, ideological, economic, social, and religious—was demanded.

Eugene Boardman has noted that the Taiping use of biblical materials was quite restricted, even after the leaders had access to the entire Bible in Chinese translation, focusing mainly on the first five books of the Hebrew Bible, some New Testament concepts of the nature of God, and general ideas about heaven, hell, Satan, and demons—basically the materials collected in "Good Words" (1952, 53-87). Significantly, the Golden Rule and teachings of love and forgiveness were conspicuously lacking from Taiping publications (Boardman 1952, 107-9).

5. Jonathan Spence coined this phrase in his recent excellent biography of Hong.

6. The Taipings' hatred of the Manchus was vitriolic and openly racist, leading to nativistic scapegoating worthy of the Nazis or the Christian Identity movement. Like many nativist movements, the Taipings sought to achieve their millennial kingdom through an imported "foreign" ideology.

## The Movement

Hong's following grew slowly at first but picked up momentum as Hong's cousin Feng Yunshan, an early convert, developed his considerable skills as a traveling evangelist. By the late 1840s, thousands of "God Worshipers" had formed societies all across the rough hill country of Guangdong and Guangxi.[7]

As the societies grew in visibility and strength, conflicts with the established order inevitably arose, especially because the God Worshipers often destroyed the shrines and images of popular religion. Hong and his followers were quickly identified as a threat by local elites, who were constantly on the lookout for potentially seditious groups. (The Chinese had long outlawed all "heterodox sects"—a broad category that included many benign, nonviolent organizations—and harshly persecuted their members.)

Apologists for the Taiping Revolution have cited the harassment of the local elites and attacks by government troops as primary causes for the insurrection (see Cheng 1963, 4), and Taiping leaders themselves exploited the escalating persecution to motivate the faithful to prepare for revolt (Michael 1966, 37–38), but it appears certain that Hong had imperial aspirations years before his following felt compelled to organize for self-defense. Unlike those long-suffering millennial groups that are forced by persecution to rebel, Hong intended to overthrow the Qing dynasty from the beginning of his religious outreach mission, perhaps as early as 1844, when the full import of his visions finally became clear (Boardman 1952, 15). It seems likely that there was very little that the civil authorities could have done to prevent the uprising, other than to intervene earlier. There was no plausible nonmilitary response to the growing movement that might have defused the revolutionary thrust of Hong and his coconspirators.

## Sources of Authority

Though the movement received its original impetus from the visions of Hong Xiuquan and although Hong remained the figurehead of

7. These God Worshiping Societies shared many generic features with the more traditional secret societies and mutual defense groups also flourishing in the area. What made Hong's converts so distinctive was their earnest attempt to reject all Buddhist, Confucian, and Taoist influences in their worship and ritual.

the movement until his death and the revolution's collapse in 1864, almost from the start others vied for power in the movement's leadership. Hong's voyage to heaven was too distinctive to be imitated by rivals, at least with any degree of plausibility, but mediumship was still a possibility, for nothing in Hong's vision precluded it. Furthermore, the Hakka community was very comfortable with the phenomena of possession. Soon ambitious members of the movement's hierarchy began receiving "visitations" from both God and Jesus (Boardman 1952, 58–59; 68).

In 1848 Yang Xiuqing, a leader of the local charcoal burners and a military strategist of real talent, entered a trance state and began speaking in the voice of the Heavenly Father. Later that year Xiao Chaogui, another peasant convert, began channeling messages from Jesus, who was Hong's older brother and therefore, by Chinese standards, his senior in status and authority. Hong appeared to accept the mediumistic messages as valid, at least at first, especially because their content tended to confirm the authenticity of his visions and special status as the Heavenly Father's son. However, it soon became clear that both Yang and Xiao had great ambitions of their own. The voice of Jesus was silenced in 1853, when Xiao Chaogui was killed while leading an attack on the walls of Changsha, the capital of Hunan. Yang continued in his efforts to undermine and usurp the authority of the Sovereign, until 1856, when he and as many as eight thousand of his followers were murdered, at Hong's command, in the Taiping capital Nanjing. In retrospect, the bloodbath accompanying the death of Yang was one of several critical turning points in the Taiping Revolution that, taken together, ensured the demise of the insurgency.

The Taiping movement devoured its elite, or so it appears to outsiders. The constant warfare in which the Taipings were involved was certainly an important factor in the thinning of the upper ranks, but palace intrigues and violent coups took a harsh toll as well, as many talented military leaders were purged by the increasingly paranoid Hong and his inner court. Had the best generals and strategists received proper support and recognition, the Taiping Revolution might well have swept all of China and profoundly altered the contours of the modern world.

### The Revolution

When the Taiping leaders began their uprising in 1851, their ragtag army was met by imperial Chinese troops that were poorly organized and ineptly led. Though the Taipings were inexperienced and badly armed, they were usually more than a match for their opposition. The Taipings were also fast learners; they rarely made the same mistake twice. Within a few months, the Taipings had designed their own highly effective system of organization that included a common treasury of pooled resources and celibate, sexually segregated armies. Their opponents had developed a healthy respect for the Taiping's military prowess and had christened the Taiping soldiers "long-haired demons"—"long-haired" because of the Taiping's rejection of the Manchu-imposed queue and "demons" in recognition of their seemingly superhuman fortitude in battle.[8]

The basic direction of the early Taiping march was northward, toward the centers of wealth and power. Though the rebel armies suffered from numerous delays and military setbacks, they were able to maintain their momentum for several years, recruiting many new members for every original believer lost in battle. Even in the midst of their march, the Taipings found the time and energy to destroy nearly all the images, shrines, and temples they encountered in their path, alienating many Chinese who might otherwise have found their racist anti-Manchu campaign appealing. These affronted members of the educated gentry class later mobilized and led the provincial armies that ultimately defeated the Taipings.

By the time the Taipings reached the Yangtze River basin, their number was estimated to be more than one million. Bandits, secret society members, and starving peasants all were swept up in the momentum of the rebels' swift advance. With so many new recruits, maintaining religious indoctrination must have been a problem, especially since most new members were presumably drawn more by the attractions of a common treasury and assured supply of food than a natural affinity for celibacy and Hong's foreign theology (Michael 1966, 68). Nonetheless, the Taiping leadership made a great investment in religious education, suggesting to most observers that the leadership was sincerely motivated by religious concerns, not cynically exploiting the superstitious credulity of the masses to gain purely secular ends.

8. When the Manchus conquered China in the seventeenth century, they demanded that all Chinese males adopt the Manchu "queue," upon pain of execution. Many thousands of Chinese looked at the high-shaven forehead and braided pigtail the Manchus were requiring, weighed their options, and chose death.

Curiously, the troops of the second century "Taiping Dao" were also called "demon soldiers."

The Manchu capital, Beijing, seems to have been the ultimate destination of the Taiping leaders, but once in the Yangtze basin the relative speed and ease of travel by water caused a reevaluation of short-term plans. The massive Taiping ground armies were transformed into giant flotillas that followed the current downstream toward Nanjing, the old capital city of the Ming dynasty (1368–1644). By 1853 Nanjing had been taken and renamed the "Heavenly Capital" of the "Taiping Heavenly Kingdom." Nearly half the population of China had felt some impact from the passing Taiping hordes and perhaps as much as one third of the Middle Kingdom was now under Taiping influence. An expedition was sent north to capture the Manchu capital city, but after a promising start it foundered on the cold open plains of the north. More than seventy thousand dedicated rebel soldiers died in the debacle. At later points, the Taipings revived plans for capturing Beijing, but their momentum had been lost. Scholars agree that with the failure of the northern expedition, the Taipings lost their best chance to conquer all of China.

Once settled in Nanjing, the Taiping leaders established palatial living quarters for themselves and began accumulating harems, one of the traditional perquisites of power in traditional China, while regular members of the movement were still required to be celibate—even married couples. (Until the ban on sex was lifted in 1855, sexual intercourse between the faithful was punished by death.) An ever widening gap developed between the leaders' official pronouncements and their personal lifestyles. Although total dedication to the cause, including unswerving allegiance to the Bible-based Taiping moral code, was expected of the rank and file, many of the leaders slowly sank into lives of dissipation and petty intrigue. This is not to say that the movement was necessarily doomed. There were still vibrant military commanders fired with a sense of mission, but increasingly they found themselves fighting rearguard battles designed to shore up crumbling defenses and reopen severed supply lines. The many innovative plans the Taipings formulated to replace the old tax systems and judicial infrastructure of the Qing were increasingly just fantasies—sometimes clever and even visionary in scope—but given the realities of a shrinking area of control and ever diminishing popular support, no more solidly grounded than castles in the clouds.

Hong Xiuquan seems to have lost all concern with the physical details of his revolution soon after establishing his capital in Nanjing. The last eleven years of his life were apparently spent mostly on theological speculation and sex, as the day-to-day affairs of administration were taken over by incompetent sycophants and relatives. He may have descended into madness, as well. At the very least, he lost touch with the political reality of his movement.

Though the fall of Nanjing seemed inevitable by the late 1850s, the Taipings had some surprises left; the ingenuity and valor of their peasant troops kept the movement alive until 1864. In the end, the rebels' failure to gain the support of the Western powers; their alienation of the Chinese gentry, the very people needed to extend their control into the countryside; their failure to pursue their promised land reform and develop sustainable systems of taxation in a secure base area, and a number of other intractable problems and errors of judgment combined to seal their fate. Besieged by hundreds of thousands of Qing troops, all supply lines cut, stockpiles depleted, foraging for edible weeds in vacant lots, the citizens of the Heavenly Capital slowly starved, until their massively fortified city walls were blown open by Qing demolition experts, and invading troops poured in. At least one hundred thousand of the defenders were slaughtered in the next three days. Hong Xiuquan had died of disease weeks before, supremely confident even in his last moments that the Heavenly Father would allow no ill to befall his Heavenly Capital (Spence 1996, 325).

That the Taiping Heavenly Kingdom survived until 1864 seems almost miraculous. It is a tribute to the dedication, tenacity, and creativity of the Taiping faithful that the movement survived as long as it did, and an implicit critique of the Taiping leadership that the movement did not conquer all of China in 1853, when it was a real possibility.

The causes underlying the stagnation of the Taiping movement after the capture of Nanjing and the ultimate failure of the revolution have never been established conclusively. Why, when the conquest of all of China appeared imminent, did the leaders settle down in Nanjing, sending a relatively small expeditionary force north, instead of launching a full-bore assault on the Manchu capital? Certainly, if the Taipings were savvy political revolutionaries, cynically using a religious front to manipulate their superstitious peasant followers, they would, or should, have been perceptive enough to continue their march toward Beijing. This failure to drive forward provides us with strong evidence undercutting all attempts to deny the fundamentally religious and millenarian nature of the Taiping Revolution.

Rudolf Wagner provides the best explanation for the failure of the Taiping Revolution to progress once the Heavenly Capital had been established. Wagner believes that Hong's *visions,* not external factors, provide the essential clues necessary to understand Taiping motives, strategies, and behaviors. He concludes that Hong was a reluctant rebel who felt compelled to launch his revolution because the Heavenly Father had commanded it, and because the visions had revealed the Heavenly Father's great plan for China (1982, 4–5). Hong surely felt himself to be a major player in this plan, but he was by no means its author; his role was that of the obedient son following his father's dictates.

For the first few years of the revolution, the Heavenly Father's plan unfolded beautifully. Perhaps some of the battles were tougher than expected, and certainly the loss of key Taiping leaders was disappointing, but as a million or more victorious Taiping troops floated down the Yangtze in awe-inspiring formations, Hong and his faithful followers had concrete proof that the vision was being actualized here on earth. God was establishing his kingdom, and the demons were in retreat.

The failure of the movement coincides with the limitations of the vision (Wagner 1982, 5). The accounts of Hong's visions end with the charge to return to earth to kill demons and instruct humankind in the proper worship of the Heavenly Father. Hong was told that he was the true Sovereign of China but apparently was not given any specific information about what he must do to gain his rightful throne. In the early years of the insurgency, Hong's expectations were met. The Taipings battled the demons and generally prevailed. Huge numbers of Chinese joined their movement, worshiping the Heavenly Father and following his will. Once the Heavenly Capital had been established and Hong was enthroned, the visions' guidance ended. The detachment that Hong displayed from that point on is explained by his sense of completion; he had done everything the visions prescribed. If any further action was required, it was up to the Heavenly Father to take the initiative; at the very least he would have to provide new instructions.[9] No further guidance was forthcoming, and so Hong sat in state, supremely confident in his role as the Heavenly Father's son, oblivious to the decline of his kingdom as it collapsed around him. He may have expected the Heavenly Father to annihilate the Manchus or send a divine force to destroy and remake the world, but if so our sources are silent on the matter.

---

9. Other members of the Taiping leadership took a far more activist stance toward the creation of the Heavenly Kingdom. Hong Rengan, a cousin of the Sovereign who reached Nanjing in the revolution's last years, developed a remarkable set of modernizing reforms that, if implemented, would have utterly transformed the Taiping Heavenly Kingdom. The Sovereign ignored his proposals.

## Conclusions

Hong Xiuquan's shamanic visions and their "Christian" interpretation led to a vast millennial revolution that swept across much of China, leaving unprecedented devastation in its wake. In most regards, Hong's movement displayed the traits of catastrophic millennialism: a polarized, dualistic worldview, pitting us versus them, good versus evil, Chinese versus Manchus, believers (humans) versus demons; a teaching that evil is rampant in the world and must be destroyed; a faith in earthly salvation in a remade world. However, it is not clear that Hong's Heavenly Father was personally expected to intervene in any dramatically supernatural way to create the new world—at least not after providing Hong with the visionary instructions that gave the revolution its initial impetus—though the Taipings presumably sensed the Father's unseen hand in their early victories.

In other ways Hong's theology hints at a progressive millennial worldview. The Taipings saw their revolution as a cooperative venture between the Heavenly Father and the armies of the faithful. Together they would create an earthly paradise. True, it was necessary to kill many demons and destroy hundreds of thousands of pagan shrines and images, but there was nothing particularly catastrophic about this destruction from a Taiping perspective; it was just vigorous housecleaning. In addition, there was a fundamental optimism about the world implicit in the Taipings' rejection of "original sin." For them sin was simply the failure to comply with the Heavenly Father's commands, not a cosmic principle of evil. Therefore, it could be eliminated (Boardman 1952, 75–76). This belief in the potentially redeemable nature of humans (Manchus excluded) is usually associated with progressive millennialism.

In Hong we have a Christian visionary whose dualistic theology and self-proclaimed divine inspiration led to millions of deaths and unprecedented destruction. In this case it is clear that mild progressive millennial leanings do not inhibit initiating violent revolution, at least not when other aspects of the teaching require it.

### Chairman Mao's Millennial Movement

There are several difficulties that surface when Mao Zedong (1893–1976) is viewed as a prophet of millennial thought. The most obvious is that Mao was an avowed atheist who did not so much despise religion as dismiss its relevance to the modern world.[10] (The fact that Mao was an atheist did not mean that he was immune to being worshiped as a deity.) Furthermore, as a dedicated, if idiosyncratic, Marxist, Mao was committed to a "scientific" ideology that ostensibly left no room for romantic and idealistic illusions, including all "utopian" dreaming.[11] Unlike many of the millennial movements studied by scholars, at the time when the Maoist movement displayed its most fervent and militant millennialism, Maoism was not a persecuted minority grounded in conscious opposition to the established state. It was the state itself. This last fact opens up interesting new angles for would-be interpreters, for many models of millennialism presuppose that the movements are struggling against an entrenched power structure. With Mao we have an opportunity to see what happens when the established secular order is itself a significant source of the millennial hysteria that transforms an entire society.

### Historical Background

Almost from the moment of its founding in 1921, the Chinese Communist Party (CCP) found itself struggling with the historical determinism fundamental to the Marxist understanding of social evolution. If socialism and its end product—communism—can occur only as the culmination of a long historical evolution, with capitalism an essential intermediate state, then China was decades, if not centuries, away from the goal. This was clearly unacceptable to the impatient young revolutionaries joining the party. As Wolfgang Bauer has noted, "from the early twenties on, this rather mechanistic view of history was gradually supplemented in Marxist circles by a voluntaristic one" (1976, 376). The extreme voluntaristic position was that "consciousness" and proper determination could triumph over any and all material conditions, no matter how daunting. By this reasoning, China could be transformed from a primitive agrarian society to an advanced socialist state in a matter of years or even months, if only the people's consciousness could be

10. Mao seemed more tolerant of religion than other early leaders of the Chinese Communist Party (CCP), often speaking nostalgically of his mother's simple faith. However, Mao expected religion to disappear as China progressed politically and economically. When it did not, he became annoyed.

11. Marx was well aware of the dangers of utopian speculation and restricted himself to restrained, prosaic descriptions of the ultimate goal of history: communism. In the late 1950s and 1960s Mao and his followers excerpted the most visionary passages in Marx, and especially Engels, to support their increasingly wild predictions.

raised high enough and every member of society would strive heroically. Though a far cry from Marx, this extreme position was frequently championed by Maoists in the following half century.

## The Chairman

By 1949, the year the People's Republic of China was founded, Mao Zedong, the Chairman of the CCP, had ample experience of the power of the will and consciousness to defeat the odds. His party had been repeatedly battered by hostile forces during its first two decades— it had been nearly annihilated during the six thousand-mile "Long March" from Jiangxi to Yanan, Shaanxi—only to rise again, triumphant. Now it was the dominant power in the most populous nation on earth, and to the extent that Mao was the party, the power was his.

Other ranking party members worked to prevent Mao from becoming the sole force behind CCP directives. Through the 1950s and 1960s, there were many periods when Mao was temporarily eclipsed by others. Yet, Mao repeatedly managed to gain ascendance over his rivals. Though he often stumbled, Mao always caught himself before falling, tricking and outmaneuvering his enemies, real and imagined, enlisting the peasant masses of China in his battles against the bureaucrats, and repackaging his ideology for the changed circumstances, thereby ensuring that supreme power was never far from his grasp.

Chairman Mao was a complex man. Part earthy, coarse peasant, part philosopher and intellectual, both charming and ruthless, he was a consummate actor and inspired manipulator who was seemingly born to reign. According to his personal physician and confidant, Li Zhisui, Mao spent much of his free time studying the old Chinese dynastic histories. He especially loved the many picaresque tales of guile, subterfuge, and deceit, admiring most the very emperors the Chinese have collectively detested as corrupt, cruel despots. In Mao's view these traditional villains were the true heroes of Chinese history, because they brought "progress" by charging ahead resolutely, not allowing themselves to be distracted by sentimental hand wringing over the human costs that revolutionary change always requires. Mao found them to be inspiring role models (Li 1994, 122–25). It was thus entirely in character that Mao showed no discernible signs of guilt over the suffering he created. Even when the masses were starving in 1959–62, during a famine for which he was largely responsible, Mao was untroubled, finding ample time for his dancing parties and sexual adventures, inviting as many as four or five young peasant women to his enormous bed at a time (Li 1994, 358, 517). He used and discarded both friends and foes, humiliating and imprisoning former lovers, allies, and comrades-in-arms without a trace of remorse. If the memoirs of his physician are to be believed, Mao displayed many of the behavioral traits diagnostic of narcissistic and antisocial personality disorders.[12]

Some scholars are tempted to discount the millennial element in Mao's thought, seeing it as simply a convenient means to his one over-riding goal: securing and holding power. By this reasoning, the content of Mao's thought is so secondary to its use—the control and manipulation of others—that it is hardly worth analyzing. I would argue, however, that Mao was remarkably consistent in his thinking over time; the content did matter. Mao killed as much for ideology as revenge; he believed in "Marxist-Leninist-Mao Zedong Thought" as fervently as any Red Guard fanatic.[13]

### The Great Leap Forward, 1958–1962

By the end of 1957 Mao was convinced that China had made the momentous breakthrough into socialism, yet at the same time he felt that the bureaucrats running the country were backsliding into reaction-ary entrenched positions that would make them virtually indistinguish-able from the traditional Chinese power elite. His response was to invoke the theory of "permanent revolution" and strive immediately to realize the next inevitable step, the transition to communism—the final utopia in which the hierarchical power of the state will "wither away" and everyone's needs will be met effortlessly in a "workers' paradise"—rather than attempt to consolidate the gains that had so recently led to socialism.

To anyone else, China's economic backwardness might have seemed an insurmountable obstacle to rapid social and economic progress, but Mao characteristically sensed opportunity in adversity. The fact that so-cialism had barely arrived in a country struggling to advance beyond the

---

12. Having no expertise in psychiatry, I simply examined the DSM IV, a standard diagnostic manual, running down the lists of behaviors and comparing Mao's actions with the traits described. Mao strongly matches the profiles of narcissistic and sociopathic personalities.

13. Maoism's major deviations from "orthodox" Marxism are clearly illustrated by the Great Leap. Mao insisted that the peasantry, not just the urban proletariat, can function as the leading class in revolutionary struggle and that revolution can succeed even when few of the essential historical prerequisites for socialism or communism are present.

primitive agrarian economic stage suggested to him that it was both right and reasonable to move quickly on to communism. As Mao saw it, the Soviet Union was mired in the relatively less advanced condition of "state socialism"—characterized by massive governmental centralization and state-owned heavy industry—because of the Soviets' timid desire to stabilize their progress instead of fearlessly charging ahead (Meisner 1977, 227–28).

Mao viewed China's huge, uneducated peasant population as a blank slate on which progressive political thought could be written. With the proper guiding ideology, China could leap into the front ranks of the developed world. Soon party propagandists were promoting slogans such as "Overtake Great Britain in fifteen years" and "Make steel production jump to ten or twenty times that of Belgium" (Chesneaux 1979, 85). Increasingly strident exhortations to work harder and longer for the common good were judged adequate replacements for an earlier emphasis on material rewards. The Chinese were assured that "three years of struggle" would certainly yield "a thousand years of communist happiness," as party propagandists enthusiastically blended the languages of millennialism and Marxism in their proclamations (Meisner 1977, 229).

When Chairman Mao embarked on a cross-country tour to promote his new policy of rapid economic development, telling the peasants that they were the political vanguard of the nation and could make the leap happen with their rural fertilizer factories and backyard steel mills, the country was gripped by a frenzy of remarkable proportions. Events soon slipped out of the control of the central authorities, as regions vied to present the rosiest economic projections imaginable. The sky was apparently the limit, with local cadres claiming anticipated grain harvests of thirty thousand pounds per mu (.0667 hectares, or 0.165 acres). This translates to roughly ninety tons per acre, an absurd figure, yet given the mood of the moment few dared to be openly skeptical, for to do so was to risk being seen as negative, or "rightist."

Though Mao himself was at first skeptical that high-quality steel could be produced in backyard furnaces, he allowed himself to be convinced by his underlings that it was indeed possible. Small homemade furnaces were set up all across the country, both in cities and in rural areas, and everything from scrap metal to tools and household utensils was soon being melted down into worthless lumps of slag. Most Chinese appeared to have been infected by a virulently contagious "utopian hysteria"—even those who certainly knew better—and in the fever of the moment it seemed to many that the ideal age of true communism was dawning (Li 1994, 277).

Spontaneously at first, rural agricultural communes began to be formed. When Mao publicly voiced his approval of the new collectives, they spread like wildfire. By late September of 1958 an estimated 90 percent of the Chinese countryside had been organized into "people's communes" (Meisner 1977, 233). The people's communes were expected to realize the utopian goals of Marxist social transformation immediately. China scholars describe the nation's mood in the fall of 1958 as "chiliastic" (example 232–35).

Touring the country in his private train, Mao saw astonishingly dense fields of grain by day and the glowing fires of thousands of backyard furnaces by night. He became convinced that China was being transformed by the power of the people's will and political consciousness. What he did not realize was that he was witnessing an extraordinary fraud, a "Potemkin Village" of continent-wide proportions, staged to deceive the supreme leader and head utopian cheerleader of China. Li Zhisui recounts his amazement when he learned that rice shoots had been transplanted at such unhealthy densities in the fields along the railway lines that only the constant blowing of electric fans could prevent the closely packed plants from rotting, and that furnaces had been intentionally clustered along the Chairman's route to provide the illusion of explosive development (1994, 278). By this time, regional officials realized that the nation had deluded itself into accepting impossible production quotas, but no one was willing to take the responsibility for blowing the whistle. Mao was notorious for punishing the bearers of bad news.

Despite the fact that China had indeed grown a bumper crop of most staples, food shortages were felt in the capital of Beijing by November of 1958 and grew progressively worse in the following months. The reasons for disaster were many. One of the most obvious was that, although crop growth had been excellent, so much energy was squandered developing rural industries that peasants were simply too exhausted to harvest their bumper crops before they rotted in the fields. The waste was widespread and horrific in a country that has long struggled to feed its people from year to year. Even worse, the central government assessed annual grain taxes on the basis of the wildly inflated production estimates. In areas where overly enthusiastic officials had produced absurd crop statistics, almost all the available grain was requisitioned by the government as taxes. The central government then promptly exported the "surplus" grain to pay off foreign debts.

Rural industrialization projects also failed, despite the qualified success of small-scale fertilizer factories and some light manufacturing plants. Huge losses came from the attempt to produce steel in backyard furnaces. Coal and iron ore were unavailable in most rural areas, yet everyone was expected to manufacture steel. As a result, desperate communes fired their furnaces with charcoal and used whatever metals were available locally as "ore." The results were massive deforestation, as China's last remaining woods were clear-cut to make charcoal, and tool shortages, owing to the smelting of almost all available metals—pots, pans, cooking utensils, knives, hoes, rakes, sickles, shovels, doorknobs, locks—the basic implements needed to run farms and homes. Much like true believers in Melanesian cargo cults, the Chinese peasants were so sure that a communist paradise was imminent that they destroyed the very tools needed to survive in the present. Not only were communes short of food, many were unable to cook the grain they had, for all their metal cooking vessels had been melted down, and they had no fuel.

Famine and famine-related illness soon raged across wide areas of the country. The economic ravages of the "Great Leap" were felt for several more years, despite desperate attempts to restore economic sanity and agricultural productivity. Between 1959 and 1962, it is estimated that between 20 and 40 million people died from starvation or malnutrition-linked disease (example Li 1994, 507).

### Political Fallout

Mao's response to the collapse of the "Great Leap" was to look for the hidden enemies who had sabotaged his millennial experiment. It did not occur to him that the theoretical underpinnings of the "Great Leap" might have been flawed. Mao did not question his progressive millennial vision, though he conceded that it had been a mistake to proceed too rapidly. Despite the setbacks, Mao retained unlimited faith in his vision, the "Great Leap," and the power of the Chinese masses (Li 1994, 286). The "Great Leap" failed only because it was too ambitious and had been undercut by the evil machinations of "right opportunists."

The party leaders who understood the folly of the "Great Leap" used the famine and resulting economic disruption to attack Mao. For several years they had limited success. However, by launching the even more disruptive "Great Proletarian Cultural Revolution" in 1966, Mao triumphed once again, this time by sending young students and workers into the streets to destroy all surviving elements of the "old culture."

Soon Mao's "Red Guard" followers began to attack his former comrades, eliminating Mao's most powerful opponents one by one, punishing several million "rightists," and, almost incidentally, destroying China's
remaining cultural artifacts, historic monuments, and economic infrastructure. Through the chaos Mao reigned as a supreme leader—and for
some a divinity—until his death in 1976.[14]

## Conclusions

The belief in progress and evolution imported from the West in the
guise of Marxism at first offered a tremendously hopeful vision of human
possibilities. Yet, when the Maoist millennium faltered because of hysteri-
cally inflated expectations, utterly unrealistic timetables, self-deceiving
leadership, and incredibly bad planning, blame was placed on hidden
opponents, not flawed theory. The subsequent human and environmental costs exceeded those known from any catastrophic millennial movement, though the direct personal violence was arguably less.

A century earlier, the Taiping Revolution had also attempted to
reinvent Chinese society, partly on the basis of Western texts and ideology. Notable for their dualistic worldview, harsh militarism, and uncom-
promising iconoclasm, the Taipings attempted to exterminate the
Manchus, while destroying the literature, temples, shrines, and sacred
objects of traditional Chinese culture.

Although Mao and Hong lived in very different times and were
motivated by ideologies that disagree on many basic points, their lives are
uncannily similar in outline. Bright, ambitious peasant boys with few
prospects, both developed imperial ambitions and unshakable confidence
in the exalted roles they felt destined to play in China's unfolding future.
The palpable charisma both displayed inspired their peasant-based military movements to struggle and prevail against enormous odds. Once in
power, both went into mental and physical decline. Cloistered in their
palaces, surrounded by sycophantic courtiers, they indulged their enormous libidos, intriguing against subordinates and hidden enemies, and

14. The Chinese have long deified great individuals, worshiping them as gods.
Mao's apotheosis began during the Great Leap when Mao was seen as a socialist "savior"
leading his people into a new era. During the Cultural Revolution, Mao worship reached
an intensity reminiscent of charismatic Pentecostal services (for a marvelous description of
this, see Liang and Shapiro 1983, 121–25). Fading after his death, the cult of Mao
experienced a modest revival in the 1990s.

writing increasingly irrelevant theoretical screeds—all the while being worshiped by the multitudes. Most importantly, both rejected Confucian "orthodoxy" while still young and discovered the keys to their missions—the liberating insights that freed them to envision and then attempt to realize China's political and spiritual regeneration—in imported Western millennial ideologies.

Through the centuries, China has seen many homegrown catastrophic millennial rebellions, but before Mao Western-style progressive millennialism was largely unknown. Despite the surface optimism implicit in a progressive millennial vision, China's recent experience suggests that the capacity for violence and social disruption is stunning when a progressive millennial ideology holds sway. As Maoism demonstrates, progressive millennial movements can flourish without reliance on a divine plan; the inexorable force of the historical dialectic, the guiding light of a secular "messiah," and the power of the masses' consciousness can serve just as well.

# 11

# *Nazism as a Millennialist Movement*

ROBERT ELLWOOD _____

On September 5, 1934, Adolf Hitler declared at Nuremberg that the Third Reich would last a thousand years. The German dictator thereby identified his creation with the millennialist expectations of the ages. Nazism fell far short of that ambition, enjoying only twelve years in power. But millennialist movements have often been spectacularly unsuccessful in real time. Was Nazism nonetheless a millennialist enterprise?[1]

The answer has to be yes and no. Behind this equivocation lie observations that may be helpful in understanding not only the Nazi phenomenon but also the secularization of religious impulses and the spiritualization of political impulses in the modern world. My position in this chapter is that Nazism was a peculiarly modern blend of the political and the religious. Nazism could have taken the form it did only in its own

---

1. The major study to date dealing with Nazism as a millennial movement, and one of the best books exploring the deeper social, psychic, and spiritual roots of Hitlerism, is James M. Rhodes, *The Hitler Movement: A Modern Millenarian Revolution* (1980). Drawing chiefly on the work of Michael Barkun (1974), Norman Cohn (1970), and Eric Voegelin (1952, 1958) for theoretical perspectives on millennialism, Rhodes perhaps too narrowly follows only a few medieval and biblical models of the type. But his two basic premises are on target: first, that to understand Nazism one must take seriously the rhetorical language the Nazis themselves used over and in speeches and writings; second, that this language—replete with such words as *collapse, catastrophe, slavery, awakening, rebirth, salvation, choseness, the eleventh hour, the new man,* together with what Rhodes refers to as the Nazi "Neo-Manichaean race cosmology" (106–11)—can be understood only as encoding a sort of secular gnostic millennialism. The reader is referred to Rhodes's book for a fuller exposition of many of the themes raised in this chapter.

time toward the end of the modern era. But though it was peculiar to
that time it was not unique. Other comparable movements, both of the
Left and of the Right, shared characteristics of modern millenarianism
with the German party, and a study of Hitler's upsurge can help us
understand them and their times. They are all heirs of the Enlightenment
and its notions of progress, of good and evil as having social sources, of
revolution as a virtually sacramental rite of accelerating progress to apocalyptic rate and thereby totally transforming the social equation to produce only good. Yet, modern millennialism also owes much to
romanticism's emotional reconstruction of the Age of Reason to super-
charge its values with the power of myth, imagination, and nonrational
will. Here is where modern fascism and communism make contact with
the ancient millennial impulse.

Catherine Wessinger has defined millennialist movements as "the
expectation of an imminent and collective earthly salvation accomplished according to a divine or superhuman plan" (1997a, 48). Norman
Cohn states that a millenarian movement hopes for a salvation that is
(a) *collective*, to be enjoyed by all its followers as a group; (b) *terrestrial*,[2]
to be realized on this earth; (c) *imminent*, to come soon and suddenly;
(d) *total*, to transform life on earth completely; and (e) *miraculous*, to
be brought about by, or with the help of, supernatural agencies (Cohn
1970, 15). The German National Socialist, or Nazi, movement can fairly
be said to meet all these criteria insofar as they could be met by a cause
that was racist and political rather than fully religious in the conventional
sense. Its collectivity—the *völksgemeinschaft*, or people's community, of
which Nazis continually spoke—was made up of those whom it chose to
define as authentically German or "Aryan"; its paradise was to be realized

2. Whether millennialist movements should be necessarily defined as "terrestial" or
"this worldly" in their eschatology is doubtless a matter of choice. Some movements, such
as Heaven's Gate of 1997, have features in common with millennialism as usually understood, but do not meet this criterion. Heaven's Gate's paradise was otherworldly—in the
literal sense of being on another planet—rather than this-worldly. However, in this chapter
we will retain a distinction between otherwise similar movements that emphasize individual
or collective salvation after death or by some kind of ascension or transportation, and those
that are truly "terrestial" in their soteriology, looking mainly for a total transformation of
this earth or a portion thereof as well as of people in it. This distinction is of heuristic value.
For one thing, distinguishing between this-worldly and otherworldly salvation movements,
and reserving the term millennialism for the former, is of particular help in understanding
a political (as well as spiritual) millennialist movement such as Nazism and its quasi-
religious character, for a *political* movement of any stripe could hardly be entirely
otherworldly.

on this earth, in Germany and a world dominated by Germany; that realization would come in accordance with an indefinite but fast-paced timetable; and it certainly sought to transform life for the better for Germans, considerably for the worse for others, as completely as would be possible by this-worldly political and military processes. But the miraculous or supernatural element was present only to the extent, though this was to a significant degree, that Nazi belief in the superior qualities and destiny of the Aryans took on the nature of nonrational, transcendentally-sanctioned, self-validating faith. For although some Nazis, including Hitler, at times made rhetorical references to God, it is clear that their real divinity was in the blood rather than in the sky.

### Millennialist Praxis

Let us turn now to praxis, or the specific ways in which a millennialist movement functions to fulfill its agenda, or perhaps one should say allows a supernatural reality (again, in the Nazi case, race as a transcendent reality) to accomplish through them its goal (attainment of a *völksgemeinschaft*, a true organic community from which all pollutants have been expelled). Here I would like to list several millennialist features besides those already cited.

1. *Prophecy, and a single key charismatic prophet as its voice.* From the Taiping Revolution and its prophet Hong Xiuquan to the Ghost Dance and the prophet Wovoka, millennialism has gestated amid waves of prophecy: that the Great Peace was about to come, or that vast herds of buffalo would once again return to the plains. Powerful millennial movements have almost inevitably been centered on the cries of a central prophetic figure, who then becomes the major oracle, spiritual leader, and often practical leader of the movement. Adolf Hitler, who sometimes almost seemed to be in a state of trance, clearly was such a prophet.

2. *Special knowledge or revelation.* The millenarian prophecy contains secret knowledge—one might say gnosis—of the prophesied results and how they must be attained. In the Nazi case, this would include special information about the racist interpretation of world history, such as that conveyed in Hitler's *Mein Kampf* (1925, 1943) or Alfred Rosenberg's *Der Mythos des XX. Jahrhunderts* (The myth of the twentieth century, 1930).

3. *The use of symbolic or magical acts as means to fulfillment of the prophecy.* Virtually all millennial movements display tokens of the antici-

pated realization of their hopes. In Nazidom, the eagle and swastika of the new order were seen everywhere, as though the community of the Aryan people they represented was already completely fulfilled. These acts are essentially magical; that is, in the expression of G. K. Nelson, they exemplify use of nonempirical means to achieve empirical ends, in contrast to religion's nonempirical means and ends and science's empirical means and ends (Nelson 1969, 132). Magic, in other words, uses words and acts of a purely symbolic order to accomplish tangible, rationally understandable ends. Often these acts are symbolic of the destruction of the old order that is necessary before the new can come in. One thinks of the practice common in Melanesian cargo cults of destroying utensils or garments that will no longer be needed, or refusing to work in fields whose crops would be superseded by the new abundance about to arrive. Or one may perceive magic symbols of the new order suggesting it is already here if only to the eye of faith: special dress emblematic of the saved and transformed faithful, dances such as the Ghost Dance to welcome returning spirits of ancestors and buffalo.

The list of Nazi quasi-magical acts, cargo cultlike destruction of the old, and symbolic enactment of the new is almost endless. There were the book burnings and the replacement of an old flag with the new hooked-cross banner. Uniforms were in every street: the brown shirts of the SA, the black of the SS, the field-green of the revived army, the various party armbands and pins, all suggesting new identities to go with a new kingdom. The grandest enactments of all were no doubt the great pageants and rallies mounted by the party with masterful skill. The Nazis were particularly effective with pageantry incorporating night and death: the famous torchlight parades; memorial displays of a "blood flag" honoring fallen "old fighters" for the cause.

4. *Political or revolutionary action to "force" the coming of the paradise, or at least the appearance of a decisive sign of its imminence.* Symbolism alone is not enough. The Taipings relied not only on magic and faith but also on armies believed endowed with spiritual power. Indeed, millennialist fervor very easily blends with the mystic warrior mentality to produce troops capable of fighting tirelessly and with a sense of invincibility. One thinks of the "Boxers" of the Chinese rebellion of 1900, actually a Taoist sect who believed they possessed magic capable of stopping the bullets of the westerners. Not entirely dissimilar as an quasi-magical army was the Nazi SS, which possessed its own arcana of mystical lore and rituals. The Reichsführer-SS, Heinrich Himmler, who was en-

amored of occultism,[3] dreamed of molding his elite corps into a merciless and mystical order of racial warriors on the pattern of the medieval Knights Templar, which he idealized.

5. *Self-purification.* Millennialist movements need continually to define rigorously the boundaries between themselves and unbelievers, or enemies representing the old order, and to expel or destroy the old order. These acts are meant to confirm faith, and to maintain a high level of spiritual intensity within the movement. After the Jewish Holocaust, as well as the extermination of countless other perceived undesirables and dissidents by the Nazi terror, it is hardly necessary to say more about this aspect of the movement.

### Nazism and Millennialist Characteristics

The Nazi movement clearly exemplified all the preceding characteristics. Adolf Hitler, as he personified the *führer-prinzip,* embodied the charismatic prophet. The Führer may have appeared more than a little ridiculous to outside observers, but he established a potent bond with the German masses through the charm of which he was capable and his impassioned oratory. As several scholars have noted, charisma is not some indefinable mystical quality but a social relationship in which a leader is recognized because he evokes an intellectual or emotional predisposition already in the situation (Worsley 1968, xii). Hitler himself said in *Mein Kampf* that "the interest of the totality... is not served by the domination of the unintelligent or incompetent, in any case uninspired masses, but solely by the leadership of those to whom Nature has given special gifts for this purpose ... the folkish state must free all leadership and especially the highest ... entirely from the parliamentary principle of majority rule—in other words, mass rule—and instead absolutely guarantee the right of the personality [of the one leader]" (446, 449). In his own eyes, and those of his swept-away followers, the Führer surely met Wessinger's definition of a messiah as "an individual with divine or superhuman powers who will bring about the millennium" (1997a, 53). For visual images to go with such statements, the reader is advised to

3. Occultism refers to hidden but powerful and significant knowledge about little-known laws of nature or of human nature. Occult teachings are usually thought of as concealed within a particular tradition, in which they are communicated through special texts or initiations or both.

review Leni Riefenstahl's great propaganda film of the 1934 Nuremberg party rally, *Triumph of the Will,* and the repeated ecstatic shouts of the slogan, "Ein Völk, ein Reich, ein Führer!" (One people, one nation, one leader!)

The maker of that film presents in her memoirs as good an evocation as any of the kind of impression Hitler could make. Leni Riefenstahl declared in that much later work (1987) that while she was obviously impressed with Hitler's personality, and desperately hoped he could do something about the terrible economic conditions of Germany in 1932, when six million were unemployed, she never accepted his racism. Nonetheless, she does not shrink from describing the experience of a Hitler rally in terms that could hardly be more religious and millenarian in tone.

> When I returned to Berlin . . . the city was filled with posters announcing that Adolf Hitler would be giving a speech at the Berlin Sports Palace. On the spur of the moment I decided to attend. I think it was late February 1932. I had never before been to a political rally.
>
> The Sports Palace was so mobbed that it was hard to find a seat. Finally I managed to squeeze in among people so excited and noisy that already I regretted coming; but it was almost impossible to leave, for the crowds blocked the exits. At last, after a brass band played march after march, Hitler appeared, very late. The spectators jumped from their seats, shouting wildly for several minutes: "*Heil, Heil, Heil!*" I was too far away to see Hitler's face but, after the shouts died down, I heard his voice: "Fellow Germans!" That very same instant I had an almost apocalyptic vision that I was never able to forget. It seemed as if the earth's surface were spreading out in front of me, like a hemisphere that suddenly splits apart in the middle, spewing out an enormous jet of water, so powerful that it touched the sky and shook the earth. I felt quite paralysed. Although there was a great deal in his speech that I didn't understand, I was still fascinated, and I sensed that the audience were in bondage to this man.
>
> Two hours later I stood freezing on Potsdamer Strasse. The rally had had such a profound impact on me that I felt unable to hail a cab. No doubt about it, I was deeply affected. New and unexpected thoughts shot through my mind. (Riefenstahl 1992, 101)

The message of such a prophet contained teachings that could certainly be regarded as special knowledge, unrevealed to those outside the circle of the faithful, particularly non-Germans. It was a wisdom of the blood, which only a real German Aryan could understand. Those for whom the message was intended would respond with nonrational awareness of its truth. The communiqué involved exhilarating information concerning the privileges and destiny of the Aryan race, and the identity of its enemies, especially the Jews. Besides the speeches of Hitler, his propaganda minister, Joseph Goebbels, and other Nazi stalwarts, the two great texts of this gnosis were Hitler's *Mein Kampf* and, until he fell somewhat out of favor after the beginning of World War II, Alfred Rosenberg's turgid racist history of the world, *The Myth of the Twentieth Century*. Hitler tells us that the trouble with the older anti-Semitism was that it was based on religion rather than race, thus providing Jews with a way out: "If the worst came to worst, a splash of baptismal water could always save the business and the Jew at the same time" (119–20). But in fact, "Blood sin and desecration of the race are the original sin in this world and the end of a humanity which surrenders to it" (249).

Discourse like this suggests a secular gnosis combined with a quite cynical view of religion. Such an observation would be largely correct, except that "blood" acquired a sacred meaning, and inspired sacrificial holocausts more than equal to any offered on the altars of humankind's gods.

## Intimidation and Symbolism

The movement did not sustain itself by symbolism and sacrifice alone. It also used roughhouse politics of the grossest sort, complete with bullying and fear of concentration camps or death to maintain itself in power at home, and military might to spread its power abroad. We must always keep in mind that any presentation of National Socialism as a spiritual movement, millennial or otherwise, is at best no more than half the story. The Nazi rampage can just as well be perceived as a political gangster activity that never received a real majority in free elections, came to power through miscalculations on the part of the aged President von Hindenburg and others who should have known better, and kept itself there by means of raw terror combined with cynical manipulation of what passed for the spiritual and intellectual side of a virulently antirational movement.

Both halves of the bizarre Nazi world are necessary to see the whole picture. The secular half was certainly real. Yet, there was also fervent faith by at least some Nazi leaders, including the monomaniac Hitler himself and Heinrich Himmler, the austere and mystical high priest of the Jewish Holocaust; it extended to the wild-eyed, ecstatic crowds who are seen cheering the Führer in a hundred old newsreels and documentaries, and the soldiers who fought and died for him on many far-flung fronts with apparently few doubts about their mission.

Judging from the collection of letters and journals of frontline soldiers in Hitler's war assembled by Stephen G. Fritz, the spiritual— indeed, the millenarian—nature of their cause sustained them amid terrible hardships and in the face of death. Horstmar Seitz wrote in 1942, "Perhaps one must lose all in order to gain one's self. . . . We must throw away all culture and education, all false pretenses that hinder us from being ourselves. . . . For us there is only one thing: to begin completely anew, to erect new values and create new forms." The war was thus an occasion for transfiguration and redemption. Another anonymous soldier wrote in 1944, "We have recently been frequently debating over the present war and have realized that it is the greatest religious war, for an ideology is the new stamp for the word religion. I draw faith from [Nazi ideology] that the struggle will end in victory." The millennialist dream of a new society, with the leveling of all Germans into a *völksgemeinschaft* under a true leader, rather than the hierarchical society of old, remained a powerful inspiration to the end. As late as October 1944, Sebastian Mendelssohn-Bartholdy wrote, "Despite all its frightfulness, the appearances of this war are only of a secondary character. The primary thing, of course, is the necessity of a new social order in the world to overcome the present contrast between acquired and inherited property, between manual and intellectual labor, between followers and leaders who move in the dazzling light" (Fritz 1995, 189, 212, 213).

On the other side of the gender gap, one finds uncomfortable but honest postwar testimonies such as this one of a woman, born in 1915, who had been a leader in the Bund deutscher Mädel, the girls' branch of the Nazi youth movement:

> Hitler understood how to fascinate women. . . . I still remember that
> before the whole thing with Hitler happened, I'd said to a girlfriend,
> "In our generation there is nothing going on with heroes and nothing going on that one can really stand up for." And then came
> Hitler. And he did it right for us young people. He said "Volk und
> Vaterland" and "We must bring our people together" and . . . that
> somehow had value for young people. . . . We did love our Führer,
> really!" (Owings 1994, 173)

## Expulsion and Pollutants

As it combined magical, psychological, and practical means for the accomplishment of its goal, Nazism was comparable to other millennialist and quasi-millennialist movements. One thinks again of the Taipings; or of the Anabaptist utopia established by the visionary Melchior Hoffmann in Münster, Germany, in the early 1530s, when mass frenzy and apocalyptic openings all too soon turned into a reign of terror within the city while armies besieged it from without (Cohn 1970, 257). One also recalls the Crusaders, who had millenarian prophets and dreamers among them, and especially the role of the Knights Templar with which Himmler liked to compare his SS.

Finally, the Nazi movement was eagerly involved in purification of itself and its environment. In theory it was an attempt to establish the *völksgemeinschaft* community, a folk community based on blood ties, rather than a nation founded on legalistic structures. The ideal was articulated by Adolf Hitler in these words:

> Thus, the highest purpose of a folkish state is concern for the preservation of those original racial elements which bestow culture and create the beauty and dignity of a higher mankind. We, as Aryans, conceive of the state only as the living organism of a nationality which not only assures the preservation of this nationality, but by the development of its spiritual and ideal abilities leads it to the highest freedom. (394)

This would make the volkish community comparable, again in theory, to what Mary Douglas would call a strong group, weak grid community (1973). In her system, "group" refers to social pressures based on boundary definitions and internalized sense of identity, while "grid" denotes the systems, classifications, and symbols, like caste in India, by which a hierarchical society orders itself. Every society has both group and grid, but their relative strength may vary.

Millennialist and revolutionary societies tend to emphasize strong group rather than grid features, because of the spirit of equalizing, "we're all in it together" group coinherence, and the role of charismatic rather than structured leadership, that are generally necessary to their success. The French Revolution with its leveling dependence on common French citizenship rather than the old aristocratic hierarchical patterns, as well as movements such as the Taiping Revolution and the Ghost Dance, all exemplify this principle. The Nazi living-organism, *völksgemeinschaft* ideal, clearly representing strong group characteristics, was repeatedly proclaimed by its advocates against the traditionally hierarchical, bureaucratic, and tightly controlled German social order of the past with its strong grid characteristics. Despite leadership compromises with the traditional establishment behind the scenes, the importance of the leveling, egalitarian theme for selling the Nazi "revolution" to ordinary Germans can hardly be overemphasized. A strong group society, according to Douglas, is much concerned with purity, believing that the society and even individual bodies are under attack and in great danger of pollution. There is emphasis on expelling "witches" (pollutants) and ritually establishing group boundaries, even as revolutions have a tendency continually to devour their children.

No lack of examples obtain in the Nazi world. The most egregious example of all was the expulsion and attempted extermination of the Jews, as well as of Rom ("gypsies"), mental defectives, homosexuals, and other alleged undesirables. The "night of the long knives," June 29–30, 1934, when Hitler used murder to eliminate SA head Ernst Roehm and a thousand or more other rivals, was a purging of the party itself. All of this, needless to say, required a thorough steeling of the will through dedication to the cause, through an inner asceticism not entirely unknown to religion as well. Rudolf Hoess, commandant at the Auschwitz extermination camp, who ought to know, put it like this:

> I had to appear cold and indifferent to events that must have wrung the heart of anyone possessed of human feeling. I might not even look away when afraid lest my natural emotions got the upper hand. I had to watch coldly, while the mothers with laughing or crying children went into the gas chambers. . . . I was repeatedly asked how I and my men go on watching these operations, and how we were able to stand it.
>
> My invariable answer was that the iron determination with which we must carry out Hitler's orders could only be obtained by a stifling of human emotion. . . . Indeed . . . I almost came to regard such emotions as a betrayal of the Führer. (Hoess 1959, 170–72)

As Hitler made clear over and over, the philosophy behind the racial community state was founded not on reason, but was validated simply by unshakable belief, the power of will to make true what it wills, the self-authentication of that which is achieved through struggle, and acceptance of truth through submission or leadership and authority from above. Recurrently in *Mein Kampf,* the aspiring führer referred to these principles: "There must be no majority decisions, but only responsible persons, and the word 'council' must be restored to its original meaning. Surely every man will have advisors by his side, but *the decision will be made by one man"* (449).

This quasi-theological doctrine of "the triumph of the will," in the title of the greatest movie made about Nazism, can be understood only in the light of the original nonrational premise of *völksgemeinschaft* as the supreme good. There is a sense in which Hitler, in his own quest of the great white whale of racial purity, could have said with Captain Ahab, "All my means are sane; my motives and object mad." For deep feelings in the blood giving rise to political messianism and millenarianism are no doubt better expressed in an absolute leadership principle than democratic process; in it nonrational means, if not exactly sane, are at least appropriate to the vision and the object.

### Nazism and Modernism

All of this emphasizes the peculiar nature of Nazism as a modern millenarian movement. To interpret its similarities and differences with the classic, cargo cultlike millennialism, let us look at how Nazism was also an ill-begotten child of the modern era. In this respect I would like to use the term *modern* in a rather limiting sense, to define the era from the Enlightenment to the 1960s. According to the French postmodernist philosopher Jean-François Lyotard, this era was dominated by two "meta-narratives": the emancipation of humanity through progress; and the unity of knowledge, that is, that all knowledge worth knowing can be put into the abstract, universal categories of such disciplines as the natural sciences and the social sciences, and then given technological application (1984, ix) Modern concepts of progress as well as archaic eschatological mythology can be seen in the Nazi idea of history as leading toward a racial paradise. For *Mein Kampf,* however tendentious its historical notions, is not pure mythology but is replete with a sense of political and social history in the modern sense. There is also a Nazi version of the unity of knowledge: the theme that race is the key to meaning and power within modern history.

At the same time, Nazism had a profound concern with the idea of "decadence" in society: democracy "perverted" into excessive individualism, progress into materialism, freedom into license and anomie. Yet, these alleged perversions are in fact perversions of modernity, inexplicable in their modern Nazi meaning without reference to Enlightenment and post-Enlightenment concepts of progress and science. It is important to realize that Nazism was not only a throwback to some sort of primitivism, or even to the excesses of nineteenth-century romanticism but was also grounded in key ideas of the eighteenth-century Enlightenment. The egalitarian *völksgemeinschaft* society opposed to clericalism and feudal hierarchy but led by a *Führer* owes much to the Rousseauian "general will" articulated by a leader of "divine genius."

Nazi racism would not have been what it was without the modern zoological and anthropological sciences so much advanced by the savants of that era, not to mention nineteenth-century evolutionary theory of the "survival of the fittest" sort. Nor would its nationalism, nor its idea of revolution as the means to national redemption and transfiguration, have had much resonance without the French Revolution as an upsurge of the leveling *gemeinschaft* aspect of society and all that it meant to modern consciousness. Indeed, the eminent scholar of fascism, Stanley Payne, goes so far as to say, "All of Hitler's political ideas had their origin in the Enlightenment. These included the concept of the nation as a higher historical force, the notion of superior political sovereignty derived from the general will of the people, and the idea of the inherent racial differences in human culture. . . . The cult of the will is the basis of modern culture, and Hitler merely carried it to an extreme" (1995, 203; see also Birken 1995).

All this is another way of saying that Nazism, as a modern millennial movement, was political as well as religious, and in fact can be characterized as making the political into the crypto-religious. It needed, on the face of it, to be political, for another characteristic of post-Enlightenment modernity is the politicization of subjective and spiritual change. Purely inward conversion of individuals is not enough, in the modern mind, to effect significant social change and the national redemptions or transfigurations that follow. For the Enlightenment assumes, with John Locke, that consciousness in its pure state is a tabula rasa upon which it is society that writes, and the script can be modified. Enlightenment rationalism taught that the sources of good and evil are to be found in the objective social environment rather than in the psyche, and so require political rather than religious solution. At the same time, the notion of progress inculcates that political changes can indeed affect subjective consciousness, and moreover that they can be irreversible in a millennialist sense—the thousand-year Reich. Social change can be total as well as permanent if wrought with sufficient revolutionary force. The idea of revolution as total, purifying, transformative, and redemptive has haunted the modern mind since the glorious days of 1789 in Paris. Revolution, too, has taken on a sacred meaning even as it is ostensibly enacted within secular history. Revolution is progress speeded up to an apocalyptic rate, creating a mood of almost unbearable tension and hope. All this is highly visible in the rapture of the 1930s Nazis as they talked of their "revolution."

Nazism indeed had roots in the Enlightenment. It also can be traced to romanticism with its more nonrational ideas of the power of will and imagination. Romanticism in turn invested nationalism, as in the German "völkisch" movement, with strong emotive meaning associated with will and imagination, and idealized folklore and mythology as expressions of a popular will beyond rationality. (Indeed, paradoxically, German nationalism as a romantic "volkish" cause was much abetted by German resistance to the French upheaval, especially in its Napoleonic phase.)

According to the philosopher of romantic views of mythology, F. W. J. Schelling, and his intellectual kin, myths were not the products of individual poets or philosophers but of "the people." They presented a deep wisdom, based on experiences of nature and the cosmos, and of human feeling often conflated with nature, that in humanity's earliest stage of development could only be communicated in stories. Myth instilled a sense of wonder and an almost indefinable kind of insight, like mystical experience. In the end its exaltations transcended the individual, and even the dualism of the human and the natural (De Vries 1967, 57; Beach 1994).

The "folk psychology" of Adolf Bastian and Wilhelm Wundt recognized that collective folk wisdom could adhere in all distinctive, "rooted" peoples. "Rootedness," suggesting the superior worth and wisdom of peasant agricultural peoples who lived generation after generation on the same soil, was to have a baleful influence on Nazi ideology. Different folk, according to Bastian and Wundt, have diverse national or cultural ways of thinking, expressed in national myths (Wundt 1916). A community is more than a collection of individuals. It has a life of its own, and its products are distinctive from individual creativity and those of other nations.

Reactionary volkish thought, familiar to many through its reflection in the operas of Richard Wagner and in the propaganda of the Third Reich, rebelled with increasing vitriol against the international world of reason, science, and progress adumbrated by the Enlightenment and reinforced by the industrial revolution. That world, often personified in the Jew, was deeply destructive in this Germanist view. The volkish antidote that was frequently the proclaimed Nazi ideal called for Germanic distinctiveness and a simple, close-to-the-soil way of life.

## Reactionary Modernism

Rusticity was not always Nazi practice, however. Life is complicated, and that is especially the case when the "green" ideal confronted the availability of an advanced technological society's mechanical means of clearing space for the Aryan pastoral idyll. A cultural movement closely related to Nazism has been aptly named "reactionary modernism" by Jeffrey Herf. It was, Herf states, "the embrace of modern technology by German thinkers who rejected Enlightenment reason." They did not, however, think of themselves as reactionary but "viewed themselves as cultural revolutionaries seeking to consign materialism to the past. In their view, materialism and technology were by no means identical" (1984, 1, 2). Enlightenment and romantic sources of the Third Reich here began to curdle each other. The idea of a folk community became more and more mystical and antidemocratic, although it might be held that modern means on the purely technical level could be used in its defense, or its enhancement. It was now the social ideological stratum of modernity that was most to be rejected: its supposed atomistic quality, its production of faceless "mass man" (in Ortega y Gasset's and Carl Jung's term), and, if one may use the term, its "spiritual materialism," its attachment to material objects not as means or even as artistic creations, but as ends in themselves for human gratification.

Reactionary modernism was willing to build the German autobahns and the Volkswagen, on which the Nazis understandably prided themselves, not for "materialistic" purposes but only for the well-being of the folk and the enriching of its communitarian life. One could also detect an element of appreciation—for Hitler and other leading Nazis considered themselves aestheticians of the highest quality—of what Andrew Hewitt has called "Fascist Modernism" (1993). This was a style of art that loved the "post-decadent" irrationalism and imperialism it saw in powerful machines, spectacles, the dramatic gesture, the aesthetics of struggle. Its kind of art was better expressed in dynamic movement than the nineteenth-century sort of stationary scene; it therefore adored technology, movement, the new art of the cinema, all well exploited in the propaganda of the new order. Hitler's taste, and therefore Nazi taste, ran to such things: the cinematic triumphs of Leni Riefenstahl, the great pageants at Nuremberg, the shining steel armor of a new Wehrmacht. It also embraced the image of the Aryan hero, and of women worthy of such a hero; Nazi art of the human form was much given to scenes suggestive of male bonding, and to male and female nudity, not excluding a soft eroticism.

The aesthetics of war, however, took pride of place. The most important writer in this genre was Ernst Jünger, who shared with others of his type the *fronterlebnis*, frontline experience, in the Great War, and found—as did Adolf Hitler—that war could be the forge of heroes and a profoundly transformative and liberating experience. In such books as *Der Kampf as inneres Erlebnis* (Battle as inner experience, 1922) and *Feuer und Blut* (Fire and blood, 1926), Jünger celebrated the heroic, spiritual dimensions of war together with the technology of modern combat, with its "storms of iron" and vulture-like bombers. Jünger did much to prepare German consciousness for Nazidom, though he himself never joined the party; he found the Nazis too plebeian, lacking his level of aristocratic refinement in contemplating the aesthetics of blood and death on the field of honor. (He did, however, enjoy a comfortable position with the German occupation regime in Paris during the war, and was virtually the only important German writer to serve the New Order.)

German science fiction during the Nazi era affords peculiar insights into popular consciousness on several issues. An interesting example is Dietrich Kärrner's *Verschollen im Weltall* (Vanished in the cosmos, 1938). The hero, a Nordic superhero named Gösta Ring, first defeats a mass of Asiatic hordes futilely attempting to subdue the white race. He then leads a fleet of spaceships into outer space, where he defeats an evil, dark-skinned race that was trying to subjugate the light-skinned inhabitants of a distant world in the Möki galaxy. Finally returning to earth, Ring puts several evil capitalists in their place and is recognized by the world, or at least the dominant race, as its "Führer."

Then, at the end of the novel, there is another significant development. Under the benign guidance of their leader, the peoples of earth realize how ugly and wicked the old urbanized, technological world really was. They voluntarily abandon the cities, with their smokestacks and pavements, turning them into parks, and settle once more in the countryside, enjoying nature's idyllic peace and the beauty of Nordic forests, mountains, and seas (Hermand 1992, 259-60). Thus, after an instrumental technology apparently advanced enough to traverse interstellar space has done its job, it is left behind on behalf of an intentional return to a volkish paradise of smiling fields, "rooted" farmsteads and villages, and exalted natural splendor. This genre has sometimes been called "Aryan Green"; it resolves on the fantasy level the deep and painful tension Germans, like other moderns, felt between various contradictions of modernity, and between dreams of a pristine past (and future?) and so-called modern progress.

Literature of this sort is important to the millenarian theme in that it points to what Germans were increasingly seeing as a torturous dichotomy between material progress and spiritual fulfillment, and no less between spiritual and historical experience. Like many other moderns, they had come to the painful realization that material attainment did not always bring happiness, much less spiritual joy. Perhaps the material had to be rejected for the sake of the spirit, but there was also the possibility that the two needed merely to be properly prioritized, with the material put in its place and brought solely into the service of spirit. If then by spirit one meant the wondrous sense of "rootedness," community, and mystic ancient wisdom so much extolled by the volkish writers, that could only mean material means not in the service of reason or the individual or crass monetary gain, but in the service of the folk. In a deep sense, this kind of thinking would be in the millenarian tradition, with its idea that goods—cargo, buffalo—are not evil in themselves, but signs of divine blessedness. But they must be the reward of spiritual purity first rightly expressed by the rejection of individualism, and even the destruction of goods only associated with the old order. They must come as the reward not of individual enterprise, but of coinherence in tribe or movement, accompanied by faithful expectation of the new millennium. About this same time, in the early Weimar era Oswald Spengler's famous *Der Untergang des Abendlandes* (The decline of the west, 1926–28) came out, with its calls for the defeat of democracy, liberalism, and money in favor of a "life energy" that is "blind and cosmic" but racially bound to the soil, and carried by an elite of "higher men" who make "great decisions" (Spengler, 1922–23, 1002, 1008–9; Herf 1984, 57). Their dictatorship will be regarded, this prophet said, as a salvation, but in it "blood must flow, the more the better" (Friedrich 1986, 351). The saving blood, one assumes, was of atonement, redemption, and chastisement for sin. Clearly, the German consciousness was preparing itself for a tremendous upheaval, like that engineered by any millennial movement, to cleanse itself of past impurity and undergo a national resurrection.

For Nazism also had its twisted roots in modern historical dissonance and the seeming disconfirmation of nationalist and völkish ideas in the defeat of Germany in World War I, and then of other modern ideas, especially democracy and purely material progress, in the Weimar period. Historical dissonance, like individual disequilibrium, is not seldom the background of calls for radical, magical means of rectification—that is, of overcoming what went wrong by sheer power of the will affirming that the contradiction does not, cannot really exist. All this created the conditions for the final apocalypse of 1945. It also created within Nazism credence in a sort of modern gnosticism, a secret knowledge capable of overcoming what the outer world sees as ordinary knowledge. For, as we have seen, belief in special access to secret or gnostic knowledge is one key to the inner meaning of millennialism.

## Modern Gnosticism

In this connection, I would like to refer to the use of the term *gnosticism* in Eric Voegelin's *The New Science of Politics* (1952). Voegelin, a political philosopher seeking to discover the root causes of the ills of the twentieth century, pointed his finger at troublemakers he labeled gnostics. They were those who strove to rise above nature and find salvation through hidden knowledge of the political and psychological laws by which history secretly works. Modern belief in progress and unity of knowledge had impelled a modern search, sometimes eager and sometimes desperate, for that supreme arcanum of human knowledge. For what could bestow more joy, or more power, than the almost magic world-insight, beyond one's fondest dreams otherwise, that would *really* make for irreversible progress leading to ultimate world-transformation? Yet, the basic modern ideas, progress and knowledge-unity, whose truth seemed well demonstrated, suggested this final treasure of modern gnosis was possible.

Modern examples of the political/social gnostic were Auguste Comte, Karl Marx, Friedrich Nietzsche, Georges Sorel, and the Nazis and the communists, with their ideological credence that through understanding the secret laws of human history and nature—those of, say, the metaphysical meaning of race or "dialectical materialism"—human nature could be radically changed and perfected. Political gnosticism, Voegelin claimed in his onslaughts against that illusion, substitutes various dreams for reason because it disregards the way world history actually works. Above all, it ignores the hard fact that no human social or political construction is permanent or permanently changes human nature. Nonetheless, fired by ideological myths, modern gnostics fantasize that by human effort based on suprarational knowledge of the ultimate goal, their kind can create a society that will come into being but have no end, an earthly paradise equal to God's (1952, 166–67).

Voegelin went so far as to define all modernity as gnosticism, a term that encompassed such diverse phenomena as progressivism, Marxism, psychoanalysis, fascism, and German National Socialism (1952, 125). Later he clarified the position to the extent of revealing that modern persons who hold to "the Gnostic attitude" share six characteristics: dissatisfaction with the world; belief that the ills of the world stem from the way it is organized; surety that amelioration is possible; belief that improvement must evolve historically; belief that humans can change the world; conviction that knowledge—gnosis—is the key to change (1968). In his most memorable statement, Voegelin, who had himself lived under the Third Reich before going into exile, and who knew Europe's ideological wars at close range, put it well enough when he alluded to "the massacres of the later humanitarians whose hearts are filled with compassion to the point that they are willing to slaughter one-half of mankind in order to make the other half happy" (1995, 28–29).

Voegelin held that at base modernity's confidence did not rest in science and technology so much as in a gnostic belief that supreme power lay in knowledge of the true nature of the world. Physical science gave modernity part of that ruling knowledge. But the human engineering aspect of managing history called for another science and other means of knowing. To the true gnostic, ancient or modern, the ultimate knowledge that is power is not about elemental forces but is intrapsychic; it is knowledge of the true nature of humans and so of right politics and social organization.[4] Thus, for most National Socialist enthusiasts, including the reactionary moderns and even the Nazi science fictioneers, material achievements however wondrous were always subordinate to the · power of the will and the spirit; in the believers' eyes they did not create social or cultural realities but only implemented them under the command of sovereign will. So it was that the Nazis and other fascists adamantly insisted, often to the bewilderment of outsiders, that theirs was a profoundly spiritual movement.

---

4. It should perhaps be pointed out that Voegelin's use of the term gnosticism for the modern quest for political, social, and historical wisdom is misleading in relation to the ancient gnostics from whom the term is derived. The ancients sought only that "gnosis" that would enable them to attain salvation out of this world, and had no discernible interest in political or social change within or even after historical time here below.

Assuming that the idea humans can irreversibly change the world for the better is essentially modern, the social ideology of the political antimoderns is paradoxically very modern at the same time, for the fascist and the communist take to the ultimate degree the notion that by secret knowledge—*political* and *historical* gnosis—they could transcend history and make a new and irreversible paradisal world. Nazi racial ideology was clearly parallel on the profoundest level to the purely religious special revelation claimed by classical millennialism. In both cases a unique insight into what can change the world totally and for good was advanced. The Nazis had a true believer's confidence in their ability to know the world secret, whether enshrined in *Mein Kampf* or in myth. As Stephan A. McKnight has put it, for Voegelin the key gnostic belief is that the gnostic has direct knowledge of ultimate human nature, and so knows how to overcome alienation. Therefore, thought such as that of Comte or Marx is no more than political gnosticism, and modernity is not truly secular but a new form of religion, with its appropriate myths and rituals (1995, 137–38).

As millenarian revolutionaries, the Nazis considered that historical change can come by magical (nonrational, symbolic) means, by the power of a charismatic leader, through tribal group identity, and control of access to knowledge. Like any strictly religious millenarian groups, they knew they could not force the coming of the kingdom, or of the final savior—Christ, Maitreya, or the Aryan racial paradise—yet they could anticipate the nature of the kingdom and prepare the way. Like many other millenarians, when they finally did attain power, they hardly knew what to do, so much more accustomed were they to working anticipatory magic than to pragmatic administration. All they could easily manage, in fact, was to keep themselves in power, expand their realm of power, and repeat symbolic magical acts. So it was with the Nazis after 1933, as they rearmed and purified the nation of pollutants, and so it was especially in the supreme magical acts of war and Holocaust.

The large-scale violence of World War II was virtually inevitable given the nature of the Nazi movement. Politically, bloodshed was really predetermined, for Hitler was riding a tiger; the extravagant hopes and deep fissures the passions of the movement had cut into German society were so profound that the Führer had to keep producing greater and greater triumphs amid storms of excitement or he would likely topple in a backlash of disillusionment.

Spiritually, much the same was true. By its very nature, a millennial movement is like placing a bet for the highest possible stakes against the

game of history. The movement is wagering that history's ordinary des-
ultory flow can be stopped dead, and through a convulsive religious/
revolutionary act the river of destiny raised into a high sparkling-pure
stream running under divine power, never again subject to the downward pull of gravity. If the wager fails and normal time again returns,
then all is lost and the movement is discredited in most eyes. To keep
the wager going, therefore, all the prophet's resources must be continually placed on the table: money, persons, armaments, the energies of
sacred wars, even human sacrifice. The ultimate gamble requires the
ultimate in commitment. In the end the bet can prevail only if spirit can
prove itself truly superior in historical time to the way of all flesh, if grace
can be shown greater than gravity in our time and space, for millennialism
means this-worldly, not other-worldly, salvation. Therefore, the stakes
call for war to make millennialist will triumph even if, by the laws of the
flesh, the millennium seems likely to lose on the field of battle; only thus
can the power of spirit in this historical moment be tested. The Nazis
gambled everything because they could do no other in the light of their
original premises about the superiority of their race, their leader, their
community, and their spirit; and they lost.

# 12

# *Japanese* Lotus *Millennialism*

## From Militant Nationalism to Contemporary Peace Movements

JACQUELINE STONE

Some of the most compelling millennial visions to emerge in modern Japan have come from the Buddhist tradition of Nichiren (1222–82), which takes the *Lotus Sutra* as its sacred scripture. In this chapter I introduce some examples of Nichiren Buddhist millennial thought during Japan's modern imperial and post-World War II periods. This material suggests two hypotheses: first, millennialist strands in a given tradition are not necessarily violent or pacifistic in themselves but can shift from one orientation to another in response to circumstances; second, millennial thinking need not be confined to individuals or fringe movements isolated from or antagonistic to the larger society but may represent particularly intense expressions of more widely held concerns. Before considering modern Nichiren Buddhist millennial ideas, however, we must briefly refer to their remote beginnings.

### Medieval Origins in Nichiren's Thought

Buddhists in Japan's medieval period generally believed that the world had entered an era of decline, known as the Final Dharma age (*mappō*), predicted in sutras (Buddhist scriptures) and commentaries and said to have begun two thousand years after the death of the historical Buddha.[1] By that time, many thought, the world had moved so far from

---

1. Traditional East Asian Buddhist eschatology divides the process of Buddhism's decline into three successive periods following the Buddha's final nirvana: the True Dharma

the Buddha's age, and human delusion had accumulated so greatly, that attaining liberation through traditional paths of study and discipline was all but impossible. Japanese Buddhists calculated that *mappō* had begun in 1052, and over the next two centuries, social and political upheaval and recurrent natural disasters combined to convince many that they were indeed living in the fifth five-hundred-year period following the Buddha's nirvana, which began the dreaded "last age."

Nichiren was originally a monk of the Tendai school, which reveres the *Lotus Sutra*, with its promise of universal Buddhahood, as the Buddha's highest teaching. Like other teachers of his time, Nichiren saw the unique soteriological problems of *mappō* as demanding an exclusive commitment. Abandoning the traditional Buddhist position that values different practices as suitable to people of differing capacities, he taught that now in *mappō*, men and women could realize Buddhahood only by embracing faith in the *Lotus Sutra* and chanting its *daimoku* or title in the formula *Namu-myōhō-renge-kyō*. These seven characters were for Nichiren not merely the name of a text but embodied the seed of Buddhahood and the essence of all Buddhism. In this age, he held, because only the *Lotus* could lead to enlightenment, other teachings were ineffectual. Nichiren therefore urged the necessity of *shakubuku*, an assertive form of proselytizing that explicitly criticized and rejected other Buddhist teachings. This stance incurred hostility and even persecution for himself and his followers, but in his view, meeting such hardships for the sutra's sake proved the validity of one's faith and guaranteed one's eventual Buddhahood.

The *Lotus Sutra* presents itself as the Buddha's ultimate teaching, designated for the "evil age" after his nirvana. Nevertheless, it is not a millennial or apocalyptic text. It was through the lens of Nichiren's teachings that certain modern Buddhists came to read it in a millennialist light. Here let us consider some specific elements in Nichiren's thought that fueled these later millennialist readings.

### Risshō ankoku

The phrase *risshō ankoku*, "establishing the right [teaching] and [thus] bringing peace to the land," derives from the title of Nichiren's

---

age *(shōbō)*, the Semblance Dharma age *(zōhō)*, and the Final Dharma age *(mappō)*. According to the chronology most commonly accepted in Japan, the True and Semblance Dharma ages last for one thousand years each, and the Final Dharma age, for ten thousand years and more (Nattier 1991, 65–118).

famous memorial *Risshō ankoku ron*, submitted in 1260 to the retired shogunal regent, Hōjō Tokiyori, virtual head of the military government of the day. In this treatise, citing scriptural passages describing the calamities that befall a country where the True Dharma (Law or teaching) is neglected, Nichiren argued that Japan was being ravaged by epidemics and other disasters because its people had abandoned the *Lotus Sutra* in favor of lesser teachings. If the people embraced faith solely in the *Lotus*, Nichiren asserted, then calamities would at once be banished and the country restored to peace. But if "slander of the *Lotus Sutra*" were allowed to continue, then further disasters—civil strife and foreign invasion—would occur without fail. Nichiren's exclusivistic claims and his harsh criticims of other Buddhist traditions incurred the wrath of the authorities, who exiled him twice. Nevertheless, an attempted coup d'état led by the regent's half-brother Hōjō Tokisuke in 1272 and the Mongol invasion attempts in 1274 and 1281 lent credence to his predictions and won him the name of prophet.

Nichiren's doctrine that faith in the *Lotus Sutra* would make the land peaceful draws on two sources. One is the old tradition of "nation protection" (*chingo kokka*), a belief in the magical power of Buddhism to ensure safety and prosperity in the realm. By Nichiren's time, the *Lotus* had already enjoyed a long history as one of three "nation-protecting sutras," having been transcribed, recited, and expounded for centuries in the belief that the merit of such deeds would ward off calamities and secure the country's peace and stability. A second source for Nichiren's *risshō ankoku* concept lay in Tendai metaphysical thinking about the nonduality of subjective and objective realms and the immanence of the Buddha land in this present world. In Nichiren's reading, the nonduality of self and environment, of this world and the Buddha land, did not stop at subjective, personal insight; wherever the *Lotus Sutra* was embraced, he taught, the phenomenal world would actually be transformed. Thus, the *Risshō ankoku ron* states that when one has faith in the *Lotus*, "the threefold world will all become a Buddha land" and "the ten directions will all become a treasure realm" (Risshō 1988, 1:226).[2]

How exactly did Nichiren envision the Buddha land that faith in the *Lotus* could manifest in this world? Although his extant writings contain little specific description, we can point to one passage, often cited in modern millennialist readings:

2. The "threefold world"—of desire, form, and formlessness—indicates the realm in which unenlightened beings transmigrate.

When all people throughout the land enter the one Buddha vehicle, and the Wonderful Dharma [of the *Lotus*] alone flourishes, because the people all chant Namu-myōhō-renge-kyō, the wind will not thrash the branches nor the rain fall hard enough to break clods. The age will become like the reigns of [the Chinese sage kings] Yao and Shun. In the present life, inauspicious calamities will be banished, and people will obtain the art of longevity. When the principle becomes manifest that both persons and phenomena "neither age nor die," then each of you, behold! There can be no doubt of the sutra's promise of "peace and security in the present world." (*Nyosetsu shugyō shō* in Risshō 1988, 1:733).

This seems to suggest a conviction on Nichiren's part that faith in the sutra could bring about an age of harmony with nature, just rule, and in some form, a transcending of impermanence. This conviction, that faith in the *Lotus* could outwardly transform the world, represents one of his most important legacies that supports the millennial thinking of modern followers.

### The Position of Japan

Nichiren's writings reflect considerable ambivalence about his country. On the one hand, he saw Japan as an evil place, full of people who slandered the Dharma by placing other teachings above the *Lotus Sutra,* and who were therefore destined to suffer great miseries such as attack by the Mongols. On the other hand, the Tendai tradition had long postulated a unique karmic connection between Japan and the *Lotus Sutra*. Nichiren carried this further in regarding Japan as the very place where—in his own person, as the Buddha's messenger—the Great Pure Dharma for the time of *mappō* had first appeared. Thus far, he said, the Buddha-Dharma of India had spread from west to east. But its light was feeble; it could never dispel the darkness of the degenerate Final Dharma age. In the time of *mappō*, the Buddha-Dharma of Japan would rise like the sun, moving from east to west, and illuminate the world (*Kangyō Hachiman shō* in Risshō 1988, 2:1850). This image of a new Buddhism emanating from Japan like a resplendent sun was to prove compelling when, six centuries later, Japan began the struggle of defining its place in the modern international community.

Especially in his later years, Nichiren seems to have recognized that the spread of his teachings would take time. His chief concern was not so much the imminent world transformation characteristic of millennial thought as establishing the exclusive validity of the *Lotus Sutra* for the

Final Dharma age. Nevertheless, under the historical circumstances of the modern period, the elements outlined above would inspire full-fledged millennial expectations among some of his later followers.

## The *Lotus Sutra* and Militant Nationalism

The first fully developed modern millennial visions claiming inspiration in the *Lotus Sutra* and Nichiren's teachings emerged around the turn of the century and persisted until the end of World War II. With various permutations, these visions identified faith in the *Lotus Sutra* with Japanese nationalistic aspirations and looked forward to a world harmoniously unified under Japanese rule. This imperialist *Lotus* millennialism had its roots in the historical pressures of the Meiji period (1868–1912). First was the acute need for Japan to gain economic and political parity with Western powers if it was not to be exploited by them. Educators, opinionmakers, and spokesmen of the new Meiji government sought to rally citizens to the cause of transforming Japan into a modern industrial country by promoting a strong sense of national identity. Growing nationalistic sentiment in turn placed strain on the Buddhist community. For some time, Shinto and Confucian ideologues had criticized Buddhism as institutionally corrupt, a superstitious relic of the past, a drain on public resources, and a noxious foreign import that had oppressed the indigenous Japanese spirit. The Meiji Restoration also brought an end to the state patronage that Buddhism had enjoyed under the previous Tokugawa regime (1600–1868); the authority of the Buddhist establishment was further undermined by a brief but violent anti-Buddhist movement (ca. 1868–71) and by the institution of state Shinto as a national creed. Buddhism faced the need both to reform internally and prove its relevance to an emerging modern nation (Ketelaar 1990). Throughout the modern imperial period, virtually all Buddhist institutions, of all denominations, supported nationalistic and militaristic aims, sending chaplains abroad to minister to Japanese troops, missionizing in subjugated territories, and promoting patriotism and loyalty to government among their followers. Within Nichiren Buddhist circles, however, Nichiren's mandate to spread the *Lotus Sutra* and thus realize the Buddha land in this present world was assimilated to imperialist aspirations in a way that inflated the latter to millennialist proportions.[3] A short

---

3. Of course, for some ultranationalists, the aim of imperialist expansion acquired a millennial character independently of any explicitly religious associations.

chapter cannot detail all the clerics, scholars, and other prominent lay figures who promulgated nationalistic interpretations of Nichirō and the *Lotus Sutra* during this period. I will focus on three individuals in whose writings such interpretations assume a decidedly millennialist character: Tanaka Chigaku, Kita Ikki, and Ishiwara Kanji.[4]

## *Tanaka Chigaku*

Tanaka Chigaku (1861–1939) is known for initiating the ideological movement known as Nichirenshugi ("Nichirenism")—not the traditional Nichiren Buddhism of temples and priests, but a popular Nichiren doctrine welded to lay Buddhist practice and modern national aspirations.[5] As a youth in training for the Nichiren priesthood, Tanaka was disturbed by the accommodating attitude displayed by sectarian leaders toward other Buddhist denominations. In the time of *mappō*, Nichiren had taught, only the *Lotus Sutra* could protect the country; Tanaka became convinced that it was now time to revive the founder's strict spirit of *shakubuku* and declare the exclusive truth of the *Lotus*. Abandoning his priestly training in 1879, Tanaka embarked on a lifetime career as a lay evangelist. In 1881 he founded the Rengekai (Lotus Blossom Society) to propagate Nichirenshugi ideals. It was reorganized in 1885 as the Risshō Ankokukai, and again in 1914 as the Kokuchūkai or "Pillar of the Nation Society" (after Nichiren's words, "I will be the pillar of Japan.") The Kokuchūkai would in time win the support of ranking government officials, army officers, leading intellectuals, and large numbers of the public. Some of Tanaka's more famous followers included scholar of religion Anesaki Masaharu (1873–1949), instrumental in introducing Japanese religion to the West; Inoue Nisshō (1886–1967), agrarian reformer and founder of the civilian terrorist organization Ketsumeidan (League of Blood); and Gen. Ishiwara Kanji (1889–1949), of whom more will be said below. Others briefly attracted to Tanaka but who later rejected his nationalistic readings of Nichiren include the lit-

4. Japanese names are given in traditional order, with the surname first.
5. Another key figure in promoting Nichirenshugi was Honda Nisshō (1867–1931), leader of the small Nichiren denomination Kenpon Hokkeshū, who founded a number of lay societies to combat socialism, promote nationalism, and provide "good guidance" for citizens. Honda took the lead in forging ties with government officials, as seen, for example, in his successful negotiations to have Nichiren awarded the posthumous title of "great teacher" by the imperial court in 1922. Tanaka, however, was the movement's leading propagandist and thus the focus of discussion here.

erary figure Takayama Chōgyū (1871–1902) and the poet Miyazawa Kenji (1896–1933).

In 1901 Tanaka published a tract called *Shūmon no ishin* (Restoration of the [Nichiren] sect), a blueprint for radical sectarian reform. Here was the first Nichirenist millennial vision of modern times, combining shrewd plans for innovative evangelizing with a wildly improbable agenda. *Shūmon no ishin* outlined a detailed fifty-year plan for converting Japan and the world to Nichirenshugi. Tanaka envisioned proselytizing throughout the country: by the roads, in halls and auditoriums, at hot-spring resorts. Lay women would be organized into nursing corps and charitable hospitals established, winning the sect both public respect and converts by its works of practical compassion. The sect would publish a daily newspaper and evangelical materials in colloquial Japanese. Passengers on ships operated by the sect would also be proselytized; eventually, thousands of such vessels would fill the international shipping lanes with the sound of voices preaching the Dharma. Colonies of Nichiren adherents would be established in Hokkaido, Taiwan, and overseas countries as bases for evangelizing abroad. The growing financial capital of the sect, conscientiously invested, would make Nichiren Buddhism a significant economic force and contribute to the nation's wealth and power. Tanaka worked out detailed projections over ten five-year periods of the number of converts, income, and expenditures required by this colossal undertaking. In twenty to thirty years, he predicted, Nichirenshugi sympathizers would dominate both houses of the Diet. Realizing the fusion of Buddhism and secular law, Nichiren Buddhism would assist the imperial court in its enlightened rule. Other nations, coming to revere Japan's example of justice and benevolence, would abandon their barbaric quarrels. The righteousness of Nichiren Buddhism being made clear, other religious bodies would announce their own dissolution (Tanaka 1931, 93–134; Lee 1975, 26–27).

It was not, however, in this extravagant, narrowly sectarian form as the worldwide propagation of Nichiren Buddhism per se that Tanaka's millennialist vision was to exert wide appeal. Rather, its attraction would lie in his increasing identification of this goal with the spread of Japanese empire. The beginnings of this identification are already evident in *Shūmon no ishin:*

> Nichiren is the general of the army that will unite the world. Japan
> is his headquarters. The people of Japan are his troops; the teachers
> and scholars of Nichiren Buddhism are his officers. The Nichiren

creed is a declaration of war, and *shakubuku* is the plan of attack. . . . The faith of the *Lotus* will prepare those going into battle. Japan truly has a heavenly mandate to unite the world. (Tanaka 1931, 16; trans. from Lee 1975, 26)

From about the time of the Russo-Japanese War (1904–5), the *Lotus Sutra* became increasingly fused in Tanaka's thought with the idea of the Japanese *kokutai,* or national essence, the ideological pillar of Meiji nationalism, said by many nationalist thinkers to have descended in an unbroken line from the Sun Goddess and her divine grandson, Emperor Jinmu, legendary founder of Japan. "The truth of the *Lotus Sutra* and the Japanese national essence form one another, like front and back, and are mutually dependent, like essence and function. Truly, this is the Great Way of nonduality," he declared (Tanaka 1936, 163). Tanaka developed a Japan-centered hermeneutic by which he read the *Lotus Sutra* as a revelation of national destiny. For example, the word "thus" of "Thus have I heard" in the sutra's opening passage he interpreted as the Japanese national essence; the "heavenly drums [that] resound of their own accord" when the Buddha preaches, as Japan's mission of world unification; and the Buddha's supernatural powers, as Japan's military victories against China and Russia (102, 103, 107; Tanabe 1989, 199-206). Tanaka began to invoke the rhetoric of the mythic origins of the Japanese state—also prominent in the discourse of state Shinto—when he spoke of Japan's "heavenly task" of world unification as a mandate inherited from Emperor Jinmu, whom he saw as reincarnated in the Meiji emperor. Though he urged the revival of Nichiren's spirit of *shakubuku,* in making these ideological moves, Tanaka radically departed from Nichiren, who had strictly subordinated to the *Lotus Sutra* both the Japanese deities and the ruler's authority. Tanaka's identification of the *Lotus Sutra* with the Japanese national essence raised the latter to a status of universal significance and in effect equated the spread of Nichiren Buddhism with the extension of Japanese empire. It also served to justify militarism and aggression on the Asian continent (Lee 1975, 28–33; Nakano 1977, 165–72, 189–95; Tokoro 1966, 78–79).

The Kokuchūkai was not a marginal organization. Tanaka has even been credited with showing Buddhists a way to overcome their religion's exclusion from political affairs, following the establishment of state Shinto (Lee 1975, 33–34). The leader of a lay association, he was able to reach the public in a way the traditional Nichiren temple structure could not. As promised in his original vision, the Kokuchūkai published a magazine and a daily newspaper, providing material about Nichiren Buddhism in the vernacular language and interpreted in terms of immediate national concerns. Although his organization had its economic base largely among the lower middle class, Nichirenshugi ideology attracted politicians, businessmen, military officers, and scholars. The Kokuchūkai represents a case where millennialist thinking was an intensified form of already heightened sensibilities of patriotism, nationalism, and support for military ventures.

### Kita Ikki

Tanaka and the Kokuchūkai endorsed war in a "righteous" cause—extending the sacred Japanese *kokutai* to all peoples. There were also individuals, not necessarily affiliated with religious bodies, for whom imperialist aspirations, inflated to the proportion of millennial visions, inspired and legitimated violence. This was especially evident in the 1930s, a time of economic depression, affecting especially agrarian workers, and of a perceived inability of bureaucrats to deal with problems at home and abroad. This period saw a number of political assassinations and attempted coups d'etat led by disaffected military officers and other right-wing elements seeking to remove "corrupt" officials intervening between the emperor and his people and "restore" direct imperial rule. Ultimately unsuccessful, their actions nonetheless had the effect of increasing the political power of the military and of right-wing influence in government. Some of these insurrectionists drew selective inspiration from the new Nichirenist millennialism, such as Tanaka's equation of *shakubuku* with territorial conquest, as well as from Nichiren's own emphasis on readiness to sacrifice one's life if needed for the spread of Dharma (on Nichirenist-inspired terrorism, see Tokoro 1972, 174–88).

An important example is the revolutionary Kita Ikki (1883–1937), who advocated national socialism and strong imperial rule (Tokoro 1966, 189–222; Wilson 1969). Kita's millennial vision first emerged in his *Shina kakumei gaishi* (Unofficial history of the Chinese revolution, 1915–16) (1959a). A sinophile and ardent sympathizer with Chinese nationalism, Kita had gone to China and taken part in the Chinese revolution of 1911. His *Gaishi*, while analyzing the Chinese revolution, also sharply criticized Japan's leaders for their foreign policy of alignment with Western interests. Japan's destiny, in Kita's view, was to lead the rest of Asia in throwing off the yoke of Western imperialism and to spearhead a world socialist revolution.

In making this proposal, Kita clearly saw himself as a second Nichiren, remonstrating with government leaders in an attempt to save the country from disaster. Both the *Gaishi*'s introduction and final chapter—titled "The Mongol Invasion by Britain and Germany," a reference to European interests in China—speak of the *Gaishi* as the "Taishō ankoku ron": Just as Nichiren had risked his life to warn the authorities of foreign invasion in the thirteenth century, Kita now sought to protect the nation by warning against the threat posed by Western imperialism in the Taishō era (1912–26) (1959a, 4, 203). By the 1930s variations on the theme of a Japan-led Pan-Asianism had gained wide support; Kita was among the first to connect it with the new *Lotus* millennialism.

Kita's vision also entailed aggressive military conquest culminating in world peace, with Japan presiding over a union of nations. Like Tanaka Chigaku, who may briefly have influenced him, Kita equated Nichiren's teaching of *shakubuku* with the forcible extension of empire. The specifically Nichirenist elements in Kita's vision had less to do with the ideal world that would be achieved under Japanese rule than with the new Nichirenshugi rhetoric of *shakubuku* as legitimating the violence necessary to accomplish it. The Buddha, Kita said, had manifested himself as the Meiji emperor, and "clasping the eight volumes of the *Lotus Sutra* of compassion and *shakubuku*," waged the Russo-Japanese War. Now China, too, was "clearly thirsting for salvation by *shakubuku*" (161, 154).

> Just as the Lord Śākyamuni [Buddha] prophesied of old, the flag bearing the sun, of the nation of the rising sun, is now truly about to illuminate the darkness of the entire world. . . . What do I have to hide? I am a disciple of the *Lotus Sutra*. Nichiren, my elder brother in the teachings, taught the Koran of compassionate *shakubuku*, but the sword has not been drawn.[6] He preached the doctrine of world unification but it has yet to reach China or India. . . . Without the *Lotus Sutra*, China will remain in everlasting darkness; India will in the end be unable to achieve her independence, and Japan too will perish. . . . Drawing the sword of the Dharma, who in the Final Dharma age will vindicate [the prediction of] Śākyamuni? (201, 203, 204)

Similar rhetoric occurs in Kita's later work, *Nihon kaizō hōan taikō* (A plan for the reorganization of Japan, 1923) (1959b), a blueprint for

---

6. Popular associations of the Koran with holy war had earlier been assimilated to the *Lotus Sutra* by Tanaka in *Shūmon no ishin* (1931, 21).

social, political, and economic reform calling for a purge of corrupt bureaucrats and business cliques and the establishment of direct imperial rule. Industry was to be nationalized, private property restricted, and with the nation's economic base thus secured, Japan could proceed with its destiny to conquer and unite Asia. This work excited the admiration of a cadre of young army officers who envisioned the "restoration" of a stronger Japan under the emperor's direct rule. In 1936, leading some fourteen hundred men, they attempted a coup d'état, assassinating several government officials and seizing the center of Tokyo. (This incident inspired Mishima Yukio's famous short story "Patriotism.") Along with the insurrectionist leaders, Kita was arrested for complicity and executed the following year.

### Ishiwara Kanji

The potential influence of one individual's violent millennialist vision is yet more vividly illustrated by the example of Ishiwara Kanji (1889–1949). In the early 1930s Ishiwara was operations officer of the Kuantung Army, a Japanese force that had been stationed in Manchuria to protect lands leased from China after the Russo-Japanese War. This military presence was a source of continual friction between Japanese and local interests. With Chinese nationalism and accompanying anti-Japanese sentiment on the rise, voices within the middle echelons of the Japanese military began calling for a more assertive policy in Manchuria. Ishiwara played a leading role in the so-called Manchurian Incident of September 18–19, 1931, an unauthorized attack on the Chinese garrison at Mukden that committed Japan to a policy of military takeover in Manchuria and fed currents of growing nationalism, military buildup, and hostility in foreign relations. Though his action was not sanctioned by civil or military officals in Tokyo, Ishiwara was hailed by many as a hero for his "decisive solution" to the Manchurian problem. Ishiwara's action in this affair seems to have been rooted in his millennialist convictions that united Nichirenshugi ideals with his own views, as a military historian, about the evolutionary role of war in human history.

Then a captain newly graduated from the War College, Ishiwara had joined the Kokuchūkai in 1920. At the time, he was seeking a theoretical grounding for his personal faith in the Japanese *kokutai*, instilled by his military training, that could explain how loyalty to the *kokutai* differed from the ordinary patriotism that inspires heroism in the soldiers of any nation, and also provide a clear moral ground upon which he, as an officer, could legitimately require the sacrifice of mens' lives in battle (Iokibe Feb. 1970, 133–34, n.30; April 1970, 76–77). Ishiwara was convinced by Tanaka's theory, which, by identifying the Japanese *kokutai* with the essence of the *Lotus Sutra,* elevated it to a principle of universal import. In the relatively liberal Taishō era, when an influx of Marxist, pacifist, democratic, and other Western ideologies seemed to threaten the moral supremacy of the Japanese *kokutai* and the prestigious position achieved by the military during the Meiji period, Ishiwara found in Nichirenshugi a justification—indeed, a divine mandate—for his military calling.

Nichiren, as we have seen, had accepted the traditional theory of Buddhist decline occurring over five five-hundred-year periods. This scheme provided Ishiwara with a framework for his views on the "final war," a concept he had begun developing in the early 1920s and to which he would devote most of his life (Peattie 1975, 53–74). War, for Ishiwara, was a driving force of historical progress, in which the struggles of nations and peoples to impose their ideologies on their neighbors led to higher levels of civilization. By the present time, Ishiwara believed, these competing cultures and ideologies had aligned themselves along two polar axes: the West, led by the United States, which followed the "way of dominance," and Asia, to be headed by Japan, which followed the "way of righteousness." The conflict between these two was destined to end in Japanese victory ushering in everlasting peace. Ishiwara drew support for his theory from Nichiren's statement that in the fifth five-hundred-year period following the Buddha's nirvana—that is, at the beginning of the Final Dharma age—"a great war, unprecedented in prior ages, shall break out in the world" (*Senji shō* in Risshō 1988, 2:1008). Nichiren was referring to the Mongol invasion, which he saw as divine punishment for Japan's neglect of the *Lotus.* For Ishiwara, however, Nichiren's "unprecedented great war" signified the final war that would pit the imperialistic West against an East Asia united under Japanese leadership in a conflict of apocalyptic proportions. To prepare for this cataclysm, Japan would need to mobilize the resources of China and Manchuria—an argument Ishiwara used to justify Japanese military agression on the Asian continent. Through this war to end all wars, "Our powerful enemies will be vanquished, the glorious spirit of the Japanese *kokutai* will come home to the hearts of the peoples of all nations, and the world will enter an era of peace under the guidance of the imperial throne" (Ishiwara 1968, 1:431; trans. from Peattie 1975, 74).

As Ishiwara struggled with the chronology of his eschatologial theory, modern Buddhological scholarship confronted him with an unexpected obstacle. Nichiren, like most of his contemporaries, had accepted the traditional Chinese date corresponding to 949 B.C.E. for the Buddha's nirvana and thus believed that he was living in the fifth five-hundred-year period that began the Final Dharma age. Today, however, though the Buddha's dates are by no means agreed upon, scholarship tends to place him much later, in the fifth or sixth century B.C.E. If one were still to assume that the Final Dharma began two thousand years after the Buddha's death, then Nichiren would have lived, not in the Final Dharma age at all, but toward the end of the Semblance Dharma age. To resolve this difficulty, Ishiwara formulated his novel "dual theory of *mappō*" (1986, 56–58). He concluded that the Buddha by his supernatural power had skillfully intended the "first five hundred years of *mappō*" in two senses, and that the messenger of the *Lotus Sutra* was to appear twice. The first time he had come as the monk Nichiren to establish the True Dharma. While Nichiren's age had not in strictly chronological terms coincided with the fifth five-hundred-year period, because the Japanese of that time were convinced that it did, this first advent was absolutely necessary. The second advent of the sutra's messenger, however, would fall within the actual historical period of the fifth five hundred years, when he would appear as a "wise ruler" to realize the Dharma in reality and "unify the world."[7]

Although not sanctioned by Nichiren orthodoxy, Ishiwara's solution enabled him to fix his timetable for the final war firmly within the 2,500-year framework of traditional Buddhist eschatology. Writing in 1939, Ishiwara calculated that about 2,430 years had passed since the Buddha's nirvana; thus, within the next seventy years—before the first five hundred years of *mappō* would have expired—the final war would break out and world unification be accomplished (1967, 307-8).

Here one man's violent millennialism literally affected nations and was instrumental in setting Japan on a tragic course. Although Ishiwara acted independently, his idiosyncratic vision of a "final war" that would unite all humanity was not all that removed from more widely held imperialistic aspirations.

---

7. Ishiwara here subverted a passage in which Nichiren predicted a "wise ruler," meaning, not the ruler of Japan, but an enemy sovereign who would punish Japan for slandering the *Lotus Sutra* (*Kanjin honzon shō* in Risshō 1988, 1:719).

## Summary

During Japan's modern imperial period, intense nationalism, militarism, and war were assimilated to new millennial visions of a world harmoniously united under Japanese rule. Certain elements in the teachings of the medieval Buddhist teacher Nichiren were appropriated to these visions. His discourse about Japan as the place where a new Dharma would arise to illuminate the world was given an imperialist reading; his advocacy of assertive proselytizing or *shakubuku*—which for Nichiren had meant preaching and debate—was adopted as a metaphor for armed force; and his emphasis on giving one's life for the *Lotus* became a celebration of violent death in the imperial cause. Such millennialist appropriations inspired not only extremists committed to political assassination or coups but also broadly legitimated the violence that pitted Japan as a whole against other Asian countries and the West.

## A World Without War

It is little exaggeration to say that ultranationalistic *Lotus* millennialism died in August 1945 in the flames of Hiroshima and Nagasaki. But even before these ruined cities had been rebuilt, a new *Lotus* millennialism had risen to take its place. Postwar *Lotus* millennialism envisions a time when, by awakening to the universal Buddha nature, people everywhere will live in harmony and with mutual respect. Different Nichiren- and *Lotus*-related religious groups offer variations on this basic theme, but on one point they all agree: in that future time, there will be no war. Nuclear weapons, in particular, will be abolished.

### The Rejection of Violence

One of the earliest articulations of postwar *Lotus*-inspired millennial hopes for peace can be found, astonishingly enough, in the last writings of General Ishiwara Kanji. Ishiwara, who lived to see Japan's defeat, did not relinquish his "final war" theory easily. For a while he seems to have believed that Japan might yet be able to wage the final war through the efforts of scientists working secretly on yet unimaginably powerful weapons (Peattie 1975, 347–48). In a long memorandum to General MacArthur, he alternatively suggested that he had mistaken the participants in the final conflict, and hinted that such a struggle might still be waged between the United States and the communist bloc (Fujimoto

1964, 309). Purged from public life and in failing health, Ishiwara retired in 1946 with a group of disciples to the village of Nishiyama on the Japan Sea, where he devoted his remaining years to pondering how Japan and the world might be regenerated through Nichiren's teaching. Before his death, he arrived at a new *Lotus*-inspired millennial vision, one that broke utterly with the violence he had previously advocated.

Ishiwara's new vision called for establishment of a modern agrarian society in which the tasks of production would be performed communally by village units of about a dozen families and where men and women would rank equally, a person's work being decided on the basis of ability rather than gender. In a long tract dictated shortly before his death in 1949, Ishiwara interpreted Nichiren's prediction of a time when "the wind will not thrash the branches nor the rain fall hard enough to break clods" in terms of a future society in which science, politics, and religion were perfectly harmonized. Science, "having obtained the Buddha wisdom," would enable control of the weather and eliminate the ravages of storms. Homes, villages, and factories, engineered by the new science, would be pleasantly integrated into a natural environment of forests and streams. For a few hours each day, everyone, even the imperial family, would work wholeheartedly in the fields, factories, or at other tasks. Then, in the ample leisure afforded by rational social management, people would devote themselves to study, art, dance, sport, or other pursuits. An abundance of commodities would eliminate all inequity of distribution. Acute illness would be conquered by science, and chronic disease would vanish with a way of life that had "returned to nature." Advances in flight technology would make the world smaller, "like a single town," and through mixed marriages based on natural affection, "all humanity will gradually become a single race" (Ishiwara 1949, 128–30).

What had not changed in Ishiwara's thinking was the notion of a unique role for Japan:

> Our vows and efforts for *rishō ankoku* will surely be achieved in a few decades. The time when, throughout the world, all will embrace the Wonderful Dharma is approaching before our eyes. At this time, we who once tasted the wretchedness of defeat have gained the good fortune of receiving the supreme command to lead the world in establishing a nation without armaments. . . . Cleansing ourselves of the dross, both material and spiritual, of humanity's prior history, we shall create a new Japan as a literal treasure realm, an actualized Buddha land, setting a correct course for human civilization. This will not only

work to atone for the crimes against humanity committed in the
Pacific War; it is the one, sole way by which to live. (1949, 126)

The community of Ishiwara's followers remained marginal and did
not give rise to a large-scale peace movement. But his vision is significant
in that it demonstrates how quickly, and in what ways, wartime *Lotus*
millennialism was refigured as the peaceful *Lotus* millennialism of the
postwar world. It also illustrates how failure to achieve the millennial
goal in one way (i.e., through military conquest) led, not to the aban-
donment of the goal, but to revised notions of how it should be achieved.

A similar shift to a millennialism of world peace can be seen in the
Nichiren Buddhist monastic order Nihonzan (or Nipponzan) Myōhōji
Sangha founded in 1918 by Rev. Fujii Nichidatsu (1885–1985). During
the war, Fujii and his followers were committed nationalists who supported Japanese expansion on the continent (Tokoro 1966, 226–27).
After the war, however, appalled by the atomic devastation of Hiroshima
and Nagasaki, Fujii came to embrace a doctrine of absolute nonviolence
on the Gandhian model. Today, the monks and nuns of this order are
engaged peace activists, especially committed to the antinuclear weapons
movement. Their courage at demonstrations, even in the face of police
brutality, and their refusal to align themselves with any political camp
have made Nihonzan Myōhōji leaders respected arbiters within the Japanese peace movement (223–47; Kisara 1997, 51–83).

Fujii discovered a Buddhist model for absolute nonviolence in the
*Lotus Sutra* in the person of Bodhisattva Never Despising (Sanskrit,
Sadāparibhūta; Japanese, Jōfukyō), who "practiced only obeisance," bow-
ing in reverence to all he met for their innate Buddha-potential and
never yielding to anger, even when scorned or struck.[8] Fujii was harshly
critical of the modern state, which he identified primarily with Western
civilization, where economic considerations hold preeminence and the
authority of laws rests ultimately on force. Instead, he envisioned an ideal
future society united by "practicing only obeisance," free of all violence
and killing and based on mutual aid and respect stemming from reverence for the Buddha in everyone. Such a society in his view would
embody the "civilization of the East," whose essence he claimed was
embodied in the precept "not to kill others" and in the words *Namu-
myōhō-renge-kyō* taught by Nichiren (1980, 25–28).

8. A *bodhisattva* is one on the path to enlightenment who has vowed to strive for
the liberation of all beings.

Like Ishiwara, however, Fujii retained a belief in Japan's unique mission in realizing the millennial goal. In his view, the atomic bombings had in one sense demonstrated curses "returning to their originators," in the sutra's words (1965, 354). But in another sense, they represented a noble sacrifice offered by the Japanese people to demonstrate the tragedy of atomic weapons and thus prevent the extermination of humanity (1980, 119). Japan now had an obligation, not only to uphold the Peace Constitution but also to set an example of absolute nonviolence.

### "Managed Millennialism"

A millennial vision of "world peace" is also central to the two lay Buddhist organizations, Sōka Gakkai and Risshō Kōseikai, the largest of Japan's so-called New Religions and both based on the *Lotus Sutra* and the teachings of Nichiren. Risshō Kōseikai claims six million members; Sōka Gakkai, ten million. Founded before the war, both achieved their greatest growth in the postwar decades. Though the millennialism of these two organizations overlaps that of Japanese new religions in general (Blacker 1971), they may also be seen as participating in a distinctive tradition of *Lotus*-related millennialist thinking. In these associations, members' personal religious practice of reciting the sutra, chanting the *daimoku,* and proselytizing is complemented by organizational activities for peace. Both groups hold NGO (nongovernmental organization) status in the United Nations and have worked on behalf of refugees; Kōseikai has been active in famine relief, while Sōka Gakkai has launched a grassroots education movement on the sufferings engendered by war. Sōka Gakkai also founded a political party, the Komeitō, or Clean Government Party, to implement Buddhist ideals in politics (Métraux 1994, 39–69).

The two groups have different understandings of how the ideal society is to be achieved (Stone 1997). Sōka Gakkai maintains that only the spread of Nichiren's teachings can bring about world peace; in the light of Nichiren's *Risshō ankoku ron,* adherence to other, "false" religions is ultimately blamed for the tragedy of Japan's defeat in World War II. This conviction underlay the organization's aggressive missionizing in the postwar years. Risshō Kōseikai, for its part, takes an ecumenical approach; the *"Lotus Sutra"* is understood as the fundamental truth—God, Allah, or the one vehicle—at the heart of all great religions. Its cofounder and longtime president, Niwano Nikkyō (1906–), was active in promoting worldwide interfaith cooperation for peace. Central to both organizations, however, is a progressive millennialism, pursued, not through the transformation of existing social structures (as advocated in Ishiwara's postwar millennialism), nor through civil protest (as practiced by Nihonzan Myōhōji), but by personal religious cultivation and by working within the system for social improvement. Both groups hold that war and other social evils have their roots in the greed, anger, and delusion of individuals; therefore, it is individual efforts in self-cultivation and promoting harmony in everyday relations—rather than diplomatic or political efforts—that will fundamentally establish world peace. What is needed, in Sōka Gakkai parlance, is not social revolution but "human revolution," the positive transformation of character said to come about through Buddhist practice. If this approach tends to discourage social or political activism, on the personal level it empowers tremendously, infusing the individual's smallest acts with deep significance by connecting that person to a cause greater than himself or herself. The doctrines of both Risshō Kōseikai and Sōka Gakkai free their adherents from impotent frustration in the face of nuclear stockpiling and other global problems. One person *can* make a difference. To quote Ikeda Daisaku, president of Sōka Gakkai International:

> The individual human revolution will never stop with just that person. It represents a moment that surely encompasses all humanity. . . . As a single drop or water of speck of dust, each of you must win the trust of those around you, acting on the basis of our common humanity, and steadily advance the movement of a new awakening of life. Your own awakening will give rise to the next awakened person, who in turn will be followed by two, three, and ten in succession, becoming a great ocean of nirvana and a great mountain of wondrous enlightenment, just as the Great Saint [Nichiren] teaches. (1977, 170–71)

For the members of these groups, the humblest actions and interactions of daily life, performed conscientiously and with a sense of their greater purpose, all become *bodhisattva* practice and karmic causes linked directly to the realization of world peace. What governments and diplomacy have failed to accomplish, ordinary believers are in fact achieving. It is here, in the heightened sense of personal meaning, the conviction that one has a "mission" to fulfill, that the millennial visions of these movements exert their appeal.

Neither Sōka Gakkai nor Risshō Kōseikai has set specific timetables for the realization of world peace but maintain this goal on a horizon that recedes in pace with organizational advance. After the initial fervor of postwar expansion, they have settled down into what might be termed a "managed millennialism": world peace, it is suggested, can be realized soon enough that individual members' efforts will make a difference; this enables the mustering of collective energy to support organizational programs. At the same time, however, the goal is not arriving so soon as to disrupt the fabric of daily life or social responsibilities. In these groups, we find a millennialism that in general works to endorse rather than threaten the status quo, and is fully consonant with broader aspirations for peace and social stability.

Risshō Kōseikai and Sōka Gakkai, too, preserve the idea of Japan's unique mission in realizing the *risshō ankoku* ideal. On the one hand, this is seen as an act of atonement for wartime hostilities against other Asian countries. On the other hand, Japan is said to be uniquely qualified to lead the way to world peace, being the only nation to know firsthand the full horror of atomic warfare and to have a constitution explicitly renouncing war. This theme of Japan's unique role represents a complex element in postwar Nichiren Buddhist millennialism. It may be seen as a refiguring, in a manner consistent with the postwar rejection of violence, of the conviction of Japan's sacred destiny that underlay much earlier imperialist ideology. It may additionally be read as an attempt to come to terms with guilt over Japanese wartime atrocities; as a revisionary coopting of the humiliation of defeat and an externally imposed constitution; and as expressing an ongoing concern about Japan's place in the international community. It also occurs in a number of modern Japanese religious movements unrelated to Nichiren Buddhism and is linked to an ethnocentric element common to much Japanese peace theory (Kisara 1997, 25, 41). Outside Japan, however, it is not emphasized among non-Japanese converts to Sōka Gakkai or Risshō Kōseikai, suggesting that this part of the millennial vision, too, is susceptible to revision.

## Conclusion

Nichiren Buddhist millennialist thinking of the modern period, in both its imperial and postwar incarnations, shares a common structure drawing on elements in Nichiren's teaching, especially the power of faith in the *Lotus Sutra* to bring about an ideal world, and the importance of Japan as the place from which the Buddhism of the Final Dharma age shall spread. However, under different historical circumstances, these elements have been interpreted in radically different ways. The first phase of *Lotus* millennialism initially arose in response to an urgently felt need to "catch up" with the industrialized West and resist the threat of Western domination; later it came to reflect (and to legitimate) the militant imperialism of the times. Its second phase represented a response to the threat of global atomic warfare—a threat at first bound up with the horror, ruin, and dislocation experienced in World War II, and more recently seen also as symbolic of alienation, loss of meaning, and other problems associated with modernity. In his essay in this volume, Ian Reader discusses how the initially progressive, rather optimistic millennialism of Aum Shinrikyō turned catastrophic as the group consistently failed to achieve its projected growth. Postwar *Lotus* millennialism may be seen as an opposite case, in which a failure, brought about by Japan's defeat, to realize a millennial vision through military conquest led to a refiguring of that vision in pacifistic terms. The rapid transformation of *Lotus* millennialism from an ideology of empire to the driving force of a peace movement strongly suggests that violent millennialist energies are not necessarily integral to the millennial vision itself, but, under different circumstances, can be redirected in peaceful and constructive ways.

What also strikes one in considering modern Lotus millennialism is how close it lies to mainstream aspirations. Perhaps a romantic advocate of direct imperial rule, such as Kita Ikki, whose ideas were appropriated in the service of a military insurrection, cannot be considered a mainstream figure; nor perhaps can the followers of Nihonzan Myōhōji, who advocate passive resistance and reject nonviolence even in self-defense. But their millennial visions were at the moment of their emergence not so very remote from the hopes of large segments of the population, being intimately connected to widespread desires, respectively, for a strong Japanese empire in the 1930s and for abolition of the atomic threat in the immediate postwar period. This is all the more true in the case of the large Nichiren Buddhist lay movements, such as the Kokuchūkai, Risshō Kōseikai, and Sōka Gakkai. Tanaka gave voice to the patriotic sentiments of many and elevated them to a holy status in his rhetoric of Nichirenshugi; the support his movement won from government bureaucrats and military leaders shows that his vision was useful to official agendas. In the postwar period, Risshō Kōseikai and Sōka Gakkai articulate a widespread revulsion against war and fears about the continuing nuclear threat, offering a path by which the common citizen can contribute to their eradication. Such examples suggest that millennial thinking is by no means limited to the marginal or disenfranchised, but can serve to legitimize the actions of armies and politicians, and also give expression—albeit in intensified form—to aspirations shared by a majority.

# 13

# Time, Authority, and Ethics in the Khmer Rouge

## Elements of the Millennial Vision in Year Zero

RICHARD C. SALTER _____

In 1975 the Communist Party of Kampuchea, labeled by Prince Norodom Sihanouk the "Khmer Rouge,"[1] defeated the American-backed Khmer Republic forces of Lon Nol, renamed Cambodia Democratic Kampuchea, and instituted a program of total social transformation. Ideologically, the Khmer Rouge was guided by a combination of Marxism, ultra-Maoist notions of cultural revolution and autarchy, and various other social theories from Fanonism to Stalinism (Quinn 1989; Jackson 1989). Much of the ideological underpinning of the revolution was brought from the West, especially France, where many of the Khmer Rouge leaders had studied; at the same time, the leaders of the revolution thought the Cambodian situation was unique, and that communism could be achieved there in a single moment without any transition stages.

The Khmer Rouge leadership, referred to primarily as the Angkar (the "organization," or, more loosely, the party elite), carried out its revolution largely through peasant cadres, and attempted a complete leveling and reorganization of society through forced evacuations of cities and forced labor. It sought to wipe out all traces of foreign influence (especially Western and Vietnamese), all foreign dependency, all class distinctions, and all possible resistance to the Khmer Rouge regime. The notorious result was the "killing fields" in which about 1.5 million people

---

1. The Khmer are the largest ethnic and linguistic group in Cambodia.

died through starvation and, to a lesser degree, political purges and executions. In 1979 the reign of the Khmer Rouge ended when the Vietnamese army invaded and installed a puppet regime.

How could such a militant and violent Marxism take hold in a nation with an extremely strong state-supported Theravada Buddhist tradition? How could Cambodians, whom the French reported as being a complacent and peaceful people, have become so violent?

In fact, the historical record shows Cambodia to have been less peaceful than the French reported. Among other things, there was a tradition of revolution in Cambodia, and it was directly connected to Khmer Buddhist cosmology and notions of kingship. This tradition re-appeared in an analogous form in the Khmer Rouge revolution.

Democratic Kampuchea was officially an atheist state, and the persecution of religion by the Khmer Rouge was matched in severity only by the persecution of religion in the communist states of Albania and North Korea, so there were not any direct historical continuities of Buddhism into the Democratic Kampuchea era. But Khmer Buddhist influences did persist and are recognizable in the Khmer Rouge worldview, particularly in notions of time, authority, and normative ethics. It makes sense that revolutions in Cambodia would share similar structures, for it is hard to imagine a revolution or ideology as comprehensive as that of the Khmer Rouge gaining support in Cambodia without any connection to a traditional base.[2] Stanley Tambiah (1970) has argued that "for the common people at large [religious] texts and knowledge have a referential and legitimating function, even if they themselves have no direct access to them" (4). Thus, even when religion has been "eradicated," it still exerts an influence on culture, legitimating practices, structuring perceptions, and providing a framework for understanding the cosmos.

These influences persist in several ways. Frank Smith (1989) wrote about Cambodian refugees using traditional Cambodian beliefs to make sense of the Khmer Rouge years. His monograph largely focused on refugees' retroactive use of traditional beliefs to make sense of a Cambodian theodicy: how could such horror occur to us? Ponchaud (1989, 152) addressed the relationship of traditional beliefs to the rise of the Khmer Rouge. He suggested that "some (but not all) Buddhist beliefs facilitated the rise and dominance of the Khmer Rouge." His focus was on parallels in what is valued in Buddhism, such as the extinction of the

---

2. Regarding differences of opinion on the consistency of Khmer Rouge ideology, see Barnett 1983; Vickery 1983; and Kiernan 1983.

self, and what was valued by the Khmer Rouge, such as complete submission of the self to the collectivity. In contrast, in this chapter I will focus on the structural affinities of the Khmer Buddhist and Khmer Rouge worldviews and how those structural affinities facilitated the emergence of the Khmer Rouge. By "structural affinities" I mean there existed a complementary relationship underlying the way the two movements conceived of time, authority, and normative behavior, and that these underlying notions legitimated and shaped the direction of social change in Cambodia.

In presenting his analysis of the relationship of the Khmer Rouge to Buddhism, Ponchaud (1989, 172) reminded us not to "overemphasize these connections between Khmer Marxism and Buddhism any more than the connection between fascism and Christianity or communism and Christianity in the European context." This warning notwithstanding, to make my thesis clear, I state it here in strong form: Though the Khmer Rouge officially was nonreligious, its worldview, especially its notions of time, authority, and its normative ethics can be understood as structural parallels to the Buddhist worldview. Thus, for some segments of the population, Khmer Rouge ideology and practices supplanted Buddhism and functioned in the same structural capacity. In effect, this made the Khmer Rouge a secular Marxist ideology grafted onto Khmer Buddhist roots. These roots helped shape the specific direction of Khmer Marxism (especially its emphases on starting over and purity); it made Khmer Rouge ideology understandable to the cadres; and it legitimated the Khmer Rouge attempt to totally remake society.

Sociologically, the confluence of Marxist and Buddhist worldviews was possible because the Khmer Rouge combined an intellectual class educated in France with peasants, whom French colonization, inattentive leaders, and American bombing had marginalized. When the French left Cambodia, the elites were excluded from politics and persecuted, and following a pragmatic and ancient pattern of Khmer kingship, they fled to the forest. Though their beliefs were Marxist, their practices in fomenting revolution and the structure of the change they advocated were analogous to the traditional Righteous Ruler returning from a purification in the forest to eliminate corruption and re-create the Khmer kingdom. Like the previous triumphant kings, the Khmer Rouge elites gained support from the marginalized rural population, whose worldview was substantially like theirs. Ultimately, then, the emergence of the Khmer Rouge was related to both the demise under French colonization of the traditional relationship of Buddhism and the Cambodian state, and to the affinities of Khmer Rouge and Buddhist worldviews, which helped shape and legitimize the Khmer Rouge.

## Worldviews: Affinities of Khmer Marxism and Khmer Buddhism

Worldview, according to Clifford Geertz (1973, 127), is a peoples' "picture of the way things in sheer actuality are, their concept of nature, of self, of society. It contains their most comprehensive ideas of order." I will focus my discussion on three aspects of worldview that were particularly important to the Khmer Rouge: conceptions of time (which underlie all understandings of change), construals of authority (which legitimate change), and normative ethics (which are among the important things guiding change).

### Time

What was the relationship of the Khmer Buddhists' and the Khmer Rouge's conceptions of time? They seem to stand in opposition, for Marxists view time linearly while Buddhists view time cyclically. The Khmer Rouge possessed a linear concept of time in the belief it could construct society and could progress to a final utopia (i.e., its "super great leap forward"), but its forcing evacuation of cities, returning to mainly manual agricultural production, and its extraordinary focus on national self-sufficiency suggested also a cyclical notion of time that allowed nations to begin anew. In essence, the Khmer Rouge presented an optimistic progressive millennialism rooted in the belief that Cambodians could build their collective future, but rooted in a cyclical notion of time. This may not be our typical understanding of millennialism, but as Catherine Wessinger (1997a) has pointed out, millennialism does not require a "linear view of time." "The average person is concerned with achieving well-being in the here and now, so whether there is a linear or cyclical conception of time is beside the point" (55). The Khmer Rouge notion of time was an amalgam of Buddhist cyclical conceptions of time and Marxist/Christian linear concepts of time; it was a millennialism that sought a one-time return to a new starting point from which a golden age could be constructed.

A conceptualization of time was crucial to Khmer Rouge ideology as it must be for all Marxist ideologies. As an interpretation of history that focuses on the dialectical clash and synthesis of classes, and the progression of history, Marxism stresses a linear vision of time; history marches from primitive communism through the social conflicts inherent in each successive stage of material production. In the end, class conflicts resolve themselves through revolution into an advanced communism in which private property is abolished, the proletariat triumphs, and the coercive power of the state is no longer necessary.

At least since Karl Lowith wrote *Meaning in History* (1949), some scholars have asserted that the Marxist worldview is in essence a secularized Christian millennialism; society moves from a blissful prehistory (Eden or primitive communism) through corruption (the Fall or the division of labor and the fragmentation of society into classes based on production) and with the help of a metaphysical or quasi-metaphysical agent (God/Christ or the laws of dialectical materialism), humanity is redeemed from corruption (salvation or pure communism). Implied in this is the linear concept of history so typically associated with Christianity, progressing from a onetime starting point to a onetime end (see especially Marx and Engels 1978).

In practice, communist parties have needed to lend history a helping hand, suppressing bourgeois reactionaries, using the power of the state to maintain a dictatorship by the proletariat, and building socialism according to plans and in stages. These practical concerns are consistent with the Marxist worldview, for to the Marxist, even though the human is self-focused, producing one's world with one's own hands, and building one's own future, the individual does so only in relation to the surrounding material forces of production. Thus, according to the Marxist materialist's view of history, history proceeds in stages corresponding to production.

This notion of time is also recognizable in the ideology of the Khmer Rouge. But there were distinctive elements of Khmer Rouge ideology and practice that seem inconsistent with Marxist philosophy. First, the Khmer Rouge did not recognize the need for stages in the revolution; instead, it would be a onetime total revolution. This led to practices that would be unusual based upon a typical understanding of Marxism, such as evacuation of cities, forced agricultural labor imposed on urban dwellers, and extreme focus on self-sufficiency. Marxism generally associates revolution with industrial classes and these typically reside in cities. Moreover, industrial production, not agricultural production, makes possible the rise of the proletariat and movement to the classless society. Marxism views communism as the culmination of a succession of stages of production, not as a return to an earlier form of production.

How is this Marxist vision related to the Khmer Rouge communist vision, which Ponchaud and others have described as a return to "Year Zero" in an effort to entirely remake society? How could one version of social change be so decidedly linear, while the other implied this sense of "starting over?" Where did this sense of starting over come from?

An answer is found by comparing the Khmer Rouge view of time to an underlying Khmer view of time. To Khmer Buddhists, history was not linear, but cyclical. Smith (1989, 18–25) noted how this view of history helped peasant refugees of the Khmer Rouge regime make sense of what happened in Democratic Kampuchea as part of a cosmic cycle in which the Khmer Rouge period was a "dark period" predicted in *put tumniay* (Buddhist predictions). We can imagine that for those who supported the Khmer Rouge, the promised revolution was the beginning of a golden era following in cyclical fashion on the weakness and shame of the colonial period. Chandler (1983, 44) cited a parallel between the reign of Jayavarman VII (r. 1178–1220) and the Democratic Kampuchean regime, because, among other things, "In both regimes history was thought to have ended and begun afresh after a ruinous war."[3] The Khmer Rouge focus on expelling foreign influence might also be taken as evidence for such a belief, for it was not just vengance that provoked such attacks but the belief in the reemergence of something authentically Khmer and pure.[4] This too implied a sense of starting over.[5]

Destroying corruption corresponds to building up something good and pure. This cyclical view of change is confirmed in the Khmer Rouge use of the word *kasang* (to build). Marston (1994, 115) describes how it was used not only in the sense of construct but also in the sense of

3. To take the connection to Jayavarman VII a step further, I would note that the ideology motivating him (Mahayana Buddhism) and that motivating the Khmer Rouge connect at more than a few points. The idea that nirvana (release) is found in samsara (the realm of rebirth and suffering) when one is imbued with the spirit of concern for others is strikingly like the Khmer Rouge idea that release is found through labor through which the individual is best able to assimilate into the collectivity. The collectivity is supreme for the Khmer Rouge, and the individual disappears. Mahayana Buddhism similarly stresses the collectivity by emphasizing interconnectedness and the immanence of the Buddha nature.

4. For instance, one of the immediate actions of the Khmer Rouge in Phnom Penh was to destroy the Catholic Cathedral. Interestingly, it was disassembled stone by stone so that no trace of it was left. The object was to utterly remove foreign influence. See Kiernan 1988a, 4; Hawk 1989, 213.

5. Reynolds 1985, 204–5 includes these episodic re-creations in his definition of Buddhist cosmogonies. Using his definition of Buddhist cosmogony, the Khmer Rouge Revolution could be considered a cosmogonic event.

tearing down, criticizing, or destroying.[6] The conflation of the meanings "to destroy" and "to build" can be understood as referring to a cyclical pattern in which rebirth always follows death, such as was the case with Cambodian cities. In most Khmer Rouge literature, Phnom Penh was referred to as "corrupt," and reeducation was seen as an effort to cleanse individuals of bourgeois and Western influences (a renewal). The implication was that people had become corrupt, but with the right practice, they could return to a more pure state. The Khmer Rouge reverence for the extinct Kingdom of Angkor as a model for future glory suggested the same relationship of past and future.[7]

In the end, though the cyclical concept of time motivated Khmer Rouge practices, it was not the only understanding of time, for Khmer Rouge ideology was still indelibly stamped with Marxism. The revolution of 1975 was conceived as the final revolution, ushering in a golden age of communism that would not end.

### Authority

*Traditional Buddhism-State Relations.* The traditional Buddhism-state relationship in Cambodia sheds light on how cyclical views of time could be reconciled with an ostensibly Marxist Khmer Rouge worldview. Traditionally, purity, powers of creation and renewal, and insight were crucial elements in legitimating a Cambodian ruler's authority. Central to the notion of authority in pre-Democratic Kampuchea was the role of the king as maker and maintainer of the world, a "god-king," or *devaraja*, who was also a righteous ruler, or *dhammaraja*. The practical circumstances facing the Khmer Rouge leaders had placed them in the forest, occupying a position like that occupied by challengers to the throne in

6. In this sense it has some of the meaning of the English "reconstruct." It is interesting to note how common the conflation of destruction and creation are in revolutionary movements. One thinks of Bakunin's famous dictum, "Destruction is creative," or Frantz Fanon's (1963, 94) more modern counsel, "At the level of individuals, violence is a cleansing force. It frees the native from his inferiority complex and from his despair and inaction; it makes him fearless and restores his self-respect."

7. For details on Angkor's part in the self-conceptions of the Khmer Rouge, see Marston 1994, 108–9. Marston stated, "The idea that a symbol associated with the Angkor empire would be invoked during Democratic Kampuchea is consistent with the fact that, during that period, pictures of Angkor Wat were displayed in public places, and songs drew parallels between the glories of the new regime and those of Angkor." He also suggested that the effort to "build up the irrigation system was related to a conception that irrigation was the basis of the glories of Angkor." For a slightly different view see Chandler 1983.

Cambodian history. Not only did they occupy a similar structural posi-tion as those challengers but their authority flowed from similar sources. They too emphasized purity, powers of creation and renewal, and in-sight, and increasingly the role of the Angkar paralleled that of the *devaraja* and *dhammaraja*.[8]

The relationship of Buddhism and the state in Cambodia was never as passive as the French reported. Theoretically, Buddhism and the state were supposed to be separate. Yang Sam (1987) described the relation-ship with a metaphor of the two wheels of a chariot:

> [I]n the Buddhist view, the nation was represented by a chariot of two wheels: one representing the Buddhist world and the other the State. Both wheels must turn harmoniously in order for the chariot to advance smoothly. . . . Buddhism was to limit its scope to moral and spiritual issues and leave politics to the State. This separation of the State and Buddhism was clearly defined theoretically, but in actuality both institutions assisted each other all along. (40)

In reality, the king derived much of his power from the Buddhist tradition. When Theravada Buddhism became the dominant religion of Cambodia in the thirteenth century, a kingship tradition emerged that was like that which emerged in other Theravada nations; there was a complementary differentiation of the community of monks *(sangha)* from the king, with authority following from an interpretation of the Buddhist text, *Aggana Sutta*.

Like other kings in Southeast Asia, the Cambodian king was re-sponsible for the perpetuation of the kingdom through ritual performed in the capital. He was a "world maintainer," who regularly stabilized a precarious world through both ritual action and merit gained by exem-plary behavior. The virtuosity of the ruler in perpetuating the *dhamma* (Buddhist path or doctrine) was required for the prosperity of the king-dom, so the virtue of the ruler was linked directly to the success or failure of the country, and his success in perpetuating the kingdom.

This corresponded to the Cambodian attitude to religious virtuos-ity in general. In normal times, the king's virtuosity had the power to

---

8. It is interesting to note here the parallel position of the Angkar to divine heroes in Cambodian Buddhism. Cambodians read the (Hindu) *Ramayana* as a Buddhist text, and in the *Ramayana*, the prince Rama spends a time of purification in the forest before coming forth to fight a transformative war and take his rightful role as king. Thanks to Joseph Walser for offering this insight.

bring prosperity to the kingdom. When the king was unable to perform his ritual function, or when his virtuosity declined, his power grew correspondingly weaker. Challenges to the king, either by other princes or by pretenders, arose when the ruler no longer possessed the authority to maintain order and prosperity in the kingdom. When this occurred the king was challenged, and if defeated was replaced by another king who could renew the world. Religious virtuosity was therefore a necessary ingredient of authority.

When the king was unable to rule in his proper function, opposition often arose in the countryside where challengers lived in the forest, moving from village to village gaining support and demonstrating virtuosity. Traditionally, this relationship between religion and the state functioned as an integrating mechanism of forest and capital keeping the two in balance. Because of the strength of caste/status distinctions in Cambodia and the persistence of Hindu and animist traditions in the countryside, the distinction between forest and city was even more dynamic than in other places. Successful resolution of the tensions between the two regions was the key to Cambodian political stability.

In the Khmer worldview, the capital represented the kingdom; it was the *axis mundi,* or center of the world, and in the capital the king performed the rituals necessary to sustain the country. But the capital was worldly, profane, and reflected worldly pleasure, so despite the king's presence there, if he did not maintain his virtue, the capital would disintegrate. In contrast, the forest was austere, and was a place for gaining virtue through renunciation, adherence to the *vinaya* (Buddhist code of ethics), and the acquisition of insight. The Buddha spent time in purification and renunciation in the forest; therefore, when kings spent time in the forest, or when challenges to the throne came from the forest, kings and challengers were symbolically linked to the Buddha. Time spent in the forest also linked kings and challengers with Cambodia's tradition of holy men, or *achars,* who often spent time in the forest. Revolts coming from the periphery used the authority associated with the forest to call for the regeneration of the corrupt capital. Thus, the primary symbol for revolutionary change in Cambodia was the vanquished king or prince who fled into the forest, gained virtue and insight through his time spent there, and returned triumphant as the righteous ruler *(dhammaraja)* to re-create the kingdom.

Although the image of the righteous ruler existed throughout Southeast Asia, the tradition was particularly strong in Cambodia, where the absence of a consistent capital before French rule meant that the triumphant king reconstituted the kingdom through the establishment of a new capital upon his return. The role of world maintainer was thus also at first a role of world creator, a role that would be reassumed with each new king. Each new king may have subtly altered his relationship with the gods, perhaps by showing direct matrilineal descent from the gods and claiming to be a god, or by claiming to be the connection to the gods, but regardless of the specifics of the relationship, he retained the power of creator, maintainer, defender of Cambodian tradition, and connection to the heavens as *devaraja*.[9]

During the past two hundred years, the political situation in Cambodia was never entirely stable. Violence was a part of Khmer politics at the start of the modern period with King Ang Chan (1806–34). The chief problem for Ang Chan was the two neighbors of Cambodia, Siam and Vietnam, who both wanted to expand. This remained a problem for Cambodian royalty until 1860, when Prince Norodom "requested" French assistance in staying the Vietnamese and the Thais. Then the problem for kings shifted to one of maintaining status as *devaraja* and *dhammaraja* in the face of French colonization.

To those in the countryside, the appeal to the French represented a decrease of the king's power and challengers initiated a series of rebellions against the capital. As French influence grew, the status of the king continued to decline. The French had no taste or patience for the Buddhist cosmology, which legitimated the king, and therefore they had no desire to maintain the status of the king as world preserver or to retain the king's capital as *axis mundi*. However, they did recognize the stabilizing function of the king. Therefore, desiring to modernize Cambodia, the French began to use the Buddhism-state relationship to usurp power from the king. By giving military aid to Prince Norodom in exchange for gradually increasing French rights of governance and administration, the French simultaneously supported the king, but undermined his authority in the eyes of the populace. Further revolts from the countryside ensued, the king appealed to the French, and the cycle continued.

As the French gained a more active influence in the affairs of the Cambodian government, the structure for forest/capital integration (and

9. See Kulke 1978. Another distinguishing aspect of the Cambodian *devaraja* tradition was the connection between authority and maternal lineage, a dual legacy of Cambodia's Hindu tradition and pre-Hindu traditions. See Chakravarti 1982.

renewal) was dismantled, and the authority of the king became more and more precarious. Many rural Cambodians grew dissatisfied with an ineffectual king.

The French set themselves up in opposition against the superstition and tradition of the Buddhist revolutions. They believed in progress, not cycles. Revolts from the countryside arose, but they did not succeed, in part because the French put them down, so power did not transfer symbolically from the forest to the capital, but from the forest to the French. When the French left Cambodia there was a power vacuum, for the kingship was perceived as weak, especially in the outlying regions, and did not have the legitimacy to rule. The door was left open for a revolution from the forest imbued with the merit of renunciation and purity that life in the forest brought.

*Authority in the Khmer Rouge.* The similarities of the Khmer Rouge revolution and the earlier forest-based revolutions are consistent with the general structure of rebellion in Cambodia. Perhaps the most striking similarities are the emergence of the Khmer Rouge from the forest, the power, titles, and successes it attributed to itself, and its self-perception as world creator.

The Khmer Rouge was primarily made up of two classes of people. On the one hand, the party was led by Cambodian intellectuals, mainly educated in French schools and sharing an elite status in a nation that was deeply status conscious. The Khmer Rouge cadres were rural, forest-based peasants, particularly the Khmer Rouge cadres following Pol Pot, who came primarily from the southwest district and exhibited both the most extreme ideological fervor and discipline (Vickery 1983, 112–15). The leaders of the movement might be seen as structurally like the leaders of past revolutions—urban elites who were vanquished to the periphery when they became a threat. The cadres also had a position like those participating in revolutions in the past; they were drawn from areas that were displaced and marginalized and had been ignored by the capital. They were also the groups who had suffered most under King Sihanouk and the Lon Nol regimes, and the ones who suffered the worst effects of American carpet bombing. They had good reason to view the government as weak and uncaring. In fact, the government was weak in respect to American and French influence, and it ignored the countryside. The city elites (at least those who remained in the city) were seen as corrupt, a condemnation that appeared again and again in Khmer Rouge propaganda. The forest, on the other hand, was valorized, consistent with the village/forest dialectic of traditional revolutions in Cambodia.[10]

The role of *devaraja* was filled by the Angkar which increasingly came to be seen as omnipotent, omniscient, and omnipresent, though also connected to the people. For example, Khmer Rouge speeches referred to the omnipotence of the Angkar. What I want to point out is the structural parallel of the Angkar and the *devaraja*. Regardless of its root cause, Khmer Rouge omnipotence was an omnipotence no less than the *devaraja*'s, striving "to make the people 'masters of the earth and of water,' 'masters of the rice fields and plains of the forests and all vegetation,' 'masters of the yearly floods,'" by way of their agricultural projects (Ponchaud 1989, 167). John Marston (1994, 108) related a quote from May Someth: "We were masters of our work. There was no more exploitation. We could do whatever we wanted. The canals were the veins of the *Angkar*. We were no longer reliant on rain. We could produce as much rice as we wanted." Again, this omnipotence corresponded to the role of the world-creator remaking the world, and world-maintainer beyond the vicissitudes of weather. As masters of the earth, Angkar assumed the structural role of the *devaraja*.[11] It was no wonder that so much propaganda was devoted to declaring the success of the regime, the growth of yields, and the absolute self-sufficiency of the country. These were the same sort of factors that demonstrated the success of the Cambodian kings.

The Angkar also assumed a role like the *devaraja* in respect to its subjects. Ponchaud (1989, 164) noted that the relationship of king to subjects was patriarchal, with king as lord-father *(samay pouk-me)* and subjects as children-grandchildren *(kaun-chau)*. Interestingly, this usage reappeared with the Khmer Rouge. Thus, the status of king as lord-father was taken over by the Angkar: "Nor is it all that surprising that *Angkar,* or more precisely all adults, came to be addressed as the 'dad-mom' *(pouk-me)* of the people, even if such an expression had not been used in such paired form in the past." The Angkar is also widely reported

10. Simply living in the country did not give religious status. In fact, rural peasants were looked down upon by many middle-level peasants. See Smith 1989, 30. But the Khmer Rouge valued its period in the forest for many of the same reasons forest time was valued in Buddhism: it was a period of renunciation, to gather strength, to purify oneself.

11. Angkar was usually referred to as a group of people. In at least one place, it was thought to refer to Pol Pot himself, who was leader of the Khmer Rouge during the Democratic Kampuchea years. This made the parallel to the *devaraja* even closer. See Kiernan 1988b, notes 109 and 112, 340–41.

to have arranged and organized marriages as a parent would. Finally, as had traditionally been the case with the king, who like a father had a personal relationship with his subjects, in Democratic Kampuchea it was also possible for one to address questions, or to petition the Angkar directly, though it is hard to imagine anyone daring to do so.[12]

Further, Angkar was omniscient; not only did its philosophy unerringly reveal history, but it also could see in all directions including into the hearts and minds of the Cambodian people. As a metaphor described, "*Angkar* has the eyes of a pineapple," that is, it had eyes that pointed in all directions (Marston 1994, 107). Reports of the self-criticism sessions, the *kasang* sessions, emphasized how one could be betrayed by one's own words and actions. Angkar had a better awareness of one's political beliefs than one did oneself. This facilitated purges, allowed Angkar to attribute motives (and torture people until they confessed), and made it easier for Angkar to rewrite history.

Like political challengers in Cambodia before it, the Khmer Rouge derived its authority from two sources. On the one hand, it was a forest-based group, having gained insight and purity from its life of renunciation and virtuosity (thus, it assumed the place of *dhammaraja*). On the other hand, the Khmer Rouge leadership assumed the place of the *devaraja*, and it derived its authority from its power, insight, and successes (real or propaganda) in assuring the material well-being and purity of the Khmer nation.

*Ethics*

There were also similarities in the normative ethics of Khmer Buddhists *(Viney)* and the Khmer Rouge *(Angkarviney)*,[13] and this too connected the Khmer Rouge to Buddhism and legitimized the movement in the eyes of some of the peasantry (Ponchaud 1989, 173). By normative ethics I mean the types of behaviors considered good or bad rather than a more abstract ethical concept of what "the Good" is. Regarding the latter, there were clear differences between the groups.

At the same time, though their notions of "the Good" differed, some of the actual behaviors advocated by each were surprisingly similar.

12. See Kiernan 1988b, note 112, 341.

13. In saying that the Khmer Rouge had a notion of ethics, I do not mean to imply that their actions were moral by our standards. The consequence clearly show they were not.

Ponchaud (174) noted affinities between the wandering Buddhist beggar and the Khmer Rouge work brigade, both having renounced all possessions, family, etc., to extinguish the self. Like Buddhist monks in Cambodia, all Khmer Rouge cadres dressed the same. As Buddhist monks were not to touch money, so the Khmer Rouge was proud to have taken the most radical step of all socialist regimes—the elimination of all money. Ponchaud also noted the parallels between Buddhist concepts of renunciation and Khmer Rouge concepts of renunciation, including the renunciation of family, self, forsaking of pride, extinction of sexual desire, and extinction of appetite. One of the most famous of the Khmer Rouge precepts was that of no sex outside of marriage, a crime reported to have been punishable by death. Overeating and pride were similarly condemned. Picq (1989, 102) recounted admonitions to extinguish the individual and remove all pride. Only then was the true liberation promised by the revolution possible. For Cambodian Buddhists, these practices led one away from the illusion of individuality. They did the same for the Khmer Rouge, but with the additional function of building the community.[14]

Several parts of the Buddhist Eightfold Path have parallels in Khmer Rouge ethics. The fourth Noble Truth of Buddhism states that the Eightfold Path is the way by which one can escape suffering. The Eightfold Path includes: (1) Right Knowledge; (2) Right Intention; (3) Right Speech; (4) Right Conduct; (5) Right Means of Livelihood; (6) Right Effort; (7) Right Mindfulness; and (8) Right Concentration. The focus here is on one's mental state, especially introspectiveness and discipline. This would seem unrelated to a materialist concept of correct behavior. But if we consider Khmer Rouge ethics a secularized parallel to Buddhist ethics functioning to legitimate similar behaviors, the relationship between the two sets of normative ethical behaviors becomes clear.

At the risk of presenting a laundry list of parallels, let me mention some affinities between behaviors advocated by the Eightfold Path and those emphasized by the Khmer Rouge.[15] Right Knowledge for the Buddhist is knowledge of the Four Noble Truths, an idealist way of

14. The confluence of ethical behavior and creating a new world is significant for Buddhism. See Reynolds 1978, 1985 on the relationship of various ethics and cosmogonies in Theravada Buddhism.

15. Another way to compare Buddhist and Khmer Route virtues is to compare the vices they are meant to combat. Reynolds (1985, 208) lists ignorance, craving, and grasping as the central vices important in structuring phenomenal reality according to Buddhism. Insofar as these can be compared to "false consciousness" and bourgeois and Western desires and notions of the self, they are strikingly like Khmer Rouge vices.

understanding the world. For the Khmer Rouge, there was a similar focus on right knowledge, but it was knowledge of dialectical materialism, also a way of understanding the world. Right Intention has its analogue in the Khmer Rouge in dedication to the goal of building a communist society. Right Speech in the Buddhist context has the connotation of not telling lies and conserving speech. The Khmer Rouge also focused on speech, eliminating status connotations from the Khmer language, requiring everyone to address one another by a family name. The way one spoke influenced who one was, so all speech had to be considered carefully. Right conduct for both meant not indulging the senses, including overeating, oversleeping, or illicit sex. Right Livelihood for Buddhists means pursuing a livelihood that does not harm others. The Khmer Rouge analogue was a positive injunction to work to build communism, remake the self, and remove bourgeois influences that hurt others. Right effort for the Khmer Rouge could be construed as support for Angkar and the revolution. Right Mindfulness for Buddhists means undertaking actions for the right reasons and in the right way. For the Khmer Rouge, there was a similar emphasis on consciousness of intentions. As Picq (1989, 107) described: "Thoughts had as much value as actions. To be on the right track, one had to imbue oneself with the ideas of the party in such a way that the mind was perpetually mobilized to the party's service, without hesitation and without wasting time, like a machine." Right Concentration for the Buddhist implies both losing one's self in what one is doing and being fully present, without distraction, in the moment. The Khmer Rouge asked for the same; one had to totally immerse oneself in work, ignoring its effects on the self, to build communism.

These parallels in the normative ethics of the Khmer Rouge and Buddhists *may* have made the Khmer Rouge acceptable to peasants. At times the connection to Buddhism was made explicit. Vickery (1984, 180) reported that some Khmer Rouge officials presented their ideology as another religion *(sasana)*, like Buddhism, but with the additional insight of class analysis. "For some lower-level cadres, and it seems in particular for those who had once followed a religious vocation as monks or *achars,* the rejection of Buddhism did not represent a change to non-religion . . . but a flight from an inferior one to a superior one." Again quoting Vickery (1984, 181), "Within his cooperative C. H. said that one of his cadres, a former *achar,* also explained Communism as a new *sasana* superior to the old. In that cadre's view Buddhism was particularly bad because it encouraged 'feudalism' and class distinctions."

Yang Sam (1987) reported that the Khmer Rouge consciously played out its similarity and superiority to Buddhist ethics. He reported a speech given by a Khmer Rouge cadre which reflected this effort:

> To his view the conduct of the Communist Party's members was far more perfect than the practices of monks. As a comparison, each Khmer Rouge Cadre observed more than ten *sila* in the Buddhist teachings. He/she persevered in improving his/her personality by loving and respecting people, being honest, protecting people's interest, confessing his/her misdeeds, using modest and polite words, and avoiding adultery and polygamy, avoiding drinking, avoiding gambling, and avoiding thievery. To the positive, they emphasized being servile and self-sacrificing, being constructively critical, being self-reliant, being always alert and conscious, being master of one's work and respecting collectivism. . . . Furthermore, a revolutionary member worked hard and contributed to the progress of the people and the nation, while monks' lives depended on the people's sweat. (70)

Thus, whatever their reasons for advocating such standards, the normative ethics of the Khmer Rouge coopted virtue through the meritorious conduct of the cadres.[16] Though they disavowed religion, they followed many of the same patterns of historical Khmer ethics, and their adherence to these previous patterns lent the movement legitimacy.

## Conclusion: Structural Continuities, Violence, and the Need for Historically Rooted Meaning

It would be irresponsible and incorrect to suggest that Buddhism was in any way responsible for the "killing fields" of Cambodia. But the underlying worldviews of Khmer Buddhism and Khmer Rouge Marxism are similar in their conceptions of time, authority, and normative ethics. In understanding these similarities, and the structural roles these concepts played in the different regimes, we are better able to understand how the Democratic Kampuchea years could have happened.

---

16. This is not to deny any of the atrocities attributed to cadres. I would point out, however, that those atrocities differed widely region to region in Cambodia. In the most ideologically rigorous region (associated with Pol Pot) it has been said that there were fewer atrocities, at least in the beginning (see Vickery 1983).

The Khmer religious worldview can be seen in the strands of Khmer Marxism, which stressed building Cambodia again from the ground up. The authority claimed by the Angkar to undertake this project was underpinned by claims that were analogous to claims to authority made in past Cambodian revolutions. Buddhist and Marxist emphasis on similar normative behaviors underscored the authority of the cadres and further legitimated the movement. Worldview, notions of authority, and normative ethics remained fundamentally similar throughout modern Cambodian history, but the forms in which the worldview was acted out, or the "ethos" (Geertz 1973) of Cambodia, changed considerably with the nation's political situation.

An essay by David Apter, "Political Religion in the New Nations" (1963), suggests that all totalitarian systems have authority structures that are analogous to religious systems. Apter draws a distinction between reconciliation systems and mobilization systems in political theory. Whereas reconciliation systems try to reconcile individual needs within a state, and recognize the individuals goals among the citizens, mobilization systems present goals and values, and try to shape society according to those preset goals and values. Apter correlates mobilization systems with theocracies. "The mobilization system is represented by valued goals laid out by higher authority and regarded as sacrosanct" (65). What Apter is saying is that mobilization systems present coherent, preconceived notions of meaning to their populations. Often the population accepts the authority of the state, because other systems of meaning, largely for practical reasons, have degenerated too far to oppose it.

The Khmer Rouge fits well into the mobilization category. Their rhetoric of rebirth, purity, development, and self-sufficiency was an attempt to create what Apter calls a "political religion." More accurately, we might see it as an attempt to reconstitute in political form, a religion, or a worldview, whose connection with the sacred had been lost in the colonial period. The Khmer Rouge drew on the worldview and symbolism of Khmer Buddhism even if it was not aware of doing so, for the Khmer Rouge was legitimized by a concept of authority that existed in Cambodia since the premodern era.

Thus understood, the Khmer Rouge can be considered analogous to a variety of monoethical, highly ascetic, peasant-oriented, millenarian movements, which so often are characterized by moments of extreme violence. Typically, members of these groups have been systematically marginalized, brutalized, or left struggling for meaning in the face of uncontrolled social change. Their response is often a tightly controlled, violent attempt to reconstruct for themselves a meaningful world that connects past and present.

What is the connection between marginalization, violence, utopian beliefs, and the desire for continuity with a submerged past? Sartre's (1963) reading of Frantz Fanon points toward a melancholy but persuasive answer: "The native cures himself of colonial neurosis by thrusting out the settler through force of arms. When his rage boils over, he rediscovers his lost innocence and he comes to know himself in that he himself creates his self" (21).

# 14

# Real Paranoids Have Real Enemies

## The Genesis of the ZOG Discourse in the American National Socialist Subculture

JEFFREY KAPLAN

> Liberals will buy anything a bigot writes. In fact, they really SUPPORT hatemongers. George Lincoln Rockwell, the leader of the American Nazi Party, is probably a very knowledgeable businessman with no political convictions what so ever. He gets three bucks a head and works the mass rallies consisting of nothing but angry Jews, shaking their fists and wondering why there are so many Jews there. And Rockwell probably has only two real followers—and they're deaf. They think the swastika is merely an Aztec symbol.
> —Lenny Bruce, ca. 1965[1]

> Why is it that such small groups of young people have attracted so much attention? Hard-core neo-Nazi skinheads are very few, even though some of their records, cassettes and discs have sold well. The same question was asked in 1975 with even greater justification in regard to a handful of terrorists. Although they numbered no more than a few dozens, their deliberately outrageous behavior brought them enormous publicity, which of course, was what they wanted. In the end, there was a book and several articles on terrorism for every active European terrorist, and learned treatises were written about their psychology, social origin and general motivation.
> —Walter Laqueur 1996a, 130

---

1. E-text, "Lenny Bruce." See <http://infoweb.magi.com/~mbein/lennyb.html> for connections to this and other repositories of the wit and wisdom of Lenny Bruce. See Cohen 1967, 81–82.

We know "Armageddon," which many (we included) believe is the
biblical word for race war, will climax a tribulation period at which time
the bankers will close their doors. What we have been attempting to
determine now is a possible trigger incident that will cause the bankers to
close their doors

—Rick Cooper 1993, 1[2]

These epigraphs, separated in time by almost forty years, point to a single
preeminent truth about the American postwar neo-Nazi movement—the
coverage that it receives and the very real fear that it engenders is far out
of proportion to its actual size and political potency. In truth, American
National Socialism (NS) is composed of a minuscule and deeply divisive
community of true seekers who are, if they manage to survive the byzantine
infighting of the movement and the social and political ostracism that
invariably accompanies fealty to the swastika, fully cognizant of the futility of their quest. Why then do they persevere? What ultimate dream
is so powerful, so all consuming, that a tiny band of believers will sacrifice
all in its pursuit?

In this chapter I will look at only one aspect of this quest: the
apocalyptic *zeitgeist* that, in the self-view of the adherents, makes the
dominant culture unbearable—a multicultural cesspool of corruption
from which the faithful's only hope of succor is a chiliasm that has for
millennia been the final refuge of the persecuted and the hopeless. In
this future promise of a cleansed and chastened world of savage purity, the NS community puts its abiding faith. Moreover, until this
dream of future terrestrial power is fulfilled, the ragtag forces of
American National Socialism seek primarily to survive in the contemporary world, which, for them, is a place of testing in which persecutions great and small are their lot and—as with martyrs of old—their
glory.

2. This apocalypticism is typical of National Socialists on every side of the strategic
divide that separates the quietest majority who dream of a mass white awakening and thus
a popular revolution with the adherents of revolution NOW. A similar sentiment is expressed
by long-time activist James Mason below. Rick Cooper holds fast to this 1993 prognos-
tication, believing that the apocalypse will be signaled "when the bankers close their doors"
and in the ensuing chaos, race war will break out in the cities and the terrified white masses
will flock to the swastika banner, under which the Jews and the radical minorities will be
dealt with as the prelude to a chiliastic paradise (conversation with Rick Cooper July 15,
1997).

But objectively speaking, how real is this perception of unremitting persecution, which in its internal discourse has been reified into the all-pervasive malevolence of ZOG, the Zionist Occupation Government? To understand this self-view, we must move beyond the all too accurate outsider observations of the comedian Lenny Bruce in the 1950s and the social scientist Walter Laqueur in the 1990s. Rather than to gaze from without at the movement, let us take an intuitive leap from the angry crowd to the speaker's podium and view the world for a moment from a National Socialist perspective. What would we see? Let us begin at the beginning, with the Commander, George Lincoln Rockwell (1918–67),[3] as he gazes out on just the kind of angry crowd described by Lenny Bruce as composed primarily of Jews among whom a handful of National Socialist true believers are scattered. Here is how such a scene is described in movement hagiography:

**Nordic NS Hero George Lincoln Rockwell Battles the Red Rats in Jew York City!**

ROCKWELL LIVES!

Ten thousand incensed Jews swarmed into New York City's Central Park where the man they hated most planned to speak in the "free forum area." The huge mob was swollen with overwrought people loudly screaming for his blood. They brandished lead pipes and pieces of broken pavement in the best Old Testament traditions of free speech. No one really expected him to show up in the face of such demented numbers, so the frothing Chosen turned the event into an anti-Nazi celebration. They clapped and sang "Havanaglia" and performed round-dances in the street. But at the height of their vengeful hysteria, at the appointed time, a big man standing tall and alone in the very midst of the insane rabble threw off his long, concealing overcoat. As if by black magic, George Lincoln Rockwell

---

3. In truth, Rockwell was somewhat predated by an inveterate anti-Semitic rabble-rouser and street orator named James Hartung Madole and his National Renaissance Party (NRP). Some of the earliest followers of Rockwell's successor, Matt Koehl, graduated through NRP ranks. Madole is of interest today primarily for his 1960s-era contacts with such American Satanist groups as Anton LaVey's Church of Satan and the Detroit-based Order of the Black Ram, thus blazing a path for today's occult-oriented National Socialists. On Madole, see House Committee on Un-American Activities (1954); George and Wilcox (1996, 324–26); Aquino (1993, 272); Kaplan and Weinberg (1998); and *Nexus* (1995).

appeared in full Stormtrooper uniform in the eye of an emotional
hurricane, surrounded by enemies too stunned to move. Incredibly,
he began to taunt them, deriding them to their camelfaces as cow-
ards and fugitives from lunatic asylums.

He had shown up, he said, at their request, so let's see how
tough they really were. No one made a move against the formidable
ex-U.S. Navy Commander. He strutted smiling among them, ridicul-
ing their false promises to prevent his New York speech. It was a very
personal confrontation between Aryan man and his Jewish opposites,
between racial matter and anti-matter. An explosion was inevitable.

The Jews Go Nuts

Only by degrees did the Hebes belatedly psych themselves up to
sufficient hysteria. In a convulsive, screaming lunge they fell on
Commander Rockwell. But he had the psychological advantage of a
larger-than life personal courage. In an utterly one-sided battle too
incredible for anyone who has not actually witnessed or fought
through such a moment, he bashed and throttled his way into the
shrieking crowd. The grasping, spitting devils fell on all sides, as the
lone hero of the White race cut a path of blood and broken bones
across New York City. They never knocked him off his feet and he
never tired of splitting enemy jaws.

Alarmed and inspired by such Herculean bravery, a squad of
policeman crashed into the howling throng swinging night sticks.
Kosher casualties mounted rapidly, as the cops obviously relished
their sport. They blazed a path of splattering gore to the ever-
battling Rockwell, and escorted him over the blubbering bodies of
fallen Jews. He emerged with only a few cuts and minor bruises.
Even his uniform was in relatively good shape.[4]

Here is the Commander as the NS equivalent of the *marj al-taqlid*,
the Shi'i term for a model for emulation—a superhuman figure heroically
doing single-handed battle for the ultimate fate of the white race. Here
as well is the truth of Lenny Bruce's mordant observation that the Jewish
presence at Rockwell's media events ultimately confirmed the movement's

4. "Nordic NS Hero George Lincoln Rockwell Battles the Red Rats in Jew York
City!" (E-text widely disseminated throughout far right). Rockwell's physical confrontations with American Jews were frequent from the late 1950s through the early 1960s. This
phase of Jewish opposition to Rockwell's movement ended at that point with the adoption
of a more sophisticated strategy by the organized Jewish community. This will be considered below.

epic self-view as the righteous remnant standing fast amid a sea of per-secution and, not coincidentally, to keep the ever empty American Nazi Party (ANP) coffers sufficiently stocked to allow at least for the next month's round of expenses at the chronically impoverished "Hate House" aka "Hatemonger Hill," in Arlington, Virginia (Rosenthal and Gelb 1967).

For their part, the organized Jewish community gradually came to understand what Bruce grasped intuitively. Strident Jewish opposition to the tiny and isolated American Nazi Party, while understandable in the light of the Holocaust, was ultimately counterproductive. At that mo-ment, Rockwell's real troubles began, and he would find no answer to the dilemma until the day in 1967 when he was felled by an assassin's bullet. If a point of conception for the ZOG discourse can be posited, it may well have been at this fateful moment.

In the late 1940s, the American Jewish Committee (AJC) held a position very much akin to that of the Anti-Defamation League today. That is, one of the functions of the AJC was to monitor the doings of anti-Semites who might present a threat to the American Jewish commu-nity. At the head of this effort was Rabbi Solomon Andhil Fineberg. At the time, Rabbi Fineberg was concerned with the high-profile activities of the surviving depression-era demagogues, in particular Gerald L. K. Smith. In conjunction with other Jewish organizations, Rabbi Fineberg developed and championed what he called a "quarantine policy" (Fineberg 1946, 1947; Jeansonne 1988).[5] Quarantine meant exactly what the word implied—an attempt to sever the lines of transmission through which the anti-Semites' message could be disseminated.

In dealing with Rockwell, "Quarantine" was renamed "Dynamic Silence," but the objective was the same. When a Rockwell media event was planned, local Jewish organizations would seek to limit the impact of the performance. This involved on the one hand securing the coop-eration of local newspaper editors and broadcast journalists in ignoring the event. To facilitate this process, every effort was made to make the event less newsworthy. This involved limiting the kind of angry confron-tations lionized above, for it was precisely these theatrical clashes that drew the press in the first place. Thus, the primary impediment to the success of the Fineberg policy were chapters of the Jewish War Veterans who were the most militantly committed to physical confrontations with the Nazis. In the end, despite much internal dissension, Rabbi Fineberg's

---

5. In arguing for the adoption of this policy, Rabbi Fineberg noted that it was successful in regard to the anti-Semitic activities of Gerald L. K. Smith.

policy was adopted, the Jewish War Veterans reluctantly stopped attending Rockwell's rallies, and an increasingly frustrated Commander was left to try to devise ever more outrageous publicity stunts to publicize his movement (Simonelli 1999).

Rockwell was well aware of the success of the Dynamic Silence policy, but knew all too well that there was little he could do about it. In his famous *Playboy* interview, the Commander opined:

> In the *Columbia Journalism Review* about three months ago, Ben Bagdikian, a frequent writer for the Anti-Defamation League, wrote an article called "The Gentle Suppression"; which asked the question, "Is the news quarantine of Rockwell a good thing?"; Bagdikian openly reveals that the press maintains as much silence as possible about our activities. So you see, the Jew blackout on us is as real as a hand over my mouth. They know we're too poor to buy air time or advertising space, so they ban our publications from all channels of distribution, and they refuse to report our activities in the daily press. I could run naked across the White House lawn and they wouldn't report it. I'm being facetious. But I'm dead serious when I say that the only kind of free speech left in this country is that speech that doesn't criticize the Jews. If you criticize the Jews, you're either smeared or silenced. They have that same kind of "free speech" in Cuba, Red China and Russia and every other Communist country: You can say anything you like as long as it doesn't criticize the dictator. The Jews are never going to let me reach the people with my message in the American press; they can't afford to. (*Playboy* 1966)[6]

As Rockwell's ANP faithful struggled in vain against the media blackout, the movement's convoluted internal intrigues increasingly took up the Commander's attention. And little wonder, for seldom has so idiosyncratic a band of followers been assembled under one roof as the group at "Hate Monger's Hill." The few intelligent and capable adherents that the ANP managed to attract were subsumed by the ANP's more typical mediocrity and madness. What could a Rockwell, or a William Pierce,[7] hope to accomplish in such a milieu (Simonelli 1998; George and Wilcox 1996; Rosenthal and Gelb 1967; Cooper n.d.)? Rockwell's

---

6. The text of the interview is most readily available today through the *Playboy* Web site: <http://www.playboy.com>.

7. William Pierce, the pseudonymous author of the incendiary novel *The Turner Diaries,* is arguably the most influential figure in American National Socialism today. He will be considered further below.

successor, Matt Koehl, was (and is) universally reputed to be a homo-sexual—a not uncommon condition despite the movement's widely trum-peted homophobia. Political education officer Dan Burros, the author of the ANP's basic training document, the *Official Stormtrooper's Manual,* committed suicide in 1965 when apprised of an upcoming exposé in the *New York Times* revealing him to be Jewish (Rosenthal and Gelb 1967), and the list goes on (and on and on). Indeed, Frank Collin, the com-mander of the Chicago area for the National Socialist Party of America, would hit the trifecta when, in the course of his arrest and subsequent incarceration for homosexual pedophilia, it was discovered that he was half Jewish, and that his father had in fact nearly perished in the Holo-caust (George and Wilcox 1992, 360–61; Kaplan 1997a, 36)![8] Nor was this all of the Commander's troubles. The active but always fractious members of the West Coast branch of the ANP were, as usual, at one anothers' throats and continually calling on the Commander to mediate their endless squabbles. His World Union of National Socialists, despite the presence of a few capable national leaders in Europe and Canada, foundered from the same internal dissension and rank incompetence that doomed the ANP (Simonelli 1997; 1999). The problem then, as now, remains the same and is encapsulated in the recent observation of loqua-cious veteran National Socialist Harold Covington: "I have stated in earlier articles that our Movement has two basic problem areas: leader-

---

8. Within the movement, none of this is any secret, and is in fact the subject that perhaps takes up much of internal movement discourse. Collin's Jewish roots were in fact demonstrated in the National Socialist White People's Party newspaper, *White Power,* when the paper printed copies of his father's naturalization documents. Today, only Harold Covington refuses to believe that Collin was in fact Jewish. In a letter to the author dated November 29, 1997, Covington asserts: "As odd as it may seem despite what it eventually turned out that he WAS, there was never any documented proof that Frank Collin was a Jew. Mike Royko never actually produced any proof and simply repeated the allegation parrotwise from time to time; there were in fact some serious discrepancies in Royko's accounts over the years regarding when Max Collin came to this country, whether or not he was a so-called 'concentration camp survivor,' etc. The 'immigration papers' alleged to be those of Collin's father published by the Arlington group were a clumsy forgery, and were created by a man named John Logan who was later expelled by Cedric Syrdahl when he was revealed to be a homosexual himself. . . . I am one of the few people in the Movement who actually had occasion to meet Max Collin, and he did not strike me as particularly Jewish. I am well aware that this 'Collin was a Jew' thing has assumed the status of a holy and sacred doctrine among the Movement and the Antifa industry alike, and like all religious doctrines it is based on faith and pointless for me to dispute it, but like so much you people believe about us, it seems to be one of your own hoaxes which has been enshrined as fact

ship and membership. Our leadership is largely incompetent and corrupt, and our most active and visible members are mostly dysfunctional scum. This has to change."[9]

How did the Commander persevere in the face of these obstacles? The answer is little known, and the subject of much debate both within the movement and among the even less numerous (but arguably no less idiosyncratic) cadre of interested scholars. However, no scholar of religion could mistake the power of a true conversion experience, and that is precisely what Rockwell appears to have undergone. In a scene that the Commander would confide to a bare handful of his most trusted confidants, Rockwell describes his fortuitous discovery of the soteriological promise of Adolf Hitler, and the religious significance of the National Socialist dream. This should come as little surprise, as for Rockwell, National Socialism was already his religion in every sense of the term and he reverenced Hitler as a racial martyr (Rhodes 1980; Kaplan 1998). In his autobiography, *This Time the World!*, and even more openly in the writings of two generations of movement hagiographers, Rockwell describes his conversion to National Socialism in explicitly religious terms (Rockwell 1963; Pierce 1969; New Order n.d.).

---

through constant monotonous repetition and assumed a life of its own. Collin was unfortunate in his physiognomy—he actually did NOT have the classically Jewish features, he was just a damned ugly little cuss with a big nose. All of the preceding is moot, of course, in view of his habit of buggering little boys" (original punctuation has been retained).

For the sordid details of this controversy, see "Frank Collin" in Jeffrey Kaplan, *Encyclopedia of White Power* (Santa Barbara, Calif.: ABC-CLIO, forthcoming). For a semi-public movement view, see Rick Cooper, "A Brief History of the White Nationalist Movement," E-text available from a number of NS Web sites or from Cooper's National Socialist Vanguard. Cooper's history is available in slightly updated form as an appendix to the *Encyclopedia of White Power*. The findings of the report were confirmed and amplified in the author's conversation with Rick Cooper, July 15, 1997. The Nationalist Socialist Vanguard publishes the widely read *NSV Report*, which Cooper disseminates as a kind of in-house newsletter for the NS faithful. The *NSV Report* is available from the NSV at P.O. Box 328, The Dalles, Oregon 97058. NS-oriented Web sites are many, but often short lived. A good starting point for the curious would be the granddaddy of them all, Don Black's Stormfront site <http://204.181.176.4:80/stormfront/>. Even more interesting is the Bizarre Pages site <http://stop-the-hate.org/bizarre.html>; a frequently updated jumping-off point for a variety of radical right-wing Web sites. The Bizarre Pages site is maintained by an antiracist who believes that the best way to combat hate on the net is simply by exposing people to racist sites and letting the natural revulsion of most visitors do the rest.

9. E-mail message from Covington's latest vehicle, the reconstituted National Socialist White People's Party, July 9, 1997. The NSWPP's frequently spammed E-mail list is intended as a private discussion group, and it would therefore be inappropriate to provide the group's E-mail address here.

First, there was the motif of the spiritual quest—in this case in the San Diego public library in a frantic search for the truth underlying the dross of everyday events. Then there was the discovery of *Mein Kampf* on a back shelf in a musty bookshop. This was a truly life-changing experience, and William Pierce's description of Rockwell's fascination with the book eerily presages the scene in his influential apocalyptic novel *The Turner Diaries*, in which the protagonist, Earl Turner, is allowed to read the Organization's Holy Book, which, like Rockwell's reading of *Mein Kampf*, suddenly drew away the veil of illusion that masked the numinous realities of the world (Macdonald 1978). In Pierce's accounts, neither Rockwell nor the fictional Turner would ever again see the world in the same way after this deeply mystical experience (Pierce 1969, 12). But there was more. According to intimate comrades, Rockwell confessed to having a series of extraordinarily vivid and nearly identical prophetic dreams in which, in a variety of everyday contexts, he was called aside from crowded commonplace situations to a private room where standing before him was his newfound god, Adolf Hitler (15–16).[10] It was not long before Rockwell was moved to build a literal altar to his deity, hanging a Nazi flag that covered an entire wall of his home, under which he placed a table containing a bust of Hitler, three candles and candleholders, and:

> I closed the blinds and lit the candles, and stood before my new altar. For the first time since I had lost my Christian religion, I experienced the soul thrilling upsurge of emotion which is denied to our modern, sterile, atheist "intellectuals" but which literally moved the earth for countless centuries: "religious experience." I stood there in the flickering candlelight, not a sound in the house, not a soul aware of what I was doing—or caring (New Order n.d.).

William Pierce, an intimate of Rockwell and the publisher of the ANP's party organs, waxes lyrical over this experience. Describing it in terms familiar to any student of mysticism, East or West, Pierce writes:

> It was a religious experience that was more than religious. As he stood there he felt an indescribable torrent of emotions surging through his being, reaching higher and higher in a crescendo with a peak of unbearable intensity. He felt the awe inspiring awareness for a few moments, or a few minutes, of being more than himself,

10. Pierce dates these dreams as occurring in 1957–58.

of being in communion with that which is beyond description and beyond comprehension. Something with the cool vast feeling of eternity and of infinity—of long ages spanning the birth and death of suns, and of immense, starry vistas—filled his soul to the bursting point. One may call that Something by different names—the Great Spirit perhaps, or Destiny, or the Soul of the universe, or God—but once it has brushed the soul of a man, that man can never again be wholly what he was before. It changes him spiritually the same way a mighty earthquake or a cataclysmic eruption, the subsidence of a continent or the bursting forth of a new mountain range, changes forever the face of the earth. (Pierce 1969, 18)

Armed with this new-found insight into the deeper truths of this world, Rockwell would until his death soldier on against impossible odds. But at the same time, the Commander's struggle could not help shifting from a contest for political power into the timeless cosmic drama of good and evil, which posits every event in absolute terms. Thus, the success of Rabbi Fineberg's dynamic silence toward all things Rockwellian was a two-edged sword. For perched atop the speaker's platform, shouting to be heard over the strident protests of the movement's many, many opponents, Rockwell would gaze out at flesh and blood foes. But as the angry crowds dwindled to the merely curious, and as the opposition of the Jewish community became more subtle, more diffuse, so too did the movement's perception of the "other" come to conceptualize a superhuman entity whose control of the levers of power in this world—the government and the mass media—was so complete that the Commander would remark in his *Playboy* interview that the Jews could openly boast of their dominion! This vision of Jewish control, and of the malevolence underlying that domination, is the essence of modern anti-Semitism from the *Protocols of the Elders of Zion*[11] to Elizabeth Dilling's *The Plot Against*

---

11. *The Protocols of Zion* are a controversial early twentieth-century document that contains the broad outlines of the conspiratorial anti-Semitism normative in American NS circles today. According to Binjamin Segel in 1924 (see 1995/1924) and Norman Cohn in 1969, the document itself probably originated in an obscure German novel, *Biarritz*, by a no less obscure petty clerk, Herman Goedsche. Since Segel and Cohn's work, a massive two-volume study of the *Protocols* has been published by Pierre André Taguieff (1992), which holds that the original sources of the *Protocol's* scenario was an 1864 book, *Dialogue aux Enfers entre Machiavel et Montesquieu*. In the Taguieff work, the nefarious conspirators were the Bonapartes, not the Jews, but the story was a good one and infinitely adaptable.

Massimo Introvigne, to whom I owe a debt of gratitude for providing this information on the history of the *Protocols,* notes that "Goedsche wrote AFTER Joly and there

*Christianity,* and this perception of Jewish power and gentile passivity is conveyed in the ZOG discourse (Marsden n.d.; Dilling 1983; Cohn 1969; Aho 1994, 68–82). In this view, the faithful are victorious if they merely stand fast in the face of the unremitting enmity of the Jewish powers that be.

After Rockwell was gunned down by a disgruntled National Socialist named John Patler, the perception of a potential threat—however fanciful that perception may have been in retrospect—faded. The American Jewish community no longer needed a Rabbi Fineberg to orchestrate a campaign of dynamic silence as American National Socialism turned in on itself with a fury that has yet to abate. In late 1966 an important change—or a devisive split, depending on whose recollection one relies on—occurred in the American Nazi Party.[12] At issue was Rockwell's realization that the public—and much of the American radical right—was simply too repelled by the history of German National Socialism to listen to anything a leader under the swastika banner might have to say. At a party conference in June 1967, it was resolved to change the name of the American Nazi Party to the National Socialist White People's Party on January 1, 1967.

With Rockwell's death on August 25 of that year, however, Koehl was able to emerge as the preeminent American National Socialist

---

is little doubt that most of the main ideas of the Protocols come from Joly (some of them in fact make little sense if referred to the Jews and perfect sense if referred to the Bonapartes). Be it as it may be, I would support Taguieff's conclusion that it is an established fact among scholars that the Protocols were fabricated in Paris in 1897–1898 under the direction of Pierre Ivanovitch Ratschkovsky, at that time head of the Russian intelligence service in Paris" (E-mail from Massimo Introvigne, Dec. 10, 1997). Whatever their origin, the modern *Protocols,* complete with a mysterious midnight meeting in a graveyard of the shadowy "Sanhedrin," suggests an age-old Jewish conspiracy to subvert and conquer the world. The document was brought to the United States under the name of Victor Marsden, a writer and reporter who offered various accounts of how he obtained it. It was popularized by, and became the basis of, the *Dearborn Independent's* depression-era "International Jew" series. The convoluted history of the *Protocols* is recounted in Cohn 1969; Taguieff 1992; Levy 1995; and is summarized in Aho 1994.

12. What follows is somewhat controversial in American NS ranks. The confusion arises from a party conference held in June 1967 in which the decision to distance the party from the German NS model was taken. This included the change of name, and an effort to bring Karl Allen back to the party as Rockwell's putative successor. Allen had for some time been estranged from Rockwell, but the June meetings held the promise of bringing him back into the fold, and in the process easing Hitler cultist Matt Koehl to the sidelines. Rockwell was assassinated only days before a final reconciliation meeting with Allen was to take place. The June conference did, however, set the course for the creation of the

leader.[13] Within a short time after this, the few capable adherents the Commander had attracted to the movement resigned or were purged. Some went on to found their own small NS organizations in a bitterly contested battle for members and dollars. Thus was born the era of the "little Führers" of whom only one, William Pierce and his National Alliance, in any way approximates the viability of Rockwell's ANP. Others, men such as Christian Identity and later Odinist figure James Warner, abandoned overt National Socialism for other radical right theological redoubts. Others, less well known, after a period of drift, simply left the movement altogether and tried to pick up the pieces of their lives in the dominant culture.

In truth, it mattered little what went on in the National Socialist world in the decade following Rockwell's death. The country changed, the state security apparatus shifted its resources to other more immediate left-wing threats, and the Jewish community's watchdog functions underwent a sea change as well.

The late 1960s and early 1970s were the era of the far left's domination of media attention. As with fears of the far right of an earlier day, the popular dread of the few terrorists spawned by the American radical left turned out to be, as Walter Laqueur notes, much exaggerated. However, the Weathermen, the Symbionese Liberation Army, and especially the Black Panthers came to be seen as a genuine threat to the state, and the radical right in the public mind faded into obscurity (Rapoport 1971).

In these years, the primary watchdog role undertaken on behalf of the American Jewish community passed from the AJC to the Anti-Defa-

---

National Socialist White People's Party (NSWPP), which Koehl was selected to head after Rockwell's death.

Although this much is clear, the machinations of NS internal politics are difficult to untangle with any certainty at this remove. Rick Cooper, for example, today recalls no such splits in 1967, and states that "Rockwell felt that his Party would receive wider support, financially and otherwise, and would be more palatable to the White public if he changed the name of the Party from the American Nazi Party to the National Socialist White People's Party. The name change was effective January 1, 1967" (comments from Rick Cooper on an early draft of this article, received Aug. 28, 1997). For a good summation of the case for a divisive split in the party around the issue of the German NS model, and for an early, highly negative portrayal of Matt Koehl that would soon become ubiquitous in the world of American National Socialism, see the twelve-page letter from the pseudonymous Max Amann (actually Max Surry, who with his wife were ANP members from Texas) to all supporters of George Lincoln Rockwell, titled "White Party," June 1968.

13. Matt Koehl's ascension to the leadership and his eulogy delivered at Rockwell's funeral are recounted in the Autumn 1967 issue of *The Stormtrooper Magazine*.

mation League of the B'nai B'rith (ADL). This change was important, for the ADL from the beginning was far more aggressive than the AJC—or if truth be told, the United States government—would have dared to be. Infiltration, disinformation, agents provocateurs, highly questionable (and at times illegal) means of information gathering, and a public relations approach that grotesquely caricatured the actual size and potential dangers posed by the radical right became the ADL's stock in trade (Kaplan 1997a, 127–63; Dinnerstein 1994). This despite the fact that, in the ADL's private view, anti-Semitism in America was at an all-time low and fading fast. In a 1972 internal memorandum, the ADL research director, Oscar Cohen, stated, "My own feeling is that the Jewish position in this country has probably never been as secure as it is nor has there ever been less prejudice" (Dinnerstein 1994, 229).[14]

As the denizens of the radical right came to believe that the ADL was an omnipresent—and, indeed, omnipotent—presence, the ZOG discourse became a defining characteristic of the movement.

In these desperate years, the National Socialist community's warring tribes grasped at ways to remain relevant. At issue were two very different organizational conceptions (Kaplan 1997c; Kaplan and Weinberg 1998). For the conservative majority, the Rockwellian theory of mass action remained the guiding strategy. In this distant dream, some terrible cataclysm—economic collapse, rising crime, ultimately race war—would drive the white majority to seek refuge in the ranks of National Socialism. Most adherents of mass action theory did nothing but dream their dreams of future power over a cleansed and redeemed new heaven and new earth while continuing to engage in the fratricidal infighting that characterized American National Socialism in the post-Rockwell era.

Occasionally, however, some of these adherents would surface for a march or a publicity stunt that would have done the Commander proud. One such, the 1978 march on the heavily Jewish city of Skokie,

14. Dinnerstein himself concludes from the perspective of the 1990s: "Today antiSemitism in the United States is neither virulent nor growing. It is not a powerful social or political force. Moreover, prejudicial comments are now beyond the bounds of respectable discourse and existing societal restraints prevent any overt antiSemitic conduct except among small groups of disturbed adolescents, extremists, and powerless African-Americans" (243). This trend continues to this day according to the 1997 *Antisemitism World Report*, which states: "What is clear from the last six years is that antisemitism does not resonate with significant sections of the public in the way it once did [and] that it cannot be used to mobilize anything other than small, extremist fringe groups." (See Reaney 1997. Note that the spelling of "anti-Semitism" is different in each source.)

Illinois, led by the unfortunate half-Jewish Frank Collin, noted above for his predilection for little boys and candid photography of same, garnered national publicity (and, not coincidentally, support from some quarters of the Jewish community on First Amendment grounds for the Nazis' right to march) (George and Wilcox 1992, 360–61). It was a masterful, if brief, reminder that the movement, contrary to popular opinion, still had a pulse.

A few in these years sought to emulate the far left and "seize the day" under the swastika banner. The most spectacular of these aggregations was the National Socialist Liberation Front (NSLF), led by Joseph Tommasi.[15] Tommasi, whose less than Nordic name and complexion brought him the not so affectionate nickname "Tomato Joe" from the less militant of the California NSWPP cadre from which he emerged,[16] was another victim of Koehl's ceaseless purge of party ranks (in this case for entertaining women on party premises—never a temptation to Koehl to be sure—smoking marijuana on said premises, unlawful armed paramilitary maneuvers, and misuse of the virtually nonexistent party funds).[17]

Urged on (from a safe distance) by William Pierce, Tommasi gathered a group of committed revolutionaries and daringly broke with the mass-action strategy in favor of revolution now. The party was founded in 1969, but would not have its first organizational meeting until 1973, which was attended by more than forty adherents.[18] These numbers were

15. The NSLF, a pet project of William Pierce, was originally conceived as a youth wing of the National Socialist White People's Party that would provide a radical right-wing alternative to the leftist presence on campuses in the early 1970s. The project was spectacularly unsuccessful. It did, however, attract one teenaged adherent who would spend a lifetime regretting this affiliation—David Duke. Duke was photographically immortalized as a nineteen-year-old in Louisiana staging a one-man NSLF rally on the campus of Louisiana State University. The picture has haunted him ever since (Zatarian 1990; Rose 1992).

16. Interview with former NSWPP member currently residing in Arizona, May 29, 1996. Name withheld by request.

17. Rick Cooper adds that one of the charges against Tommasi stemmed from his disobeying an explicit Koehl order against firearms and military maneuvers. Cooper comments Aug. 28, 1997.

18. The key year for the NSLF was 1973. In that year Koehl officially expelled Tommasi from the NSWPP—a move that ironically seemed to shock Tommasi, who perversely remained a Koehl loyalist to the bitter end. In any case, over Labor Day weekend, Koehl loyalists unceremoniously removed Tommasi's belongings from the NSWPP's El Monte, California, headquarters. This seems to have expedited Tommasi's resolve to make the NSLF a reality (Cooper comments, Aug. 28, 1997. Interview with James Mason, Nov. 28, 1996).

deceptive, however, as only four NSLF members were prepared to undertake immediate revolutionary violence. The futility of the plan is obvious, and within a short time Tommasi was dead—killed by an NSWPP adherent[19]—and two other revolutionaries, Karl Hand and David Rust, found themselves serving long prison sentences on weapons charges and for racially motivated violence (Mason 1992; Kaplan 1997c; Kaplan forthcoming; Kaplan and Weinberg 1998].

How could such a quixotic enterprise as the NSLF hope to overthrow the state? The answer has much to do with the impact of the 1960s on the far right—an influence that has yet to abate as virtually every adherent interviewed in the course of this research who is of an age to remember the time remains much in thrall of the era. It has much to do as well with the frustration that the increasingly hopeless mass-action strategy engendered. Moreover, it is a reaction to the vicious internal fragmentation of a movement in which more time is spent hurling calumnies at one another than in fighting the perceived enemy. And it owes much to the feeling of helplessness that is reflected in the ZOG discourse—a vision of a movement that sees itself as relentlessly persecuted by the inextricable forces of the state and the Jews, as personified in particular by the ADL. Recently, I had the opportunity to put the question to James Mason, one of the four combatant NSLF adherents, who was then incarcerated in Colorado:

> KAPLAN: I wanted to ask [a question that] . . . [y]ou could shed some light on . . . as I am sure you have given much thought to this dilemma. With the NSLF's turn to revolutionary violence, there seems to be a serious catch-22. On the one hand, the mass action strategy clearly was not going to work—it meant permanent impotence. But on the other, the idea of 4 people, or 400 for that matter, making a serious revolutionary movement that would in any way threaten the power of the state seems equally incredible. To act would, as happened in fact, merely allow the activists to imbibe the

19. Rick Cooper describes Tommasi's death as follows: "Tommasi drove by the El Monte HQ one evening, apparently shouting insults at the Duty officer, Jerry Jones. Jones 'flipped off' Tommasi. Tommasi left his car to confront Jones, a teenager, in a threatening manner. Jones drew his .45 caliber pistol and shot Tommasi in the left eye." Cooper notes as well that Jones and another NSWPP member on the scene, Clyde Bingham, drew only minimal jail sentences from the altercation, which he believes would indicate that the "cops thought Tommasi a danger" (Cooper comments Aug. 28, 1997; conversation with Rick Cooper Aug. 28, 1997).

hospitality of the prison system for much of their lives. And to add to the dilemma, there seems to be no third path that I can think of between mass action and futile violence.[20]

MASON: Your question is a tough one, but I believe I have a handle on it. Indeed [my] new book is dedicated to it and I recently sent [Tom] Metzger an article to the effect.

First, if you're going to be wasting your time, at least don't be kidding yourself or others. If you wind up in the hands of the law, at least make it worthwhile and know what it's been for.

The "mass action" strategy could have probably worked— maybe it still could. One ringer at the top did in the good efforts of those of us in the NSWPP. We had something going, no mistake. I saw how it was scuttled. (That name finally came to me—Karl Hand's one-word response when I asked him what caused him to quit the NSWPP was "Bishop," one of Koehl's hand-picked de- formed freaks).[21]

Yet to ever dream of inheriting this mess? To consider taking responsibility for it? "Careful what you wish for." Getting in line with evolution rather than standing apart from it. We can't topple the system, but neither can its pigs save it. . . .

[Charles] Manson really had the answer: Drop out all the way, not part of the way, and let it fall. That might even be called "spiri- tual" as it calls for great self-discipline. The Bible says the same for the End-Time and Babylon's Whore. . . .

. . . Blacks, browns, etc., have their crime and gang activity which isn't even "crime" in the commonly accepted sense—it's them reasserting their "tribal" ways as society dies. There is the key, Jerry Rubin said in "Do It!" that "we are nothing until the establishment moves to react to us."

Basically, the Movement needs to heed Rubin's words and do it rather than wait until the system comes to scoop them up on weapons and conspiracy charges. I hope they will learn this before too much time goes by. Unless they're terminally stupid, they will.[22]

Mason's wish for the movement to take action—any action—in the face of the overawing power of the state may be lost on the National

20. Kaplan to James Mason, June 26, 1997.

21. The "Citizen Kane"-like reference here is to an earlier conversation about Karl Hand, another of the NSLF's combatants. The "Bishop" in question is Joseph Bishop, one of a long line of Koehl factotums who served briefly and then were purged from NSWPP ranks.

22. Mason to Kaplan, July 3, 1997.

Socialist faithful in the United States. The acts of antistate violence that have taken place in recent years have emerged more from the patriot subculture, which the media has reified into the "militia movement" in the wake of Oklahoma City, than from the tiny and more divided than ever National Socialists.

In the NS subculture, the conservative majority remains focused on their ongoing feuds and remain paralyzed to undertake any action in the sure knowledge that to act is to follow the course most desired by ZOG, as undirected acts of violence against individual Jews or racial minorities—much less against the state itself—would be tantamount to accepting ZOG's open invitation to spend the prime of the activists' lives warehoused in the American prison system. Thus, while the ever prudent William Pierce can publish incendiary novels such as *The Turner Diaries* and *Hunter* in his decades-old quest to motivate younger adherents such as Joseph Tommasi to act, he himself lives the life of a gentleman farmer on his West Virginia estate and counts the royalties from the National Alliance's publishing and direct-mail sales.

Against such counsel, George Burdi, aka George Eric Hawthorne, the lead singer of the popular White Noise band Rahowa and the former publisher of *Resistance* magazine, warns:

> These sort of attacks accomplish absolutely NOTHING, and have cost us hundreds of our best men who are currently rotting away in ZOG's dungeons because they lacked the foresight and direction necessary to act as revolutionaries instead of reactionaries. Beating some worthless mud to death is not an act of revolution, it is an act of poor judgment. The *Protocols of the Learned Elders of Zion*, which is the doctrine outlining ZOG's plan for global domination, says that our enemy *can count on the White man to sacrifice long term victory for short term satisfaction*. We must stop acting in accordance with their plans and start acting in accordance with our own LONG RANGE PLAN FOR WHITE REVOLUTION. This means staying out of jail whenever it is avoidable. Remember, this is a war and you are living behind enemy lines. Act accordingly. (Hawthorne 1995, 42)

Hawthorne himself was jailed for a year for assault in 1996, although the circumstances that led to the confrontation remain murky at best.[23]

---

23. After his release from prison in 1998, Hawthorne quietly left the movement. Since then, the Swedish music label and eponymous magazine *Nordland* has sent some of its people to keep the Resistance CD business and Web site alive. The prospects for

However, the sentiments expressed in this quote—ZOG's overweening power and the superhuman guile of the Jews—are all but ubiquitous in the National Socialist world today.

What then is left but passive resignation and the timeless dream of a whiter and brighter day when the endless infighting ends and the unassailable power of ZOG crumbles? Given the condition of the American National Socialist movement today, there seems little to be done in the immediate future. Thus, the infighting has, if anything, intensified in recent years, with the tireless polemicist Harold Covington providing the most colorful purple prose through his *Resistance* newsletter (again, no relation to George Hawthorne's eponymous magazine) and most recently through his private E-mail list. Particular targets of Covington's lethal wit have been William Pierce and other members of the National Alliance (who may or may not have filed a libel suit against Covington, depending on whom you ask) and Tom Metzger, the head of the White Aryan Resistance (WAR).

Metzger has been a particularly fat target as a result of the success of Morris Dees and his Southern Poverty Law Center's civil suit against Metzger as being indirectly responsible for the beating death of an Ethiopian immigrant in Oregon. At the time the controversy began in 1995, Metzger was riding high, and appeared to be a power to be reckoned with in the world of the radical right. However, in 1995 the racialist newspaper *The Truth at Last* published the fact that as a condition of fulfilling his debt stemming from the lawsuit, Metzger was forced to cede control of the WAR mailbox to a San Diego attorney named Jim McElroy. This should have come as no surprise—Dees himself broke the news in his book *Hate on Trial* (Dees and Fiffer 1993, 276–77).[24]

Reading this, Harold Covington immediately undertook a long-running campaign warning anyone who would listen (and many who would not) of the danger to the movement caused by Metzger's silence on the issue. Soon, Covington even produced a martyr, a skinhead named Mark Lane, whose written threats of violence in a letter to WAR were reportedly delivered to Dees, who passed them on to the authorities, who in turn arrested and incarcerated Lane.[25] The damage done to Meztger's reputa-

---

*Resistance* magazine at this writing are considerably less than sanguine (information communicated by E-mail from Swedish sources close to Nordland, Apr. 2, 1998).

24. The relevant issue of *The Truth at Last* is 380 (1995). Covington's laudatory response was printed in the undated issue 385.

25. See, for example, *Resistance* 40, July 1994; "An Open Letter to Morris Seligman Dees," *Resistance* 51 (June 1995); and "The Ongoing Farce," E-mail from Harold

tion from all this is incalculable—so much so that Rick Cooper took it upon himself to launch an independent investigation. Cooper found that although it was true that Metzger's mailbox is (or was, Cooper is not certain of the current situation) probably under the control of Morris Dees through the San Diego attorney, Lane's troubles were the result of his having sent the incriminating letter to another organization—also named WAR—under the leadership of Bill Riccio, who is widely thought to be a government informant, and is in any case incarcerated at the moment as well.[26]

The point of all this is, however, not the ups and downs of Tom Metzger or to demonstrate the jungle telegraph by which news is disseminated throughout the movement. Rather, the extraordinary divisiveness of the National Socialist world makes its reticence to act all the more understandable. If a figure of the stature of Tom Metzger can be brought down and forced to cooperate with the movement's most implacable foes, who then is safe? Who is beyond the reach of ZOG? And who in the movement can be trusted?

There are, however, other, albeit little-traveled, paths that may promise greater things in revolutionary action. These delve into the occult tributaries of contemporary National Socialism. In truth, it is a minority path—much demonized by the conservative majority of the movement (Goodrick-Clark 1992, 1998). It involves a relative handful of seekers world wide—adherents known more for their talents in the underground world of music and the arts than for their revolutionary ardor. Some of these movements have a decidedly Satanist cast. The British-based Order of the Nine Angles (ONA) and its black mass dedicated to raising the shade of Adolf Hitler and its central dogma of human sacrifice is but one example. The Swedish Black Order, which is heavily influenced by ONA dogma and whose Gothenberg branch is much addicted to the murder of homosexuals, is another group that comes to mind (Kaplan 1998; Selwyn 1990).[27]

---

Covington, June 11, 1997, which states Covington's positions on the Metzger controversy and the theoretical lawsuit that may or may not have been filed against him by the National Alliance.

26. On Cooper's findings, Cooper conversation with me, July 15, 1997. Cooper noted that such are relations in the radical right that Metzger, unsatisfied with less than total vindication, wrote Cooper and declared, in so many words, "you are not my friend anymore." Metzger later softened and the two are back on speaking terms. For Covington's reaction to the Cooper report, see "Damning with Faint Praise: Rick Cooper's Report on the Tom Metzger Situation," *Resistance* 52 (July 1995).

27. Interview with the ONA's Christos Beest, June 20, 1996. In 1996 the ONA released an updated set of guidelines for human sacrifice titled "A Gift for the Prince—A Guide to Human Sacrifice"; "Culling—A Guide to Sacrifice II"; "Victims—A Sinister

Although space does not permit a thorough consideration of this fascinating tributary of contemporary National Socialism, one preeminent figure should be mentioned as a central source of contemporary NS occultism. Savitri Devi, born Maximiani Portas in Lyons, France, in 1905 is a fascinating figure (Goodrick-Clark 1998; Kaplan forthcoming). The only woman to achieve global renown in the patriarchal world of postwar National Socialism, she moved to India in 1932 to study the roots of Aryan religion and philosophy. Adopting the name Savitri Devi in honor of the Aryan sun goddess, by 1935 she fell under the spell of Adolf Hitler—a fascination that she would take to her grave. After a brief imprisonment in Germany after the war for pro-Nazi activities, she began in about 1960 to correspond with Rockwell, who reportedly became fascinated with her and her mystical approach to National Socialism. She and Rockwell met for the first and last time in 1962 at the Cotswold Conference in England that formed the groundwork for the World Union of National Socialists (Simonelli 1999).

Savitri Devi was a prolific—if sometimes impenetrable—writer. So taken were Rockwell and the editor of the ANP's various publications, William Pierce, with her work, however, that most of the premier issue of *National Socialist World*[28] was devoted to her 1956 masterpiece, "The

---

Exposé"; and "Guidelines for the Testing of Opfers." Opfers are, in ONA terminology, candidates suitable for sacrifice.

The Swedish Black Order led by third-generation National Socialist Gurran Gullwang was in 1997 in some difficulty, according to several Swedish sources, stemming from a recent ritual reportedly involving human sacrifice that was aimed at raising the shade of Heinrich Himmler. The Swedish government takes a rather dim view of these expressions of religiosity. Raids on the group's Gothenburg headquarters in late 1997 and early 1998 recovered ritual implements, a video of the girlfriend of the leader bathing in blood à la Countess Bathory, and human bones. The bather we are assured was immersed in animal blood only and the bones were artifacts "harvested" in a cemetery rather than taken from living people. At this writing (in 1998), Gullwang remains free but most other Black Order adherents are incarcerated.

Finally, in a snippet from his forthcoming book, James Mason writes: "Among my personal friends—respected and capable Movement captains—are formalized and legitimate High Priests of the Church of Satan. You'd undoubtedly be amazed" (Mason 1998, 20).

28. The American Nazi Party under Rockwell put out three major publications. *The Stormtrooper* and *The Rockwell Report* were both for internal consumption and intended as recruiting vehicles for like-minded white radicals. *National Socialist World,* however, was very much a William Pierce vehicle and aimed at a more intellectual audience. The articles in the *National Socialist World* dealt with political philosophy, racial theory, and through Savitri Devi, religion, philosophy, and speculations dealing with the "Golden Age" history of the Aryan race.

Lightning and the Sun." The story, dedicated "To the godlike Individual of our times; the Man against time; the greatest European of all times; both Sun and Lightning: ADOLF HITLER," is an imaginative history of Aryan man, which culminates, not surprisingly, with Hitler and the "tragedy" of 1945 (Savitri Devi 1966, 13). Savitri Devi's "Gold in the Furnace," originally published in 1959, excerpted in *National Socialist World* in 1967, and "Defiance," excerpted in the same publication in 1968, were more frankly autobiographical. Her remarkable "Impeachment of Man," originally written in 1959, was republished in 1991 by Willis Carto's Noontide Press and is particularly recommended for her juxtaposition of Eastern and Western spirituality—and for her devotion to what would be called in a later day "animal rights" (1991). Savitri Devi's influence on postwar National Socialism—and particularly on the occult byways of the movement—is incalculable.

Yet, although these occult NS movements are minuscule even by the standards of American National Socialism, they are nonetheless important, for they represent a vital trend that was in German National Socialism from its very inception. The finest student of this esoteric world, Nicholas Goodrick-Clark, puts the case well:

> For historians trained exclusively in the evaluation of concrete events, causes, and rational purposes, this netherworld of fantasy may seem delusive. . . . However, fantasies can achieve a causal status once they have been institutionalized in beliefs, values and social groups. Fantasies are also an important symptom of impending cultural changes and political action. (1992, 1)

Of these tiny NS movements, the most important—and from a historical point of view, the most interesting—is the Universal Order. The Universal Order is a direct outgrowth of Tommasi's NSLF combatant group, and is led today by the infamous Charles Manson from prison and organized by James Mason. Mason describes in rich detail the history of the Universal Order:

> The [Universal Order is the] operational front adopted at the direct suggestion of Charles Manson by James Mason, the publisher and editor of *Siege*, which had been a newsletter of the National Socialist Liberation Front (NSLF) beginning in 1980.
>
> Mason had been a member of first the National Socialist White People's Party and then the NSLF, but had been growing increasingly disillusioned with the conservative, legalistic stance of the hard

right wing organizations and their apparent lack of relevance and impact upon national and world events. Having run the entire gamut of political extremism, Mason sensed that by 1980 there existed no conventional political solution to the dilemma of Whites in America, i.e., increasing non-White presence and Jewish domination of government and media.

In 1980, Mason was moved to contact Manson Family members Lynette Fromme and Sandra Good, confined at the Federal Women's Penitentiary at Alderson, West Virginia, and Charles Manson himself at the state prison at Vacaville, California. The heavy exchange of letters and telephone calls which resulted led to a visit to Alderson in March 1981 and, due to the input of Manson's ideas, the formal move away from the NSLF and to the Universal Order by mid-1982.

It was also Charles Manson's contention that there was no political solution to the world's problems which, in his view, extended well beyond the parameters of government and race, encompassing such issues as the poisoning of the earth's environment and the deadly damage being done to the human psyche by the modern, materialistic society. In line with this greater reality, Manson suggested that the name National Socialist Liberation Front was no longer valid and put forth Universal Order instead to reflect the philosophy and program itself.

Along with the change of name, Manson proposed a new symbol for the effort. Rather than a Swastika positioned with an M-16 rifle, it would now be a Swastika superimposed over the scales of justice. In deference to Manson, Mason utilized a leftward-revolving Swastika in the new symbol. At the same time, Manson reversed the direction of the Swastika in his forehead to now revolve to the right.

From 1982 until it ceased publication in 1986, *Siege* promoted Manson's philosophy as the logical extension of Hitler's philosophy as it applied to today's world. Despite much initial rejection on the part of traditional Movement stalwarts on the basis of imagery and the lack of orthodoxy, the sentiments, priorities and strategies of Manson gradually came to pervade areas of the US radical right over the following decade.

Though few would realize or admit it, the gradual move away from "White Supremacy" toward White Separatism, from any hopes of recovering the US government, toward establishing new, independent regions, is precisely what animated the creation of the Manson enclaves in Death Valley during the 1960s. At issue is bare survival as a species as the world system begins to crumble and die. (Mason forthcoming)

The Universal Order's approach to National Socialism may best be described as a work in progress. Mason has recently taken the case for Charles Manson as the natural leader of the National Socialist movement to a variety of movement forums—most recently to George Eric Hawthorne's *Resistance* magazine (Mason 1995). Its reception in these quarters has been less than universally enthusiastic. Yet, at the heart of the Universal Order's appeal is a markedly millenarian, strongly chiliastic zeitgeist based on the inevitability of race war and on a radical environmentalism that predated—and according to the Manson Family provided a model for—the later Earth First! brand of ecological activism, which the Manson group dubs ATWA (Air Trees Water Air) (Kaplan 1997b).

## Conclusion

> All the places I've been
> Make it hard to begin
> To enjoy life again on the inside
> But I mean to . . .
>
> Here on the inside
> The outside's so far away . . .[29]
> —Jethro Tull

Let us return for a brief concluding glance from the speaker's platform once manned by the Commander George Lincoln Rockwell, and look at the world from the inside of the contemporary American National Socialist scene. What do we see? The crowds are gone now. The frantic heckling has all but died away. A National Socialist event now ranks with an appearance by the Ku Klux Klan as a magnet for determined, organized opposition by the no less minuscule and isolated denizens of the radical left (George and Wilcox 1992, 361).[30] The American economy is strong and the American public seems unusually self-satisfied

---

29. Jethro Tull, "Inside," from the compact disc *Living in the Past*.

30. Usually, this leads to much pushing and shouting and overtime pay for overworked police officers. On one occasion, however, the results were tragic. In Greensboro, North Carolina, in 1979, a contingent from the Communist Workers' Party decided to confront a group of demonstrators from the local Ku Klux Klan, two of whom were also members of the National Socialist Party of America, then led by Frank Collin and Harold Covington. Shooting broke out and five members of the Communist Workers Party were killed.

with their place in the post–Cold War world. If there is a White riot going, it is at the ballot box and not in the streets. Contrary to the movement's apocalyptic prognostications, affirmative action, for example, is being voted and legislated out of existence and even the power of the presidency seems helpless to slow the trend.

Where once an opportunity appeared to beckon under the leadership of a charismatic figure such as Rockwell to expand NS influence into the disparate tribes of the right—and perhaps into the heart of a mainstream America frightened by rapid social change, by integration, and by rising crime—today there is only the dream of the future promise of an apocalyptic reversal of fortunes. Too, there is the sure knowledge that the state—and the Jewish power that the NS faithful are convinced lurks behind every machination of the American government—allows you to dream your dream on sufferance. With every hand turned against you, with almost every channel of communication effectively closed (Eatwell 1996; Anti-Defamation League 1996; Back, Keith, and Solomos 1998; Capitanick and Wine 1996; Kleim forthcoming),[31] and with the movement riddled with agents and informers, the true believers can do little but persevere and hold fast to the age-old millennial hope.

31. There was some initial hope that the Internet and the White Power music scene would offer at least the younger and more technologically literate of the faithful a way to as last break through with their message. An interesting case in point is provided by Milton John Kleim Jr. Kleim and several other individuals were the main theorists behind the use of the Internet as a Neo-Nazi recruiting tool. His widely disseminated essay, "On Strategy and Tactics for the Usenet," was the blueprint for the effort. Tellingly, Kleim and the other theorists have all left the movement (E-mail from Milton Kleim Jr. Nov. 15, 1996).

The White Power music scene is even more interesting. Its market share in some European countries is remarkable, although it seems almost in inverse proportion to the number of adherents the movement manages to attract. A soon-to-be released Swedish government survey of all Swedish high school students demonstrates this rather conclusively, but the point was better made in a disgusted E-mail from Matti, the lead singer of the Swedish White Noise band Svastika (Aug. 27, 1997). Another Swedish activist, Tommy Rydén put it succinctly: "[E]veryone who has studied Sun-Tzu's writing on the art of war will understand . . . (the others will continue to listen to their compact disks and understand nothing)" (fax from Tommy Rydén, Apr. 13, 1997).

# 15

## The Justus Freemen Standoff

### The Importance of the Analysis of Religion in Avoiding Violent Outcomes

JEAN E. ROSENFELD _____

> In Numbers 25, verses 1-9, . . . the People of "Israel" played the *"harlot" with the daughters of Moab,* and a Man of Israel brought a *Midianite woman* to his family, in the sight of Moses and the whole congregation, whereby *a Priest took up the spear and killed them both for the sin of mixing with other races.* Kind after Kind. For this sin [plague] of race mixing, *24,000 Israelites were killed that day for playing the harlot with other races.* ". . . and when We move into a new land, *We are to kill all of the inhabitants of the other races,* Numbers 33:55
> —Rodney Skurdal 1994, 4[1]

### Introduction

In Numbers 25 in the Old Testament, Phinehas the priest halts a plague sent by God to punish the Israelites for cohabiting with Moabites by slaying an intermixed couple. God rewards Phinehas and his descendants with a "covenant of a perpetual priesthood," and Israel unleashes holy war against Moab. The Phinehas paradigm of zealotry has inspired an assortment of millenarian groups, from the Sicarii of first-century Palestine to the Aryan Nations of Hayden Lake, Idaho, and the Justus Freemen of Montana. Claiming they were sovereign "Characters" solely under

---

1. An earlier version of this article was published as "The Importance of the Analysis of Religion in Avoiding Violent Outcomes: The Justus Freemen Crisis," *Nova Religio: The Journal of Alternative and Emergent Religions* 1, no. 1 (Oct. 1997): 72–95.
    Skurdal's "Edict" (1994) is a summary of Christian Identity theology by the co-founder of the Freemen movement.

the jurisdiction of their Common Law courts,[2] the Freemen launched a paper assault on public officials, threatening to bankrupt or hang some of them.

In this chapter I demonstrate how the analysis of religion was employed to avoid a violent outcome of the eighty-one day standoff between the FBI's Critical Incident Response Group (CIRG) and the Justus Freemen. The chapter reflects the perspective of three religious studies scholars, Catherine Wessinger, J. Phillip Arnold, and I, who formed a consultative team after CIRG requested our advice.[3]

On January 27, 1994, a group of Freemen took over the Garfield County courthouse in Jordan, Montana, to announce that they were setting up their "Supreme Court of Garfield County-comitatus." They were led by Rodney O. Skurdal, an activist from neighboring Musselshell County, and Richard E. Clark, whose wheat farm had been threatened with foreclosure for failure to make payments on $710,000 in federal loans (Pitcavage 1996). It was sold at auction on April 14, 1994, but the Clark family[4] was not evicted (*Billings Gazette Online* Apr. 24, 1996). Throughout the early 1990s Ralph and Emmett Clark had contacted various "prophets," including Freemen founders Rodney Skurdal and LeRoy Schweitzer, for help with their financial and legal problems (Pitcavage 1996).

In October 1994, Rodney O. Skurdal filed an "Edict" at the Musselshell County courthouse and set up a local Common Law court. The "Edict" expatiated on racial purity doctrines of Aryan Nations' ideology and attracted the notice of Montana human rights organizations. A year later Skurdal and Leroy M. Schweitzer led an armed convoy of Freemen from their cabin in Musselshell County to the 960-acre Clark wheat farm (henceforth referred to as a ranch) in Garfield County near Jordan. In December 1995 federal prosecutors charged twelve Freemen and their followers with fifty-one counts of conspiracy, mail fraud, and threatening the life of a federal judge. On March 25, 1996, the FBI captured Schweitzer and Daniel E. Petersen Jr. on the perimeter of the

2. From 1992 to 1996 Rodney O. Skurdal and LeRoy Schweitzer taught paying clients how to set up an idiosyncratic, Common Law court system in their various communities.

3. Other scholars were also consulted.

4. The branch of the Clark family aligned with the Freemen included brothers Emmett (67) and Ralph (65); Ralph's son, Edwin (45); and Edwin's son, Casey (21). Ralph's wife, Rosie (70), and Emmett's wife Kay (65) were on the farm during the standoff, but were not charged with any crime after the standoff was concluded.

Clark property, triggering a standoff between the FBI and twenty-one Freemen remaining on the ranch. Between March 26 and June 13 more than one hundred FBI agents ringed the Clark ranch while CIRG negotiators patiently sought a peaceful resolution of the crisis.

That this critical incident near Jordan, Montana, did not result in bloodshed is noteworthy. Standoffs between the state and groups claiming allegiance to the higher authority of God tend to result in violence. It was not clear to CIRG personnel at the outset that the Jordan group that called itself Justus[5]—a pun on "just us" and "justice"—was a religious movement. During the incident the FBI consulted with many outside experts, but only a few were scholars of religion.[6] To scholars who had studied similar movements the uppermost question was, how could a nonviolent resolution of the standoff be negotiated with a group that would not compromise its claim to absolute truth?

The Justus Freemen standoff resembled previous confrontations between sectarians and governments that had culminated in lethal conflict, a lamentable history that prompts the question: How and why do groups that can be identified as millenarian behave differently from hostage takers or ordinary criminals?

## Scholars and the FBI

After the clash between federal agents and Branch Davidians began and ended in tragedy near Waco, where at least eighty-six people died during the initial dynamic entry and final assault by federal agencies that bracketed a 51-day siege in 1993, the FBI "tried a fundamentally different approach" (AP News Online REF5434, June 14, 1996). Attorney General Janet Reno and FBI Director Louis Freeh developed a new "critical incident response management policy" calling for three changes: (1) "When the FBI reacts in a crisis situation, the reaction must be commensurate with the facts as we know them"; (2) "our negotiations drive our strategy"; and (3) "the FBI must never hesitate to go outside of government to seek other experts or other people who might help us peacefully [resolve] a crisis situation" (CNN "Breaking News" 1996,

---

5. Heidi Rankin (1996, 1) asserted that "Justus" also stands for the surname of Jesus (Col. 4:11).

6. FBI Director Louis Freeh revealed that in addition to contacting "a wide variety of experts," the FBI worked with "45 different third-party intermediaries" (TPIs), ranging from members of the Patriot movement to a state legislator (CNN "Breaking News)," June 13, 1996, 29).

29). Implementing the new approach, CIRG contacted religious studies experts between March 25 and June 13, 1996.

After the Waco tragedy, Dr. J. Phillip Arnold of the Reunion Institute in Houston formed the Religion-Crisis Task Force, a network of scholars willing to advise law enforcement agents. Dr. Catherine Wessinger of Loyola University, New Orleans, wrote letters to Attorney General Janet Reno resulting in some contacts in the FBI. Arnold and Wessinger communicated with the FBI from April through June 13, 1996. I was called by CIRG on May 7 and remained in daily contact with Catherine Wessinger until the end of the standoff.

Shortly after the Jordan story broke in late March, I had obtained information about the Freemen from Christine Kaufmann of the Montana Human Rights Network and Susan DeCamp of the Montana Association of Churches. However, at the beginning of May, Wessinger, Arnold, and I still did not have sufficient information to answer such questions as: Are the Justus Freemen an apocalyptic group? Would they react violently to a tightening of the FBI perimeter? CIRG agents invited us to forward to them any ideas we formulated about avoiding a violent outcome and resolving the crisis peaceably. In May and June we studied the Justus Freemen's sectarian views and assessed their potential for violence. We applied provisional knowledge derived from former cases to an unfolding, volatile situation, tapped other sources of data, and pooled our resources.[7] Michael Barkun[8] and Phillip Arnold were given access to Freemen videos, tapes, and documents.[9] Years later important differences between religious studies scholars and FBI analysts still remained despite our fruitful collaboration during the Montana crisis. Catherine Wessinger observed, "As we have expressed to each other on a number of occasions, it is increasingly apparent that the FBI once again is overlooking the religious dimension to this case. . . . The challenge here . . . is to convince FBI and Justice that religion, a religious worldview with [an] ultimate goal, has to be dealt with in order to resolve the standoff" (personal communication, Oct. 3, 1996).

In the fall of 1996, I submitted an early draft of this paper to CIRG for peer review. Mindful that internal sources of information may contain

7. I am indebted to Linda Collette, Paul de Armond, David Niewert, and Professors Michael Barkun, David C. Rapoport, and S. Scott Bartchy, with whom I communicated during the standoff.

8. A leading expert on Christian Identity, Prof. Michael Barkun, was also consulted by the FBI between April 8 and June 13, 1996.

9. CIRG at first promised me data they did not send.

sensitive material, I have limited my citations in this account to sources in the public domain, except for one interview. A preponderance of data supports my argument in this chapter that knowledge about the singular characteristics of religiously motivated groups contributed significantly to a nonviolent outcome in the Freemen case.

On June 13, 1996, FBI Director Louis Freeh thanked "all who aided the quest for a peaceful solution" including "outside experts" (CNN "Breaking News" 1996, 21), but news accounts of how the crisis was settled failed to mention the religion factor (*Billings Gazette Online* June 22, 1996). *If we are to construct a body of knowledge that may be applied to prevent or resolve any future confrontation between a new religious movement and the state, we need to know why and how the analysis of religion serves as a useful technique for ameliorating such critical incidents.* The analysis of religion was not heeded at Waco (Tabor and Gallagher 1995, 4-5, 13-14, 217 n.28; Carstarphen 1995). It was requested and used at Jordan.

## Yahweh's Barrier

Federal negotiators were unaware that religion motivates people to act differently from con men and hostage takers. On the assumption that those who had engaged in criminal fraud were not religious, negotiators asked religious studies experts to divide the individuals on the ranch into those who were religious and those who were not. A Freeman they labeled a "scam artist" told Bo Gritz[10] that "Yahweh has placed an invisible barrier around this sanctuary that foreign enemies cannot penetrate."[11] Based upon the following analysis of that statement, I replied that all were taking a religious position of ultimacy and might defend it to the death. Ultimacy, expressed as an ultimate concern or goal, is what human beings live their lives by and express willingness to die for

The use of God's holy name, Yahweh, revealed that the Freemen worship the warrior God of Exodus, who accompanied his people to the promised land. Yahweh is a celestial deity. Just as sky gods dispense divine laws to govern a new world, so the Freemen dedicated themselves

---

10. Bo Gritz founded "Almost Heaven," a Christian Patriot community in Idaho. He was the running mate of klansman David Duke during Duke's 1988 campaign for president.

11. Alternatively reported as "Yahweh has placed an invisible barrier around their sanctuary that no more enemies can penetrate" (AP News Online, May 1, 1996).

to replacing United States law with their Common Law to establish a theocratic polity of local townships. The Freemen accepted the doctrine of antigovernment Constitutionalists[12] and the theology of the "two-seedline" Christian Identity movement.[13] They believed that Common Law "pursuant to the Word of Almighty God" is Yahweh's divinely instituted law (Skurdal 1994, 1).

The Freemen were acting as if Yahweh's "invisible barrier" separated them from a sinful world and guaranteed them immunity from harm, much like some Native American ghost dancers believed their ritual would shield them from bullets. Nativists seek to separate their land and people from alien, that is, enemy, influences. Setting boundaries around native ground is a religious act (Douglas 1996). Inside "Yahweh's barrier" Rodney Skurdal was spreading the Freemen gospel by mean of the Internet and shortwave radio.

The choice of the word "sanctuary" for the Clark ranch marked it as a sacred place where Yahweh dwelt. A sanctuary shelters those who flee from pursuers, and trespassers risk God's punishment at his hand or at the hands of sanctuary guardians.

The "foreign enemies" referred to the evil power of Baal (Satan), who is struggling with the power of God for dominance over the world, according to Skurdal's "Edict." The Freemen identified themselves with Elijah in 1 Kings 18:17–40, who battled and executed the 450 prophets of Baal—who symbolized U.S. "public servants," "state legislators," and "our so-called congress" (Skurdal 1994, 10). Cosmic and ethical dualism—the division of the cosmos into good and evil factions and influences—is a formal feature of apocalyptic movements.

Because the Freemen had retreated to a sanctuary guarded by Yahweh, we advised CIRG that they were likely to respond violently to any move across the perimeter that separated them from federal agents. We emphasized that all of the twenty-one Freemen were acting as a persecuted religious group. Some of those charged with criminal complaints had been members of the Church of Jesus Christ of the Latter-day Saints, a persecuted sect that fled to Utah Territory in the nineteenth century—a pattern replicated by Freemen, who retreated to the Clark ranch. Skurdal believed that his ancestors had left the Jordan River in

12. Constitutionalists generally acknowledge the legitimacy of only the pre-Civil War form of the United States Constitution.

13. "Two-seedline" Christian Identity religion teaches that the white race descended from Adam, but Jews are the "spawn of Satan," with whom Eve mated to produce Cain.

ancient Palestine to found Denmark (Skurdal 1994, 6), and it was likely that Jordan, Montana, connoted the ancestral homeland. Migration to its symbolic center of the world is sometimes undertaken by a millenarian group.

## The Specter of Waco

Catherine Wessinger advised the FBI in early April that there was a "millennial component" in the Freemen worldview. In May CIRG asked religious studies scholars if the Justus Freemen were an apocalyptic group. Behind their question lingered the specter of Waco, the concern that the Freemen would meet tactical pressure with force or commit suicide rather than surrender.

In fact, there were significant differences between the Justus Freemen and the Mount Carmel Davidians, an offshoot of the Seventh-day Adventist church, whose prophet, David Koresh, believed he was the "Lamb of God" of the New Testament book of Revelation. Koresh was reading signs of an imminent end of the world and anticipated persecution for interpreting the Seven Seals described in Revelation. Christianity teaches that the world will end violently at a time known only to God, but Koresh was convinced the time was at hand. Unlike the Davidians, the Freemen did not follow a single charismatic leader. The Freemen believed a heterodox interpretation of biblical prophecy that teaches followers they will endure a time called the Tribulation that precedes the final war before God's thousand-year kingdom is established on earth. Unlike the Davidians, the Freemen did not appear to be reading signs for the end of the world. In early May 1996 there was little evidence that the Freemen expected an imminent apocalypse, although we noted unsettling references to "the last days" in Freemen writings. However, by setting up Common Law courts, juries, and townships, the Freemen were symbolically transforming the quotidian world into a Bible-based polity.

Studies of millennialism tend to focus on prophet-led groups, but not all movements belong to the same type. When a charismatic prophet like Koresh claims divine authority, we can evaluate his movement's propensity for violence by noting if the mythical figure he emulates is violent or peaceable.[14] In a decentralized movement, violence may be committed

14. Koresh took the name of Cyrus the Great, a benefactor who released the Jews from captivity, while Eleazar ben Jair, the first-century leader of the Jews at Masada, emulated Phinehas, the proponent of holy war.

by rogue leaders and may be less foreseeable. During the standoff, Leroy Schweitzer was in jail, where he initiated a hunger strike (Pitcavage 1996). Cofounder Rod Skurdal remained inside the perimeter, but no single Freeman assumed the authority to negotiate with the FBI until early June.

## Con Artists

Although the FBI's assessment of the Freemen as criminals and hostage-takers did not waver, CIRG adhered to its new policy of time and caution. The misconception that "con artists" cannot be religious derives from the conventional wisdom that religion is intrinsically good and would not allow followers to endanger their children, undermine the government, sanction mass suicide, or teach that "racial mixing" is a capital offense. Some FBI analysts argued that intransigent, seditious, or violent behavior did not qualify as religiously motivated behavior. However, *religion is, among other things, a construction of ultimate reality by means of an elaborate, self-consistent system of interpretation that is regarded as absolute truth.* Religion may justify almost any behavior, and millennialists follow higher laws that claim to supersede all other ideas of morality (Rapoport 1988, 202).

## Catastrophic Millennialists

FBI agents believed the diverse individuals inside the perimeter had little in common. Scholars disagreed, and set about finding out if all of them were equally committed to defending their position to the death. For a closer look at the Justus Freemen, on May 29, 1996, I spoke to a pastor in the town of Jordan who had ministered to the Freemen before and during the early part of the standoff.

The pastor's report of the Freemen's shared beliefs contributed to our growing understanding of them as millennialists. They had told the pastor that only Justus Township followed God's law, and the whole world needed to convert to their creed. Between fall 1995 and spring 1996 about seven hundred people had come from all over America to attend Freemen seminars at the Clark ranch. They were advised to return with weapons if government officials threatened the Freemen.[15] The men

15. On May 3, 1996, AP News Online reported from the Spokane *Spokesman-Review* that "A nationwide FBI alert is warning of a militia extremist plan to wage war on the government and the media if the Freemen are attacked."

and women at the ranch spoke of this time as the advent of God's millennial kingdom, proclaiming, "This is heaven. We have established God's law on earth. This is what heaven is." The Freemen celebrated the growth of their movement, boasting that "Common Law is established all over the country already." They wore guns, had gas masks, and talked about violence. Many had sacrificed their possessions by refusing to pay taxes or support usury (a biblical injunction) by paying interest on federal loans. In behavior reminiscent of Melanesian "cargo cults," whose members abandoned ordinary activities to wait for ships or planes bearing material goods, the Justus Freemen laid claim to surrounding federal lands, and set up a "bank" that issued checks and paper currency. They expected a "Jubilee," a time when all debts would be canceled and every "true Israelite" would benefit from a redistribution of property. The pastor described the Freemen as "the latest incarnation of the Posse Comitatus,"[16] a Christian Identity movement that originated around 1969 and advocated a "theocratic and radically decentralized" new government (Barkun 1994, 222). The pastor's observations placed the Freemen worldview in Catherine Wessinger's category of "catastrophic millennialism":

> Catastrophic millennialism is the belief that God (or a superhuman agent) will destroy the hopelessly sinful world in order to subsequently create the kingdom of God on earth. In this earthly salvation, the limitations (the "fallenness") of the human condition will be overcome. Catastrophic millennialism involves a pessimistic view of human nature. Humanity is so evil, that it must be destroyed except for a remnant of the righteous elect, who will enjoy the earthly salvation. The catastrophe is the necessary preliminary to the establishment of the millennial kingdom. (E-mail, Oct. 3, 1996)

Thus, by May 29 the Freemen appeared to be an apocalyptic religious group, even though they differed from the Branch Davidians. *Each millenarian sect has its own myth, which must be understood on its own terms before one can assess whether or not it may resort to aggression or defensive violence.*

16. Daniel Levitas traced the origins of the Common Law court movement to Henry Lamont "Mike" Beach's "Blue Book" in the late 1960s. Beach founded the Posse Comitatus (Burghart and Crawford 1996, 2, 3).

## Patriot Intermediaries

For five days (April 27–May 1) two Christian Patriot leaders, Jack McLamb and Bo Gritz, were allowed inside the perimeter to negotiate with Freemen as third-party intermediaries, but their efforts failed despite the FBI's willingness to make concessions. Between May 15 and May 21 Colorado state senator and Christian Patriot (AP News Online REF5977, May 22, 1996) Charles Duke initiated face-to-face negotiations between FBI agents and Freemen that ended in stalemate and the brandishing of guns on May 21. Duke vented his frustration to the press, urging, "The time for negotiations is over. . . . They need to feel some pain" (REF5261, June 6, 1996).

The Christian Patriot movement includes diverse groups—Freemen among them—that believe the United States government has been taken over by forces that plot to undermine individual freedom and Christian civilization.[17] If Gritz, McLamb, and Duke were Christian Patriots like the Freemen, why did their mediation efforts fail? One possible reason is that a movement that tolerates the autonomy of local leaders is often beset with internecine squabbles. Duke, Gritz, and McLamb may have considered the Freemen's activism a liability to their own goals (Paul de Armond, personal communication). In 1995, for example, after moving toward collaboration, the Justus Freemen and the Militia of Montana had a falling out, perhaps because Freemen offenses provoked too much law enforcement attention.

## Millennialism, Apocalypticism, and Violence

Even after concluding that the Freemen were millennialists, the religious studies scholars needed time to decipher their precise worldview, especially after negotiations broke down on May 21 and the FBI pondered taking more aggressive action. An independent researcher assessed the Freemen as bullies who would quickly fold under the pressure of a tactical assault. Robert Crawford of the Coalition for Human Dignity warned that the Freemen were expecting "an Armageddon to establish this white Christian republic." A police siege consultant advised swift action to end a standoff that was becoming "more volatile every day," because "a peaceful ending is less likely the longer it drags on" (AP News

17. The forces may be one or more of the following: Jews, bankers, judges, Catholics, secret societies, the United Nations, their sympathizers.

Online REF5443, Apr. 3, 1996). In fact, this standoff proved that *it was time and patience, not dynamic intervention, that enabled the FBI to devise a peaceful resolution that the Freemen would accept.*

An expectation of the apocalypse is not sufficient cause for a group to engage in violence. The facile presumption that any apocalyptic sect intends murder and mayhem may encourage tactical intervention by law enforcement agents that could trigger armed defense or group suicide. *To assess whether or not catastrophic millennialists will resort to violence, one must determine from their writings, communications, and behavior what role they believe they are called to play at the end of time.*

Historical studies of millennial groups support the hypothesis that they fall into at least three types that vary in their propensities for violence: (1) groups that believe that the imminent and total transformation of the world will take place only if the "elect" bring it about through a deliberate, violent strategy (Rapoport 1988); (2) groups that believe that there will be a cosmic war, but their mission is to wait and watch as supernatural forces fight the battle; and (3) groups that believe they must separate from mainstream society and institute a divinely sanctioned polity in a designated place.[18] Type 1—groups that *intend* violence—are the most rare and dangerous. Typical of type 2 are the early Christians who believed that their role at the end time was to wait and watch, not fight. Type 3 millennialists may also believe their assignment is to watch and wait, unless they are directly assaulted by "satanic" forces. They may fight to the last person, because they trust that the outcome must be part of God's divine plan. Type 3 groups, such as the Branch Davidians, are on their guard, and like a coiled snake will attack if provoked.

After the breakdown in negotiations on May 21 in Montana, the question, Is this an apocalyptic group? prompted another: And, if so, is it likely to respond violently to *any* tactical initiative? This was a vital question because after May 21 the FBI was considering shutting off electricity to the ranch and displaying their tactical superiority.

At this low point in late May we recommended that religious studies scholars go to Jordan to assess the Freemen's potential response to FBI pressure. CIRG invited Michael Barkun and Phillip Arnold on site. Although Barkun was out of the country, he continued to communicate with CIRG. Arnold went to Montana and spoke to negotiators and

---

18. This typology does not cover all possible permutations; a group may mutate from one type to another.

Freemen family members during the tensest part of the standoff. He also kept in touch with colleagues.

## The Religion Factor

Ultimacy is a formal feature of religion (Tillich 1957, 1–4). The religious studies scholars agreed that the Freemen were motivated by an "ultimate concern" that they lived by and would die for: eliminating the allegedly illegitimate, "satanic" United States government and replacing it with the Common Law, biblical rule of Yahweh. As a condition of settlement, the Freemen insisted at the outset that they be allowed to present their voluminous evidence against the government before a "grand jury" of their "peers." Phillip Arnold cautioned negotiators that if they analyzed the Freemen's behavior solely as a means to the ends of money, power, or ego, they would be out of step with the Freemen's perception of reality. *He observed that it is the story (myth or worldview) as a whole that determines a group's actions and that the FBI should factor the Freemen's worldview into a settlement.* Thus, we strongly advised that any agreement would have to take the Freemen's ultimate concern into account. We were unaware at this time that the CAUSE Foundation had proposed a similar approach to the FBI in April (N. H. Payne 1996, 1-3). CAUSE is an acronym for Canada, Australia, United States, South Africa, and England—all countries that until recently were ruled by northern European populations that Christian Identity religion regards as "true Israelites." The Southern Poverty Law Center, which opposes white supremacists, listed CAUSE in 1995 as a "hate group." The CAUSE Foundation describes itself as "an international civil rights legal foundation that defends the rights of the unpopular, the powerless, and the politically incorrect" (AP News Online June 11, 1996).

While FBI personnel on site in Montana continued to assess the twenty-one individuals in terms of behavioral psychology, we searched Freemen writings for clues to what was uppermost in their minds. The most worrisome problem was how to facilitate the departure of three children inside Justus Township. Catherine Wessinger suggested that the memory of Waco focused the attention of CIRG on the fate of innocents inside the barrier; their safety was uppermost in everyone's minds.

Gloria Teneuvial Ward, mother of two little girls, and her common law husband, Elwin Ward, had arrived at the ranch in January 1996, seeking help from LeRoy Schweitzer. Gloria had violated a court custody order by taking two of her daughters out of Utah to join the Freemen.

Elwin Ward was a charismatic Christian who trusted in revelations from God to guide his important decisions.[19] Gloria grew up in a polygamous household and had joined a Mormon sect called the House of Chaney. Although the FBI thought the children were being kept on the ranch against their will, we believed that Gloria had backed down from an earlier agreement to leave with the girls because she was waiting for spiritual guidance from her jailed pastor, John Perry Chaney.[20] Thus, we advised that if the Wards could be convinced that *God* wanted them to exit the ranch, they would leave.

Phillip Arnold discussed Gloria's dependence on her religion at length with her sister, Lynn Nielsen, and Nielsen appealed to Gloria's pastor, who then wrote to the Wards conveying that "he had a revelation she should not stay with the Freemen" (AP News Online REF5526, June 7, 1996). On June 6, one week before the final settlement, Gloria received Chaney's letter, and the Wards immediately left the ranch with the two girls. Charles Duke called this the "turning point," believing that "that success convinced [Edwin] Clark to press the others to surrender" (CNN "Daybreak" June 17, 1996, transcript #1421 Segment #1). A few days later sixteen-year-old Ashley Taylor left Justus Township, and the Freemen reengaged in talks with the FBI that resulted in a peaceful resolution.

Only a month earlier, we had seen scant possibility that the Freemen would exit without violence. On June 6 violence still could have erupted had the FBI tried to end the standoff by tactical means. Neighbors in Jordan had gathered two hundred signatures urging the use of "reasonable force," while militia leader John Trochmann was quoted as saying that militias would rush to the Freemen's defense if the FBI took forceful action (AP News Online REF5511, June 6, 1966).

### Discerning the Leader

After the standoff ended on June 13, the FBI acknowledged the key role played by Edwin Clark in brokering a resolution. FBI negotiator Dr. Dwayne Fuselier told the press that during the talks in early May, he

---

19. James Aho (1990, 53, 177) determined that fundamentalist Christians provided a disproportionate number of recruits to Christian Identity in Idaho.

20. Chaney was awaiting trial in Utah on charges of aiding and abetting, and conspiracy to commit the rape of a child (AP News Online, June 29, 1996); his sect practiced marriage between adult men and underage girls.

noticed "after eight or nine meetings that Clark wanted a nonviolent resolution." But after the talks blew up and the Freemen refused to answer the telephone, the FBI decided on a "show of force" by cutting off power to the ranch and moving up armored personnel carriers in order to bring them back to the negotiating table (*Billings Gazette Online* June 23, 1996).

During this stalemate Phillip Arnold spoke at length to Edwin Clark's wife, Janet, who was going to and from Justus Township to administer medicine to their son, Casey. A CIRG agent suggested that a meeting between the Clarks and the FBI be set up in a church. "Beginning on June 5, Fuselier and other FBI negotiators met with Edwin and Janet Clark at a church building outside the Freemen compound. Clark told the FBI he believed there could be a peaceful resolution to the standoff"(*Billings Gazette Online* June 23, 1996). The Clarks' willingness to meet was potentiated by more than the show of force. Janet probably appealed to Edwin to help their son by ending the crisis. I believe the value of the analysis of religion in ending the standoff was confirmed by the results of Phillip Arnold's outreach to Lynn Nielson and Janet Clark, which Dr. Fuselier's account did not mention.

The FBI did not really gauge the depth of the Clarks' attachment to their land. After Bo Gritz reported in a *New York Times* interview (May 18, 1996) that Edwin Clark "broke down in tears as he poured out his heart full of troubles," I recommended that CIRG approach him as one of two potential leaders.

> He explained how hard they had worked the land, only to come up short, Mr. Gritz recalled the 45-year-old Vietnam veteran saying. The Freemen system of printing up bogus money orders "offered the only hope to cling to what four generations had sweat [*sic*] and bled to keep." For almost 15 years, Mr. Clark's father, Ralph, had fought off creditors, finally losing the farm in . . . 1994.

On June 5 Janet Clark drove Edwin about a mile off the ranch to meet with FBI agents (AP News Online June 6, 1996). He insisted on consulting LeRoy Schweitzer, and the FBI flew Edwin and three CAUSE lawyers on June 11 to Billings, where Schweitzer approved a "five-point agreement for resolution of the standoff" (Payne 1996, 2). FBI acceptance of Edwin's request to consult with Schweitzer allowed the Freemen to maintain their commitment to their ultimate concern (to demonstrate the alleged illegitimacy of the federal government and to replace it with a God-centered rule), while modifying their initial stance that they were "prepared to die" if necessary to "spread their message." They had at first insisted upon presenting their evidence before a "grand jury of Freemen sympathizers" (AP News Online REF5283, June 13, 1996).[21] In the final settlement the Freemen instead agreed to argue their case against the federal government in United States courtrooms (REF5460, June 14, 1996).

### Grievance Factors

What tended to get lost in the heat of the encounter were the Freemen's "legitimate grievances" (Berlet 1994, 26), which marked them as a nativist movement, one that seeks to defend a cherished territory and way of life from a perceived invasion of alien powers. Although scholars associate nativist movements with nonwhite peoples, Christian Patriots and South African Boers are also nativists.

According to Christine Kaufmann of the Montana Human Rights Network, more than one hundred thousand family farms had failed or been auctioned off in America since the mid-1980s (personal communication).[22] Largely unperceived in the politically powerful urban centers of the United States, these losses affected thousands of rural towns. Several of the Justus Freemen—the Clarks, William L. Stanton, Rodney Skurdal, and LeRoy Schweitzer—had their properties confiscated or threatened with confiscation for nonpayment of debt or taxes.

Historically, eastern Montana has been a difficult zone for farming. Enticed by the railroad and the government, which painted a rosy picture of cheap land and new beginnings, families who homesteaded along the tracks laid across Montana's drought-plagued plains had left the land in despair (Raban 1996, 60–81). Thus, Garfield County inhabitants were predisposed to be suspicious of the federal government and corporate enterprises, and Freemen ideology struck a resonant chord. Some members of the Clark family became Freemen while other members opposed them. *Like many new religions seeking converts, wherever the Common Law movement took hold, it exacerbated existing tensions and polarized society.*

---

21. The Justus Freemen wanted to protect their "massive collection of evidence" against the government that they were guarding with their lives, said Peter K. Stern, who tried to intervene before the electricity was shut down. Stern is a member of a North Carolina Common Law group (Stern June 3, 1996).

22. A causal linkage between the United States farm crisis and the rise of antigovernment movements is asserted in Joel Dyer's *Harvest of Rage* (Westview Press, 1997).

Many Americans believe that the Freemen brought catastrophe upon themselves by refusing to pay their debts. From the Freemen's dualist perspective, the religious imperative of separating themselves from a government that allegedly violated the higher laws of God leads logically to noncompliance with United States law.

## The Freemen as a Religious Sect

To become a Freeman, one completes a rite of passage by filing a "Quiet Title" or "affadavit" at the county courthouse. A Quiet Title is a declaration of independence from the United States of America and a renunciation of its jurisdiction over oneself, one's offspring, and land (Burghart and Crawford 1996, 7; Ward 1996, 6). It is "sealed" by one's fingerprint. The Quiet Title is analogous to the rite of baptism; as one's old self "dies," a new self arises in its place.

The Freemen call themselves "Characters" to emphasize that they are not "citizens" or "persons"—designations routinely used in legal documents they repudiate as fraudulent (Ward 1996, 7). This peculiar dogma inhibited negotiation during the standoff, for the Freemen did not acknowledge the legal standing of the FBI or its warrants.

Revitalization movements, whether they are millenarian, nativist, or messianic (Wallace 1956, 264–81), anticipate the total transformation of the world. Their symbolic expressions vary, but they offer a means of salvation from humiliation and despair. The myth and prophecy summarized in the "Edict" identified the present as a time of tribulation for the white race in America. Whites fear that they are being supplanted by immigrants and minorities whose numbers and influence are increasing. Christian Identity adherents feel dislocated and colonized in their own land. They express a territorial imperative, believing that Yahweh gave to them, the true descendents of the tribes of Israel, the promised land of North America (Skurdal 1994, 11).

In 1995 Freemen-style Common Law courts were set up in at least seventeen states (Burghart and Crawford 1996, 27–38). Skurdal flooded the courts of Montana with "liens" against public officials who attempted to foreclose on his property in Roundup and urged his followers to cash drafts that he issued against those liens. Although local magistrates regarded this "paper warfare" as frivolous, it tied up the courts and forced public officials to spend time and money defending themselves against Freemen legal maneuvers. The Freemen spread their faith via computer, shortwave radio, and seminars attended by hundreds of individuals seeking a means of saving themselves from economic distress. By the time the FBI surrounded the Clark ranch, Freemen tactics were spreading rapidly throughout the United States. How could the FBI, perceived as an arm of the repudiated United States government, entice the Justus group out of its sanctuary and into the hated courts of "de facto" judges clothed in the *"color of darkness, Satan's colors"* (Skurdal 1994, 13)?

## Mediating a Resolution

The CAUSE Foundation first contacted the FBI in late March and at the FBI's invitation had drafted a proposal for resolving the standoff (Payne 1996, 1). Their initiative was revisited by the FBI on May 28 when CAUSE attorneys were enlisted to craft an agreement that entrusted Montana State Representative Karl Ohs with the Freemen's documentary evidence against the "de facto" United States. Karl Ohs had "acted as a mediator" (AP News Online REF 5384, June 13, 1996) throughout the standoff. Unlike Gritz, McLamb, and Duke, Ohs maintained a requisite critical distance from any personal or political agenda while simultaneously understanding the Freemen's perspective. All other settlement initiatives failed, we believe, because they did not acknowledge the paramount importance of the Freemen's ultimate concern: *that they be heard in a setting where they and they alone could present their case before the country without compromising their observance of God's laws.* According to the CAUSE Foundation, after LeRoy Schweitzer decided "it was time to take this fight to the courts," the final agreement was adopted (Payne 1996, 2). The agreement stipulated that Representative Ohs would be given protective custody of the Freemen's legal documentary evidence and that any Freeman who wished attorney representation would retain 51 percent control of his or her case with cocounsel (*Billings Gazette Online,* June 19, 1996). In other words, the Freemen were assured that they could control their presentation of evidence in court. Consistent with their establishment of Common Law institutions at Justus Township, after they left the ranch, the Freemen have challenged the federal courts' jurisdiction in their cases on the grounds that they are governed solely by Common Law (Roots 1996, 1, 6).

Their behavior is not delusional, but magical. The Freemen regard symbolic words and acts as efficacious means that bring a new world into being. Filing legal documents and writing drafts against a fund allegedly derived from liens against local magistrates is a kind of magical activity.[23] The written word in Freemen documents is sacred; diacritical marks, capitalized words, boldfaced type, and underlined portions possess the power to create a new reality. Only by knowing what their doctrines teach—that only Common Law courts may legitimately exercise their jurisdiction over Freemen "Characters"—can one contextualize their behavior and use this knowledge to defuse a critical incident.

The Justus Freemen seemed impervious to rational offers to reduce criminal charges if they would surrender. Bo Gritz reported they had taken an "oath to God" not to leave the ranch (AP News Online May 1, 1996). The FBI moved carefully and persistently. Unlike the initial engagement between the Bureau of Alcohol, Tobacco, and Firearms personnel and the Branch Davidians, the Freemen standoff began without casualties. The FBI's problem after the May 21 stalemate was how to reestablish communication with the Freemen and conduct a fruitful negotiation. Phillip Arnold advised that the Freemen had to feel that any agreement would preserve their dignity. For eighty-one days the Freemen bore witness to their gospel from the Clark ranch. Only after CAUSE attorneys drafted terms that permitted them to represent themselves in court did the Freemen exit. From the Freemen's viewpoint, they did not surrender to "Satan." FBI negotiators, whether or not they realize it, factored the Freemen's ultimate concern into the final resolution, as religious studies experts had advised.

Terms of settlement included the promise that felonious custodial interference charges against Gloria Ward would be dropped and that the Freemen could defend themselves in court (AP News Online REF5099, June 25, 1996). Ward later lost custody of her children after a Utah court refused to accede to the terms (REF5749, June 9, 1996). Elwin Ward was not allowed to choose someone other than an attorney to advise him in his own defense (REF5371, June 25, 1996). Objecting to the federal court's jurisdiction, sixteen Freemen disrupted their hearings with appeals to Common Law, prompting the judge to remove them to holding cells where they watched on closed-circuit televisions while court-appointed attorneys represented them.

## Symbolic Expression

Media coverage of the Freemen's departure from Justus Township showcased the religious significance of numbers and dates. On June 13

---

23. Catherine Wessinger made this observation.

CAUSE attorneys Kirk Lyons and Lourie Salley removed an American flag the Freemen had flown upside down as a "distress signal"[24] to the outside world since May 21, and replaced it with a thirteen-star Confederate flag from the ranch schoolroom. Lyons and Salley explained that "to those in the know, the raising of the Confederate battle flag sent a signal that the CAUSE team had been successful. It meant that everyone would be coming out" (Payne 1966, 3). CNN reported that "a Freeman" had called their station to say that the flag symbolized the "tribe of Jacob, one of the tribes of Israel [*sic*]" and that there were "13 tribes of Israel" (CNN "Breaking News" 1996, 20)

"The number 13 has great significance to the Identity movement and to the right wing groups," observed Prof. Allen D. Sapp (1986, 25). According to Christian Identity doctrine, Moses led thirteen tribes out of Egypt, and the thirteenth tribe of Manassah imigrated to the American colonies, where on July 4, 1776, Yahweh's allotted "punishment time" for their sins expired (6, 7). *The change of flags on June 13, 1996, signaled the triumph of the thirteenth tribe, the "true Israelite" Freemen ancestors who fought for American independence, to their supporters outside the ranch.*

The ritual commemoration of sacred dates is a formal feature of religion. An adversarial sect's dependence on symbolic expression can provide civil authorities with exploitable opportunities to combat their activities (Rapoport 1984). Phillip Arnold had wondered what dates the Freemen held sacred, aware that they might favor a specific date for exiting the ranch (Arnold, personal communication).

While investigating possible origins of Skurdal's ideology, I chanced on the importance of the number 13 in the "Nehemiah Township Charter," a document filed by a coalition of Christian Identity leaders at an Idaho courthouse on July 12, 1982, to claim land for the Aryan Nations in Kootenai County (Floyd Cochran, personal communication). Its call for a "National Jury" of "thirteen of our own Judges in the [white Christian] Nation from our many communities" also helped set the Freemen's "grand jury" demand in the larger context of the Christian Identity movement.

The Freemen's legal and financial schemes may have been prompted by Article 14 of the Charter, which advocated a renewal of an archaic Germanic system of *wergild*, a compensation paid by a killer to the

---

24. Christian Identity proselytizers have used the upended flag to attract the attention of potential recruits.

victim's family to atone for his crime and avoid reprisals. In the Nehemiah Township Charter *wergild* referred to compensation owed by one who violated the rights of a freeman.

> Every white freeman shall have a WERGILD to be held against the world and all individuals and entities at large including juristic and corporate ones. . . . The Wergild shall be enforced after mere violation of a right, absence of damages notwithstanding. . . . All State, Federal, local, municipal, and foreign employees, agents, grantees, etc. shall be subject to trials in our own Common Law Courts for damages arising out of their personal, professional, and/or official duties, acts and omissions. (quoted in Sapp 1986, 3 of 4)

Freemen threats against public officials and their filing of "liens" for millions of dollars in compensation for the "acts and omissions" of magistrates, judges, sheriffs, and county attorneys are consistent with the *wergild* provision of the Nehemiah Township Charter.

## The Social Context of the Freemen Movement

An avowed determination to establish Yahweh's rule is espoused by a sizeable cohort of disaffected Americans, many of whom are sophisticated in the use of weapons and electronic technology. Tax protesters, militiamen, Constitutionalists, and Common Law advocates believe that they have been dislocated from their position in the world relative to women, minorities, and immigrants. In their eyes, the traditional boundaries that separated women and men, minorities and whites, urban and rural dwellers, homosexuals and heterosexuals, public lands and private property, employees and corporate executives have been violated with impunity by liberals, feminists, environmentalists, and public officials. They are convinced that the culture of white, Christian, rural, working, male Americans is declining precipitously. Holding on to their slipping position, their dignity, and their voice seems less possible than ever. They perceive themselves as forced to relinquish their privacy, property, guns, jobs, and roles—in sum, all that defines their lives—in a lethal submission to the humiliations of history.

## Provisional Conclusions

Based on data revealed about the Freemen movement during and after the "critical incident," one may conclude that they are a potentially violent subset of Christian Identity religion; this judgment should be tempered by the observation that their paper assault on civil authority has been magical and nonviolent,[25] in marked contrast to the physical assaults of rogue terrorist groups.

Like the earlier Posse Comitatus movement, the Justus Freemen intended to establish theocratic rule by white, Christian males at the county (township) level. They recruited those who felt persecuted by government, teaching them how to renounce their citizenship. Believing that Yahweh's thousand-year kingdom on earth would restore their privileged status as his chosen people, they awaited a war between "God's children" and "the Corporate United States (a bankrupt nation which has enslaved all Americans by fraudulent purposes)" (Ward 1996).

Christian Identity religion exhibits an intense nostalgia for the antebellum South's devotion to a time when women deferred to their husbands' authority over holdings and chattel. Identity adherents' nativist doctrine draws upon a mythic construction of the past to reorder the present and ensure their preeminent position in Christ's millennial kingdom. Identity Christians appear willing to witness to their beliefs (become martyrs) and die for them.

Understanding a given millenarian movement's symbolic expressions of myth, practice, time, and space helps us ascertain whether or not and under what conditions it will engage in violence. The analysis of a group's apocalyptic myth helps us understand what they perceive their role to be in the endtime. Millenarians set up a counterworld with borders and rules that challenge civil law and prevailing conventions. New religious movements are frequently derided as "cults," whose "bizarre" behavior and "rambling" discourse are indecipherable, but, in fact, their theologies are usually systematic and coherent. *Because most millennial movements are not aggressive, we need to attain a level of knowledge about them that will enable us to identify with greater precision the few that promote violence and terror, keeping in mind that over time even the most threatening movements may become benign.* Many Patriot groups are convinced that a New World Order—a global, Jewish/United Nations conspiracy—already commands the Zionist Occupation Government (ZOG) of the United States. Because they expect a war between good and evil powers to break out, "two-seedline" Christian Identity groups should be approached with great caution.

25. They were suspected of plotting to kidnap officials and issued verbal threats, but did not carry them out.

The foregoing argument from evidence in the public domain confirms that an analytic understanding of the religion that motivates catastrophic millennialists facilitated a nonviolent outcome of the Justus Freemen standoff. At Jordan, Montana, the use of outside experts in religion, trustworthy intermediaries, and a patient new policy resulted in a peaceful ending of "the longest armed siege in modern U. S. history" (AP News Online REF5384, June 13, 1996).

## Part Five

## Implications for Law Enforcement

# 16

# A Brief History of Millennialism and Suggestions for a New Paradigm for Use in Critical Incidents

## A Presentation to the Los Angeles Police Department

JEAN E. ROSENFELD ⎯⎯⎯⎯⎯⎯⎯⎯⎯⎯⎯⎯⎯⎯⎯⎯⎯

Millennialism is a belief in the archaic myth of a total transformation of the ordinary world into a golden age of peace and justice.[1] It may be found in various religious traditions around the world as well as in Christianity. The word "millennium" is Latin and refers to the Roman division of history into thousand-year periods. Jews and Christians in the Roman world conceived of these millennia as a set of seven or a "week" of ages, and of the final age as a "Sabbath rest." The last book of the Christian Bible, the Apocalypse or Revelation, prophesied that after the world is purged at the end of history, the resurrected saints will be incorporated into the Millennium, Christ's thousand-year kingdom on earth. The approach of dates that mark the end or beginning of a thousand-year period may stimulate the formation of religious movements that expect a divine cleansing and renewal of society.

1. This summary derives from the paradigmatic understanding of religions in the work of Joachim Wach, Gerardus van der Leeuw, and Mircea Eliade, as well as that of Bernard McGinn, Paul Tillich, Kees W. Bolle, Anthony F. C. Wallace, Michael Barkun, David C. Rapoport, S. Scott Bartchy, Jayne S. Docherty, Ian Reader, and Thomas Robbins.

*Apocalypsis* is a Greek word that means "veiled" or "hidden." An apocalypse was a written text that revealed in code or symbols what would happen in the last days. The Hebrew Bible, or Old Testament, also contains an apocalypse, chapters 7–12 in the book of Daniel. There are references throughout the Bible to a "day of the Lord," a "jubilee," and a time of "tribulation" that Christian churches and sects have associated with the Millennium. Followers of millennial groups often are intensely involved in interpreting apocalyptic texts in esoteric ways that appear bizarre, but are quite systematic.

Millennial groups in the United States may organize their lives around the expectation that the world is about to be totally transformed. Convinced that a divine or abstract Power controls all events both great and intimate, they believe that God intervenes directly in their lives through manifestations and signs that only the spiritually chosen or purified can correctly interpret. Besides waiting for the final age of peace and justice, Christian groups expect a messiah to rule over the Millennium.

The word *messiah* means "anointed one," or king. All the kings of Israel who ruled before Babylon destroyed the first temple in Jerusalem in 586–87 B.C. were messiahs anointed by the Lord through a priest or prophet. The first non-Jewish messiah in the Old Testament was Cyrus the Great of Persia, who liberated the Jews from captivity in Babylon. Branch Davidian leader Vernon Howell adopted the names of two biblical messiahs, David and Cyrus, to become "David Koresh."

Christianity began as a messianic movement that proclaimed that Jesus of Nazareth was the risen anointed one who would return in the final age to save the saints after the good news of resurrection had been preached to all people on earth. In the book of Revelation, Christ as the figure of the Lamb of God opens up Seven Seals on a scroll that release plagues and terrors upon the entire world. The Seven Seals also represent the seven periods in the final age that lead up to the culminating event of world transformation.

Millennialism, apocalypticism, and messianism are related phenomena in Christianity, the parent religion of many new millennial movements, some of which, such as the Seventh-day Adventists, the Latter-day Saints, and Roman Catholicism, have evolved into established churches that expect the Millennium at an unspecified future time.

Christianity's latent millennial doctrines may become reactivated when there is societal upheaval or confusing changes. For example, in the fifth century A.D. after Rome was sacked by Germanic tribes, St. Augustine wrote the *City of God* to answer pagan critics who blamed Christianity for the decline of the Roman Empire, and Christians who falsely expect an imminent apocalypse. Again during the sixteenth and seventeenth-century Reformation in Europe, numerous millennial sects sprang up, including Taborite terrorists. In Russia thousands of monks and peasants committed suicide after the Russian Orthodox Church tried to enforce new, top-down reforms.

Active millennial, apocalyptic, and messianic groups present a unique challenge to civil authorities because they proclaim allegiance to the allegedly "higher law" of a divine Power that may contravene the mores of society and the statutes of the state. Although most millennial groups do not engage in violence or terrorism, the few that do undermine social stability. Millennial movements tend to fall into three broad categories, but any given group may mutate over time from one type to another or present itself in a novel way.

Type one includes relatively few millennial groups that believe they must act as the "hand of God" to bring about world destruction and renewal through extralegal violence. Examples include the first-century Zealots/Sicarii, who assassinated priests and nobles in Palestine; Muslim Shiite Assassins—named because they consumed hashish—who martyred themselves while killing their targets in the eleventh and twelfth centuries; Russian anarchists of the late nineteenth century; and the Japanese sect of Aum Shinrikyō.

Type two groups expect to see armies of light and darkness fight a cosmic battle in heaven and earth while they watch and wait. Christian Fundamentalists believe they will be caught up in the clouds in a "rapture" before the war breaks out. Christian Identity groups believe they must prepare themselves to survive the imminent tribulation which includes war, plagues, and terror.

Groups of the third type withdraw from ordinary space and society to establish their own little kingdom that is modeled after their religious interpretation of the millennial kingdom. By separating themselves from the profane world, they mark off a portion of territory as sacred space within which God dwells with the community of the faithful.

The first type fosters an elite membership that is pledged to die, if necessary, to provoke "holy war." Groups of the second type tend to be nonviolent or pacifist, but may change if they receive a revelation from God that instructs them to take on a militant defensive or offensive role in endtime events. Groups that form a model of the millennial kingdom may engage in behavior that is intended to transform society by other than violent means, but, in doing so, they may attract suspicion. Groups that establish a sacred space may defend their perimeter to the death if it is breached.

To evaluate whether or not a millennial group that adheres to religious law is a threat to society, one must understand its worldview, ultimate concern, unique evolution, rituals, sacred calendar, and divine models. The mainstream Christian myth of the Millennium is an inherently violent one, but very few Christian millennialists engage in violence. Too often, misinformation about a group escalates into a confrontation with civil authorities that, in turn, provokes a lethal conflict that might have been avoided.

Hostage negotiation teams are instructed by models of hostage-taking incidents. However, hostage-taking incidents differ significantly from religious confrontations. The following points outline some of these significant differences.

1. Religious standoffs, by definition, do not include the taking of hostages. Children of the group should not be considered hostages in order to redefine the incident as a hostage incident. Persons or groups who do take hostages should be approached according to a hostage-taking model, not a religious standoff model.

2. A religious confrontation always involves more than one person, unless that person is acting on behalf of a religious community or group that acknowledges him or her as a member who is fulfilling the group's imperatives.

3. Contrary to conventional wisdom, religious leaders are no more likely to suffer from mental illness than any other person. In certain studied cases (e.g., Jonestown, Aum Shinrikyō) in which a leader's mental state deteriorated, movements did engage in violent acts. However, the data do not yet support the assertion of a causal relationship between a leader's mental illness and violence or terror. In other words, there is no reason to assume that the leader of a new religious movement is "wacky."

4. Religious groups regard perimeters as sacred boundaries that they will defend to the death. If possible, avoid confronting a group on its own ground or forcing it into an enclosure.

5. Religious standoffs always involve an ultimate concern—that which members live by and profess willingness to die for—that must be taken into consideration in crafting a peaceful resolution.

6. Even when religious groups use English, they speak a different language from the rest of society. They attach an unfamiliar set of meanings to words that seem familiar.

7. Because they occupy sacred space in a different world, religious communities adhere to divine commands over and above the ordinary rules and mores of society.

8. Because religious groups regard their laws as divine commands that take precedence over human laws, negotiators should take these laws into consideration during negotiations.

9. Religious groups engage in highly organized behavior motivated by imperatives that outsiders are not familiar with or do not value; thus, their behavior does not necessarily conform to psychologically defined categories of basic human drives and needs.

10. Religious groups may endure greater hardships and bear a higher casualty rate than nonreligious groups, because they believe that whatever happens is the will of God.

11. Negotiators may use an understanding of the group's worldview to craft a rational agreement that reduces tensions or resolves the confrontation or both. Accomplishing this requires a detailed knowledge of the group's worldview and a flexible approach to group demands.

12. Thus, time is an asset in resolving a religious confrontation, unless the group has announced a specific date on which it expects God to intervene, in which case there may be cause for concern about group suicide or mayhem.

13. The negotiation team should include worldview translators who can listen to and understand the mythology, ultimate concern, and language of the religious group. Worldview translators should maintain a neutral perspective, or critical distance, and be able to win the trust of the group.

14. Religious groups vary greatly. Within the same group individuals may have different interpretations of events. A prophet or leader may not be certain of the exact meaning of his revelation from God. Strategies for the resolution of each critical incident should exploit the religious constraints and ambiguities within the group. It is essential to decode the symbolic expression of the group in order to work toward a resolution members will accept.

15. A negotiation is likely to succeed in crafting a nonviolent outcome insofar as it allows the group to maintain its dignity as well as its ultimate concern.

# Afterword

## Millennial Violence in Contemporary America

MICHAEL BARKUN _____

### Historic Peaks in American Millennialism

The period since about 1970 has constituted the most intense and prolonged period of millenarian ferment in American history, eclipsing even the fervor of the 1830s and 1840s. The ferment also occurs at a time of growing apocalyptic consciousness in many other parts of the world. At least four major factors appear implicated in this development: increasing religious pluralism, new forms of communication, the social mobilization of fundamentalists, and the imminence of the year 2000.

American religious pluralism has increased in part because of immigration from non-European areas such as the Middle East and Latin America, but also as a result of the growth of New Religious Movements (NRMs) originally associated with the 1960s counterculture. Although such groups as the Unification Church, the Church Universal and Triumphant, and the Church of Scientology have remained extremely small, they have had visibility out of all proportion to their size and have often been successful in securing converts from among articulate urban professionals. More significant for present purposes, such groups more often than not share a millenarian sensibility.

NRMs have been able to achieve visibility not only because of the communications skills of their members but also because they have had an extraordinary range of media at their disposal: mass-market paperbacks, audio and video cassettes, cable television, and (perhaps most significantly) the Internet. The Internet combines low-capital investment with an absence of gatekeepers—a perfect combination for marginal and stigmatized groups, whose message can now be widely diffused at modest cost.

New Religious Movements are not the only millenarians on the contemporary religious horizon. They have been joined by the far more numerous Christian fundamentalists,[1] for whom millennialism is a central theological pillar (Boyer 1992). To be sure, fundamentalist millennialists have been a presence in American religion since at least the turn of the twentieth century. However, their new prominence has been due to a number of factors: the economic development of the Sun Belt, a traditional area of fundamentalist strength; their increasing affluence, educational level, and media sophistication; and their increasing mobilization on behalf of political and social causes.

The mobilization of evangelicals generally (both fundamentalist and non-fundamentalist) first became evident in the mid-1970s with the presidential candidacy of Jimmy Carter, a nonfundamentalist Southern Baptist. Previously apolitical evangelicals voted in unusually large numbers, a tendency they continued in the 1980s on behalf of Ronald Reagan. Besides their electoral mobilization, they have organized effectively in many issue areas, such as abortion, homosexuality, and sex in the media, leading some to suggest the beginnings of societal polarization between so-called orthodox and progressive forces. This "culture war" thesis (Hunter 1991) reinforces apocalyptic religious tendencies by projecting an ultimate battle between good and evil onto daily policy debates.

Finally, millennialism has benefited enormously from the approach of the year 2000 and the imminence of the new millennium itself. Millennialists have never been dependent upon the arrival of the millennial date—witness the Millerites' fixation upon dates in 1843 and 1844 (Numbers and Butler 1987).

Nonetheless, nearness to the year 2000 has proven to be a powerful amplifier of millenarian themes. This appears to be less a matter of committed millennialists making date-specific predictions, as it is the saturation of the larger culture by motifs of sudden transformation and cataclysmic upheaval.

---

1. Here and elsewhere in this chapter I employ "fundamentalist" and "fundamentalism" in the manner developed by Martin Marty and R. Scott Appleby (Marty and Appleby 1993, 3), i.e., as "a selective retrieval of doctrines, beliefs, and practices from a sacred past" by "beleaguered believers [who] attempt to preserve their distinctive identity as a people or group."

These forces have together produced a millennial ferment of unparalleled intensity. Its duration now exceeds that of the pre-Civil War period, and where the millennialism of that period was largely confined to the Northeast, contemporary chiliasm is a truly national phenomenon. There are also significant differences in the potential for violence.

The millennialism of the 1830s and 1840s was largely free of the reality or threat of violence. The signal exception was Mormon millennialism, for, as Grant Underwood's chapter makes clear, the Mormon community was the target of both mob and official violence until statehood for Utah was achieved in 1890. Particularly in the period before migration to the Great Salt Lake area, as persecution increased, Mormon millennialism intensified (Underwood 1993). Virtually all other manifestations of antebellum millennialism, however, appear to have proceeded nonviolently, with believers neither the targets nor the users of violence.

The absence of violence appears to have been due primarily to two forces: the desire of millennialists to win public acceptance and the support millennialists often enjoyed from the courts. This is particularly clear for millennialists who organized communally by setting up separate, self-sufficient communities. Although these were in part intended to separate them from a society judged to be flawed and impure, the communities were also regarded as models that outsiders were urged to emulate. These "patent-office models of society," in Arthur Bestor's evocative phrase (Bestor 1970, 230–52), were designed as alternatives to existing social institutions, but with the hope that outsiders would view them sympathetically. Thus, even when their conduct was regarded as reprehensible, as for example in matters of sexual practice, groups such as the Shakers and the Oneida Perfectionists tried to avoid confrontational postures. The religious millennialism such groups espoused was often closely related to the religious revivalism supported by mainstream Protestant churches and participated in by persons of all social classes. Their nonviolent separation was further facilitated by the fact that government in general was relatively nonintrusive by modern standards, and nineteenth-century courts, with their reverential attitude toward freedom of contract, were usually reluctant to disturb arrangements individuals made among themselves (Weisbrod 1980).

In short, the millennialism of the 1830s and 1840s sheds relatively little light on possible relationships between millennialism and violence in contemporary society, for the earlier period was not only less intense in its millennial expression; that expression was more in tune with prevailing sensibilities. Millennialist activity in America has exhibited periodic peaks and valleys (Barkun 1985); the current peak eclipses its predecessor in both its breadth and its intensity.

## Millennial Violence

A fuller understanding of the relationship between millennialism and violence has been retarded by stereotypes of millennial beliefs and behavior. Some may be found in media accounts, others in pronouncements by the "anticult" movement. In both cases, millenarians are often portrayed as irrational, "brainwashed," and violence-prone (Kaplan 1997a, 127-63). In fact, as the chapters in this volume make abundantly clear, violence involving millenarians is a complex phenomenon. As the historical record reveals, most millenarians have neither been users nor targets of violence. They have often preferred to passively wait on divine forces, while making whatever compromises are necessary to forestall persecution. Although that has been the more common approach, the contributors to this volume also demonstate that it is not the only approach, that millennial expectation has sometimes conflicted with the wishes of those who held power, and that at times believers felt that direct assault on the forces of sin was required. Whatever the relationship between millennialism and violence, however, it is not a simple one.

We may gain a better understanding of the range of possible relationships by making two distinctions. One is between those who initiate violence and those who employ it reactively. The second distinction concerns the objects against which violence may be directed, contrasting violence directed within a millennial group and violence directed at targets outside the group. These distinctions are significant not only because they contrast with the undifferentiated and uniformly threatening stereotypes referred to earlier but also because they reflect the concerns of law enforcement agencies.

Insofar as public order is concerned, it matters whether millenarians are first or second users of violence. If they initiate violence, that may require a higher level of surveillance and other preventive action. If they use violence only in response to the behavior of others, that implies the need for a comparably lower level of threat. It also suggests that millennialist violence may be at least partly controlled if others act in suitably nonprovocative ways. As far as potential objects of violence are concerned, law enforcement agencies should protect all citizens and property equally. However, violence directed within a millennialist group will usually be smaller in scale than violence directed outward, especially among the many millennialist groups that have very small numbers of adherents, and hence will be perceived as less dangerous.

The two distinctions—between initiated and reactive violence, and between violence directed within and outside the group—generate four possible permutations:

*Type 1*: group-initiated violence, directed at targets within the group. Such a situation is exemplified by the murder-suicides of the Order of the Solar Temple (discussed in the chapter by Introvigne). As Introvigne points out, however, the perpetrators may have believed that they would soon themselves be targets of state repression and hence desired to act preemptively. Much the same is true of the Heaven's Gate suicides, seemingly unprovoked. On the other hand, the Heaven's Gate Web page suggested that they feared meeting the same fate at the hands of the government as the Branch Davidians outside Waco, an episode they regarded as paradigmatic of government attitudes toward New Religious Movements. Type 1 situations, like all ideal types, therefore, can only imperfectly match the nuances of real-world situations. Such internal violence is also a product of the drive to maintain internal discipline by preventing defections and leadership challenges. This was (as Rebecca Moore points out) certainly the case in Jonestown, although, as noted in the discussion of Type 3 below, internal violence also thrives where the environment is regarded as hostile.

*Type 2*: group-initiated violence, directed at outside targets. Here the most conspicuous case is Aum Shinrikyō (discussed in the chapter by Reader). It is also a case conspicuous as much for its rarity as for its drama. To be sure, other outer-directed, violence-initiating groups may be found, such as revolutionary groups formed by white racialists (e.g., The Order[2]). While one can do little more than guess at the proportion such organizations occupy in the millennial universe, it can confidently be considered very low. Whether because of fear, lack of organizational ability, prudential calculation, or government counteraction, the violent impulses of millennialists rarely proceed beyond rhetoric. Indeed, a greater

2. The Order (also known as The Silent Brotherhood and the Bruders Schweigen) was a white racialist insurgent group that committed numerous acts of violence in the West in 1983–84 in an effort to overthrow the national government. Of the approximately forty members, about one-half subscribed to the religious orientation known as Christian Identity. The organization was modeled after the group portrayed in the racialist novel *The Turner Diaries*. By 1986 all members had pled guilty, been convicted, or killed (Barkun 1997a, 228).

danger than the groups themselves may be overgeneralization from the few actual Type 2 cases. The readiness to use violence characteristic of such organizations also makes them receptive to Type 1 violence as a way of purging those within who are thought to be disloyal or insufficiently committed. Aum in particular combined outer-directed violence with violence for purposes of internal discipline and purification.

*Type 3*: reactive violence, directed within the group. In the view of federal authorities, this would accurately characterize the Branch Davidians (discussed by Gallagher), but such a characterization depends largely upon the belief that those in the compound set the fire for purposes of self-immolation. This category raises again the issue of a group's own threat assessment, discussed earlier with regard to Type 1. Although no organized violence appears to have been directed at the Jonestown community,[3] Rebecca Moore points out in her chapter that the federal government had begun to place considerable pressure on the Peoples Temple, and its leadership clearly believed that Representative Leo Ryan's visit was a prelude to violence. Here it is the *perception* of impending violence that seems to matter, which also suggests that millennialists, accustomed to thinking in terms of a dualistic universe, may perceive themselves to be the objects of imminent violence when the authorities may have no intention of employing violence against them. There appears to be a reciprocal relationship between the perception of enemies outside and the existence of violence within. Where the external world is thought to be filled with evil forces, the need to maintain the purity of the Elect is deemed to be all the greater.

*Type 4*: reactive violence, directed outside the group. Although controversy remains about who fired the first shot at Waco, it can plausibly be argued that the ATF either did so or, through a massive display of firepower, gave every indication of preparing to do so, provoking the Davidians' volley. What distinguishes such a situation from ordinary self-defense is the millennial belief system through which information is filtered. For here (as in the other three types), violence is understood as a significant element in a progression of events deemed to have ultimate significance

---

3. In early September 1977—two months before Representative Ryan's arrival—the Jonestown community mobilized to ward off attackers amid claims that shots had been fired. The affair may well have been staged because Jim Jones had a history of contriving security threats that extended back to the early 1970s in California. Such incidents both played to and reinforced his followers' perception of the Peoples Temple as the target of violence (Hall 1987, 112, 217–18).

for believers. The instrumentality of violence does not lie in its ability to preserve believers' lives; indeed, in Type 1 cases, its purpose may be to take those lives, at least as it would be viewed by outsiders. Instrumentality here becomes the degree to which the exercise of violence can help fulfill the group's millennial "script" for the end of time. For there is always some conception of how future events will unfold. Often, these prophetic visions include acts of violence by the forces of evil as the prelude to a final battle. Hence, violence is to be embraced, not avoided, for its occurrence is deemed part of the final, endtime plan.

How are these four types of violence related to the types of groups considered in this volume—"assaulted," "fragile," and "revolutionary"? Assaulted groups, to the extent that they themselves employ violence, fit overwhelmingly in Type 4. However, precisely because they believe so fervently in their saved or sacred status, they often inadvertently adopt postures that invite state repression. Unlike martyrs, their behavior is not consciously self-sacrificing, but may well lead to "suicidal" results. Fragile groups, on the other hand, seem to cluster in Type 1. They find themselves in a cul-de-sac from which they can exit only by desperate, and increasingly violent, measures. Often the violence will be directed toward themselves, so that, like the members of the Solar Temple, they can reach a transmundane level of existence. But as their alternatives become more constrained, they may direct violence outward as a way of "forcing the end," in the manner of Aum Shinrikyō (Type 2).

Revolutionary millennial movements present the greatest difficulties. Predominantly found under Type 2, the revolutionary movements share characteristics with both fragile and assaulted groups. They may actually be fragile, but lack a sense of their own fragility; hence, their penchant for going down to defeat. At the same time, their political aspirations invite assault; yet, in most cases the revolutionary movements are able to strike first. Indeed, the distinction between revolutionary and assaulted movements is often largely one of timing: who was able to use violence first, millenarians or the state? One would intuitively believe that revolutionary movements always strike outward, toward the authority structures they wish to topple. That, however, is not always the case. It was certainly not for the suicidal Old Believers (described by Robbins), nor even for Jonestown, whose leaders saw their final act as "revolutionary suicide" that would hasten the desired societal transformation.

These observations have two important implications: first, systems of classification can focus our attention on commonalities we might otherwise miss, but they can never fully encompass the variability of actual cases. Even when they seem exhaustive, their categories are rarely mutually exclusive. Actual movements may exhibit traits that place them in one conceptual pigeonhole or another, but they are also likely to share characteristics with other varieties as well, as with Aum's manifestation of both Types 1 and 2. Second, the position of any movement within a classificatory scheme should not be regarded as permanent. As groups go through their life histories, they may be expected to migrate from one category to another, whether in terms of the four types introduced earlier or the assaulted-fragile-revolutionary trichotomy. The history of millennialism is filled with such cases, whether of once-volatile Anabaptists who metamorphosed into Mennonites, or of patriotic British-Israelites, who gave birth to antigovernment Christian Identity.

As Jean Rosenfeld points out, law enforcement personnel have been slow to appreciate the role religion plays in both the transformations and in the recourse to violence, as if violence and sincerely held religious beliefs were incompatible. For example, a pre-Waco FBI "White Paper on Cults" describes "hardcore" members as "psychopathic" or "sociopathic," led by "impulsive thrillseekers" (FBI, n.d.). One might think that the painful lessons of Waco would have eliminated such tendencies. That they have not is evident from a recent government report meant to advise local law enforcement personnel on proper threat assessment when dealing with potential assassins. The manual contains a lengthy inventory of desirable background information on suspects, including "Interest in extremist ideas and radical groups," but makes no mention of religious affiliations or beliefs. Indeed, the latter are mentioned only in connection with organizations "that might work cooperatively with the investigator to engage, neutralize, and redirect the potential attacker" (Fein and Vossekuil 1998, 41, 56).

## Millennialist Violence in Its Legal and Cultural Contexts

Although the suppression of private violence is a basic function of the state, the means available to a democratic society to do so become distinctly limited where millennialist groups are concerned. This is so because actual, threatened, or potential millennialist violence can bring the coercive apparatus of the state into collision with freedom of conscience. To what extent are millennialists, like other religious believers, protected, even when their statements or conduct seem to affront or endanger the community?

In the United States, this and related questions are inseparable from understandings of the free exercise clause of the First Amendment, with its categorical but ambiguous promise that religious exercise will not be prohibited by Congress (and, by extension, by the states). In recent years, as American religious pluralism has burgeoned, the limits of free exercise have been tested. Thus, in 1990, the United States Supreme Court, ruling on the right of members of the Native American Church to use the hallucinogenic drug peyote for religious purposes, decided that they enjoyed no such right; and that as long as the state's regulation serves some governmental interest, and only incidentally burdens religious observance, believers must yield (Employment Division, Department of Human Resources of Oregon, et al. v. Alfred L. Smith, et al., 494 U.S. 872 [1990]). Those who were troubled by the decision could take some limited comfort by a case three years later, in which an Afro-Cuban Santería church in south Florida appealed a local zoning ordinance that effectively prevented the church from constructing a new sanctuary because Santería believers employ animal sacrifices. Here the Supreme Court took the side of religionists against the state, but only because governmental regulation intentionally burdened a religious group rather than indirectly disadvantaging it (Church of Lukumi Babalu Aye, Inc. v. City of Hialeah, 508 U.S. 520 [1993]).

These murky First Amendment waters cleared briefly in late 1993, when Congress overwhelmingly passed, and President Clinton signed, the Religious Freedom Restoration Act, establishing a barrier to governmental action far higher than that articulated in the peyote case. The Religious Freedom Restoration Act asserted that government could burden religious practice only in furtherance of "a compelling governmental interest," and only if the means chosen to advance that interest were the least restrictive available (Public Law 103-141, 42 USC 200bb).

The protection this statute offered to believers, however, was short-lived, for within four years, the Supreme Court declared it an unconstitutional violation of the separation of powers, returning the meaning of free exercise to the point it was at in the peyote case (City of Boerne v. Flores, Archbishop of San Antonio 95-2074 [1997]).

The implications of this legal quagmire for both millennialists and law enforcement agencies are, as one might imagine, unclear. Yet, the lack of clarity provides no basis for evading the issues. As practical matters, both chiliasts and their potential adversaries need to address the meaning of "religious practice," "governmental interest," "free exercise," and related concepts—the more so because police and other instruments of public order desire to prevent, and not merely respond to, violence. Does that mean placing millenarian groups that seem putatively "dangerous" under surveillance? Does it mean performing "threat assessments" on religious literature? On what basis can authorities meaningfully distinguish between "belief," which is unarguably protected, and "practice," which may not be? This is not the place to try to resolve such deeply contested issues. However, their present unresolved state points up the difficulties that exist in responding to actual or potential violence that involves millennialists. The overlap in time between much of the most important recent litigation and legislation and the Waco episode constitutes a significant subtext, with judicial and legislative struggles taking place in counterpoint to the bloodiest church-state confrontation in recent American history. This provides further demonstration of the importance of more clearly charting the outer boundaries of permissible action for both millennialists and state representatives. The fact that prudent FBI action prevented violence in the 1996 Montana Freemen standoff (described by Rosenfeld) does nothing to make such legal clarification any less necessary.

In fact, it is not clear what law enforcement personnel can and cannot do when religiously based violence occurs or is believed to be likely. The legal uncertainty unfortunately coincides with a growing global concern about terrorist acts committed by the religiously committed. Walter Laqueur, an influential writer on terrorism, observes that with the approach of a new millennium, "Extremist millenarians would like to give history a push, helping create world-ending havoc, replete with universal war, famine, pestilence, and other scourges" (Laqueur 1996b). Although Laqueur's concerns may well be exaggerated, they mirror those of governments in many parts of the world, including the United States, for each new terrorist attack (and particularly those in which religious commitments appear to have played a role) raises levels of fear.

In America, that fear is often associated with religious groups that have not traditionally been part of American political and legal debate, either because of association with different cultures or because the groups are of very recent origin. Among groups associated with different cultures are such religious traditions as Islam, Santería, and Hinduism, until recently present in only token numbers or not at all, and now growing as a result of the "new immigration" from Asia, Africa, and Latin America. Among groups of very recent origin are such New Religious Movements as the Unification Church and the International Society for Krishna Consciousness, popularly stigmatized as "cults." Neither the cultural imports nor the New Religious Movements have been participants in what Martin Marty calls "the republican banquet" (Marty 1987, 53–76), the ongoing national conversation that lays out the informal (as opposed to the officially legal) understandings concerning the relationships among religious groups, state power, and civic responsibility. Rising fear of religiously based violence has combined with legal uncertainties and the proliferation of "outsider" religious groups to create an atmosphere in which millennialists are more likely to become both the users and the objects of violence.

This atmosphere has been intensified by a cultural "mainstreaming," in which millennial themes once associated with insular religious "undergrounds" now proliferate in popular culture. They make increasingly frequent appearances on television (e.g., *The X-Files* and *Millennium*) and in motion pictures (e.g, *The Rapture* and *Conspiracy Theory*). Millennial messages intended as popular entertainment coexist with more active proselytizing through such media as the Internet. The result is an increased degree of legitimization, in which repetition reduces stigma and new audiences present enhanced recruiting opportunities.

But the larger the number of millenarians, the greater the likelihood that their predictions of future transformation will become, at least in part, self-fulfilling prophecies. For growing numbers will themselves come to be viewed, as they were in the 1840s, as "signs of the times," markers of the nearness of the end. When such growth appears at a time when a calendrical end (the year 2000) is in sight, the potential for millenarian-state violence also increases. It may do so when millennialists seek to radically withdraw from the dominant society, going, as survivalists put it, "off the grid," shunning social institutions and ignoring legal mandates. It may also occur when the heady sense of millennial growth intersects with a critically important date, convincing believers and authorities alike that action is imperative before they literally "run out of time."

Popular culture feeds this sense of living in a temporal cul-de-sac, from which the only exit must be a cataclysmic end to history. Motion pictures portray "civilization as we know it" as continually at risk, whether from wayward asteroids, approaching comets, volcanic eruptions, or marauding aliens. The common thread tying these disaster scenarios together is a fascination with high impact/low probability events. Rather than feeling secure because of low probability, many feel anxious because of high impact. The emphasis is not on a disaster's low likelihood of occurrence, but on its potentially devastating consequences. The intimate association of disaster motifs with millennial expectations (Barkun 1974) may easily give rise to both selective perception and self-fulfilling prophecies: We anticipate disasters as an accompaniment to the endtime; therefore, we are sensitized to identify and emphasize stressful events; and because the cultural atmosphere of apocalyptic expectation leads so many to view the world under the aspect of calamity, they behave in ways that may help bring about the very destabilization they dread—for example, by radical withdrawal from the larger society, by creating armed, paramilitary organizations, and by regarding the environment as a source of threat rather than of support. Little wonder, then, that the path to an imagined millennium may be strewn with opportunities for violence.

*Bibliography*
*Index*

# Bibliography

Aho, James A. 1990. *The Politics of Righteousness, Idaho Christian Patriotism.* Seattle: Univ. of Washington Press.

———. 1994. *This Thing of Darkness: A Sociology of the Enemy.* Seattle: Univ. of Washington Press.

Alexander, Thomas G. 1986. *Mormonism in Transition: A History of the Latter-day Saints, 1890–1930.* Urbana: Univ. of Illinois Press.

———. 1991. *Things in Heaven and Earth: The Life and Times of Wilford Woodruff, a Mormon Prophet.* Salt Lake City: Signature Books.

Anderson, Allan. 1992. "African Pentecostalism in a South African Urban Environment: A Missiological Evaluation." D.Th. thesis: Univ. of South Africa.

Anthony, Dick, and Thomas Robbins. 1997. "Religious Totalism, Exemplary Dualism, and the Waco Tragedy." In *Millennium, Messiahs, and Mayhem: Contemporary Apocalyptic Movements,* ed. Thomas Robbins and Susan J. Palmer, 261–84. New York: Routledge.

Anti-Defamation League of the B'nai Brith. 1996. *The Web of Hate: Extremists Exploit the Internet.* New York: Anti-Defamation League.

Aoyama Yoshinobu. 1991. *Naze watashi wa taihō sarenakute wa naranakatta no ka.* Tokyo: Oumu Shuppan.

Apter, David E. 1963. "Political Religion in the New Nations." In *Old Societies and New States,* ed. Clifford Geertz, 57–104. Glencoe, Il.: Free Press.

Aquino, Michael. 1993. *The Church of Satan.* 3d ed. San Francisco: Michael Aquino.

Arita Yoshifu. 1995. *Ano ko ga Oumu ni!* Tokyo: Josei Jishin Books.

Arnold, J. Phillip. 1994. "The Davidian Dilemma—To Obey God or Man." In *From the Ashes: Making Sense of Waco,* ed. James R. Lewis, 23–32, Lanham, Md.: Rowman and Littlefield.

Arrington, Leonard J. 1985. *Brigham Young: American Moses.* New York: Alfred A. Knopf.

Asahara Shōkō. 1986a. *Chōnōryoku: himitsu no kaihatsuhō.* Tokyo: Oumu Shuppan.

———. 1986b. *Seishi o koeru.* Tokyo: Oumu Shuppan.

———. 1987. *Inishieeshon*. Tokyo: Oumu Shuppan.

———. 1988. *Supreme Initiation*. Tokyo: Aum USA Co.

———. 1989a. *Metsubō no hi*. Tokyo: Oumu Shuppan.

———. 1989b. *Metsubō kara kokū e*. Tokyo: Oumu Shuppan.

———. 1991a. *Kirisuto sengen: kirisuto no oshie no subete o akasu*. Tokyo: Oumu Shuppan.

———. 1991b. *Kirisuto sengen 2: sairin, sabaki, shūmatsu*. Tokyo: Oumu Shuppan.

———. 1991c. "Beyond the Impermanence of Things: The Path to Being a Great Winner of the Truth." *Mahayana News Letter* 24: 1–8.

———. 1992. *Declaring Myself the Christ: Essential Teachings of Jesus Christ's Gospel*. Tokyo: Aum Publishing Co.

———. 1995a. *Hiizuru kuni wazawaichikashi*. Tokyo: Oumu Shuppan.

———. 1995b. *Disaster Approaches the Land of the Rising Sun*. Tokyo: Aum Publishing Co.

———. n.d. (ca.1994). *Vajrayana kōsu. Kyōgaku shisutemu kyōhon*. Internal Aum document.

Associated Press Online. <http://www.latimes.com/HOME/NEWS/APONLONG/ NATIONAL>.

Aum Translation Committee. 1992. *Your First Steps to Truth*. Fujinomiya: Aum Publishing Co.

Back, Les, Michael Keith, and John Solomos. 1998. "Racism on the Internet: Mapping Neo-Fascist Subcultures in Cyberspace." In *Nation and Race: The Developing Euro-American Racist Subculture,* ed. Jeffrey Kaplan and Tore Bjørgo. Boston: Northeastern Univ. Press.

Baird, Robert D. 1971. *Category Formation and the History of Religions*. The Hague: Mouton.

Balch, Robert W. 1982. "Bo and Peep: A Case Study of the Origins of Messianic Leadership." In *Millennialism and Charisma,* ed. Roy Wallis, 13–72. Belfast: Queen's Univ.

———, 1995. "Waiting for the Ships: Disillusionment and the Revitalization of Faith in Bo and Peep's UFO Cult." In *The Gods Have Landed: New Religions from Other Worlds,* ed. James R. Lewis, 137–66. Albany: State Univ. of New York Press.

Ball, Bryan W. 1975. *A Great Expectation: Eschatological Thought in English Protestantism to 1660*. Leiden: Brill.

Barkun, Michael. 1974. *Disaster and the Millennium*. New Haven: Yale Univ. Press.

———. 1985. "The Awakening-Cycle Controversy." *Sociological Analysis* 46: 425–43.

———. 1986. *Disaster and the Millennium*. Syracuse: Syracuse Univ. Press.

———. 1994. *Religion and the Racist Right: The Origins of the Christian Identity Movement*. Chapel Hill: Univ. of North Carolina Press.

———. 1997a. *Religion and the Racist Right: The Origins of the Christian Identity Movement.* Rev. ed. Chapel Hill: Univ. of North Carolina Press.

———. 1997b. "Millenarians and Violence: The Case of the Christian Identity Movement." In *Millennium, Messiahs, and Mayhem,* ed. Thomas Robbins and Susan Palmer, 247–60. New York: Routledge.

Barnett, Anthony. 1983. "Democratic Kampuchea: A Highly Centralized Dictatorship." In *Revolution and Its Aftermath in Kampuchea: Eight Essays,* ed. David P. Chandler and Ben Kiernan, 212–29. Monograph series no. 25. New Haven, Conn.: Yale Univ. Southeast Asia Studies.

Barrett, Leonard E. Sr. 1988. *The Rastafarians: Sounds of Cultural Dissonance.* Boston: Beacon Press.

Bauer, Wolfgang. 1976. *China and the Search for Happiness: Recurring Themes in Four Thousand Years of Chinese Cultural History.* New York: Seabury Press.

Beach, Edward Allen. 1994. *The Potencies of God(s): Schelling's Philosophy of Mythology.* Albany: State Univ. of New York Press.

Berlet, Chip. 1994. "The Right Rides High." *The Progressive.* (Oct.): 22–29.

Bernard, Raymond. 1970. *Les maisons secrètes de la Rose-Croix.* Villeneuve-Saint-Georges, France: Éditions Rosicruciennes.

———. 1976. *Rencontres avec l'insolite.* Villeneuve-Saint-Georges, France: Éditions Rosicruciennes.

———. 1997. "Témoignage de Raymond Bernard." In *L'Ordre Rénové du Temple. Aux racines du Temple Solaire,* by Serge Caillet, 152–90. Paris: Dervy.

Bestor, Arthur. 1970. *Backwoods Utopias: The Sectarian Origins and the Owenite Phase of Communitarian Socialism in America: 1663–1829.* Philadelphia: Univ. of Pennsylvania Press.

*Billings Gazette Online.* 1996. <http://www.bigskywire.com/gazette/>.

Birken, Lawrence. 1995. *Hitler as Philosophe: Remnants of the Enlightenment in National Socialism.* Westport, Conn.: Greenwood.

Blacker, Carmen. 1971. "Millenarian Aspects of the New Religions in Japan." In *Tradition and Modernization in Japanese Culture,* ed. Donald H. Shively, 563–600. Princeton: Princeton Univ. Press.

Boardman, Eugene. 1952. Christian *Influence upon the Ideology of the Taiping Revolutionary Rebellion, 1851–1864.* Madison: Univ. of Wisconsin Press.

———. 1970. "Millenary Aspects of the Taiping Rebellion (1851–64)." In *Millennial Dreams in Action: Studies in Religious Movements,* ed. Sylvia Thrupp, 70–79. New York: Schocken.

Bourdieu, Pierre. 1990. *The Logic of Practice.* Stanford: Stanford Univ. Press.

Boyd, James P. 1891. *Recent Indian Wars, under the Lead of Sitting Bull, and Other Chiefs; with a Full Account of the Messiah Craze, and Ghost Dances.* Philadelphia, n.p.

Boyer, Paul. 1992. *When Time Shall Be No More: Prophecy Belief in American Culture.* Cambridge: Harvard Univ. Press.

Breyer, Jacques. 1959. *Arcanes solaires, ou les Sécrets du Temple Solaire.* Paris: La Colombe.

Bromley, David G., ed. 1998a. *The Politics of Religious Apostasy: The Role of Apostates in the Transformation of Religious Movements.* Westport, Conn.: Praeger.

Bromley, David G. 1998b. "The Social Construction of Contested Exit Roles: Defectors, Whistleblowers, and Apostates." In *The Politics of Religious Apostasy: The Role of Apostates in the Transformation of Religious Movements,* ed. David G. Bromley, 19–48. Westport, Conn.: Praeger.

Brooke, John L. 1994. *The Refiner's Fire: The Making of Mormon Cosmology, 1644–1844.* Cambridge: Cambridge Univ. Press.

Burghart, Devin, and Robert Crawford. 1996. *Guns and Gavels, Common Law Courts, Militias and White Supremacy.* Portland: Coalition for Human Dignity.

Caillet, Serge. 1997. *L'Ordre Rénové du Temple. Aux racines du Temple Solaire.* Paris: Dervy.

Cameron, Trewhella. 1994. *Jan Smuts: An Illustrated Biography.* Cape Town: Human and Roussouw.

Campbell, Colin. 1972. "The Cult, the Cultic Milieu, and Secularization." In *A Sociological Yearbook of Religion in Britain—5,* ed. Michael Hill, 119–36. London: SCM Press.

Campiche, Roland. 1995. *Quand les sectes affolent: Ordre du Temple Solaire, médias et fin du millénaire. Entretiens avec Cyril Dépraz.* Geneva: Labor et Fides.

Capitanick, David, and Michael Wine. 1996. *The Governance of Cyberspace: The Far Right on the Internet.* London: Institute for Jewish Policy Research.

Carr-Brown, David, and David Cohen. 1997. "Mystery of Princess Grace and the Temple of Doom." *New York Post* (Dec. 28).

Carstarphen, Nike. 1995. "Third Party Efforts at Waco: Phillip Arnold and James Tabor." Unpublished paper. Institute for Conflict Analysis and Resolution, George Mason Univ..

Carter, Stephen L. 1993. *The Culture of Disbelief: How American Law and Politics Trivialize Religious Devotion.* New York: Doubleday.

Chakravarti, Adhir. 1982. *Royal Succession in Ancient Cambodia.* Asiatic Society Monograph series 26. Calcutta: Asiatic Society.

Chandler, David P. 1983. "Seeing Red: Perceptions of Cambodian History in Democratic Kampuchea." In *Revolution and Its Aftermath in Kampuchea: Eight Essays,* ed. David P. Chandler and Ben Kiernan, 34–56. Monograph series no. 25. New Haven, Conn.: Yale Univ. Southeast Asia Studies.

Charles, R. H. 1963. *Eschatology: The Doctrine of a Future Life in Israel, Judaism, and Christianity.* New York: Schocken.

Cheng, J. C. 1963. *Chinese Sources for the Taiping Rebellion, 1850–1864.* Hong Kong: Hong Kong Univ. Press.

Cherniavsky, Michael. 1970. "The Old Believers and the New Religion." In *The Structure of Russian History,* ed. Michael Cherniavsky, 140–88. New York: Random House (reprinted from *Slavic Review* 25, no. 1, 1966).

Chesneaux, Jean. 1979. *China: The People's Republic, 1949–1976.* New York: Pantheon.

Chevannes, Barry. 1994. *Rastafari: Roots and Ideology.* Syracuse: Syracuse Univ. Press.

Chidester, David. 1988. *Salvation and Suicide: An Interpretation of Jim Jones, the Peoples Temple, and Jonestown.* Bloomington and Indianapolis: Indiana Univ. Press.

Christian, Gabriel J. 1992. "In Times Crucial: Radical Politics in Dominica, 1900–1980." In *In Search of Eden: Dominica, the Travails of a Caribbean Mini-State,* ed. Irving W. Andre and Gabriel J. Christian, 1–52. Upper Marlboro, Md.: Pond Casse Press.

Christian, Hecknell Lockinvar. 1992. *Gatecrashing into the Unknown: A Dominica Journal.* Roseau, Dominica: ACT Press.

Clark, James R., ed. 1966. *Messages of the First Presidency.* 5 vols. Salt Lake City: Bookcraft.

CNN "Breaking News." 1996. Transcript #892 (June 13), 1–39. Denver: Journal Graphics, Inc.

CNN "Daybreak." 1996, transcript #1421, Segment #1 (June 17). Denver: Journal Graphics, Inc.

Coates, Lawrence G. 1985. "The Mormons and the Ghost Dance." *Dialogue: A Journal of Mormon Thought* 18, no. 4:89–111.

Cohen, John, ed. 1967. *The Essential Lenny Bruce.* New York: Ballantine Books.

Cohn, Norman. 1957. *The Pursuit of the Millennium.* London: Secker and Warburg.

———. 1969. *Warrant for Genocide.* New York: Harper.

———. 1970. *The Pursuit of the Millennium: Revolutionary Millenarians and Mystical Anarchists of the Middle Ages.* Rev. and exp. ed. New York: Oxford Univ. Press.

———. 1993. *Cosmos, Chaos and the World to Come: The Ancient Roots of Apocalyptic Faith.* New Haven, Conn.: Yale Univ. Press.

Collins, John J., ed. 1979. *Apocalypse: the Morphology of a Genre, Semeia* 14. Missoula, Mont.: Scholars Press.

———. 1986. "Apocalyptic Literature." In *Early Judaism and Its Modern Interpreters,* ed. R. Kraft and G. W. Nickelsburg, 345–70. Chico, Calif.: Scholars Press.

Commissioner of Indian Affairs. 1891. *Sixtieth Annual Report of the Commissioner of Indian Affairs I.* Washington, D.C.: Government Printing Office.

Committee on the Judiciary, House of Representatives, and the Subcommittee on National Security, International Affairs, and Criminal Justice of the Committee on Government Reform and Oversight, One Hundred Fourth

Congress. 1996. *Joint Hearings on Activities of Federal Law Enforcement Agencies Toward the Branch Davidians.* 3 vols. Washington, D.C.: U.S. Government Printing Office.

Cooper, Rick. 1993. "No Man Knows the Date." *NSV Report* 11/3 (July/Sept.): obtained as E-text <http://www.alpha.org/nsv>.

————. n.d. "A Brief History of the White Nationalist Movement." NSV Report 11/4 (Oct./Dec.): obtained as E-text <http://www.alpha.org/nsv>.

Coser, Lewis. 1956. *The Functions of Social Conflict.* New York: The Free Press.

Crummey, Richard. 1970. *The Old Believers and the World of Antichrist.* Madison: Wisconsin Univ. Press.

Damotte, Jean C. 1996. *Le Grand Maître. Roman.* Taulignan, France: Le Regard du Monde.

Danker, Donald F., ed. 1981. "The Wounded Knee Interviews of Eli S. Ricker." *Nebraska History* 62, no. 2:151–243.

Davidson, James A. 1977. *The Logic of Millennial Thought.* New Haven, Conn.: Yale Univ. Press.

de Armond, Paul. 1996. "Christian Patriots at War with the State." (Apr.) The Public Good Project. <http://nwcitizen.com/public good>.

Dees, Morris, and Steve Fiffer. 1993. *Hate on Trial.* New York: Villard Books.

Delaforge, Gaetan. 1987. *The Templar Tradition in the Age of Aquarius.* Putney, Vt.: Threshold Books.

Delorme, Hermann. 1996. *Crois et meurs dans l'Ordre du Temple Solaire.* Saint-Alphonse-de-Granby, Quebec: Éditions de la Paix.

DeMallie, Raymond J. 1982. "The Lakota Ghost Dance: An Ethnohistorical Account." *Pacific Historical Review* 51, no. 4:385–405.

De Vries, Jan. 1967. *The Study of Religion.* Transl. by Kees W. Bolle. New York: Harcourt, Brace, and World.

Dilling, Elizabeth. 1983. *The Jewish Religion: Its Influence Today.* Torrance, Calif.: Noontide Press.

Dinnerstein, Leonard. 1994. *Antisemitism in America.* New York: Oxford Univ. Press.

*Doctrine and Covenants of the Church of Jesus Christ of the Latter-day Saints, The.* 1989. Salt Lake City: The Church of Jesus Christ of Latter-day Saints.

Dodds, E. R. 1965. *Pagan and Christian in an Age of Anxiety.* New York: Norton.

Douglas, Mary. 1966. *Purity and Danger: An Analysis of the Concepts of Pollution and Taboo.* New York: Frederick Praeger.

————. 1973. *Natural Symbols.* New York: Vintage Books.

Doyle, Sir Arthur Conan. 1888/1900. *A Study in Scarlet.* London 1888; New York: Burt.

Dyer, Joel. 1997. *Harvest of Rage: Why Oklahoma City Is Only the Beginning.* Boulder, Colo.: Westview Press.

Eastman, Elaine Goodale. 1945. "The Ghost Dance War and Wounded Knee Massacre of 1890–91." *Nebraska History* 26, no. 1:26–42.

Eatwell, Roger. 1996. "Surfing the Great White Wave: The Internet, Extremism, and the Problem of Control." *Patterns of Prejudice* 30, no. 1 (Jan.):61–71.

Edgar, Robert. 1988. *Because They Chose the Plan of God: The Story of the Bulhoek Massacre*. Johannesburg: Ravan.

Ehat, Andrew F. 1980. "'It Seems Like Heaven Began on Earth': Joseph Smith and the Constitution of the Kingdom of God." *BYU Studies* 20:253–79.

Eichler, Margrit. 1971. "Charismatic and Ideological Leadership in Secular and Religious Millenarian Movements: A Sociological Study." Ph.D. diss., Duke Univ.

*Elders' Journal of the Church of Jesus Christ of Latter Day Saints*. 1837–38. Kirtland, Ohio, and Far West, Mo.

Eliade, Mircea. 1964. *Shamanism: Archaic Techniques of Ecstasy*. Princeton, N.J.: Princeton Univ. Press.

Fanon, Frantz. 1963. *Wretched of the Earth*. Trans. Constance Farrington. New York: Grove Press.

FBI. n.d. "White Paper on Cults."

Fein, Robert, and Bryan Vossekuil. 1998. *Protective Intelligence and Threat Assessment Investigations: A Guide for State and Local Law Enforcement Officials*. Washington, DC: National Institute of Justice.

Fineberg, Rabbi Solomon Andhill. 1946. "Checkmate for Rabble-Rousers: What to Do When the Demagogue Comes." *Commentary* (Sept.): 220–26.

———. 1947. "Quarantine Treatment." Memorandum published by the Community Service Department of the American Jewish Committee.

Firmage, Edwin Brown, and Richard Collin Mangrum. 1988. *Zion in the Courts: A Legal History of the Church of Jesus Christ of the Latter-day Saints, 1830–1900*. Urbana: Univ. of Illinois Press.

"Folk-Lore Scrap-Book." 1891. *Journal of American Folk-Lore IV*, no. XIII: 160–65.

Friedrich, Otto. 1986. *Before the Deluge: A Portrait of Berlin in the 1920's*. New York: Fromm International.

Fritz, Stephen G. 1995. *Frontsoldaten: The German Soldier in World War II*. Lexington: Univ. of Kentucky Press.

Fujii Nichidatsu. 1965 [1950]. *Risshō ankoku*. In *Gendai Nihon shisō taikei 7: Bukkyō*, ed. Yoshida Kyūichi, 354–76. Tokyo: Chikuma Shobō.

———. 1980. *Buddhism for World Peace: Words of Nichidatsu Fujii*. Trans. Yumiko Miyazaki. Tokyo: Japan-Bharat Sarvodaya Mitrata Sangha.

Fujimoto Haruki. 1964. *Ishiwara Kanji*. Tokyo: Jiji Tsūshinsha.

Fujita Shōichi. 1995. *Oumu Shinrikyō jiken*. Tokyo: Asahi News Shop.

Furniss, Norman F. 1960. *The Mormon Conflict, 1850–1859*. New Haven: Yale Univ. Press.

Geertz, Clifford. 1973. "Ethos, World View, and the Analysis of Sacred Symbols." In *The Interpretation of Cultures*. New York: Basic Books.

George, John, and Laird Wilcox. 1992. *Nazis, Communists, Klansmen, and Others on the Fringe*. Buffalo: Prometheus.

———. 1996. *American Extremists, Supremacists, Klansmen, Communists, and Others*. Buffalo: Prometheus Books.

Gill, Sam. 1987. *Native American Religious Action: A Performance Approach to Religion*. Columbia: Univ. of South Carolina Press.

Givens, Terryl L. 1997. *The Viper on the Hearth: Mormons, Myths, and the Construction of Heresy*. New York: Oxford Univ. Press.

God—The Supreme Being. 1997. *God's Descending in Clouds (Flying Saucers) on Earth to Save People*. Garland, Tex.: Kingdom of God.

Godfrey, Kenneth W. 1965. "Causes of Mormon and Non-Mormon Conflict in Hancock County, Illinois, 1839–1846." Ph.D. diss. Brigham Young Univ.

Goodman, David G., and Masanori Miyaza. 1995. *Jews in the Japanese Mind: The History and Uses of a Cultural Stereotype*. New York: The Free Press.

Goodrick-Clarke, Nicholas. 1992. *The Occult Roots of Nazism*. New York: New York Univ. Press.

———. 1998. *Hitler's Priestess: Savitri Devi, the Hindu-Aryan Myth, and Occult Neo-Nazism*. New York: New York Univ. Press.

Hall, John R. 1987. *Gone from the Promised Land: Jonestown in American Cultural History*. New Brunswick, N.J.: Transaction.

———. 1995. "Public Narratives and the Apocalyptic Sect: From Jonestown to Mt. Carmel." In *Armageddon at Waco: Critical Perspectives on the Branch Davidian Conflict*, ed. Stuart A. Wright, 205–35. Chicago: Univ. of Chicago Press.

Hall, John R., and Philip Schuyler. 1997. "The Mystical Apocalypse of the Solar Temple." In *Millennium, Messiahs, and Mayhem: Contemporary Apocalyptic Movements*, ed. Thomas Robbins and Susan J. Palmer, 285–311. New York: Routledge.

———. 1998. "Apostasy, Apocalypse, and Religious Violence: An Exploratory Comparison of the Peoples Temple, the Branch Davidians, and the Solar Temple." In *The Politics of Religious Apostasy: The Role of Apostates in the Transformation of Religious Movements*, ed. David G. Bromley, 141–70. Westport, Conn.: Praeger.

Hamberg, Theodore. 1854. *The Visions of Hung-Siu-Tshuen and Origin of the Kwang-si Insurrection*. Hong Kong.

Hansen, Klaus. 1967. *Quest for Empire: The Political Kingdom of God and the Council of Fifty*. East Lansing: Michigan State Univ. Press.

Hanson, Paul D. 1979. *The Dawn of Apocalyptic: The History and Sociological Roots of Jewish Apocalyptic Eschatology*. Rev. ed. Philadelphia: Fortress Press.

———. 1985. "Apocalyptic Literature." In *The Hebrew Bible and Its Modern Interpreters*, ed. Douglas H. Knight and Gene M. Tucker, 465–88. Chico, Calif.: Scholars Press.

Hawk, David. 1989. "The Photographic Record." *In Cambodia: 1975–1978: Rendezvous with Death*, ed. Karl D. Jackson, 209–14. Princeton, N.J.: Princeton Univ. Press.

Hawthorne, George Eric. 1995. "News and Views." *Resistance* 4 (Spring): 42.

Heinerman, John, and Anson Shupe. 1985. *The Mormon Corporate Empire*. Boston: Beacon Press.

Herf, Jeffrey. 1984. *Reactionary Modernism*. Cambridge: Cambridge Univ. Press.

Hermand, Jost. 1992. *Old Dreams of a New Reich: Volkish Utopias and National Socialism*. Trans. Paul Levesaque. Bloomington: Indiana Univ. Press.

Hewitt, Andrew. 1993. *Fascist Modernism*. Stanford, Calif.: Stanford Univ. Press.

Hill, Marvin S. 1989. *Quest for Refuge: The Mormon Flight from American Pluralism*. Salt Lake City: Signature Books.

Hitler, Adolf. 1925. *Mein Kampf.* München: Verlag Franz Eher. 1943 English trans. Ralph Manheim. Boston: Houghton Mifflin.

Hodgson, Janet. 1982. *The God of the Xhosa: The Study of the Origins and Development of the Traditional Concepts of the Supreme Being*. Cape Town: Oxford Univ. Press.

Hoess, Rudolf. 1959. Commandant of Auschwitz. Trans. Constantine FitzGibbon. Cleveland: World Publishing Co.

Honychurch, Lennox. 1995. *The Dominica Story*. London: Macmillan Education Ltd.

House Committee on Un-American Activities. 1954. *Preliminary Report on Neo-Fascist and Hate Groups*. U.S. Government Printing Office. (Dec. 17).

House of Representatives. 1996. *Investigation into the Activities of Federal Law Enforcement Agencies toward the Branch Davidians: Thirteenth Report by the Committee on Government Reform and Oversight Prepared in Conjunction with the Committee on the Judiciary Together with Additional and Dissenting Views*. Report 104–749, Union Calendar No. 395. Washington, D.C.: U.S. Government Printing Office.

Howell, Vernon W. (David Koresh). 1985a. "Judge What I Say."

———. 1985b. "The Identity of the Ancient of Days and the Son of Man."

———. 1987a. "Study on the Assyrian."

———. 1987b. "Study on Joel and Daniel 11."

———. 1987c. "Confusion."

———. 1989a. "Vernon's Dream."

———. 1989b. "The Foundation."

Hughes, Lindsey. 1990. *Sophia, Regent of Russia: 1657–1704.* New Haven, Conn.: Yale.

Huguénin, Thierry. 1995. *Le 54e*. Paris: Fixot.

Hunter, James Davison. 1991. *Culture Wars: The Struggle to Define America.* New York: Basic Books.

Ikeda Daisaku. 1977. "Ikeda Kaichō no gosho kōgi *(Senji shō)*." *Daibyakurenge* 320 (Nov.):163–72.

Introvigne, Massimo. 1990. *Il cappello del mago. I nuovi movimenti magici dallo spiritismo al satanismo.* Milan: Sugar Co.

———. 1995a. "Ordeal by Fire: The Tragedy of the Solar Temple." *Religion* 25:267–83.

———. 1995b. *Idee che uccidono. Jonestown, Waco, il Tempio Solare.* Pessano (Milan): MIMEP-Docete.

———. 1997a. *Heaven's Gate. Il paradiso non può attendere.* Leumann, Turin: Elle Di Ci.

———. 1997b. "The Solar Temple Strikes Back: Comments and Interpretations after the Second Tragedy." *Theosophical History,* 6, no. 8:298–308.

———. 1998. "De la dérive vers le suicide et l'homicide. L'Ordre du Temple Solaire." In *Nouveaux mouvements religieux et logiques sectaires,* ed. Françoise Champion and Martine Cohen. Paris: Seuil.

Introvigne, Massimo, and J. Gordon Melton, eds. 1996. *Pour en finir avec les sectes. Le débat sur le rapport de la commission parlementaire.* 3d ed. Paris: Dervy.

Iokibe Makoto. 1970. "Ishiwara Kanji ni okeru Nichiren shūkyō." *Seikei ronsō* 19 (Feb.), nos. 5–6:121–47; and 20 (Apr.), no. 1:69–100.

Ishiwara Kanji. 1949. *Nichirenkyō nyūmon.* Osaka: Seikakai.

———. 1967 [1939]. *Sekai sensōkan.* In *Ishiwara Kanji shiryō, Meiji hyakunenshi sōsho,* vol. 18, ed. Tsunoda Jun, 297–308. Tokyo: Hara Shobō.

———. 1968 [1934]. *Ōshū kosenshi kōgi.* In *Ishiwara Kanji shiryō, Meiji hyakunenshi sōsho,* vol. 17, ed. Tsunoda Jun, 49–433. Tokyo: Hara Shobō.

———. 1986 [1940]. *Saishū sensōron.* In *Ishiwara Kanji senshū,* ed. Ishiwara Rokurō and Tamai Reiichirō, vol. 3, 19–98. Tokyo: Tamaira-bō.

Itagaki Eiken. 1995. *Oumu Shinrikyō to shūkyōseiji sensō.* Tokyo: Sanichi Shobō.

Jackson, Karl D. 1989. "Intellectual Origins of the Khmer Rouge." In *Cambodia: 1975–1978: Rendezvous with Death,* ed. Karl D. Jackson, 241–50. Princeton, N.J.: Princeton Univ. Press.

Jeansonne, Glen. 1988. *Gerald L. K. Smith: Minister of Hate.* New Haven, Conn.: Yale Univ. Press.

Jessee, Dean C., ed. 1989. *The Papers of Joseph Smith.* Vol. 1 *Autobiographical and Historical Writings.* Salt Lake City: Deseret Book.

Jessee, Dean C., and David J. Whittaker., eds. 1988. "The Last Months of Mormonism in Missouri: The Albert Perry Rockwood Journal." *BYU Studies* 28 (Winter):1–41.

Johnson, Clark V. 1992. *Mormon Redress Petitions: Documents of the 1833–1838 Missouri Conflict.* Provo, Utah: BYU Religious Studies Center.

Johnson, W. Fletcher. 1891. *Life of Sitting Bull and History of the Indian War of 1890–91.* Edgewood Publishing Company.

*Journal of Discourses.* 1851–86. Liverpool, England. 26 vols.

Kajima Tomoko. 1996. *Oumu no "onibaba" to yobarete.* Tokyo: Kindai Eigasha.

Kaplan, David E., and Andrew Marshall. 1996. *The Cult at the End of the World: The Incredible Story of Aum.* London: Arrow Books.

Kaplan, Jeffrey. 1997a. *Radical Religion in America: From the Far Right to the Children of Noah.* Syracuse: Syracuse Univ. Press.

———. 1997b. "The Postwar Paths Of Occult National Socialism: From Rockwell and Madole To Manson." Paper for the conference "Rejected and Suppressed Knowledge: The Racist Right and the Cultic Milieu." Stockholm, Sweden. (Feb. 13–17).

———. 1997c. "Leaderless Resistance." *Terrorism and Political Violence,* 9, no. 3 (Fall).

———. 1998. "Religiosity and the Radical Right: Toward the Creation of a New Ethnic Identity." In *Nation and Race,* ed. Jeffrey Kaplan and Tore Bjørgo. Boston: Northeastern Univ. Press.

———. Forthcoming. *Encyclopedia of White Power.* Goleta, Calif.: ABC-CLIO.

Kaplan, Jeffrey, and Leonard Weinberg. 1998. *The Emergence of a Euro-American Radical Right.* Rutgers, N.J.: Rutgers Univ. Press.

Kelley, Dean M. 1995. "Waco: A Massacre and Its Aftermath." *First Things* 52 (May 18):22–37.

Kelly, William Fitch. 1971. *Pine Ridge 1890: An Eye Witness Account of the Events Surrounding the Fighting at Wounded Knee.* Ed. and comp. Alexander Kelley and Pierre Bovis. San Francisco: Pierre Bovis.

Kenney, Scott G., ed. 1983–85. *Wilford Woodruff's Journal 1833–1898.* 9 vols. Typescript ed. Midvale, Utah: Signature Books.

Kern, Phil, and Doug Wead. 1979. *Peoples Temple, Peoples Tomb.* Plainfield N.J.: Logos International.

Ketelaar, James Edward. 1990. *Of Heretics and Martyrs in Meiji Japan: Buddhism and Its Persecution.* Princeton: Princeton Univ. Press.

Kiernan, Ben. 1983. "Wild Chickens, Farm Chickens, and Cormorants: Kampuchea's Eastern Zone under Pol Pot." In *Revolution and Its Aftermath in Kampuchea: Eight Essays,* ed. David P. Chandler and Ben Kiernan, 136–211. Monograph series no. 25. New Haven, Conn.: Yale Univ. Southeast Asia Studies.

———, trans. 1988a. "Decisions of the Central Committee on a Variety of Questions." In *Pol Pot Plans the Future: Confidential Leadership Documents from Democratic Kampuchea, 1976–1977,* ed. David P. Chandler, Ben Kiernan, and Chanthou Boua, 1–8. New Haven, Conn.: Yale Center for International and Area Studies.

———, trans. 1988b. "Planning the Past . . . the Forced Confessions of Hu Nim." In *Pol Pot Plans the Future: Confidential Leadership Documents from Democratic Kampuchea, 1976–1977,* ed. David P. Chandler, Ben Kiernan, and Chanthou Boua, 227–317. New Haven, Conn.: Yale Center for International and Area Studies.

Kilduff, Marshall, and Ron Javers. 1978. *The Suicide Cult: The Inside Story of the Peoples Temple Sect and the Massacre in Guyana.* New York: Bantam.

Kiriyama Seiyū. 1995a. *1999 nen shichigatsu ga kuru: unmei no hi no yogen to yochi.* Tokyo: Hirakawa Shuppan.

———. 1995b. *Oumu Shinrikyō to Agonshū.* Tokyo: Hirakawa Shuppan.

Kisala, Robert. 1996. "Protecting the State from Religion?: Religion, Politics, and the Law after Aum." Paper presented at the American Academy of Religion, New Orleans, Nov. 25, 1996.

Kisara Robāto (Kisala, Robert). 1997. *Shūkyōteki heiwa shisō no kenkyū: Nihon shinshūkyō no oshie to jissen.* Tokyo: Shunjūsha.

Kita Ikki. 1959a. *Shina kakumei gaishi.* In *Kita Ikki chōsakushū,* vol. 2, 1–213. Tokyo: Misuzu Shobō.

———. 1959b [1923]. *Nihon kaizō hōan taikō.* In *Kita Ikki chōsakushū,* vol. 2, 283–351. Tokyo: Misuzu Shobō.

Kleim, Milton John, Jr. Forthcoming. "Internet-Recruiting." In *Encyclopedia of White Power,* by Jeffrey Kaplan. Goleta, Calif.: ABC-CLIO.

Koch, Klaus. 1983. "What Is Apocalyptic: An Attempt at a Preliminary Definition." In *Visionaries and Their Apocalypses,* ed. Paul D. Hanson, 16–36. Philadelphia: Fortress Press.

Koresh, David. 1993a. "Untitled March 2 Radio Address."

———. 1993b. Apr. 14 letter to attorney Dick DeGuerin.

———. 1993c. *The Seven Seals of the Book of Revelation.* In *Why Waco? Cults and the Battle for Religious Freedom in America,* James D. Tabor and Eugene V. Gallagher, 191–211. Berkeley: Univ. of California Press.

Krause, Charles, with Laurence M. Stern and Richard Harwood. 1978. *Guyana Massacre: The Eyewitness Account.* New York: Hawthorne.

Kromminga, D. H. 1945. *The Millennium in the Church: Studies in the History of Christian Chiliasm.* Grand Rapids, Mich.: Eerdmans.

Kulke, Hermann. 1978. *The Devaraja Cult.* Trans. I. W. Mabbett. Southeast Asia Data paper no. 108. Ithaca, N.Y.: Cornell Univ.

Kumamoto Nichinichi Shinbun, ed. 1992. *Oumu Shinrikyō to mura no ronri.* Fukuoka: Ashi Shobō.

Kure Tomofusa, Hashizume Daisaburō, et al. 1996. *Oumu to kindai kokka: shimin wa Oumu o kyoyō suru ka.* Tokyo: Nanpūsha.

Kyōdō Tsūshinsha Shakaibu, ed. 1997. *Sabakareru kyōso.* Tokyo Kyōdō Tsūshinsha.

Lamy, Philip. 1996. *Millennium Rage: Survivalists, White Supremacists, and the Doomsday Prophecy.* New York: Plenum.

Landes, Richard. 1996. "Apocalyptic Expectations Around the Year 1000." Center for Millennial Studies. <http://www.mille.org/1000–br.html>.

———. n.d. "The Apocalyptic Dossier: 967–1033." Center for Millennial Studies. <http://www.mille.org/1000–dos.htm>.

Laqueur, Walter. 1996a. *Fascism: Past, Present, Future*. New York: Oxford Univ. Press.

———. 1996b. "Postmodern Terrorism." *Foreign Affairs* 75 (Sept.–Oct.): 24–36.

Lee, Edwin B. 1975. "Nichiren and Nationalism: The Religious Patriotism of Tanaka Chigaku." *Monumenta Nipponica* 30, no. 1: 19–35.

Le Forestier, René. 1987. *La Franc-Maçonnerie templière et occultiste au XVIIIe et XIXe siècles*. Reprint. 2 vols. Paris: La Table d'Eméraude.

Levering, Miriam Lindsey. 1981. "Millenarian Movements." In *Abingdon Dictionary of Living Religions*, ed. Keith Crim, 480–81. Nashville: Abingdon.

Levy, Richard S., ed. 1995. *A Lie and a Libel: The History of the Protocols of the Elders of Zion*. Lincoln: Univ. of Nebraska Press.

Lewis, James R., ed. 1994. *From the Ashes: Making Sense of Waco*. Lanham, Md.: Rowman and Littlefield.

Li, Zhisui. 1994. *The Private Life of Chairman Mao*. New York: Random House.

Liang, Heng, and Judith Shapiro. 1983. *Son of the Revolution*. New York: Random House.

Lindsey, Hal. 1970. *The Late Great Planet Earth*. Grand Rapids, Mich.: Zondervan.

Long, E. B. 1981. *The Saints and the Union: Utah Territory During the Civil War*. Urbana: Univ. of Illinois Press.

Lowith, Karl. 1949. *Meaning in History: Theological Implications of the Philosophy of History*. Chicago: Univ. of Chicago Press.

Lucas, Phillip. 1994. "How Future Wacos Might Be Avoided: Two Proposals." In *From the Ashes: Making Sense of Waco*, ed. James R. Lewis, 209–12. Lanham, Md.: Rowman and Littlefield.

Lucas, Phillip Charles. 1997. "Shifting Millennial Visions in New Religious Movements: The Case of the Holy Order of MANS." In *The Year 2000: Essays on the End*, ed. Charles B. Strozier and Michael Flynn, 121–32. New York: New York Univ. Press.

Lyotard, Jean-François. 1984. *The Postmodern Condition: A Report on Knowledge*. Trans. by Geoff Bennington and Brian Massumio. Minneapolis: Univ. of Minn. Press.

Maaga, Mary McCormick. 1996. "Triple Erasure: Women and Power in Peoples Temple." Ph.D. diss., Drew Univ..

———. 1998. *Hearing the Voices of Jonestown*. Syracuse, N.Y.: Syracuse Univ. Press.

Macdonald, Andrew (William Pierce). 1978. *The Turner Diaries*. Arlington, Va.: National Vanguard Books.

———. 1989. *Hunter*. Arlington, Va.: National Vanguard Books.

Maha Khema (Ishii Hisako). 1991. "Welcome to the Astral World." *Mahayana News Letter* 24:93–110.

Mahayana News Letter, 1989. No. 14:2–3, 24–25.

———. 1990. July: 29.

Mainichi Shinbun Shūkyō Shuzaihan, ed. 1993. *Kiseimatsu no kamisama*. Tokyo: Tōhō Shuppan.

Marsden, Victor E., trans. and ed. n.d. *The Protocols of Zion.* n.p.

Marston, John. 1994. "Metaphors of the Khmer Rouge." In *Cambodian Culture Since 1975: Homeland and Exile,* ed. May M. Ebihara et al. Ithaca, N.Y.: Cornell Univ. Press.

Marty, Martin E. 1987. *Religion and Republic: The American Circumstance.* Boston: Beacon Press.

Marty, Martin E., and R. Scott Appleby. 1993. *Fundamentals and the State: Remaking Politics, Economics, and Militance.* Chicago: Univ. of Chicago Press.

Marx, Karl, and Frederick Engels. 1978. "The German Ideology." In *The Marx-Engels Reader,* ed. Robert C. Tucker, 146–200. 2d ed. New York: W. W. Norton and Company.

Mason, James. 1992. *Siege.* Denver: Storm.

———. 1995. "Charles Manson: Illusion vs. Reality." *Resistance* 4 (Spring): 20–22.

———. 1998. "1-800-Hell-Yes." *Ohm Clock Magazine* 5 (Spring):20–21.

———. Forthcoming. "National Socialist Liberation Front." In *Encyclopedia of White Power,* by Jeffrey Kaplan. Goleta, Calif.: ABC-CLIO.

Mayer, Jean-François. 1997. *Il Tempio Solare.* Updated Italian ed. Leumann, Turin: Elle Di Ci.

———. 1998. "Les Chevaliers de l'Apocalypse. Quelques observations sur l'Ordre du Temple Solaire et ses adepts." In *Nouveaux mouvements religieux et logiques sectaires,* ed. Françoise Champion and Martine Cohen. Paris: Seuil.

———. 1999. "Our Terrestrial Journey Is Coming to an End': The Last Voyage of the Solar Temple." *Nova Religio: The Journal of Alternative and Emergent Religions* 2, no. 2 (Apr.): 172–96.

McConkie, Bruce R. 1982. *The Millennial Messiah.* Salt Lake City: Deseret Book.

McGillycuddy, Julia B. 1941. *McGillycuddy Agent.* Stanford, Calif.: Stanford Univ. Press.

McKnight, Stephen A. 1995. "Voegelin and Gnostic Features of Modernity." In *The Allure of Gnosticism,* ed. Robert A. Segal, 136–46. Chicago: Open Court.

Meisner, Maurice. 1977. *Mao's China: A History of the People's Republic.* New York: Free Press.

Melville, J. Keith. 1960. "Theory and Practice of Church and State During the Brigham Young Era." *Brigham Young Univ. Studies* 3:33–55.

Merton, Robert K. 1968. *Social Theory and Social Structure.* New York: The Free Press.

Métraux, Daniel A. 1994. *The Soka Gakkai Revolution.* Lanham, Md.: Univ. Press of America.

Michael, Franz. 1966. *The Taiping Rebellion: History and Documents.* Vol.1, *History.* Seattle: Univ. of Washington Press.

———. 1971a. *The Taiping Rebellion: History and Documents.* Vol. 2, *Documents and Comments.* Seattle: Univ. of Washington Press.

Massie, Robert. 1980. *Peter the Great.* New York: Knopf.

———. 1971b. *The Taiping Rebellion: History and Documents*. Vol. 3, *Documents and Comments*. Seattle: Univ. of Washington Press.

Mihailova, Yulia. 1996. "The Aum Supreme Truth Sect in Russia." *Bulletin of the Japanese Studies Association of Australia* 16, no. 3:15–34.

Miliukov, Paul. 1942. *Outlines of Russian Culture. Part One: Religion and the Church in Russia*. Philadelphia: Univ. of Pennsylvania.

Millard, Joan. 1997. "The Bulhoek Tragedy," 25, no. 3: 418–28.

Miller, Joaquin [Cincinnatus Hiner]. 1881. *Danites in the High Sierras*. Chicago: Jansen and Co.

Mills, Jeannie. 1979. *Six Years with God: Life Inside Rev. Jim Jones's Peoples Temple*. New York: A&W Publishers.

Mooney, James. 1896/1973. "The Ghost-Dance Religion and the Sioux Outbreak of 1890." *Fourteenth Annual Report of the Bureau of Ethnology*. Washington, D.C.: Government Printing Office. Reprint. *The Ghost-Dance Religion and Wounded Knee*. New York: Dover Publications.

Moore, Carol. 1995. *The Davidian Massacre: Disturbing Questions about Waco Which Must Be Answered*. Franklin, Tenn., and Springfield, Va.: Legacy Communications and Gun Owners of America.

Moore, Rebecca. 1985. *A Sympathetic History of Jonestown: The Moore Family Involvement in Peoples Temple*. Lewiston, N.Y.: Edwin Mellen Press.

———. 1986. *The Jonestown Letters: Correspondence of the Moore Family 1970–1985*. Lewiston, N.Y.: Edwin Mellen Press.

Moorehead, Warren K. 1891. "The Indian Messiah and the Ghost Dance." *The American Antiquarian and Oriental Journal*. XIII: 161–67.

Moorhead, James H. 1978. *American Apocalypse: Yankee Protestants and Civil War, 1860–1869*. New Haven, Conn.: Yale Univ. Press.

———. 1979. "Social Reform and the Divided Conscience of Antebellum Protestantism." *Church History* 48:416–30.

Moorman, Donald R., and Gene A. Sessions. 1992. *Camp Floyd and the Mormons: The Utah War*. Salt Lake City: Univ. of Utah Press.

Morioka Kiyomi. 1994. "Attacks on the New Religions: Rissho⁻ Ko⁻seikai and the 'Yomiuri Affair.'" *Japanese Journal of Religious Studies* 21, nos. 2–3:281–310.

Mullins, Mark R. 1997. "The Political/Legal Response to Aum-Related Violence in Japan." *Japan Christian Review* 63:37–46

Murvar, Vatro. 1971. "Messianism in Russia: Religious and Revolutionary." *Journal for the Scientific Study of Religion* 14, no. 3:229–57.

Nakano Kyōtoku. 1977. "Tanaka Chigaku: Hōkoku myōgōron kara Nihon kokutairon e no tenkai." In *Kindai Nichiren kyōdan no shisōka*, ed. Nakano Kyōtoku, 148–98. Tokyo: Kokusho Kankōkai.

Naquin, Susan. 1976. *Millenarian Rebellion in China: The Eight Trigrams Uprising of 1813*. New Haven, Conn.: Yale Univ. Press.

Nattier, Jan. 1991. *Once upon a Future Time: Studies in a Buddhist Prophecy of Decline*. Berkeley, Calif.: Asian Humanities Press.

Naud, Yvon. 1997. "Rapport d'investigation du Coroner A-109231: Didier Quèze." Quebec: Gouvernement du Québec, Bureau du Coroner.

Nelson, Geoffrey K. 1969. *Spiritualism and Society*. New York: Schocken Books.

New Order. n.d. *The Religion of Lincoln Rockwell*. Milwaukee: New Order.

*New York Times*. 1996. (May 18).

*Nexus*. 1995. "James Hartung Madole: Father of Post-War Fascism" (Nov.): 1–4.

*Nightline*. 1993. Journal Graphics transcript. June 9.

Nugent, John Peer. 1979. *White Night: The Untold Story of What Happened Before—and Beyond—Jonestown*. New York: Rawson, Wade.

Numbers, Ronald L., and Jonathan M. Butler, eds. 1987. *The Disappointed: Millerism and Millenarianism in the Nineteenth Century*. Bloomington: Indiana Univ. Press.

Ōkawa Ryūhō. 1990a. *Taiyō no hō*. Tokyo: Kōfuku no Kagaku Shuppan.

———. 1990b. *Nosutoradamusu no shinyogen*. Tokyo: Kōfuku no Kagaku Shuppan.

———. 1990c. *The Laws of the Sun*. Tokyo: Kōfuku no Kagaku Shuppan.

———. 1990d. *The Laws of Gold*. Tokyo: Kōfuku no Kagaku Shuppan.

O'Leary, Stephen. 1994. *Arguing the Apocalypse: A Theory of Millennial Rhetoric*. New York: Oxford Univ. Press.

Oliver, W. H. 1978. *Prophets and Millennialists: The Uses of Biblical Prophecy in England from the 1790s to the 1840s*. Auckland, New Zealand: Auckland Univ. Press.

Order of Nine Angles. n.d. "A Gift for the Prince—A Guide to Human Sacrifice." n.p.

———. n.d. "Culling—A Guide to Sacrifice II." n.p.

———. n.d. "Guidelines for the Testing of Opfers." n.p.

———. n.d. "Victims—A Sinister Exposé." n.p.

Overholt, Thomas W. 1978. "Short Bull, Black Elk, Sword, and the 'Meaning' of the Ghost Dance." *Religion* 7–8:171–95.

Owings, Alison. 1994. *Frauen: German Women Recall the Third Reich*. New Brunswick, N.J.: Rutgers Univ. Press.

Palmer, Susan. 1994. "Excavating Waco." In *From the Ashes: Making Sense of Waco*, ed. James R. Lewis, 99–110. Lanham, Md.: Rowman and Littlefield.

———. 1996. "Purity and Danger in the Solar Temple." *Journal of Contemporary Religion* 11, no. 3 (Oct.):303–18.

Payne, Neill H. 1996. "Shades of Waco." *The Balance: A Newsletter of Civil Rights and Current Events* 7/2 (Summer):1–3.

Payne, Stanley G. 1995. *A History of Fascism 1914–1945*. Madison: Univ. of Wisconsin Press.

Peattie, Mark R. 1975. *Ishiwara Kanji and Japan's Confrontation with the West*. Princeton, N.J.: Princeton Univ. Press.

Peires, J. B. 1987. *The House of Phalo: A History of the Xhosa People in the Days of Their Independence*. Johannesburg: Ravan.

———. 1989. *The Dead Will Arise: Nongqawuse and the Great Xhosa Cattle-Killing Movement of 1856–7*. Johannesburg: Ravan

Pelchat, Martin. 1993. "Jouret avait été écarté de l'Ordre du Temple Solaire." *La Presse* (Montreal), (Mar. 18).

Penrose, Charles. 1909. "O Ye Mountains High." In *Deseret Sunday School Songs*, 198. Salt Lake City: Deseret Sunday School Union.

Peterson, Paul H. 1989. "The Mormon Reformation of 1856–57: The Rhetoric and the Reality." *Journal of Mormon History* 15:59–87.

Picq, Laurence. 1989. *Beyond the Horizon: Five Years with the Khmer Rouge*. New York: St. Martin's Press.

Pierce, William L. 1969. *Lincoln Rockwell: A National Socialist Life*. Arlington, Va.: NS Publications.

Pitcavage, Mark. 1996. "Every Man a King: The Rise and Fall of the Montana Freemen." (May 6) Militia Watchdog. <http://www.greyware.com/authors/pitman/freemen. htm>.

*Playboy*. 1966. "George Lincoln Rockwell: A Candid Conversation with the Fanatical Fuhrer of the American Nazi Party." (Apr.):obtained as E-text <http://www.playboy.org>.

Ponchaud, François. 1989. "Social Change in the Vortex of Revolution." In *Cambodia: 1975–1978: Rendezvous with Death*, ed. Karl D. Jackson, 151–77. Princeton, N.J.: Princeton Univ. Press.

———. 1978. *Cambodia: Year Zero*, trans. Nancy Amphoux. New York: Holt, Rinehart, and Winston.

*Proclamation of the Twelve Apostles of the Church of Jesus Christ of Latter-day Saints. To All the Kings of the World; To the President of the United States of America, To the Governors of the Several States; And to the Rulers and People of all Nations*. 1845. New York.

Quinn, Kenneth. 1989. "Explaining the Terror." In *Cambodia: 1975–1978: Rendezvous with Death*, ed. Karl D. Jackson, 179–208. Princeton, N.J.: Princeton Univ. Press.

Quinn, Michael D. 1980. "The Council of Fifty and Its Members, 1844–1945." *BYU Studies* 20:163–97.

Raban, Jonathan. 1996. "The Unlamented West." *The New Yorker* 20 (May):60–81.

Rankin, Heidi. 1996. "The Montana Freemen: The Untold Story." *Jubilee* 9/1 (Sept./Oct.):7.

Rapoport, David C. 1971. *Assassination and Terrorism*. Toronto: Canadian Broadcasting Corporation.

———. 1984. "Fear and Trembling: Terrorism in Three Religious Traditions." *American Political Science Review* 78/3 (Sept.): 471–92.

———. 1988. "Messianic Sanctions for Terror." *Comparative Politics* 20/2 (Jan.):195–213.

Reader, Ian. 1988. "The 'New' New Religions of Japan: An Analysis of the Rise of Agonshu." *Japanese Journal of Religious Studies* 15, no. 4:235–61.

———. 1991. *Religion in Contemporary Japan.* Honolulu: Univ. of Hawaii Press.

———. 1996. *A Poisonous Cocktail? Aum Shinrikyō's Path to Violence.* Copenhagen: NIAS Books.

———. 2000. *Religious Violence in Contemporary Japan: The Case of Aum Shinrikyō.* London and Honolulu: Curzon and Univ. of Hawaii.

*Reader's Digest Illustrated History of South Africa: The Real Story.* 1988. Cape Town: Reader's Digest.

Reaney, Patricia. 1997. "Antisemites Find New Ways to Convey Message." Reuter wire report. (July 18).

Reavis, Dick J. 1995. *The Ashes of Waco.* New York: Simon and Schuster.

Reynolds, Frank E. 1978. "The Holy Emerald Jewel: Some Aspects of Buddhist Symbolism and Political Legitimation in Thailand and Laos." In *Religion and the Legitimation of Power in Thailand, Laos, and Burma,* ed. Bardwell Smith, 175–93. Chambersburg, Pa.: Anima Books.

———. 1985. "Multiple Cosmogonies and Ethics: The Case of Theravada Buddhism." In *Cosmogony and the Ethical Order: New Studies in Comparative Ethics,* ed. Robin W. Lovin and Frank E. Reynolds, 203–24. Chicago: Univ. of Chicago Press.

Rhodes, James M. 1980. *The Hitler Movement: A Modern Millenarian Revolution.* Stanford, Calif.: Hoover Institution Press.

Riefenstahl, Leni. 1987. *Memoiren.* München: Albrecht Knaus; 1992. *The Sieve of Time.* London: Quartet Books.

Rigdon, Sidney. 1838. *Oration Delivered by Mr. S. Rigdon on the 4th of July, 1838.*

Risshō Daigaku Nichiren Kyōgaku Kenkyūjo, ed. 1988 [1952–59]. Rev. ed. *Shōwa teihon Nichiren Shōnin ibun.* 4 vols. Minobu-chō, Yamanashi Prefecture: Minobusan Kuonji.

Robbins, Thomas. 1986. "Religious Mass Suicide Before Jonestown: The Russian Old Believers." *Sociological Analysis* 41, no. 1:1–20.

———. 1989. "The Antecedents of Jonestown: The Sociology of Martyrdom." In *New Religious Movements, Mass Suicide, and Peoples Temple,* ed. Rebecca Moore and Fielding McGehee, 51–70. Lewiston, N.Y.: Edwin Mellen.

———. 1997. "Religious Movements and Violence: A Friendly Critique of the Interpretive Approach." *Nova Religio: The Journal of Alternative and Emergent Religions* 1, no. 1 (Oct.):13–29.

Robbins, Thomas, and Dick Anthony. 1995. "Sects and Violence: Factors Enhancing the Volatility of Marginal Religious Movements." In *Armageddon in Waco: Critical Perspectives on the Branch Davidian Conflict,* ed. Stuart A. Wright, 236–59. Chicago: Univ. of Chicago Press.

Robbins, Thomas, and Susan J. Palmer, eds. 1997a. *Millennium, Messiahs, and Mayhem: Contemporary Apocalyptic Movements.* New York: Routledge.

———. 1997b. "Introduction." In *Millennium, Messiahs, and Mayhem: Contemporary Apocalyptic Movements,* ed. Thomas Robbins and Susan J. Palmer, 1–27. New York: Routledge.

Rockwell, George Lincoln. 1963. *This Time the World!* Arlington, Va.: Parliament House.

Roots, Roger. 1996. "Judge Recognizes Freemen Court." *Jubilee* 8/6 (July/Aug.):1, 6.

Rose, Douglas D., ed. 1992. *The Emergence of David Duke and the Politics of Race.* Chapel Hill: Univ. of North Carolina Press.

Rosenberg, Alfred. 1930. *Der Mythos des XX. Jahrhunderts.* München: Hoheneichen-verlag.

Rosenfeld, Jean E. 1997. "The Importance of the Analysis of Religion in Avoiding Violent Outcomes: The Justus Freemen Crisis." *Nova Religio: The Journal of Alternative and Emergent Religions* 1, no. 1 (Oct.):72–95.

———. 1999. "Response to Mayer's 'Our Terrestrial Journey is Coming to an End.'" *Nova Religio: The Journal of Alternative and Emergent Religions* 2, no. 2 (Apr.):197–207.

Rosenthal, A. M., and Arthur Gelb. 1967. *One More Victim: The Life and Death of a Jewish Nazi.* New York: New American Library.

Russell, Samuel, ed. and comp. 1913. *The Millennial Hymns of Parley Parker Pratt.* Cambridge: Univ. Press.

Samples, Kenneth, Erwin DeCastro, Richard Arbunes, and Robert Lyle. 1994. *Prophets of the Apocalypse: David Koresh and Other American Messiahs.* Grand Rapids, Mich.: Baker.

Sandeen, Ernest R. 1970. *The Roots of Fundamentalism: British and American Millenarianism.* Chicago: Univ. of Chicago Press.

Sapp, Allen D. 1986. "Ideological Justification for Right Wing Extremism: An Analysis of the Nehemiah Township Charter Document." Unpublished paper. Center for Criminal Justice Research, Central Missouri State Univ..

Sartre, Jean-Paul. 1963. "Preface." In *The Wretched of the Earth,* by Frantz Fanon. Trans. Constance Farrington, 7–31. New York: Grove Press.

Savitri Devi. 1966. "The Lightning and the Sun." *National Socialist World* 1 (Spring):14–90.

———. 1967. "Gold in the Furnace." *National Socialist World* 3 (Spring):59–71.

———. 1968. "Defiance." *National Socialist World* 6 (Winter):64–87.

———. 1991. *Impeachment of Man.* Costa Mesa, Calif.: Noontide Press.

Scheffel, David. 1991. *In the Shadow of Antichrist.* Peterborough, Ont.: Broadview Press.

Segel, Binjamin W. 1995 [1924]. *A Lie and a Libel: The History of the Protocols of the Elders of Zion.* Ed. Richard S. Levy. Lincoln: Univ. of Nebraska Press.

Séguin, Rhéal. 1997. "Autopsies Seek Clues to Deadly Ritual." *The Globe and Mail* (Toronto) (Mar. 24).

Selwyn, Elizabeth. 1990. "The Right Wing Left Hand Path." *Black Flame* (Winter): obtained as E-text from private individual associated with the Church of Satan.

Serizawa Shunsuke. 1995. *Oumu genshō no kaidoku*. Tokyo: Chikuma Shōbo.

Shepherd, Gordon, and Gary Shepherd. 1984. *A Kingdom Transformed*. Salt Lake City: Univ. of Utah Press.

Shimada Hiromi. 1995. *Shinji yasui kokoro*. Tokyo: PHP.

Shimazono Susumu. 1995a. *Oumu Shinrikyō no kiseki*. No. 379. Tokyo: Iwanami Booklets.

———. 1995b. "In the Wake of Aum: The Formation and Transformation of a Universe of Belief." *Japanese Journal of Religious Studies* 22, no. 3–4: 343–80.

———. 1997. *Gendai shūkyō no kanōsei: Oumu Shinrikyō to bōryoku*. Tokyo: Iwanami Shoten.

Shupe, Anson D., and David G. Bromley. 1981. "Apostates and Atrocity Stories." In *The Social Impact of New Religious Movements*, ed. Bryan Wilson, 179–215. New York: Rose of Sharon Press.

Shupe, Anson, and David G. Bromley, eds. 1994. *Anti-Cult Movements in Cross-Cultural Perspective*. New York: Garland Publishing.

Shupe, Anson, David G. Bromley, and Edward Breschel. 1989. "The Peoples Temple, the Apocalypse at Jonestown, and the Anti-Cult Movement." In *New Religious Movements, Mass Suicide, and Peoples Temple: Scholarly Perspectives on a Tragedy*, ed. Rebecca Moore and Fielding McGehee III, 153–78. Lewiston, N.Y.: Edwin Mellen Press.

Simonelli, Frederick J. 1997. "Thriving in a Cultic Milieu: The World Union of National Socialists, 1962–1992." Paper delivered at the conference "The Radical Right and the Cultic Milieu," Stockholm, Sweden. (Feb. 13–17).

———. 1998. "The World Union of National Socialists and Post-War Transatlantic Nazi Revival." In *Nation and Race: The Developing Euro-American Racist Subculture*, ed. Jeffrey Kaplan and Tore Bjørgo. Boston: Northeastern Univ. Press.

———. 1999. *American Fuehrer: George Lincoln Rockwell and the American Nazi Party*. Univ. of Illinois Press.

Skurdal, Rodney O. 1994. "Edict." (Oct. 28) Unpublished document available through the Montana Human Rights Network, P.O. Box 1222, Helena, MT 59624.

Smith, Frank. 1989. *Interpretive Accounts of the Khmer Rouge Years: Personal Experience in Cambodian Peasant World View*. Occasional Paper no. 18. Madison: Center for Southeast Asian Studies.

Smith, Joseph Jr. 1976. *History of the Church of Jesus Christ of Latter-day Saints.* Ed. B. H. Roberts. 7 vols. Salt Lake City: Deseret Book.

Spence, Jonathan D. 1996. *God's Chinese Son: The Taiping Heavenly Kingdom of Hong Xiuquan.* New York: W. W. Norton.

Spengler, Oswald. 1922–23. *Der Untergang des Abendlandes.* München: Beck. 1926–28. *The Decline of the West.* New York: Knopf.

Stern, Peter K. 1996. "Montana Siege Update." (June 3) From the Liberty Newswire, published and redistributed by release agent Peter Kawaja. Internet posting by the Assembly of IaHUShUA MaShIaChaH (iahu@efn.org).

Stone, Jacqueline I. 1997. "The Ideal of *Risshō Ankoku* in the Nichiren Buddhist Movements of Postwar Japan." Paper delivered at the Third Chung-Hwa International Conference on Buddhism, Taipei. (July).

Suksamran, Somboon. 1993. "Buddhism, Political Authority, and Legitimacy in Thailand and Cambodia." In *Buddhist Trends in Southeast Asia,* ed. Trevor Ling. Singapore: Institute of Southeast Asian Studies.

Sundkler, B. G. M. 1976 [1948]. *Bantu Prophets in South Africa.* London: Oxford Univ. Press.

*Survivre à l'an 2000.* 1986. 2 vols. Toronto: Atlanta.

Sweet, Leonard I. 1979. "Millennialism in America." *Theological Studies* 40:510–31.

Switzer [Bartlett], Jennie. 1882. *Elder Northfield's Home, or, Sacrificed on the Mormon Altar.* New York: J. Howard Brown.

Sword, George. 1892. "The Story of the Ghost Dance." *The Folk-Lorist* 1:28–36.

Tabachnik, Michel. 1997. *Le bouc émissaire. Dans le piège du Temple Solaire.* Paris: Michel Lafon.

Tabor, James D., and Eugene V. Gallagher. 1995. *Why Waco? Cults and the Battle for Religious Freedom in America.* Berkeley: Univ. of California Press.

Taguieff, Pierre André. 1992. *Les Protocoles des Sages de Sion.* 2 vols. Paris: Berg International.

Takahashi Hidetoshi. 1995. *Oumu kara no kikan.* Tokyo: Sōshisha.

Takimoto Tarō, and Fukushima Mizuho. 1996. *Habōhō to Oumu Shinrikyō.* No. 398. Tokyo: Iwanami Booklets.

Talmon, Yonina. 1962. "Pursuit of the Millennium: The Relation Between Religious and Social Change." *Archieves Européènes de Sociologie* 3: 125–48.

———. 1966. "Millenarian Movements." *Archieves Européènes de Sociologie* 7: 159–200.

Tambiah, Stanley J. 1970. *Buddhism and the Spirit Cults in North-East Thailand.* New York: Cambridge Univ. Press.

Tanabe, George J., Jr. 1989. "Tanaka Chigaku: The *Lotus Sutra* and the Body Politic." In *The Lotus Sutra in Japanese Culture,* ed. George J. Tanabe Jr. and Willa Jane Tanabe, 191–208. Honolulu: Univ. of Hawaii Press.

Tanaka Chigaku. 1931. *Shūmon no ishin.* In *Shishiō zenshū,* ed. Shishiō Zenshū Kankōkai, vol. 7, 1–152. Tokyo: Shishiō Bunko.

————. 1936. *Tanaka Chigaku jiden*. Vol. 7. Tokyo: Shishiō Bunko.

Thorpe, Shirley. 1982. "A Comparative Study of Two Millenarian Responses to Stress: The North American Indian Ghost Dance (1890) and the Xhosa Cattle-Killing (1857)." M.Th. thesis. Univ. of South Africa.

Tillich, Paul. 1957. *Dynamics of Faith*. New York: Harper and Row.

*Times and Seasons*. 1839–46. Nauvoo, Ill.

Tokoro Shigemoto. 1966. *Kindai Nihon no shūkyō to nashonarizumu*. Tokyo: Fuzanbō.

————. 1972. *Kindai shakai to Nichirenshugi*. Tokyo: Hyōronsha.

Tōkyō Shinbun Shakaibu, ed. 1995. *Oumu: Soshiki hanzai no nazo*. Tokyo: Tōkyō Shinbun Shuppankyoku.

"The Tracks of Salvation, Part 1." 1989a. *Mahayana News Letter* 13:45–55.

"The Tracks of Salvation, Part 2." 1989b. *Mahayana News Letter*. 14:46–52.

"The Tracks of Salvation, Part 3." 1989c. *Mahayana News Letter* 15:48–53.

Underwood, Grant. 1993. *The Millenarian World of Early Mormonism*. Urbana: Univ. of Illinois Press.

United States Department of the Treasury, Bureau of Alcohol, Tobacco, and Firearms. 1993. Tapes of negotiations with the Branch Davidians at the Mount Carmel Center, Mar. 1 to Apr. 19.

United States House of Representatives. 1979. *Staff Investigative Report to the Committee on Foreign Affairs of the U.S. House of Representatives*. Washington, D.C.: Government Printing Office.

Utley, Robert M. 1963. *The Last Days of the Sioux Nation*. New Haven, Conn.: Yale Univ. Press.

*Vejrayāna Sacca*. 1995. No. 9 (April).

Vernadsky, George. 1969. *The Tsardom of Moscovy*. Vol. 5, Part B. New Haven: Yale.

Vestal, Stanley. 1932. *Sitting Bull Champion of the Sioux; A Biography*. Boston and New York: Houghton Mifflin Company.

————. 1934. *New Sources of Indian History 1850–1890*. Norman: Univ. of Oklahoma Press.

Vickery, Michael. 1983. "Democratic Kampuchea: Themes and Variations." In *Revolution and Its Aftermath in Kampuchea: Eight Essays*, ed. David P. Chandler and Ben Kiernan, 99–135. Monograph series no. 25. New Haven, Conn.: Yale Univ. Southeast Asia Studies.

————. 1984. *Cambodia: 1975–1982*. Boston: South End Press.

Voegelin, Eric. 1952. *The New Science of Politics*. Chicago: Univ. of Chicago Press.

————. 1968. *Science, Politics, and Gnosticism*. Chicago: Henry Regnary.

————. 1995. *From Enlightenment to Revolution*. Durham, N.C.: Duke Univ. Press.

Wagner, Rudolf G. 1982. *Reenacting the Heavenly Vision: The Role of Religion in the Taiping Rebellion*. Berkeley: Univ. of California Press.

Waite, Gary K. 1995. "The Religious State: A Comparative Study of Sixteenth- and Nineteenth-Century Opposition: The Case of the Anabaptists and the Babis." *Journal of Baha'i Studies* 7/1: 69–90.

Walker, James R. 1992. *Lakota Society.* Ed. Raymond J. DeMallie. Lincoln: Univ. of Nebraska Press. 1982. Reprint.

Wallace, Anthony F. C. 1956. "Revitalization Movements," *American Anthropologist* 58/2 (Apr.):264–81.

Wallis, Roy. 1977. *The Road to Total Freedom: A Sociological Analysis of Scientology.* New York: Columbia.

Watanabe Manabu. 1997. "Reactions to the Aum Affair: The Rise of the Anti-Cult Movement in Japan." *Bulletin of the Nanzan Institute for Religion and Culture* 21:32–48.

Ward, Gloria Teneuviel. 1996. "'Who Has the Right,' God's Children or Satanists?" *Jubilee* 9/1 (Sept./Oct.):7.

Weisbrod, Carol. 1980. *The Boundaries of Utopia.* New York: Pantheon.

Wentz, Richard E. 1993. *Why People Do Bad Things in the Name of Religion.* Macon, Ga.: Mercer Univ. Press.

Wessinger, Catherine. 1988. *Annie Besant and Progressive Messianism.* Lewiston, N.Y.: Edwin Mellen Press.

———. 1995. "Religious Intolerance—Not 'Cults'—Is the Problem. *Communities: Journal of Cooperative Living* 88 (Fall):32–33.

———. 1997a. "Millennialism With and Without the Mayhem." In *Millennium, Messiahs, and Mayhem,* ed. Thomas Robbins and Susan J. Palmer, 47–59. New York: Routledge.

———. 1997b. "How the Millennium Comes Violently: A Comparison of Jonestown, Aum Shinrikyo, Branch Davidians, and the Montana Freemen." *Dialog: A Journal of Theology* 36/4: 277–88.

———. 1997c."Review Essay: Understanding the Branch Davidian Tragedy." In *Nova Religio: The Journal of Alternative and Emergent Religions* 1/1 (Oct.):122–38.

———. 2000. *How the Millennium Comes Violently: From Jonestown to Heaven's Gate.* New York: Seven Bridges Press.

Wicker, Christine. 1998a. "Garland Sect Prepares for God's Arrival." *Dallas Morning News* (Mar. 22):1A, 32A.

———. 1998b. "Apparent Appearances: Religious Leader Says Those Present Are God." *Dallas Morning News* (Apr. 1):23A, 28A.

Wilson, George M. 1969. *Radical Nationalist in Japan: Kita Ikki, 1883–1937.* Cambridge, Mass.: Harvard Univ. Press.

Winn, Kenneth H. 1989. *Exiles in a Land of Liberty: Mormons in America, 1830–1846.* Chapel Hill: Univ. of North Carolina Press.

Worsley, Peter. 1968. *The Trumpet Shall Sound.* New York: Schocken Books.

Wright, Lawrence. 1993. "The Sons of Jim Jones." *The New Yorker* 69:66–89.

Wright, Stuart A., ed. 1995. *Armageddon in Waco: Critical Perspectives on the Branch Davidian Conflict*. Chicago: Univ. of Chicago Press.

Wundt, Wilhelm. 1916. *Elements of Folk Psychology*. Trans. Edward Leroy Schaub. New York: Macmillan.

Yamaori Tetsuo. 1995. "Oumu jiken to Nihon shūkyō no shūen." *Shokun* 27, no. 6:34–47.

Yang Sam. 1987. *Khmer Buddhism and Politics from 1954 to 1984*. Newington, Conn.: Khmer Studies Institute.

Zatarian, Michael. 1990. *David Duke: Evolution of a Klansman*. New York: Pelican.

Zenkovsky, Serge. 1957a. "The Ideological World of the Denison Brothers." *Harvard Slavic Studies* 3:49–66.

——. 1957b. "The Russian Church Schism." *Russian Review* 16:37–58.

# Index